DARWINISM: THE REFUTATION OF A MYTH

This book provides a major historical re-evaluation of Darwinism, Neo-Darwinism and Neo-Mendelism. It proposes that Lamarck had precedent over Darwin in propounding a theory of the evolution of living forms, and that Darwin's contribution to evolutionary thought has been uncritically overrated. It also advocates an alternative macromutation theory of evolution.

By taking this critical stance and giving a detailed analysis of the ideas of neglected figures in evolutionary biology such as Lawrence, Matthew, Blyth, Hooker, Gray and Butler, as well as more established figures such as Buffon, von Baer, Geoffroy Saint-Hilaire, Chambers, Owen, Lyell, Huxley, Fisher, Bateson, Haldane and Sewall Wright, the author makes a highly original contribution to a historical and philosophical appreciation of evolutionary theory. This extends and develops the author's earlier voluminous writings over the last thirty-five years, including his books entitled *Epigenetics: A Treatise on Theoretical Embryology* and *The Phylogeny of Vertebrata*. By careful analysis of Darwinian thought, an unravelling of the epistemological relationships between Darwin, his friends, supporters and critics, exposing some of the limitations of Neo-Darwinism, and then proposing an alternative view, the book makes a major contribution to the literature on evolutionary biology.

DARWINISM:
THE REFUTATION OF A MYTH

SØREN LØVTRUP

CROOM HELM
London ● New York ● Sydney

© 1987 Søren Løvtrup
Croom Helm Ltd, Provident House, Burrell Row,
Beckenham, Kent BR3 1AT
Croom Helm Australia, 44–50 Waterloo Road,
North Ryde, 2113, New South Wales

British Library Cataloguing in Publication Data

Løvtrup, Søren
    Darwinism: the refutation of a myth.
    1. Darwin, Charles 2. Evolution
    I. Title
    575.01'62   QH366.2
    ISBN 0-7099-4153-6

Library of Congress Cataloging-in-Publication Data

ISBN 0-7099-4153-6

Filmset by Mayhew Typesetting, Bristol, England
Printed and bound in Great Britain by Mackays of Chatham Ltd, Kent

Contents

Preface

In my previous books, *Epigenetics* and *The Phylogeny of Vertebrata*, I tried to show that the currently accepted theory of evolution — called 'neo-Darwinism' or 'the modern synthesis' — is false.

Taking an interest in the history of evolutionary thought in the course of subsequent work, I made a very remarkable and unsuspected discovery: nobody, not even Darwin and his closest friends, ever believed in Darwin's theory of natural selection: *Darwinism was refuted from the moment it was conceived*. Considering that it is difficult to open a biological treatise without finding a tribute to either Darwin or natural selection we are indeed facing a very peculiar situation in the history of biology, of science in fact, a situation which demands an explanation. The present book is an attempt to provide one.

Various colleagues and friends have read the manuscript, Dr Ove Eriksson, Dr Huguette Løvtrup-Rein, Dr Gareth Nelson, Professor Marianne Rasmuson, Professor Robert G.B. Reid and Professor René Thom. Their comments have allowed many improvements, and their interest has been a source of encouragement. My wife has also helped me with the translation of various citations. For the assistance thus rendered I express my deepest appreciation. Of course, the responsibility for the shortcomings that remain is mine, and mine alone.

As this will be the last major work of mine to be published while I am still professor at the University of Umeå, I want to express my appreciation for the outstanding research opportunities I have enjoyed during my tenure here. My complete lack of interest in matters bureaucratic has surely contributed heavily to my privileged position, but this circumstance does not lessen my gratitude.

I also wish to express my thanks to the personnel at the University Library in Umeå and at the other research libraries, who have done their best to furnish the literature I needed for my work.

The manuscript has been typed, re-typed and corrected several times by Miss Eva Björk and Mrs Mabel Jonsson, and I thank them both for their patient co-operation.

"Men han har jo ikke Noget paa!"
sagde et lille Barn. ,,Herre Gud, hør
den Uskyldiges Røst!" sagde Faderen; og
den Ene hviskede til den Anden, hvad Barnet sagde.
,,Han har ikke Noget paa, er der et lille Barn, der siger,
han har ikke Noget paa!"
,,Han har ikke Noget paa!" raabte tilsidst hele Folket.

"But he hasn't got anything on!" cried a little child.
"Dear me! just listen to what the little innocent says",
said the father; and the people whispered to each other
what the child had said. "He hasn't got anything on!"
shouted all the people at last.

Hans Christian Andersen:
'The Emperor's New Clothes'

Cogitare necesse est

To: Jacques Barzun
      Paul Brien
      C.D. Darlington
      Leon Croziat
      Richard B. Goldschmidt
      Gertrude Himmelfarb
      Norman Macbeth
      Robert G.B. Reid
      Otto H. Schindewolf
      D'Arcy W. Thompson
      John C. Willis

Introduction

It is doubtful if any single book, except the 'Principia', ever worked so great and so rapid a revolution in science, or made so deep an impression on the general mind [as *On the Origin of Species*].[1]

T.H. Huxley

. . . the name of Charles Darwin stands alongside of [that] of Isaac Newton . . . and, like [it], calls up the grand ideal of a searcher after truth and interpreter of Nature . . . [The present generation] think[s] of him who bore it as a rare combination of genius, industry, and unswerving veracity, who earned his place among the most famous men of the age by sheer native power.[2]

T.H. Huxley

All educated persons are familiar with the notion that life on this planet has arisen through a process of evolution. Most people have been taught that the proper name of this theory is 'Darwinism', the reasons being that Charles Darwin was the first person to state the idea about organic evolution and furthermore originated the theory of natural selection, which unambiguously accounts for the mechanism through which the process of evolution is realised.

The concept of 'evolution' unites all branches of biology, and a person who accomplished these two feats would indeed be greatest among biologists, and might well deserve the epithet: 'The Newton of Biology'. As appears from the above quotations, Huxley did not hesitate to bestow this honour upon his friend Charles Darwin.

In fact, this comparison was no invention of Huxley's; ironically enough it appears that Alfred Wallace was the first to come upon this idea, for on 1 September 1860 he wrote to his friend George Silk: 'Darwin's "Origin of Species" . . . you may have heard of and perhaps read, but it is not one perusal which will enable any man to appreciate it. I have read it through five or six times, each time with increasing admiration. It will live as long as the "Principia" of Newton.'[3]

As might almost have been predicted, it was also heralded by Ernst Haeckel. Some few years after the publication of *On the Origin of Species*, quoting Immanuel Kant, he wrote:

'. . . it is absurd for man even to conceive such an idea, or to hope that a Newton may one day arise able to make the production of a blade of grass comprehensible, according to natural laws

1

ordained by no intention; such an insight we must absolutely deny to man'. Now, however, this impossible Newton has really appeared seventy years later in Darwin, whose Theory of Selection has actually solved the problem, the solution of which Kant has considered absolutely inconceivable![4]

Thus, Huxley was not the first, and still less the last one prepared to elevate Darwin to the pinnacles of glory in the history of biology; even today this opinion is shared almost unanimously by all who feel entitled to judge in these matters.

It is important to observe, however, that Huxley makes the comparison between Newton and Darwin with regard to two separate points: the impact of their work and their intellectual excellence. Surely, no sensible person would contend Huxley's first assertion; it is indeed true that no other book ever had the influence on the state of science commanded by *On the Origin of Species*. Is it a corollary that its author was a towering genius, foremost among biologists?

It may not be easy to give a direct answer to this question, and I shall therefore approach the problem by dealing with the two claims made above on behalf of Darwin. Thus (1) is Darwin the founder of the theory of evolution and (2) does his theory of natural selection give an acceptable explanation of the mechanism of evolution? If these two points are indeed borne out, then Darwin may well be the 'Newton of Biology' — otherwise not.

In this book I propose to show that in both instances the answer is 'no'; and if I am right, we obviously end up in a rather awkward situation as far as present-day biology is concerned. But before we reach this point it would be well to outline the issue.

The main tenet of Darwin's theory is that his natural selection accomplishes evolutionary changes through the accumulation of some of those very slight individual variations which occur in all populations of living beings. The selection of these variations, and hence the direction of evolution, is such that the organisms become better adapted to the environment in which they happen to live. Since the struggle for existence is bound to be toughest between adults, it follows that Darwin's theory is a *micromutation* theory which accounts for evolutionary innovation primarily through the modification of adult organisms.

This theory was professed *ex cathedra* when I went to school, and for many years I accepted it without contemplation or dissent. Now and then I read literature dealing with evolution, but being an embryologist I did not think that evolution was of direct concern to me. I do not know when I first began to suspect that there is something questionable in the state of current evolutionary thought, but I know who aroused my suspicions — Karl Ernst von Baer[5] and Richard B. Goldschmidt,[6] and it is *because* I am an embryologist that their teachings had this effect. These two zoologists quite clearly demonstrated that the origin of the major animal taxa must be sought in modifications of the epigenetic, and notably the morphogenetic processes through which the fertilised egg is transformed, first into an embryo or a larva, and subsequently to a slightly deformed miniature of the adult organism. (This last statement is not valid for animals that undergo extensive metamorphosis.) And the main inference from this insight is that many of the mutations which have been really important from an evolutionary point of view must have been one-stroke changes of features distinguishing disparate major taxa. In other words, the views of von Baer and Goldschmidt imply that *macromutations* have been of great significance in organic evolution.

I did not examine the consequences of this insight until I was engaged in writing *Epigenetics — A Treatise on Theoretical Biology*.[7] This work aimed at elucidating some of the epigenetic mechanisms responsible for animal ontogenesis. Only at that time did I see that phylogenesis, i.e. evolution, is of primary concern for epigenetics because phylogenetic innovations imply ontogenetic innovations. Hence I realised that my book would not be complete without a discussion of evolution, particularly a discussion of the consequences of the *macromutation* theory for our conception of the course and mechanism of evolution.

I therefore undertook a study of the literature on evolution, and made several discoveries which strengthened my conviction that the micromutation theory does not stand up to critical testing. Above all, I discovered that the so-called 'Neo-Darwinism' is fundamentally different from Darwin's theory.

Since that time I have written several publications on evolution, adding steadily to the evidence falsifying the micromutation theory. However, the most interesting discoveries were made when I began to delve into the history of evolutionary thought. First, I came to see what I should have realised at the outset, namely, that it is Lamarck, and not Darwin, who is the founder of the theory of evolution. Second, I found that the macromutation theory is older than Darwinism, if not than the micromutation theory, and that it has had supporters, in varying numbers, for about one-and-a-half centuries. Third, I came to understand that in the last century, hardly anybody, not even Darwin himself, believed that natural selection can accomplish all the events necessary for the occurrence of organic evolution. Fourth, I discovered that the history of evolutionary thought, as it is told today, contains a large number of mistakes and misrepresentations — to express it fairly mildly — all of them aimed at adulating Darwin and debunking his opponents.

Today it is still commonly claimed that Darwin's natural selection is the evolutionary mechanism *par excellence*. However, this assertion is not based on any factual evidence, for nobody has ever demonstrated that natural selection can bring about anything but events that are trivial from an evolutionary perspective. And this brings me to the fifth point. Since the publication of *On the Origin of Species*, and particularly since the Second World War, a lot of empirical observations have been made which may be used to test the evolutionary theories. And the remarkable result is that, just as Darwin found one hundred years ago, the facts obstinately corroborate the macromutation theory and falsify the micromutation theory.

These are the main discoveries I have made in the course of my studies, and I propose to present them in detail on the following pages.

The championship of a heretical point of view is a delicate matter which requires better corroboration than might otherwise be called for. For this reason I have decided to let the *dramatis personae* speak their own cases as far as possible, and therefore a large part of the following text consists of quotations. This fact does not, of course, guarantee impartiality; against accusations of inequity I can only say that I have done my best. One circumstance which may serve to support this claim is that some persons, above all the principal actor, Charles Darwin, are quoted to present divergent, even contradictory views.

Before we deal with Darwin's contribution, we shall first discuss a set of four theories, which *in my view* are required to account for organic evolution, and some aspects of the history of evolutionary thought before Darwin. Subsequently we shall deal with Darwin's theory, its reception and its fate during the following century. After that follows the presentation of an alternative theory of evolution, which stands up to the problems which have remained unsolved by Darwinism. At this stage, when, in my opinion, the Darwinian myth has been refuted, it may be appropriate to scrutinise it and try to understand why it arose in the first place.

4

1

The Four Theories of Evolution

Extravagant theories, however, in those parts of philosophy, where our knowledge is yet imperfect, are not without their use; as they encourage the execution of laborious experiments, or the investigation of ingenious deductions, to confirm or refute them.[1]

Erasmus Darwin

On sait que toute science doit avoir sa *philosophie* et que ce n'est que par cette voie qu'elle fait des progrès réels.[2]

J.-B. de Lamarck

There are two ways, fundamentally antithetic, to account for the occurrence of life on our planet. It may be the creation of God or some other supernatural power, or it may have arisen spontaneously in some relatively simple form of matter, being subsequently perfected in a process of organic evolution.

The notion of evolution may be traced far back in the history of mankind, but until the publication of *On the Origin of Species* in 1859 'Creationism' was the predominant belief, even among scientists. Darwin's book presented a theory on the *mechanism* of evolution, in Darwin's opinion the only relevant kind of evolutionary theory. Darwin reluctantly admitted the existence of other mechanisms of evolution, but he was convinced that natural selection is the most important evolutionary agent. On this point he had little company; friends and foes alike rejected his theory. In our century Darwin has ostensibly been rehabilitated — the currently accepted theory of evolution purports to be a modification of Darwin's theory, usually known under the name of 'Neo-Darwinism'.

But a curious thing happened: to the general public, and gradually even to the scientific community, Darwin came to stand as the founder of the idea of evolution, 'Darwinism' came to mean 'Evolutionism'. A hundred years ago many knew this to be a mistake and it was duly and repeatedly pointed out — but to no avail. Today very few people are aware of the mistake, and this circumstance has had a rather unexpected consequence. In recent years dissenting voices from many quarters have been raised against the ruling theory. If

5

this criticism against '*Darwinism = Evolutionism*' is correct, then the alternative appears to the Creationism. This, at least, is the argument of some Creationists who have diligently exploited the present dissidence.

For this reason it may be justified to mention even Creationism in the present context. There are two kinds of Creationists, those who do and those who do not take the Bible literally. As the Bible refers directly to the world in which we live, then the assertions made can be tested by empirical observations. Needless to say, innumerable facts are known to falsify the origin of life as related in Genesis. On the other hand, it is possible to combine the belief in the discoveries of science with a religious faith claiming that the 'prime mover' is a being whose existence cannot be perceived by human beings. This is a metaphysical theory which can neither be verified nor falsified, but the same holds for the opposite view: it is not possible to prove that God does not exist.

We have seen that in Darwin's opinion theories on evolution are theories on the mechanism of evolution. This view seems to be prevalent today, it being presumed that there is only one *kind* of theory on evolution, namely that dealing with its mechanism; the most typical examples are Creationism, Lamarckism, Darwinism and Neo-Darwinism.

At this point it is necessary to digress in order to discuss terminology. The use of the expression 'Neo-Darwinism' as the name of the ruling theory of evolution has been criticised because it was adopted by Weismann at the end of the last century to represent his particular version of Darwinism. It seems that today very few biologists are familiar with this historical fact, and therefore this objection may safely be neglected. Of much greater importance is that, as I shall argue subsequently, there is a difference between Darwin's theory and 'Neo-Darwinism' so fundamental that it is a mistake to associate the latter theory with Darwin's name. The currently accepted theory is more correctly called *Mendelian population genetics*; for convenience I shall here employ the name 'Neo-Mendelism', as suggested by Waddington.[3] This expression also has a history, for it was used by Bateson to designate the macromutation theory advocated by him. Although this meaning is the opposite of the one proposed here, I do not believe that any harm is done, for Bateson's use of the name is unknown to the majority of the biological community.

The process of evolution is a phenomenon which concerns all the levels of organisation encountered in living beings, and thus all biological disciplines. The very thought that evolution can be explained by one single theory, based on one single biological discipline, namely genetics, seems to me outrageous. In point of fact, I propose to show here that four theories are necessary to account for evolution and that each of these four theories employs empirical data from several disciplines. The first deals with the *reality* of evolution, the second with the *history* of evolution and the remaining two with the *mechanisms* of evolution.

THE THEORY ON THE REALITY OF EVOLUTION

This theory asserts that life on Earth has originated through a process of evolution. The most crucial among its implications is that the first living organisms were extremely primitive and that, with time, higher and higher forms arose. Hence, *'progress' is a logically inescapable consequence of the notion of evolution.* To believe in evolution and reject progressive evolution is a flagrant contradiction, committed, as we shall see, by Darwin and many of his successors.

I have dealt with the theory on the reality of evolution in the singular, intimating that there is only one of its kind. There seems to be only one empirical alternative to this theory, the one stating that new forms of life, in the past as in the present, arise through *spontaneous generation.* This theory was once common belief, but has now been abandoned, not the least through the endeavours of Louis Pasteur in the last century.

What evidence is available for testing the theory on the reality of evolution? First of all, the testimony left in the fossil record, which shows that living organisms have existed during milliards of years, that they have undergone substantial changes in the course of this time, and that the general direction of this change spells progress. This is the only direct and tangible evidence we have. However, among the various facts that may be mobilised in support of the three other theories of evolution which, incidentally, presume the reality of evolution, many bring indirect support to this theory. Indeed, the nature and the wealth of the corroborating evidence are such that the theory on the reality of evolution turns out to be one of the best substantiated theories in biology, perhaps in the natural sciences.

THE THEORY ON THE HISTORY OF EVOLUTION

If the reality of evolution is accepted then it follows that all living beings must be genetically related, and it also follows that this kinship must reflect the order in which the organisms have originated, that is, the history of evolution. Ever since Aristotle it has been known that living organisms can be arranged in groups on the basis of similarities and dissimilarities, and by the grade of complexity, notably in morphological features. This classification was systematised by Linnaeus, who showed that the several groups of plants and animals can be arranged in hierarchies. Linnaeus realised that the criteria chosen by him were in some cases arbitrary conventions, and that consequently his system was not 'natural'. He believed, however, that a natural system exists, although he did not know how to find it.

Linnaeus was not an Evolutionist and therefore he could not envisage the implications of the notion of 'natural system'. However, if one believes that evolution has taken place, then it becomes evident that there is a unique classification which depicts the course of evolution, and that this phylogenetic classification represents the ideal, the natural system which Linnaeus dreamed about. We shall later discuss Lamarck's and Darwin's relation to this theory of evolution. However, at this juncture we should briefly review the present status of the theory on the history of evolution.

For many years after the general acceptance of evolution as an empirical fact the interest in phylogenetic classification was quite modest, but recently it has flourished, owing mainly to the work of Hennig,[4] which has shown that phylogenetic classifications usually take the form of dichotomous dendrograms. This circumstance implies that the classifications are widely different from those established in the traditional systematics, based on Linnaean conventions.

Morphological characters are the most conspicuous ones, and originally all classifications were based on such traits. However, in recent years other kinds of characters, not the least molecular properties, have been used to an ever increasing extent. By and large this new approach has served to corroborate the original classifications, but in some cases radical revisions have been suggested.

As long as only morphological — indeed, mainly osteological — characters were used, it was easy to incorporate palaeontological data in the classifications. However, the more other characters are employed, the more difficult it becomes to classify fossil organisms.

8

In spite of the fact that the latter are of so great importance for our knowledge of the history of evolution it may well be necessary to establish phylogenetic classifications solely on the basis of existing organisms, fossil ones being only secondarily incorporated in, or adjoined to the classifications.[5]

Every phylogenetic dendrogram may assume the form shown in Figure 1. Each of the vertical lines stands for a class of organisms, a taxon. If one such taxon comprises subordinate taxa, it may be further resolved in the way outlined by the figure. The taxa united at each branching are called 'sister groups'[6] or 'twin taxa'.[7]

If it is accepted that phylogenetic classifications faithfully render the course of evolution, then they imply a very important conclusion concerning the direction of evolution: it proceeds from the superior to the inferior taxa. This inference cannot be stated correctly in the terms of Linnean systematics, but as an approximation it may be said to imply that evolution proceeds from the phyla towards the species. This state of affairs implies an incompatibility between Linnaean systematics and phylogenetic classification, as is borne out by Figure 1, which is an alternative classification of the taxon Craniata (Vertebrata). All craniates are represented, some by Linnaean classes and some by orders. However, in the Linnaean classification all classes are on an equal footing, and so are the orders, but in the phylogenetic dendrogram the taxa of the higher craniates, the reptilian orders, birds and mammals are seen to be subordinate to those of the lower ones, cyclostomes and fishes.

The species are the terminal taxa in phylogenetic classification; when we go backwards in time, that is, downwards in the dendrograms, we shall no longer find any species, but rather genera, families, orders and classes, plus a vast number of taxa which cannot be allotted Linnaean categorical rank. This fact shows that the title of Darwin's book is a misnomer, it should have been called 'On the Origin of Taxa'. To those biologists who accept the widely held view that all living beings, past or present, must belong to a species, the statements made here will be unacceptable. In the present context I shall not delve into this question; a defence of my views may be found elsewhere.[8]

Organic evolution is a unique process and thus there can be only one phylogenetic classification, and hence only one theory on the history of evolution. This does not mean that unanimity prevails concerning the actual course of evolution, for in the same classification separate characters may often indicate quite disparate paths, and thus give rise to different interpretations. Such discrepancies are of

Figure 1: Phylogenetic classification of the taxon Craniata

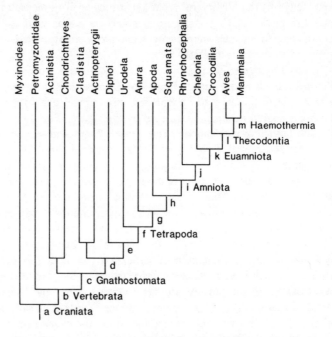

When confronted with current orthodoxy this classification comprises several heresies. Some of these have been presented some years ago,[9] and will be neglected in the present context. The new challenges to the ruling opinion are: (i) normally the taxa Urodela (salamanders and newts), Anura (frogs and toads) and Apoda (caecilians) are united into the taxon Amphibia. Since there is no binding evidence for this classification, and some data speak against it, the taxon Amphibia has been suppressed; (ii) in the work quoted I showed that there are several features shared by the taxa Crocodilia and Mammalia (crocodiles and mammals), so many indeed that it would be warranted to suggest classing the two taxa as twins or sister groups. This would by necessity lead to the classification shown here, with Aves (birds) and Mammalia as twins at the top of the hierarchy in the kingdom Animalia. This most heretic classification has recently been proposed by B.G. Gardiner,[10] and being no longer the only one to advocate this classification, I feel I can venture to publish it.

The classification comprises only the major craniate taxa; in every case but two the taxa contain a number of subordinate taxa. The two exceptions which include only one species are Actinistia, the coelacanth (*Latimeria chalumnae*) and Rhynchocephalia, the tuatara (*Sphenodon punctatus*).

It turns out that whenever a pair of twin taxa has been recognised, one of the twins is distinguished either by its primitive organisation, or by its including only a very modest number of subordinate taxa, or both. This taxon may be called the 'isolated', and its twin the 'dominant' taxon. In establishing the classification shown here the rule has been adopted that the dominant taxa is *always* placed to the right. When this is done, the dendrogram of the classification will be bordered to the lower right by a step-like line, representing a succession of major craniate taxa, some of which are named, others not. The mentioned line represents the dominant phylogenetic lineage of the taxon Craniata. A similar resolution is possible, mostly repeatedly, in all those taxa which contain more than one species.

The 'non-dominant' taxa in Figure 1 represent forms of animals which have become isolated from the dominant taxa, either by luck or by specialisation. The former generally may be distinguished by containing very few subordinate taxa — the two already dealt with plus Cladistia (bichirs) and Dipnoi (lungfishes). The taxa isolated through specialisation may be very successful indeed, as shown for instance by Actinopterygii (the ray-finned fish) and Aves (birds).

The terminal taxa in the classification which have not already been mentioned represent: Myxinoidea (hagfish), Petromyzontidae (lampreys), Chondrichthyes (cartilaginous fish), Squamata (lizards and snakes) and Chelonia (turtles and tortoises). From S. Løvtrup.[11]

little concern, for there is no limit to the number or the kind of characters which may be used in phylogenetic classification, so the search may go on until unambiguous results have been obtained.

THE THEORIES ON THE MECHANISMS OF EVOLUTION

The process of evolution involves the creation and the survival — temporarily at least — of living organisms. The mechanisms of evolution thus comprise two radically different types of event, the successive creation of novel organisms through innovations of various kinds, an epigenetic phenomenon, and their survival, an ecological phenomenon. Obviously, these two disparate phenomena cannot be explained by the same theory; rather, we need an epigenetic and an ecological theory on the mechanisms of evolution. I believe that much confusion in the history of evolutionary thought stems from the fact that this distinction is seldom made.

The epigenetic theory

Epigenetics concerns the mechanisms responsible for the onto-genetic creation of plants and animals. The phenomena dealt with by the epigenetic theory of evolution thus all take place within the confines of living organisms, from the molecular level and upwards.

11

Epigenetics is not embryology, nor even experimental embryology or developmental biology; rather, it is a branch of biology integrating biophysics, biochemistry, molecular biology, cell biology, developmental biology, morphology, genetics, etc.

The name 'epigenetics' was coined by C.H. Waddington more than 25 years ago, but it had a slow start, and it is only in the last decade that it is beginning to gain acceptance, both as a concept *per se*, and as a challenge to Neo-Mendelism. Many biologists round the world are studying problems concerning epigenetic events, but that does not mean that they consider themselves epigeneticists, or even that they are particularly well acquainted with the subject of epigenetics. For the synthesis of knowledge from many separate biological disciplines implied by epigenetics has hardly yet begun.[12]

There are two theories dealing with the origin of evolutionary innovations. One of these, the micromutation theory, affirms that all major changes are the outcome of an accumulation of numerous very slight modifications, caused by micromutations. This theory was upheld by Lamarck and Darwin; it is also championed by the current Mendelian population genetics. The second, the macromutation theory, asserts that many of the most important evolutionary events have arisen in single steps, as saltations or macromutations. This is believed to hold in particular for mutations which have interfered with various epigenetic processes, and Macromutationists are therefore found primarily among embryologists and morphologists, who often tend to be supporters of the epigenetic theory on the mechanism of evolution.

The ecological theory

The evolutionary events taking place on levels above the organismic one are dealt with by the ecological theory on the mechanism of evolution. Ecology comprises a great number of phenomena concerning the relations between members of the same species, between members of different species and between living organisms and their inanimate environment. Under these circumstances it might be envisaged that the ecological theory of evolution is as elaborate as the one dealing with the epigenetic aspects. However, I believe it is possible to formulate the problems in such a way that the theory may be greatly simplified.

I shall begin by submitting that, once created, the problem facing living organisms is their survival. If this is accepted then it follows that the ecological theory of evolution must deal with the factors which ensure the survival, or the lack of survival, of taxa in the state of nature.

We shall be concerned primarily with the influence of the organic elements of the environment. On this premise it appears that there are two circumstances that may ensure the survival of the members of a particular taxon, isolation and dominance.

Since Darwinism is primarily a theory on the *mechanism* of evolution, it follows that much of the discussion that follows will concern these two theories on the mechanism of evolution. They will therefore be dealt with in greater detail below.

2

The Pioneers

Precurseur est, sans doute, celui qui court devant tous ses contemporains, mais c'est aussi celui qui s'arrête sur un parcours où d'autres, après lui, courront jusqu'au terme.[1]

Georges Canguilhem

What is a precursor? As it turns out, when this concept is scrutinised, it becomes quite ambiguous.[2] I shall here suggest three alternative answers to the question which, without being general, may form the basis for the following discussion: (i) A is a precursor to B, if he in a vague and imperfect fashion has advanced notions which are part of a comprehensive theory later stated by B; (ii) A is a precursor to B, if the latter *independently* submits a theory previously advanced by A; (iii) A is a precursor to B, if B submits a theory previously advanced by A, and known by B.

What are the merits of being a precursor of the second kind? After all: 'A man might unaided rediscover Euclidian geometry tomorrow and still not receive much thanks for his pains.'[3] In fact, a claim on independence of existing knowledge is difficult to prove, and is more likely to raise suspicions of ignorance or dishonesty.

Yet it may be imagined that, owing to particular circumstances, a certain contribution may be overlooked, collectively, as it were; in such a situation I think the rediscoverer might deserve a share in the honour. The only biological example I know of that approximates this hypothetical case is the rediscovery of Mendel's laws in 1900 by Correns, von Tschermak and de Vries. The three of them declared that they had *rediscovered* the Mendelian laws, that is, that they had arrived at their results without knowing of Mendel's work. Suspicions have been raised on this point; in fact, de Vries was accused by Correns of attempting to conceal the existence of a precursor.[4] So if there had not been three rediscoverers, anxiously watching each others steps, perhaps 'Mendelism' would today be known as 'de Vriesism'?

The third case is quite clear-cut, supporters of B may indeed consider A his precursor, but this is false; B is a plagiarist or an epigone.

14

This exercise in semantics may seem extravagant, but it is rather important because, as we shall see, the implication is that Lamarck is no precursor of Darwin. This in turn means that he does not belong to this chapter, so the vindication of this assertion must be postponed to the following one. The only precursors to be dealt with here are of the first type, that is, the true precursors. In the course of time many authors have discussed this question, and many people have been declared precursors to Darwin. As an example I may mention that C.D. Darlington made a list of the principal characters in the history of evolutionary thought, according to which eighteen persons, beginning with Leonardo da Vinci and ending with Herbert Spencer, may be classed as precursors,[5] and this enumeration does not include persons like Etienne Geoffroy Saint-Hilaire, Karl Ernst von Baer and Richard Owen. The list may even be extended backwards to the Greeks and Romans, via the Middle Ages.[6]

In the third and subsequent editions of *On the Origin of Species* we find a 'Historical Sketch', written, it seems, at the instigation of Darwin's friends. Here he presents in brief outline a history of the theories on evolution and on natural selection, without making too great a distinction between the two topics.

In the present chapter we evaluate the importance of some of those who, directly or indirectly, have, or may be suspected to have influenced or at least anticipated Darwin's thinking. In this context the 'Historical Sketch' acquires particular interest, because it allows for a comparison of Darwin's estimation of his predecessors with that arrived at on the basis of other sources.

The people discussed here are George Louis Leclerc de Buffon, Erasmus Darwin, William Lawrence, Patrick Matthew, Edward Blyth and Herbert Spencer. It will be noticed that German-speaking people are conspicuously missing in this survey. In fact, in Darwin's 'Historical Sketch' only four Germans are mentioned, and all as minor names in the history of evolution, although one of them, Johann Wolfgang Goethe, is a giant in other contexts. This circumstance need not be a reflection of the state of evolutionary thought in the German-speaking part of Europe — Darwin's German was notoriously very poor — but it may well be, although the records concord in showing that evolution in general, and Lamarckism in particular, were familiar problems in German science. The problem is this: did the German biologists believe in a material process of evolution or only in a transcendental, *naturphilosophische* version? Both views have been contended, and it is quite difficult to settle this issue. I have decided to take it up in a later chapter.

15

GEORGE LOUIS LECLERC DE BUFFON (1707–1788)

Buffon was born into a Burgundian noble family. After studies and travels in Europe he was appointed superintendent of Le Jardin du Roi at the age of 32. For half-a-century he occupied his post, publishing alone or with the co-operation of others a large number of books on zoology; at the end of his life he was renowned as the most outstanding zoologist in Europe.

We can learn about Buffon's contribution to evolutionary thought in Samuel Butler's *Evolution, Old and New*.[7] This book, written in part as a polemic against Darwin, may not be the most reliable guide towards the truth, but it may still be more trustworthy than Darwin's own opinion on the subject.

Butler makes numerous citations to support his view of Buffon as an early Evolutionist. Thus, here is what Buffon wrote in 1753:

> The naturalists who are so ready to establish families among animals and vegetables, do not seem to have sufficiently considered the consequences which should follow from their premises, for these would limit direct creation to as small a number of forms as anyone might think fit . . . *For if it were once shown that we had right grounds for establishing these families; if the point were once gained that among animals and vegetables there had been, I do not say several species, but even a single one, which had been produced in the course of direct descent from another species; if for example it could be once shown that the ass was but a degeneration from the horse — then there is no further limit to be set to the power of nature, and we should not be wrong in supposing that with sufficient time she could have evolved all other organized forms from one primordial type . . .*
>
> But no! It is certain *from revelation* that all animals have alike been favoured with the grace of an act of direct creation, and that the first pair of every species issued full formed from the hands of the Creator.[8]

Considering the context, the first part of this quotation is surely a statement of the belief in organic evolution as candid as ever there was, but then suddenly everything is contradicted in one paragraph. It is known that on some occasions Buffon was censured for his opinions by the Theological Faculty at Sorbonne, and Butler thinks that Buffon had his tongue in cheek when he wrote the quoted addition, aimed at placating his clerical critics. Why not?

16

Otherwise it is interesting to see that, slightly illogically in our eyes, Buffon considers evolution as a process of degradation, not progression. This 'inversion' is typical also of Lamarck's early writings on evolution, and either suggests the natural inference that, without ever admitting this fact, he was inspired by Buffon, or else that both of them had the same source of inspiration, the *Scale of Nature*. As we shall see later, this latter is a very likely proposition.

One more quotation must be made:

> It may be said that the movement of Nature turns upon two immovable pivots — one, the illimitable fecundity which she has given to all species; the other, the innumerable difficulties which reduce the results of that fecundity, and leave throughout time nearly the same quantity of individuals in every species.[9]

This shows that Buffon realised the existence of a mechanism of natural selection without, however, grasping its implications for evolution.

In writing about his French precursors, Darwin sought information in the recently published work *Histoire Naturelle Générale des Règnes Organiques* by Isidore Geoffroy Saint-Hilaire.[10] We find the following statement in Darwin's *Historical Sketch*:

> Passing over allusions to the subject in the classical writers, the first author who in modern times has treated it in a scientific spirit was Buffon. But as his opinions fluctuated greatly at different periods, and as he does not enter on the causes or means of transformation of species, I need not here enter on details.[11]

True enough, Geoffroy Saint-Hilaire states that the views of Buffon on evolution have undergone changes, but when we turn the page we find that the changes did not amount to fluctuations. In fact, Buffon started out from the traditional standpoint: immutability, but around 1760 he is outspoken in favour of evolution; later on, in the 1770s, he is still an Evolutionist, but a cautious one. We are told: 'This may be thus interpreted: Buffon does not contradict, but corrects himself. In particular, he does not wriggle; he goes, once for all, from one opinion to the other.'[12] Darwin's rendering evidently was not particularly fair to this great naturalist, but worse, it is incomplete. Thus, Geoffroy Saint-Hilaire mentions Buffon's notion that the external conditions are the driving force of organic evolution. Since Darwin had himself mobilised this agent as a source of evolutionary innovation, although in 'an unimportant manner', it would have been of some historical interest to be informed about this, rather than to be told that Buffon had not considered the question. Incidentally, Darwin's theory on Pangenesis was indistinguishable from ideas submitted by Buffon a century before.

ERASMUS DARWIN (1731–1802)

In *The Structure of Scientific Revolutions*[13] Thomas S. Kuhn claims that all great advances in science are accomplished by outsiders or by young scientists, in both cases, thus, by people who have not based their reputations on the prevailing doctrines. The following pages will contain many examples corroborating Kuhn's assertion.

Indeed, if ever there were outsiders, Erasmus Darwin, Charles Darwin's grandfather, was one.[14] He was a physician, practising in Lichfield, and later in Derby, provincial towns near Birmingham. He was highly successful as a doctor; his fame was so great that King George III offered to appoint him royal physician, an honour he refused.

Gathered around him, in the 'Lunar Society' of Birmingham, was a group of friends, Matthew Boulton, Richard Edgeworth, James Keir, Joseph Priestley, William Small, James Watt and Josiah Wedgwood. This group of men was the chief intellectual driving force behind the Industrial Revolution in England and hence in the modern technological world.

Spurred in part by his friends, Erasmus Darwin made a number of ingenious inventions, some realised at the time, some remaining on the drawing board. He also made discoveries in physics and meteorology; many of his ideas were a century or two ahead of their time.

In the last part of his life he occupied himself as an author of books on botany, horticulture, medicine and — evolution; some books were written in verse, which seems to have flown easily from his hand, some in prose. This literary work began with the translation of two books by Linnaeus: *System of Vegetables* and *The Families of Plants*. Next came Erasmus Darwin's own work, *The Loves of the Plants*, appearing in 1789, and *The Economy of Vegetation*, in 1792, forming together *The Botanic Garden*. With this work, containing more than four thousand verse lines, and plenty of notes, often learned comments, Darwin won fame as a poet.

In the years 1794 and 1797 Erasmus Darwin published his two-volume work *Zoonomia, or the Laws of Organic Life*, dealing with zoology and medicine. It was immensely successful, being thought to bid 'fair to do for Medicine what Sir Isaac Newton's *Principia* has done for Natural Philosophy'.[15] The book was published in several English editions, translated into German, French and Italian, and placed by the Pope in the *Index Librorum Prohibitorum*.

Of particular interest in the present context is that Erasmus Darwin here stated his belief in organic evolution as a natural process unaided by metaphysical agents. Among the mechanisms involved he suggested sexual selection, writing: 'The final cause of this contest amongst the males seems to be, that the strongest and most active animal should propagate the species, which should thence become improved.'[16] He also discussed adaptation and mimicry, involving a mechanism similar to the one later submitted by Lamarck. Several other points show that he had formed a fairly accurate view of the process of evolution, so it is only fair to acknowledge that this 'exposition of evolution in . . . *Zoonomia* is an important advance in biology'.[17]

Phytologia, or the Philosophy of Agriculture and Gardening, another prose work, appeared in the year 1800. In this volume Erasmus Darwin also presented a number of startling observations; for instance, he recognised all the components in the process of photosynthesis and the importance of nitrate, phosphate and calcium for the plants.

His last work, a poem called *The Temple of Nature*, appeared posthumously in 1803; originally called *The Origin of Society*, it aims at presenting the evolution of life. Also here we find, mixed with mistakes, of course, many statements which biologists of today can endorse. One single example:

First forms minute, unseen by spheric glass,
Move on the mud, or pierce the watery mass;
These, as successive generations bloom,
New powers acquire, and larger limbs assume;
Whence countless groups of vegetation spring,
And breathing realms of fin, and feet, and wing.[18]

In his autobiography Darwin describes how at Edinburgh in 1826 he was introduced to Larmackian evolution by Dr Robert Grant:

I listened in silent astonishment, and as far as I can judge, without any effect on my mind. I had previously read the 'Zoonomia' of

19

my grandfather, in which similar views are maintained, but without producing any effect on me. Nevertheless it is probable that hearing rather early in life such views maintained and praised may have favoured my upholding them under a *different* form in my 'Origin of Species'. At this time I greatly admired the 'Zoonomia'; but on reading it a second time after an interval of ten or fifteen years, I was much disappointed; the proportion of speculation being so large to the facts given. (My italics)[19]

To Darwin, the Empiricist, his grandfather's work might indeed have few facts to offer, but could it not be a source of inspiration as far as ideas are concerned?

Normally a historian of science would, I presume, give prominence to contributions by his own ancestors, with pride, but, as we shall discuss in the next chapter, in Darwin's famous 'Historical Sketch' Erasmus was relegated to a derogatory sentence in a footnote. This incomprehensible behaviour has been explained in the following way: 'Despite his strong affinity with his grandfather, Charles was forced to disown him, because reviews of *The Origin of Species* . . . accused him of merely reviving the idea of his "grandsire". So Charles had to emphasize his independence.'[20]

This interpretation is also suggested by a comment upon a letter written by Darwin to Huxley: 'The history of error is quite unimportant, but it is curious to observe how exactly and accurately my grandfather . . . gives Lamarck's theory.'[21] Of this letter the editors (Francis Darwin and A.C. Seward) write: 'The date of this letter is unfortunately doubtful, otherwise it would prove that at an early date he was acquainted with Erasmus Darwin's views on evolution, a fact which has not always been recognized. We can hardly doubt that it was written in 1859.'[22] This is evidently an attempt to establish an independence far beyond that claimed in the autobiography. But even the latter is dishonest, as became known when Darwin's notebooks on transmutation were published. In the first one, opened in 1837, Darwin did not hesitate about the source of information on evolution closest at hand, for the first page is headed 'ZOONOMIA'.[23] Darwin began the collection of notes from his grandfather's book; he knew where to find information on the subject of evolution. Furthermore, all his copies of Erasmus Darwin's works were heavily marked and commented.[24] Could Charles read these books without getting hints as to 'the struggle for existence', 'sexual selection' and 'mimicry'?

On the occasion of Darwin's seventieth birthday the German

periodical *Kosmos* issued a congratulatory volume. In this was found an article by Ernst Krause dealing with Erasmus Darwin as an Evolutionist. Darwin had this work translated, and published it together with a biography of his grandfather, written by himself on the basis of various sources in his possession. It may be true that this enterprise was inspired by the fact that 'Charles was uneasy about his forced renunciation of Erasmus, and wanted to make amends.[25] But in that case one would have expected Darwin to mention at least once that his grandfather was one of his greatest predecessors, the more so because this was the claim made by Krause.[26] But Darwin only wrote: 'As Dr. Krause has so fully discussed Dr. Darwin's published writings I have but little to say about them'.[27] And then he devotes 30 pages to this subject without, so far as I can see, touching upon the subject of evolution.

Krause opens his contribution by quoting Darwin's footnote in the 'Historical Sketch' and goes on.

> Being quite aware of the reticence and modesty with which the author expresses himself, especially in speaking *pro domo*, I thought immediately that *here we ought to read between the lines*, and that this ancestor of his must certainly deserve *considerable credit in connection with the history of the Darwinian theory* . . .
>
> *Almost every single work* of the younger Darwin *may be paralleled by at least a chapter* in the works of his ancestor; the mystery of heredity, adaptation, the protective arrangements of animals and plants, sexual selection, insectivorous plants, and the analysis of the emotions and sociological impulses; nay, even the studies on infants are to be found already discussed in the writings of the elder Darwin . . .
>
> The unusual circumstance that a *grandfather should be the intellectual precursor of his grandson* . . . must of itself suffice to excite the liveliest interest. But at the same time it must be pointed out that in this fact we have not the smallest ground for *depreciating* the labours of the man who has *shed a new lustre upon the name of his grandfather*. (My italics, except for the first ones)[28]

Perhaps Darwin was making amends after all when he had this article translated into English.

Ernst Krause also wrote: 'we must . . . admit *that [Erasmus Darwin] was the first who proposed and consistently carried out, a well-rounded theory with regard to the development of the living world.*'[29] Indeed, he was a great precursor, whose work has influenced the thought of many people, including his grandson, but not, I believe, Lamarck. But this does not suffice for the final judgement of Erasmus Darwin. Desmond King-Hele, his biographer, ends his book thus:

> Though I may be biased, I regard Erasmus Darwin as the greatest Englishman of the eighteenth century. If you disagree, can you name anyone else in the past 250 years with a list of accomplishments so numerous, so notable and so varied?[30]

I do not disagree; he was unquestionably the greatest of the Darwins.

WILLIAM LAWRENCE (1783–1867)

In the second decade of the nineteenth century three persons in England published works in which the mechanism of natural selection was clearly formulated. These people were William Charles Wells, James Cowles Prichard and William Lawrence. Being medical men their interest was focused on man, and for that reason alone the question of evolution would be of minor importance.

Of the three, only Wells is mentioned in Darwin's 'Historical Sketch'. Darwin frankly admitted that Wells had stated the principle of natural selection, and that he was the first to have done so, an assertion which, as we have seen, may be contested. But Darwin emphasised that Wells had applied the principle only on man, and only on certain characters. It has been shown that Wells thought natural selection to occur also in animals,[31] but I cannot see that this makes him an Evolutionist. The same holds for Prichard and Lawrence.

Perusal of Darwin's notebooks shows that Darwin had read Prichard and Lawrence, but not Wells.[32] Offhand one might therefore expect the presence of the former two, and the absence of the latter in the 'Historical Sketch', but I shall try to show at the end of this chapter that there may be a rational explanation of the prevailing state of affairs.

Lawrence is the most interesting person in the present context, the reason being that his book, *Lectures on Physiology, Zoology and the Natural History of Man*, attracted considerable attention when it was published in 1819.

22

Lawrence was professor at the Royal College of Surgeons, and in his lectures he introduced and discussed the inheritance of physical, mental and moral differences in man, the role of mutations in the origin of human races, sexual selection, genetic isolation, 'selection and exclusions' as the means of change and adaption, eugenics and dysgenics, and the view that man must be studied as an object of natural history. He further rejected the influence of external conditions on the evolution of the various races of man.

When we recall that Erasmus Darwin's *Zoonomia* to a large extent was a textbook on medicine, highly appreciated by the English medical profession, we cannot doubt that the three physicians were influenced by the older Darwin. But still, it appears from the enumeration above that Lawrence had original ideas and that his overall view was more advanced than the one Charles Darwin offered 40 years later. C.D. Darlington claims that if Darwin had read Lawrence 'he would have been able to write a better book',[33] provided, of course, that he would permit other opinions than his own to prevail.

According to Darlington the establishment reacted with vigour to the publication of Lawrence's *Lectures*. Books were written to refute or denounce him, and the Lord Chancellor declined to allow copyright because the book contradicted the Scriptures. Lawrence chose obedience, suppressed his own book and was recompensed, becoming later President of the Royal College of Surgeons, Sergeant-Surgeon to Queen Victoria and a baronet.

This account of events has recently been contested.[34] It turns out that the suppression of the book followed shortly after its publication, upon the demands of Lawrence's employers. The court case in which copyright was denied occurred three years later and concerned royalties for a pirated edition of the book, and not the question of its publication being illicit. In fact, several editions of the book appeared.

The attacks on Lawrence were not made because he was a defender of organic evolution, for he was not, and so far as I can see nobody has made this claim. Rather, 'he had made three mistakes. He acknowledged his indebtedness to predecessors. He based his views on man. And he pointed out all the implications for the society of his day.'[35]

PATRICK MATTHEW (1790–1874)

Shortly after the publication of *On the Origin of Species*, in April 1860, an article appeared in *The Gardener's Chronicle*, in which the author claimed that he had advanced Darwin's theory on the mechanism of evolution 29 years earlier, in a book called *On Naval Timber and Arboriculture*.[36]

The author is our second outsider, Patrick Matthew, of whom very little was known until quite recently. It has now been disclosed that he had studied at the University of Edinburgh and spent most of his life managing his estate in Scotland. He travelled much, occupied himself with various political questions, contributed many articles to local newspapers and wrote two books, the first being the one mentioned here.[37]

It is in an appendix to this book that Matthew stated his theory of evolution based on a 'natural process of selection', from which it appears that his claim was correct. The work of Matthew has been quoted by several authors[38] and I shall therefore make only one citation here:

> The self-regulating adaptive disposition of organized life may, in part, be traced to the extreme fecundity of Nature, who, as before stated, had, in all the varieties of her offspring, a prolific power much beyond (in many cases a thousandfold) what is necessary to fill up the vacancies caused by senile decay. As the field of existence is limited and pre-occupied, it is only the hardier, the more robust, better suited to circumstance individuals, who are able to struggle forward to maturity, these inhabiting only the situations to which they have superior adaptation and greater power of occupancy than any other kind; the weaker, less circumstance-suited, being prematurely destroyed.
>
> This principle is in constant action, it regulates the colour, the figure, the capacities and instincts; those individuals of each species, whose colour and covering are best suited to conceal-ment or protection from enemies, or defence from vicissitude and inclemencies of climate, whose figure is best accommodated to health, strength, defence, and support; whose capacities and instincts can best regulate the physical energies to self-advantage according to circumstances — in such immense waste of primary and youthful life, *those* only come forward to maturity from the strict ordeal by which Nature tests their adaptation to her standard of perfection and fitness to continue their kind by reproduction.

From the unremitting operation of this law acting in concert with the tendency which the progeny have to take the more particular qualities of the parents, together with the connected sexual system in vegetables, and instinctive limitation to its own kind in animals, a considerable uniformity of figure, colour, and character, is induced, constituting species; the breed gradually acquiring the very best possible adaptation of these to its condition which it is susceptible of, and when alteration of circumstance occurs, thus changing in character to suit these *as far as its nature is susceptible of change.* (My italics)[39]

The wording is not Darwin's, but the thinking is. It is interesting to note that Matthew did not assume that the source of variation is inexhaustible. Elsewhere he showed that he could not accept the inheritance of acquired characters unreservedly; rather, he suggested that this point be submitted to 'examination and experiment'.[40]

The nature of Matthew's view as an evolutionary theory does not emerge clearly from the quotation given here. However, it appears that he was a Catastrophist, believing that large parts of the animal and vegetal world repeatedly had succumbed in cataclysms shaking the planet. Subsequently, with new environments created in the wake of the catastrophe, the surviving organisms could resume their evolution towards adaptation to the changed circumstances. That Matthew was a Catastrophist is hardly surprising; Lyell's work on Uniformitarianism had just appeared when Matthew prepared his manuscript.

Some recent critics[41] believe that Matthew's view on geology made his theory different from Darwin's in essence, and inferior of course. I fail to see this, for if the 'natural process of selection' and natural selection is the same force, then the outcome ought to be comparable, if not identical, whether the process of evolution is continuous or is violently interrupted from time to time. As far as the merits of the two theories are concerned it should be recalled that the Catastrophist theory fits better with the fossil record, on which, in fact, it was based. Furthermore, in recent times evidence is steadily accumlating in favour of the view that the Earth has repeatedly undergone holocausts in the course of the milliards of years it has existed.

Darwin seems to be of my opinion as far as the differences between the theories are concerned, for in the 'Historical Sketch' he wrote:

In 1831 Mr. Patrick Matthew published his work on 'Naval Timber and Arboriculture', in which he gives *precisely* the same view on the origin of species as that . . . propounded by Mr. Wallace and myself . . . Unfortunately the view was given by Mr. Matthew very briefly in scattered passages in an Appendix to a work on a different subject, so that it remained unnoticed until Mr. Matthew himself drew attention to it . . . *The differences of Mr. Matthew's view from mine are not of much importance*: he seems to consider that the world was nearly depopulated at successive periods, and then re-stocked . . . I am not sure that I understand some passages; but it seems that he attributes much influence to the direct action of the conditions of life. *He clearly saw*, however, *the full force of the principle of natural selection*. (My italics)[42]

Darwin commented upon Matthew's claim on priority in a note to *The Gardener's Chronicle*:

I freely acknowledge that Mr. Matthew has anticipated by many years the explanation which I have offered of the origin of species, under the name of natural selection. I think that no one will feel surprised that neither I, nor apparently any other naturalist, had heard of Mr. Matthew's views, considering how briefly they are given, and that they appeared in the appendix to a work on Naval Timber and Arboriculture. I can do no more than offer my apologies to Mr. Matthew for my entire ignorance of his publication.[43]

It has been asserted that Darwin must have been acquainted with Matthew's work.[44] However, the facts mobilised in support of this view are not very convincing. I personally think he was completely honest concerning his ignorance on this matter, and also that the reasons he gave were weighty enough to be accepted.[45] In this affair Darwin behaved completely irreproachably.

After Darwin's grandfather, Patrick Matthew was the first person to state the theory of evolution which is called *Darwinism*. He was indeed a true percursor, but in contrast to Darwin he did little to elaborate and corroborate his theory. This he acknowledged himself in a letter to *The Gardener's Chronicle* (12 May 1860):

To me the conception of this law of Nature came intuitively as a self-evident fact, almost without an effort of concentrated thought. Mr. Darwin here seems to have more merit in the discovery than I have had — to me it did not appear a discovery. He seems to have worked it out by inductive reason, slowly and with due caution to have made his way synthetically from fact to fact onwards; while with me it was by a general glance at the scheme of Nature that I estimated this select production of species as an *a priori* recognisable fact — an axiom, requiring only to be pointed out to be admitted by unprejudiced minds of sufficient grasp.[46]

We cannot accept Matthew's view on the ways through which advance of knowledge is ensured; the notion of natural selection also came to Darwin 'intuitively as a self-evident fact'; it had to, for no number of empirical facts would lead to it by induction.

Patrick Matthew has made a contribution to evolutionary thought, modest, but not insignificant. His reward is that he is not the entirely forgotten person he would otherwise have been.

EDWARD BLYTH (1810–1873)

Edward Blyth was of humble origin and received only a trade school education, although he developed a voracious interest in natural history. He settled as a chemist in Tooting, but was not successful in this enterprise, presumably because he devoted most of his time to zoological studies. Being advised for health reasons to move to a warmer climate, in 1841 he became curator of the Museum of the Royal Asiatic Society of Bengal. He spent 22 years in India, returning to England in 1862.

Blyth made many contributions to the natural history of Southeastern Asia; yet he could have been largely unknown today had he not been saved from oblivion by Loren Eiseley, who has suggested that Blyth was Darwin's main, but unquoted, source of inspiration with respect to the notion of 'natural selection'.[47] Eiseley arrived at this conclusion through a literary investigation. The material thus brought forward is of varying credibility, but still I think one must be a very orthodox Darwinian to be left completely untouched by Eiseley's accusation. I shall here present the most important of the discoveries made by Eiseley.

According to his *Autobiography* Darwin read Malthus' work *An Essay on the Principle of Population* in October 1838, and this, he asserts, gave him the idea that if there is a struggle of existence, then natural selection may be responsible for evolutionary change. Eiseley does not question that Darwin may have been inspired by Malthus, but finds it unnecessary that Darwin should resort to this author to hit upon the idea of 'the struggle for existence'. For besides the articles by Blyth which we shall presently discuss, this notion had been dealt with in the works of his grandfather Erasmus, in Paley's *Natural Theology*, in Lyell's *Principles of Geology* and even in Lamarck's *Philosophie Zoologique* — all works well known to Darwin. His own son, Francis, was surprised that he needed Malthus for inspiration, pointing out that Darwin had formulated the outlines of his theory in 1837, when he wrote in his notebook:

> With respect to extinction, we can easily see that a variety of the ostrich (Petise), may not be well adapted, and thus perish out; or on the other hand, like Orpheus, being favourable, many might be produced. This requires the principle that the permanent variations produced by *confined breeding* and changing circumstances are continued and produced according to the adaptation of such circumstances, and therefore that death of species is a consequence . . . of non-adaptation of circumstances. (My italics)[48]

Evidently, little is missing here to make the theory of natural selection; it is noteworthy also that at this time he held inbreeding to be an essential aspect of the mechanism of evolution.

In fact Eiseley pointed out that, considering the importance of Malthus conceded in the autobiography, it is remarkable how little this author is mentioned in the 'Sketch' of 1842 and the 'Essay' of 1844, and even in the early correspondence. For instance, in the letter to Gray in September 1857, read before the Linnean Society in July 1858, Darwin mentions De Candolle, Herbert, and Lyell as authors on the struggle for life, but not Malthus.[49] Wallace later told how his inspiration came from reading Malthus' book, and this influence is evident in Wallace's small paper from 1858, even if the name of Malthus does not occur in the text. The passage from the 'Essay' of 1844, which was selected for the Darwin–Wallace contribution at the Linnean Society, is the only one in which Malthus is mentioned, and it is possible that is was chosen 'because of its correspondence with the subject matter of Wallace's essay'.[50]

The main evidence on which Eiseley bases his case of Blyth as a precursor to Darwin concerns three articles published 1835–7 in *The Magazine of Natural History*. From these papers it appears that Blyth was aware of the struggle for existence, and also of the selection which may occur as a result. These were not very original thoughts on his part, for he had read Lawrence, Prichard and Lyell, as is made clear by his quoting them.

Thus he wrote in 1835:

It is a general law of nature for all creatures to propagate the like of themselves: and this extends even to the most trivial minutiae, to the slightest individual peculiarities . . . When two animals are matched together, each remarkable for a certain given peculiarity, no matter how trivial, there is also a decided tendency in nature for that peculiarity to *increase*; and if the produce of these animals be set apart, and only those in which the same peculiarity is most apparent, be selected to breed from, the next generation will possess it in a still *more remarkable degree*; and so on, till at length the variety I designate a *breed*, is formed, which may be very unlike the original type.[51]

Blyth thus realised that in artificial selection it is possible, through inbreeding, to bring forth various kinds of deviating form.

Discussing the conditions in nature Blyth wrote: 'It is worthy of remark, however, that the original and typical form of an animal is in great measure kept up by the same identical means by which a true *breed* is produced. The original form of a species is *unquestionably* better adapted to its *natural* habits than any modification of that form.'[52] Thus, as animals in nature are already adapted to their conditions, selection can do nothing but eliminate those harmful deviations which may survive only under domestication.

Blyth was also quite outspoken on sexual selection:

. . . as the sexual passions excite to rivalry and conflict, and the stronger must always prevail over the weaker, the latter, in a state of nature, is allowed but few opportunities of continuing its race. In a large herd of cattle, the strongest bull drives from him all the younger and weaker individuals of his own sex, and remains sole master of the herd; so that all the young which are produced must have had their origin from one which possessed the maximum of power and physical strength; and which, consequently, in *the struggle for existence*, was the best able to maintain his ground, and defend himself from every enemy. (My italics)[53]

In 1837 Blyth went a step further and asked whether the results achieved by the breeders might not, after all, occur in nature:

29

A variety of important considerations here crowd upon the mind; foremost of which is the enquiry, that, as man, by removing species from their appropriate haunts, superinduces changes on their physical constitution and adaptations, to what extent may not the same take place in wild nature, so that, in a few generations, distinctive characters may be acquired, such as are recognized as indicative of specific diversity? . . . May not, then, a large proportion of what are considered species have descended from a common parentage? . . .

There are many phenomena which tend, in no small degree, to favour the supposition, and none more so than what I have termed the localising principle, which must occasion, to a great extent, what is called 'breeding in and in', and, therefore, the transmission of individual peculiarities. We have seen, however, the extreme difficulties which most species have to encounter when occuring beyond the sphere of their adaptations; difficulties which must require human aid, in general, to render surmountable.[54]

Here again we see the idea that wild organisms represent the optimal adaption, deviations can only be disadvantageous, and therefore are removed through selection. Blyth evidently never came upon the notion later envisaged by Darwin, namely, that if the environment changes, and changes slowly, the organisms may follow suit and thus preserve their adaptation. It thus appears from his articles, and also from his later correspondence with Darwin,[55] that Blyth did not believe in evolution.

Yet, he was familiar with the phenomena of 'struggle for existence', 'sexual selection' and 'natural selection', even if he did not use the last two expressions. In these respects Blyth was certainly a precursor to Darwin. Why was this never acknowledged by Darwin? Could the omission be because Darwin had not read Blyth's articles? Considering the voracity with which he read books and periodicals in the search for evidence supporting his theory, this suggestion is utterly improbable. Indeed, Eiseley has unearthed several facts indicating that he was acquainted with the papers in question; and on this point he was right, for Darwin refers to the article from 1837 in his notebooks.[56]

There is no reason to render Eiseley's details here, except to show that even a literary detective may follow a misleading track. Eiseley had noted the odd and rare word 'inosculate', meaning 'adjoin', 'pass into' or 'merge', in Darwin's notebook from 1836, and also in Blyth's articles from 1836 to 1837, and suggested that there was here a direct association.

Another detective, Joel S. Schwartz, has taken up this lead, pointing out that Darwin hardly would have had the opportunity to read Blyth's article when he wrote in his notebook, as he was at that time on the Atlantic on his way home to England.[57] Still more important, however, is the circumstance that Darwin had used 'inosculate' in a letter to Professor J.S. Henslow in November 1832. In fact, it seems that both Blyth and Darwin may have got the word from the naturalist William Sharp MacLeay, who used it in his *Horae Entomologicae* (1819-21).[58] Elementary, Dr Watson!

Blyth was not an Evolutionist, but nor were De Candolle, Herbert and Lyell to whom Darwin referred in the letter to Asa Gray as upholders of the struggle for existence and natural selection. On this occasion Darwin might have included Blyth, and also in the chapter on the struggle for existence in *On the Origin of Species*, where these three persons are mentioned together with Herbert Spencer.[59]

Eiseley repudiates the contention that this omission was unconscious on behalf of Darwin. Perhaps; but that he was left out of the 'Historical Sketch' was undoubtedly deliberate, for it was obviously Darwin's intention to deal only with persons who had confessed their belief in evolution. On the whole, therefore, Darwin may be acquitted from the accusations of Eiseley.

HERBERT SPENCER (1820-1903)

Herbert Spencer did not receive much formal education, however he learned some science and mathematics and became a railway engineer and inventor. At the age of 20 he read Lyell's *Principles of Geology*, and, in spite of the author's reservations on this point, Spencer was converted to Lamarckism.

From 1850 onwards a never ceasing stream of articles and books took shape under his diligent pen, dealing with biology, psychology, sociology and ethics, most of them treated under the unifying concept of a 'General Law of Evolution'. This 'Law' states

. . . that the direction of the flow of events in the Universe is from simple to complex, diffuse to integrated, incoherent to coherent, independent to interdependent, undifferentiated to differentiated; from homogeneous and uniform to heterogeneous

31

and multiform; and from an abundance and confusion of motion to a regimentation and loss of motion.[60]

Prima facie, Spencer's law of evolution appears to imply a violation of the second law of thermodynamics or energetics.

Spencer's teaching was a gospel, his evolution spells progress at all levels. Perhaps this was the secret of his success (his books sold exceedingly well): for people living in the second half of the last century witnessed an unprecedented boom and might have wished to believe that this was a predetermined and inevitable phenomenon; '. . . that Evolution can end only in the establishment of the greatest perfection and the most complete happiness'.[61]

In 1852 Spencer published his first essay on evolution, and in 1864 *The Principles of Biology*[62] appeared. From this he appears to have learned from von Baer that in its development the embryo goes through stages corresponding to a passage from the general to the special, and he drew the correct conclusion:

> The embryological tree, expressing the developmental relations of organisms, will be similar to the tree which symbolizes their classificatory relations. That subordination of classes, orders, genera, and species, to which naturalists have been gradually led, is just that subordination which results from the divergence and re-divergence of embryos, as they all unfold. On the hypothesis of evolution this parallelism has a meaning — indicates that primordial kinship of all organisms, and that progressive differentiation of them, which the hypothesis alleges.[63]

This is followed by what amounts to an explicit statement of von Baer's rule (see p. 378):

> The implication is that each organism, setting out from the simple nucleated cell, must in the course of its development follow the line of the trunk, some main branch, some sub-branch, some sub-sub-branch, &c., of this embryological tree; and so on till it reaches that ultimate twig representing the species of which it is a member.[64]

And this is what he had to say on the origin and inheritance of somatic variation two years before Mendel published his discoveries and many years before Galton and Weismann pointed out the separation between the soma and the germ line:

Just as, during the evolution of an organism, the physiological units derived from the two parents tend to segregate, and produce likeness to the male parent in this part and to the female parent in that; so, during the formation of reproductive cells, there will arise in one a predominance of the physiological units derived from the father, and in another a predominance of the physiological units derived from the mother. Thus, then, every fertilized germ, besides containing different *amounts* of the two parental influences, will contain different *kinds* of influences — this having received a marked impress from one grandparent, and that from another. Without further exposition the reader will see how this cause of complication, running back through each line of ancestry, must produce in every germ numerous minute differences among the units . . .

From the general law of probabilities it may be concluded that while these involved influences, derived from many progenitors, must, on the average of cases, obscure and partially neutralize one another; there must occasionally result such combinations of them as will produce considerable divergences from average structures; and, at rare intervals, such combinations as will produce very marked divergences. *There is thus a correspondence between the inferable results and the results as habitually witnessed.* (The last italics are mine)[65]

Evidently, Spencer was a Micromutationist insisting on the necessity of macromutations, which he assumed to arise through particular combinations of micromutations. Surely, if Darwin had paid a little more heed to Spencer, he could have saved himself much trouble.

Influenced by Malthus as to the struggle for existence, he wrote in the essay 'A Theory of Population, deduced from the General Law of Animal Fertility', published in *The Westminster Review* in April 1852: '. . . as those prematurely carried off must, in the average of cases, be those in whom the power of self-preservation is the least, it unavoidably follows that those left behind to continue the race must be those in whom the power of self-preservation is the greatest — must be the select of their generation.'[66] This process Spencer called 'the survival of the fittest', the maxim later adopted by Darwin. It thus appears that Spencer had the trumps in his hand, but he lost the game. This, at least, was what he later admitted himself.

As I shall argue later, natural selection is perfectly suited for sustaining progressive evolution. But Spencer did not need selection for this purpose, progress was ensured by his general law of evolution, and therefore he made selection responsible for adaptive evolution, just like Darwin, though claiming that the latter had exaggerated the importance of this evolutionary agent. It is apparent that in this respect Spencer was strongly influenced by Lamarck, and also in the fact that he, like Darwin, believed in the inheritance of acquired characters. To an upholder of an epigenetic theory of evolution it would seem natural to presume that evolution advances through the fortuitous origination of new patterns of embryonic development, but Spencer thought that both external and internal conditions are causes of variation.

Much of what Spencer wrote may undoubtedly be classified as speculative metaphysics. But, like Darwin, he was anxious to have his views supported by empirical evidence, collected, in his case, exclusively from the literature. And he had a feeling for biological reality which by far exceeds that of Darwin. It is boring, nay, impossible today to study his endless floods of words, but from reading minor passages one comes to realise that he argues intelligently and with fewer of the contradictions which so glaringly mar Darwin's work.

Darwin wrote in the 'Historical Sketch':

Mr. Herbert Spencer in an Essay (originally published in . . . 1852 . . .) has contrasted the theories of the Creation and the Development of organic beings with remarkable skill and force. He argues from the analogy of domestic productions, from the changes which the embryos of many species undergo, from the difficulty of distinguishing species and varieties, and from the principle of general gradation, that species have been modified; and he attributes the modification to the change of circumstances.[67]

All arguments similar to Darwin's. But Darwin's survey is wanting in one important aspect, he forgot to mention 'the survival of the fittest'!

Darwin had an ambiguous attitude towards Spencer: he admired him for his intellect which he clearly realised was far superior to his own, and he despised him for the fact that he speculated too much. This is apparent on many occasions. In 1858 he wrote to Spencer:

I beg permission to thank you sincerely for your very kind present of your Essays. I have already read several of them with much interest. Your remarks on the general argument of the so-called development theory seems to me admirable. I am at present preparing an Abstract of a larger work on the changes of species; but I treat the subject simply as a naturalist, and not from a general point of view *otherwise*, in my opinion, *your argument could not have been improved on, and might have been quoted by me with great advantage.* (My italics)[68]

Darwin's ways of thought are indeed inscrutable.

In 1866 Darwin wrote to Hooker:

I have now read the last No. of H. Spencer. I do not know whether to think it better than the previous number, but it is wonderfully clever, and *I dare say mostly true*. I feel rather mean when I read him: I could bear, and rather enjoy feeling that he was twice as ingenious and clever as myself, but when I feel that he is about a dozen times my superior, even in the *master art of wriggling*, I feel aggrieved. If he had trained himself to observe more, even if at the expense, by the law of balancement, of some loss of thinking power, he would have been a wonderful man.[69] (My italics)

His deep respect for Spencer is also expressed in a letter to E.R. Lankaster in 1870: 'It has also pleased me to see how thoroughly you appreciate (and I do not think that this is general with the men of science) H. Spencer; I suspect that hereafter he will be looked at as by far the greatest living philosopher in England; perhaps equal to any that have lived.'[70] Darwin's prophesies did not come true; today Spencer is almost forgotten. One reason for this is, perhaps, that he was too ambitious. He wrote *Principles* in next to all fields of human knowledge, and anyone attempting that is bound to fail. After all, philosophy is not only a matter of compiling evidence, but also of thinking. And that takes time — the deeper it goes, the more time it takes.

But still, Spencer antedated Darwin on almost every point, publicly at least. *Vis-à-vis* Darwin he surely could claim priority as the founder of the theory of evolution, but Lamarck came before him, and he knew it. One cannot but sympathise with Spencer when he protested against the trends towards identifying Darwinism with the theory on the reality of evolution, even if he himself at times forgot that this theory rightly should carry the name *Lamarckism*.

'Herbert Spencer is second only to Chambers [and Lamarck,

35

Owen and Mivart] in the degree to which historians have denigrated [their] scientific status.'[71] Yet, 'today one would lose one's time in wanting to revise the situation. Nobody will succeed where Spencer himself lost out.'[72]

THE PRECURSORS

I will here give a brief sketch of the progress of opinion on the Origin of Species.[73]

Charles Darwin

The only time Darwin publicly paid tribute to his precursors was in the 'Historical Sketch'. Nothing published by Darwin has fared so badly as this brief survey which, as we have seen, was added as an afterthought to the third edition of *On the Origin of Species*. Thus we may read: 'Darwin wrote an "Historical Sketch". Butler described this essay as "meagre and slovenly". Its stilted phrases read indeed like an unhappy confession. It is also a gravely misleading confession';[74] and 'Darwin's "Historical Sketch" was a jewel of studied or unstudied detraction, damning many — among them his own grandfather — in little space and small type. His ambiguities, intended or unintended, were not simply baffling, but interested, deceptive, and insidious, enabling him to insinuate a claim to the discovery of evolution itself as well as of natural selection'.[75]

To most people it is an astonishing fact that Darwin did not mention a single precursor in the first edition of his book, not as precursor at least, and hardly mentioned even Wallace. One reason for this is undoubtedly that he was extremely uninterested in the history of ideas, including his own ideas. But, furthermore, to him an unsubstantiated theory was not an inspiration for empirical study, but pure speculation, metaphysics. In his view a theory comes into being, as it were, only at the moment it is 'proven' by empirical evidence. This view may sound rather strange, but Darwin could in fact point to earlier exemplars. Thus, Kepler, and in particular Newton, whom Darwin liked to use for comparison, set out to account for the movements of the planets and obtained verification by the circumstance that their theories more or less perfectly fulfilled this purpose. In neither case did an unsubstantiated theory circulate for centuries before it was verified empirically. The theory and its 'corroboration' were published simultaneously.

36

In the last century, and still today, no names in biology may be compared to that of Newton, but William Harvey has often been named in such contexts. Harvey's situation is similar to that of Newton in that his theory was made public when he reported his various observations. It therefore seems to me that Darwin to some extent was justified in upholding that a theory and its empirical verification are inseparable. And in Darwin's view nobody before him had compiled enough data to substantiate the theory on the reality of evolution, and nobody had even *attempted* to do so for the theory of natural selection, because, to the best of his knowledge, this was his own creation. Wallace had independently come upon the theory, but he had little material to support his view.

I have here given an interpretation of Darwin's stand on the problem of priority in science which, I believe, is corroborated by the letter from Darwin to Spencer quoted above on page 35. It is not one commonly accepted, and as we shall see, it was not Darwin's at the outset, that is, before he had made his particular contribution. Once he had finished his assiduous compilation of facts, this collection of data became to him the really important aspect in the history of evolutionary thought.

One may characterise this stand as self-centredness or self-delusion, but that changes nothing. And in any case, this interpretation may explain why he could write 'my theory' 45 times in the first edition of *On the Origin of Species*, referring either to Lamarck's theory on the reality of evolution, or to his and Wallace's theory on natural selection, and why he almost forgot to mention Wallace. And we may also presume that it was with some reluctance and lack of consensus that he wrote the 'Historical Sketch' and dropped most of the 'my's in the later editions of his book.[76]

If the explanation given here is accepted then it will be realised that the persons Darwin might consider for inclusion in the 'Historical Sketch' would be adherents to the theory on the reality of evolution and to the theory on the mechanism of evolution involving the participation of natural selection as the principal agent. Viewed from this angle Darwin had no reason to include Wells, Prichard, Lawrence and Blyth, who had recognised natural selection as an expedient for intraspecific normalising selection, but not for transspecific directive selection. These people were not Evolutionists, and therefore had no place in the sketch. Thus, on the premises adopted by Darwin he cannot be accused of injustice towards his precursors when he omitted a number of early Selectionists.

Apart from Wells, the remaining persons listed by Darwin had all declared their faith in organic evolution, without, however, having justified this faith. These persons can be divided into two groups, the Macromutationists (Geoffroy Saint-Hilaire, Chambers, Owen and, to some indeterminable degree, Spencer) and the Micromutationists. Darwin might of course then go one step further and divide the latter group into non-Selectionists and Selectionists. The former would comprise Buffon, Lamarck and his followers, and, presumably, Erasmus Darwin. In spite of Darwin's protests we shall include his grandfather among the Selectionists, together with Matthew, Spencer and Wallace.

But in the eyes of Darwin, as the author of *On the Origin of Species* at least, all of those mentioned here were but daydreamers, idle speculators, whose views were not theories, but merely unfounded conjecture. Here Darwin made one of his great mistakes. All of these people, except perhaps Spencer, were intimately acquainted with one or more fields of biology, zoology, botany, morphology, systematics, embryology, palaeontology, etc., and they used their knowledge as support for their views on evolution. Darwin might possibly pride himself that no one else had collected so much empirical material corroborating Lamarck's theory on the reality of evolution, but if his precursors' evidence had been added together, then his contribution would not have been impressive at all.

I have here tried to outline my view on the status of the 'Historical Sketch', a view which to some extent is an apology for Darwin. As a historical document it is defective, its philosophical ground is shaky, and Darwin underestimates his precursors' empirical contributions. However, though this be madness, yet there is method in it.

3

Jean-Baptiste de Lamarck (1744–1829)

Tout fait ou phénomène observé dans un corps vivant, est à la fois un fait ou phénomène physique, et un produit de l'organisation.[1]

J.-B. de Lamarck

Lamarck is the only major figure in the history of biology whose name has become, to all intents and purposes, a term of abuse. Most scientists' contributions are fated to be outgrown, but very few authors have written works which, two centuries later, are still rejected with an indignation so intense that the sceptic may suspect something akin to an uneasy conscience.[2]

C.H. Waddington

La pensée de Lamarck, ce malheureux auteur qu'on ne lit pas et à qui on prête des opinions qu'il n'a jamais soutenues, possède une cohérence sans faille et une rare puissance de pénétration. On est frappé par le modernisme et la justesse [de ses] idées.[3]

P.-P. Grassé

Lamarck has devoted two major works to the question of evolution, *Philosophie Zoologique* from 1809, and the first volume of his *Histoire Naturelle des Animaux sans Vertèbres*, published in 1815. This fact makes him the first great Evolutionist in the history of biology. We shall here briefly survey his life,[4] discuss his contribution to the theories of evolution and consider some aspects of the relation between Lamarck and Darwin.

Lamarck never received any academic training. He went to school in a Jesuit college at Amiens, but he was not much attracted by the prospect of a clerical career. So when his father died in 1760, he left school and enlisted in the French army, at that time engaged in war in Westphalia. Distinguishing himself, he was soon promoted to officer. After the war, he was garrisoned in Toulon and Nice, where he became fascinated by the exuberant Mediterranean flora, and got involved in enthusiastic botanical studies. As the consequence of an accident he had to resign and go to Paris for medical treatment. Later he began to work for a banker, while continuing botanical studies in his spare time. An illustration of his remarkable capacity and devotion is afforded by the fact that his famous *Flore Française* (in three volumes) was written in six months. This work was published in 1778 with the help of Buffon, who was favourably impressed by the young amateur biologist, and who continued to help him in various ways.

In 1793[7] the Musée d'Histoire Naturelle was founded. When the various chairs thus made available were to be distributed, it turned out, apparently, that no one from the established academic circle wanted to become 'professor of zoology, of insects, of worms and microscopic animals'.[5] The chair was therefore offered to, and accepted by the botanist Lamarck.

With his indomitable energy Lamarck set out to master his new field, and in 1794 he began lecturing on invertebrate zoology. One result of his studies was a classification of the animal kingdom which, so far as the invertebrates are concerned, was greatly superior to that existing at the time. It must be acknowledged that Lamarck's classification to a significant extent was based upon ideas advanced by Cuvier. This activity culminated in the monumental work on the natural history of the invertebrates. Due to blindness he was dependent upon the assistance of his daughter in the preparation of this work.

Lamarck did not limit himself to botany and zoology; he wrote on meteorology, geology, physics, chemistry — he criticised the work of Lavoisier — and even psychology. In fact, in his works one may find many shrewd observations on human behaviour. Much of this work was highly speculative, supporting the thesis that Lamarck represents eighteenth-century metaphysical rationalism. Cuvier commented in his *Eloge*:

. . . on all of these matters he entertained an assemblage of fixed ideas, original as far as he was concerned, who had conceived them by his own mind, but which he believed were likewise new to everybody else, and above all well-founded and apt to reform all the human sciences. In this respect he was like many other solitaries, who have never doubted, because they have never been contradicted.[6]

From this it appears that Lamarck had an isolated position at the museum. Why was this? Did he isolate himself, or was he isolated by his colleagues? This we shall probably never know, all we can say is that he was treated with disdain (in the Jardin des Plantes some very great scholars, whose names I will not write down, treated him as a fool!)[7] and neglect (Lamarck held such a low standing among us!).[8]

Lamarck was clearly an outsider at the Museum, and he has

remained an outsider in the history of biology. But his name at least is not forgotten.

THE REALITY OF EVOLUTION

In the year 1800 a new idea appeared in the work of Lamarck: the phylogenetic evolution of animals and plants, a notion further developed in the works mentioned above. How did Lamarck arrive at this concept? From the way he presents his views it appears that his classificatory work was his primary, perhaps his sole source of inspiration.

The general theory of evolution was stated in 1809 in the following way:

(1) That all the organised bodies of our earth are true productions of nature, wrought successively throughout long periods of time.

(2) That in her procedure, nature began and still begins by fashioning the simplest of organised bodies, and that it is these alone which she fashions immediately, that is to say, only the rudiments of organization indicated in the term *spontaneous generation*.

(3) That, since the rudiments of the animal and plant were fashioned in suitable places and conditions, the properties of a commencing life and established organic movement necessarily caused a gradual development of the organs, and in course of time produced diversity in them as in the limbs.

(4) That the property of growth is inherent in every part of the organised body, from the earliest manifestations of life; and then gave rise to different kinds of multiplication and reproduction, so that the increase of complexity of organisation, and of the shape and variety of the parts, has been preserved.

(5) That with the help of time, of conditions that necessarily were favourable, of the changes successively undergone by every part of the earth's surface, and, finally, of the power of new conditions and habits to modify the organs of living bodies, all those which now exist have imperceptibly been fashioned such as we see them.

(6) That, finally, in this state of affairs every living body underwent greater or smaller changes in its organisation and its parts; so that what we call species were imperceptibly fashioned

among them one after another and have only a relative constancy, and are not as old as nature.[9]

We cannot accept all of these statements today, but nevertheless we must admit that this first formulation of the theory on the reality of evolution possesses an unsurpassed clarity and beauty; certainly, Darwin never managed to express his ideas in a comparable fashion.

A few comments. The expression 'true productions of nature' might suggest that Lamarck was a Materialist. This is not the case, like many later Evolutionists Lamarck was a Deist, believing that Nature follows laws instigated by God. This we learn from the following quotation:

> . . . if I find that nature herself works all the wonders . . . that she has created organisation, life and even feeling, that she has multiplied and diversified within unknown limits the organs and faculties of the organized bodies whose existence she subserves or propagates . . . should I not recognise in this power of nature, that is to say in the order of existing things, the execution of the will of her Sublime Author, who was able to will that she should have this power.[10]

As far as spontaneous generation is concerned, Lamarck claimed: 'Nature, by means of heat, light, electricity and moisture, forms direct or spontaneous generations at that extremity of each kingdom of living bodies, where the simplest of these bodies are found'.[11] The notions involved in this statement are not so far from those championed by current students of the origin of life,[12] even if some reservations must be made. Thus, the first organisms endowed with life were much simpler than anything known at the time of Lamarck. And with regard to spontaneous generation two alternatives present themselves: (i) it may have happened once or a few times in the distant past; or (ii) it may go on continuously.

Logically these possibilities are equally valid, the choice between them can be made only on the basis of empirical knowledge. We now know that Lamarck made a mistake when he chose the second alternative. But Lamarck has actually stated the reason why he felt compelled to assume a constant spontaneous generation:

> Now if we consider the most imperfect of these animals, such as the infusorians, we shall see that in a hard season they all perish, or at least those of the most primitive orders. Now seeing how

ephemeral these animalcules are, and how fragile their existence, from what or in what way do they regenerate in the season when we again see them? Must we not think that these simple organisms, these rudiments of animality, so delicate and fragile, have been newly and directly fashioned by nature rather than have regenerated themselves? This is a question at which we necessarily arrive, with regard to these singular creatures.[13]

Thus, it is their frailty which made Lamarck believe in the spontaneous generation of these primitive organisms. We shall see later that his critics have suggested another reason for his acceptance of spontaneous generation.

The most compelling evidence in favour of the theory on the reality of evolution is certainly supplied by the fossil record showing how plants and animals on our planet have changed in the course of time. The fossils clearly suggest that extinction has occurred repeatedly during the history of the Earth. For reasons discussed below Lamarck did not like the notion of 'extinction', and he therefore suggested that: (i) the fossil forms may still exist in unexplored parts of the earth; (ii) if extinction has at times occurred, it may be due to the exertions of human beings; and (iii) the fossils may be earlier evolutionary stages of still existing organisms. In this way he thought he had rid himself of an embarrassment.

Whether we trace back its history two millennia or two centuries, it will turn out that the *notion* of 'evolution' was not Lamarck's creation. However, from the preceding discussion it appears that the authorities quoted at the head of the last section of this chapter are right: *the theory on the reality of evolution*, which today goes under the name of *Darwinism*, was first stated by Lamarck and *ought* to be called '*Lamarckism*', or still better *Lamarck's first theory on evolution*.

THE HISTORY OF EVOLUTION

We have seen that it follows from the theory on the reality of evolution that a classification of living organisms with respect to their phylogenetical affinities will depict the course of evolution. This was clearly realised by Lamarck who wrote:

The aim of a *general arrangement* of animals is not only to possess a convenient list for consulting, but it is more particularly to have *an order in that list which represents as nearly as possible the actual order followed by nature in the production of animals*; an order conspicuously indicated by the affinities which she has set between them. (My italics except for the first ones)[14]

Lamarck distinguished between *classification* and *distribution générale* (general arrangement), the former signifying conventional classification, the latter phylogenetic classification, the natural system. Lamarck being thus the first ever to propose a link between classification and evolutionary events, *he is indisputably the founder of the theory on the history of evolution*; the latter is therefore *Lamarck's second theory of evolution.*

One of the most important discoveries made by Lamarck while engaged in these endeavours was the necessity to distinguish between two directions in the course of evolution, upwards and sidewards, as it were. Of this finding he wrote:

> . . . I shall show that nature, by giving existence in the course of long periods of time to all animals and plants, has really formed a true scale in each of these kingdoms as regards the increasing complexity of organization; but that the gradations in this scale, which we are bound to recognise when we deal with objects according to their natural affinities, are only perceptible in the main groups of the general series, and not in the species or even in the genera . . . instead of being arranged like the main groups in a single linear series as a regularly graduated scale, these species often constitute lateral ramifications around the groups to which they belong, and their extremities are in reality isolated points.[15]

It is important to observe that by 'main groups' Lamarck here understands superior taxa like present-day phyla and classes. In fact, the preceding discussion of current phylogenetic classification shows that it conforms with Lamarck's proposition.

However, if Lamarck had known the consequences he would have been more careful with his terms, thus avoiding the notion of 'scale'. For this expression has been used again and again to prove that 'the backbone of Lamarck's theory was the "chain of being" '.[16] This is a flagrant misinterpretation of Lamarck, dating back to the time when he could protest himself, something which, it appears, has been of little avail.

The *Scala Naturae*, the *Ladder of Nature*, the *Chain of Being*,

Figure 2: A reproduction of Lamarck's attempt to establish a phylogenetic classification of the kingdom Animalia

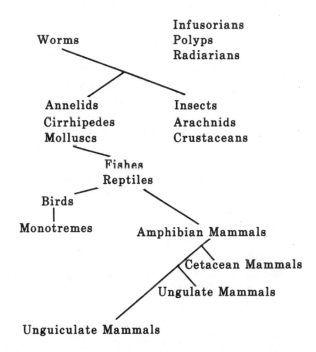

TABLE

SHOWING THE ORIGIN OF THE VARIOUS ANIMALS

Michael Ruse, who has published the original French version of this diagram, anxiously warns us '. . . being careful not to confuse Lamarck's diagram with Darwin's superficially similar diagram', the one reproduced here at page 119. I do not think there is any risk of confusion; after all, Lamarck's classification concerns animal taxa, whereas Darwin's deals with hypothetical constructs, represented by letters and numbers. As a consequence Lamarck's outline represents an empirical theory, which can be falsified; indeed, a glance shows that although far from being correct in detail, in principle it is still valid today. Making no statements about the real world, Darwin's diagram remains an unfalsifiable metaphysical conjecture. Only by reading the associated text is it possible to discover the extent to which Darwin had misunderstood the correlation between classification and evolution. After J.B. Lamarck, *Zoological Philosophy* (1914).

45

l'Échelle des Êtres, is a notion traceable back to Plato, Aristotle and the Neo-Platonians,[17] which experienced a resurgence in the eighteenth century. The salient features of this concept are three: (i) living organisms can be arranged in one single linear scale, from the humblest known organism to man and passing further, *via* the angels, to God; (ii) this scale is continuous, no gaps occur except, presumably, between the last two categories; (iii) the scale represents a passage from the top to the bottom, an uninterrupted sequence of degradation. This last point is, of course, a logical consequence of (i) and (ii), on the assumption that the scale must begin with God, the Creator. This notion of a 'chain of being' evidently was no idle speculation by the Greek philosophers, it was based on a reality, a gradation in the complexity of living organisms, which is easily distinguished by a diligent observer of Nature.

Did Lamarck accept this classical notion? Here is what he said himself:

> . . . it has been supposed that I intended to talk about the existence of an uninterrupted chain, formed by all the living beings, from the simplest to the most complex, uniting the former with the latter by characters linking them together while changing gradually . . . It has even been supposed that I would talk of a chain existing between all the bodies in nature, and it has been said that this graduated chain was nothing than an imitation of an idea advanced by *Bonnet*, and since then by many others. One might have added that this idea is of the most ancient ones, since it is found in the works of the Greek philosophers. But this very idea, whose source presumably is the obscure perception of what exists in reality with respect to the animals, but which has nothing in common with the fact I shall establish, is explicitly contradicted by observations of various kinds of bodies which are now well known.
>
> To be sure, I have nowhere talked about such a chain; on the contrary, I acknowledge that there is everywhere an enormous distance between the inorganic and the living bodies . . . I will say more; even the animals, which form the subject of the fact which I shall expound are not linked together forming a simple and regularly graduated series. Thus, what I have to demonstrate has nothing to do with such a chain, for it does not exist.[18]

Thus, Lamarck clearly and openly dissociated himself from the 'chain of being'. Can anybody acquainted with this statement claim that the classical concept forms the 'backbone' of Lamarckism?

We may conclude that Lamarck's theory is not based on the *Scala Naturae* concept. Yet, naturally enough, in his thinking and writing he was influenced by this idea, an influence from which he only gradually unfettered himself. Before we discuss this point I should mention that some of Lamarck's critics have suggested that he needed the continuous spontaneous generation of the lowest organisms because his *échelle*, functioning as an escalator, rushes the organisms upwards as soon as they are formed. So without a continuous supply from below there would soon be only human beings — or angels? — left in the universe.[19] This idea must stem from a shallow acquaintance with Lamarck's texts, for, as we have seen, he clearly asserted that the ascending evolution concerns only the superior taxa, whereas the inferior taxa are isolated side branches to his *échelle*. And from this it follows that as soon as the organisms have come to belong to one of the lower taxa the road towards perfection is forever blocked. The objection against Lamarck's critics raised here is mine, not his, and it is only approximately correct, for, in fact, one lineage of progressive evolution issues from each branching in the phylogenetic dendrograms. Nevertheless, Lamarck did not clearly realise the consequences of progressive evolution, for he declared that the primitive organisms are the youngest, and man the oldest of the creations of Nature.

It is easy to fill the chain of being with eternal species, created by God once for all. If evolution has occurred, a replete scale will obtain if the following conditions are met with: (i) evolution proceeds in small steps; (ii) extinction does not occur; and (iii) neither does divergence. Lamarck was a 'Micromutationist', that is, he believed evolution to proceed in small steps. If living beings can adjust themselves completely to their inorganic environment, then extinction can occur only through the action of other organisms or through catastrophes. Both alternatives were ruled out by Lamarck. Thus, in his *Discours d'Ouverture de l'An VIII* he states: '. . . no species predominates to the extent that it causes the ruin of another one, except perhaps in the foremost classes, where the reproduction of the individuals is slow and difficult; and as a consequence of this state of affairs one conceives that in general the species are conserved.'[20] It should be noticed that 'the foremost classes' refers to the higher animals like mammals and birds. Further, like Darwin, Lamarck was a Uniformitarian: '. . . there is no necessity whatever to imagine that a universal catastrophe came to overthrow everything, and destroy a great part of nature's own works.'[21]

However, Lamarck believed in divergent evolution, and consequently the animals cannot be classified in a single line:

> I do not mean that existing animals form a very simple series, regularly graded throughout; but I do mean that they form a branching series, irregularly graded and free from discontinuity, or at least once free from it. For it is alleged that there is now occasional discontinuity, owing to some species having been lost. It follows that the species terminating each branch of the general series are connected on one side at least with other neighbouring species which merge into them.[22]

Lamarck was aware of gaps in *his* classification, but apparently believed that most of them would be stopped with advancing knowledge. Here he was inconsistent on two points: (i) if evolution is both progressive and divergent, as suggested by himself, then it logically follows that there must be gaps *between* 'the branching series'; (ii) it is a consequence of the micromutation theory that evolution is continuous, that is, without gaps. However, there is no reason to believe that all intermediate stages have survived. Darwin correctly accepted this, referring to the fossil record for the missing forms. Although Lamarck hinted at this explanation, it appears that did not quite grasp its implications.

In his *Flore Françoise* from 1778 Lamarck was of the opinion that the 'true natural order would begin with the most complex plant and gradually descend from there to the simplest'.[23] At this time Lamarck was clearly influenced by Aristotle and the *Scala Naturae*. Evidently no theory of evolution makes sense unless it postulates a movement in the opposite direction. This was early recognised by Lamarck, for in 1802 he told his students:

> . . . I ought to begin with the presentation of the characters of the most simply organized animals, and thereafter ascend gradually to those of the most perfect animals, thus following the order that nature seems to have kept in forming them.

He did not do so, for the following reason:

> But since the former are much less familiar to you than the latter, and since it is more suitable to proceed from the known to the unknown, than to begin with something scarcely known, I shall take a direction opposite to that of nature, and follow the

organization of the animals in its ever increasing simplifications, from those which are the most perfect, the most completely organized, until those who exhibit only the slightest traces of animality.[24]

This idiosyncratic inversion of the order of Nature is continued in *Philosophie Zoologique*, in which Chapter 6 is called 'Dégradation et simplification de l'organisation d'une extrémité à l'autre de la chaîne animale, en procédant du plus composé vers le plus simple'. However, in the following 'general arrangement' the animals are presented in the inverse order, but the diagram which he proposed to account for the phylogenetic classification of the animal kingdom is again turned upside down (see Figure 2 above). With time it seems that Lamarck came to understand that progression is the important aspect, degradation only its consequence, for in *Histoire Naturelle des Animaux sans Vertèbres* we find a section called 'De l'existence d'une progression dans la composition de l'organisation des animaux, ainsi que dans le nombre et l'éminence des facultés qu'ils en obtiennent'. Still, in his demonstration of this progression he begins from the top.

Lamarck realised from the outset that the direction of his *échelle des animaux* was opposite to that of *Scala Naturae*. His treatment of the *distribution générale* as a series of degradations may be regarded as an influence by, but not an approbation of, the classical views, from which he only gradually succeeded in disembarrassing himself.

THE MECHANISMS OF EVOLUTION

We have seen that theories on the mechanisms of evolution must concern two different aspects, the epigenetic processes which give rise to new forms of life, and the ecological events which ensure their survival.

On the basis of his classifications Lamarck had arrived at the view that there are two kinds of evolution, which I have called *progressive* and *divergent*, respectively. This idea was stated in the following way in 1815:

> Everything rests here on two essential foundations which regulate the observed facts . . .
>   (i) On the *power of life*, whose results are the increasing

49

constitution of the organization, and as a consequence, the mentioned progress;

(ii) On the *modifying cause*, whose products are interruptions, diverse and irregular deviations in the results of the power of life.[25]

For reasons to be discussed later, Darwin did not believe in progressive evolution, and it seems that still today there are some people who have difficulties with grasping the implications of 'progressive evolution'. I shall therefore outline the concept with the words of an outstanding 'Neo-Darwinian', Julian Huxley:

Perhaps the most salient fact in the evolutionary history of life is the succession of what the paleontologist calls *dominant* types. These are characterized not only by a high degree of complexity for the epoch in which they lived, but by a *capacity for branching out into a multiplicity of forms*. This radiation seems always to be accompanied by the partial or even total *extinction of competing main types*, and doubtless the *one fact is in large part directly correlated with the other*

and

The distinguishing characteristics of dominant groups all fall into one or other of two types — those making for *greater control over the environment* and those making for *greater independence of changes in the environment*. Thus *advance in these respects may* provisionally *be taken as the criterion of biological progress* . . .

It is important to realize that *progress*, as thus defined, *is not the same as specialization*. Specialization . . . is an improvement in efficiency of adaptation for a particular mode of life: progress is an improvement in efficiency of living in general. The latter is an all-round, the former a one-sided advance. (My italics)[26]

In fact, it is not so difficult to demonstrate progressive evolution as claimed by Darwin and some of his successors. As shown by Lamarck the existence of this phenomenon becomes obvious as soon as organisms are classified with respect to properties which imply increase in organisation. One thing which was not realised by Lamarck, nor by Darwin, is that in an exhaustive phylogenetic classification of, say, the animal kingdom, there will be a large number of lineages of progressive evolution.

However this may be, Lamarck gave *le pouvoir de la vie* as the driving force of progressive evolution. *Prima facie*, this claim appears to suggest that he had dropped his intentions to manage without supernatural interference, falling back into metaphysic vitalism. I admit that Lamarck's assertion is vitalistic, but it is not metaphysical. For everything which goes on in living organisms, and is unknown in the inorganic world, is, of course, due to the power of life. So even 'the modifying cause', responsible for divergent evolution, must in the last instance work through the power of life. Evidently, Lamarck's explanation of the mechanism of progressive evolution is not much of an explanation. But it is not inferior to the ways used by Darwin to account for the origin of variations, for usually he assumed their existence; when he referred to the mechanisms responsible for their origin it was often followed by a statement like: 'Our ignorance of the laws of variation is profound.'[27]

In his *Philosophie Zoologique* Lamarck formulated two laws concerning the mechanism of evolution; to these were added another pair in *Histoire Naturelle des Animaux sans Vertèbres*.

Lamarck's first law states: 'Life, through its own powers, tends continuously to increase the volume of each body which possesses it, and to extend the dimensions of its parts, until an end point which she determines herself.'[28] At first sight, this law seems to refer to ontogenesis, the development of individual organisms, rather than phylogenesis, the evolution of the world of living things. But from the accompanying text it follows that it is a law of *progressive evolution* which, in modern language, might be stated as follows: *organic evolution has been associated with a steady increase in the size and the complexity of living beings.* This 'law' clearly does not explain anything, it is merely a registration of what seems to be an observable fact.

The second law states: '*The formation of a new organ in an animal body results from a new incidental need which is incessantly felt, and a new movement created and supported by this need.*'[29] When does one feel a new need? Evidently when present in a new environment, and the need in question must be an adjustment to the environment, an adaptation. So the second law may be written: *if, and when an organism invades a new environment it will gradually become adapted to the latter.* This statement formulates with great precision the fundamental contention of Darwinism except, of course, that the mechanism of selection is not involved. The way I have interpreted it, the law has a general application, but in

Lamarck's formulation it is valid only for organisms which can experience a need, thus for the higher animals. Lamarck was aware of this and wrote: 'It is true that in animals too imperfect to possess the faculty to *feel*, it cannot be to an experienced need one can attribute the formation of a new organ, this formation may then be the result of a mechanical cause, like a new movement produced in some part of the fluids in the animal.'[30] He expressed a similar reservation with respect to plants. It thus seems that the formulation of the second law was unnecessarily sloppy.

Lamarck admitted himself that the predictions of his second law were difficult to demonstrate, while being a necessary consequence of his third law: '*The development of the organs and their power of action are always related to the use of these organs.*'[31] This 'law of use and disuse' clearly must concern ontogenesis, and as such it is indeed well supported by observation, as also noted by Lamarck. In fact, if the second and the third law are combined in the transcription rendered above, then we are no longer dealing with a theory of evolution, the 'adaptation' in question being merely phenotypic adjustments achieved through training or exercise. Even if it is interpreted as an ontogenetic law, one important inference may be drawn, namely, that it is the environment which is the agent of change:

> But the second and the third of laws we are dealing with would have no effect, and consequently be useless, if the animals had always found themselves under the same circumstances, if they had generally always preserved the same habits, and if they had never changed them or formed any new ones.[32]

As noted above, Lamarck considered his third law supported by empirical observation, by the often considerable changes which use and disuse may bring about. However, if he considered this type of change to be of evolutionary import, then surely evolution should be a very fast event.

However, Lamarck's theory on the mechanism of evolution is a micromutation theory, on this point it thus coincides with Darwin's theory. Lamarck stated his view on several occasions — for instance in the following quotations:

> I know very well that for us the appearance must present . . . a stability which we believe to be constant, although it is not really so; for a rather large number of centuries may be a lapse of time

too short to make the mutations about which I speak so extensive that we can observe them.[33]

and

> I observe, however, that in cases of necessity nature passes from one system to another *without a break*, if they are closely allied; it is indeed by this faculty she succeeded in fashioning them all in turn, passing from the simplest to the most complex. (My italics)[34]

Any attempt to observe evolution in action would evidently be futile, like all endeavours to falsify the theory, except possibly indirectly. When Lamarck asserts that his theory may be empirically verified, it must therefore be concluded either that he is arguing without rhyme or reason, or else that he uses phenotypical adjustment as an *analogy*.

But this attempt to save Lamarck's theory fails when we pass to his fourth law: '*Everything* which has been acquired, outlined or changed in the organization of the individuals in the course of their life, is preserved through the reproduction, and is transmitted to the new individuals which spring from those who have undergone these changes'[35] (my italics). It fails because acquired characters are not inherited. Perhaps we may forgive Lamarck this mistake, for the inheritance of acquired characters was the then current belief.[36] Worse was that Darwin continued the tradition, for in the meantime several authors, among them Wells, Prichard and Lawrence, had rejected this idea.[37]

Lamarck did not succeed in explaining the epigenetic aspect of the mechanism of evolution. It deserves mention, however, that he was completely aware that the essential aspect of evolution is something which goes on inside the living beings, that is, epigenetic processes. To the extent that evolution is adaptive, the environment dictates the direction of change in the organisms, but in a passive way; the active aspect of evolution is carried out by the living organisms. Lamarck commented on this point in the following fashion:

> I must now explain what I mean by this statement: *the environment affects the shape and organisation of animals*, that is to say that, when the environment becomes very different, it produces in the course of time corresponding modifications in the shape

and organisation of animals. It is true if this statement were to be taken literally, I should be convicted of an error; for, whatever the environment may do, it does not work any direct modification whatever in the shape and organisation of animals.[38]

Lamarck made a significant contribution to the ecological theory on the mechanism of evolution, by his distinction between progressive and divergent, or adaptive, evolution. The importance of this distinction will appear later, here it may be mentioned that it allows us to account for the fact that organisms representing many different levels of organisation live side by side. He said himself:

It is obvious that, if nature had given existence to none but aquatic animals and if all these animals had always lived in the same climate, the same kind of water, the same depth, etc., etc., we should then no doubt have found a regular and even continuous gradation in the organisation of these animals.[39]

Lamarck is here contradicting himself with respect to what he had said about adaptive evolution (p. 52), but we may interpret the two statements to imply that adaptive evolution is dependent upon the environment, while progressive is not. It would be very difficult for Darwin to explain this situation because he operated only with adaptive evolution.

Lamarck has been much misinterpreted, for two reasons mainly. First, because of his anthropocentric vocabulary: *sentiment intérieur, besoin, volonté, habitude* and *effort*. In agreement with Lyell and many others I think this criticism is petty and irrelevant. Second, because of the examples he used to illustrate, if not demonstrate the process of evolution. I shall quote the following, which we can compare with a similar example in Darwin's book:

It is interesting to observe the result of habit in the peculiar shape and size of the giraffe (*camelo-pardalis*): this animal, the largest of mammals, is known to live in the interior of Africa in places where the soil is nearly always arid and barren, so that it is obliged to browse on the leaves of trees and to make constant efforts to reach them. From this habit long maintained in all its race, it has resulted that the animal's fore-legs have become longer than its hind legs, and that its neck is lengthened to such a degree that the giraffe, without standing up on its hind legs, attains a height of six metres.[40]

For one who has adopted the Darwinian notion that *the* theory of evolution is a theory on the mechanism of evolution, Lamarck is a failure as an Evolutionist. And in that case it may be very tempting to try to vindicate his reputation by a generous interpretation of his various statements.[41] This is a misdirected attitude, Lamarck needs no such assistance, he is a great Evolutionist on his own, who stated the theories on the reality and the history of evolution, and made an important contribution to the ecological theory on the mechanism of evolution. No other person ever made a greater contribution to the study of evolution.

PRECURSOR OR EPIGONE?

Lamarck, der geistvolle Begründer der Descendenztheorie.[42]

Ernst Haeckel

Si un mérite appartient en propre à ce grand méconnu, c'est bien d'avoir le PREMIER érigé l'évolutionisme . . . en un système explicatif de la nature vivante. Sur ce point, la priorité de Lamarck est certaine, absolue.[43]

P.-P. Grassé

The term 'Lamarckism' should in all justice be applied to evolution itself, since he was the first to advocate it as a co-ordinated system.[44]

Gavin de Beer

But Darwin might well have chosen to view himself, fairly and accurately, I think . . . a Lamarckian (with what unknown effect upon subsequent history?).[45]

Gareth Nelson

The greatest injustice was of course to Lamarck. According to Osborn, 'the disdainful allusions to him by Charles Darwin . . . long placed him in the light of a purely extravagant speculative thinker'. These disdainful allusions were all the more reprehensible that they were misrepresentations, not excusable through ignorance, and made by an unavowed part-disciple. It is clear that Darwin would not have treated a pigeon or a gastropod in this cavalier fashion, and that coming from any other man than an 'intellectual, modest, simple-minded lover of truth' the whole performance would have been damned as shamefully fraudulent.[46]

Jacques Barzun

Darwin grew up with the notion of evolution, as put forward by his grandfather, and he was introduced to the teachings of Lamarck when he studied medicine in Edinburgh 1825–7.

The next time Darwin was confronted with Lamarck's work was in Lyell's *Principles of Geology*, in which much space was devoted to the discussion and the rejection of Lamarck's theory. This he read on board the *Beagle*, and it seems that he completely shared Lyell's views at that time. For although it has been suggested that Darwin became converted to evolution during the voyage,[47] it seems certain that it was *after* his return to England he began to consider that his many and varied observations could make sense only on the assumption that organic evolution had occurred. And so he began his notebooks on transmutation of species in July 1837, and, as we have seen, he commenced by studying *Zoonomia*. But as early as page 9 we find Lamarck's name.[48]

In the second notebook we even find the following eulogy: 'Lamarck was the Hutton of Geology, he had few clear facts, but so bold & many such profound judgement that he foreseeing consequence was endowed with what may be called the prophetic spirit in science. The highest endowment of lofty genius.'

To this in more than one sense remarkable statement a comment was made by de Beer: 'It seems that the sentence should read: — Lamarck was the *French* Hutton of Geology, referring to Lamarck's Hydrogéologie . . . In this work Lamarck put forward the view that Nature had unlimited time at her disposal.'[49] This is a most uninspired interpretation. I am sure we should read: 'Lamarck was the *Hutton of Biology* (or Evolution).' This was written one year after Darwin had begun to work on the 'species problem', after having filled one-and-a-half notebooks with scattered and confused facts and speculations touching on the subject. Guess whom he at that time imagined was going to be the *Lyell of Biology*!

But at other times he was willing to assume a more modest role in the history of biology: 'State broadly *scarcely any novelty* in *my* theory, only *slight* differences, the *opinion of many people in conversation*. The whole object of the book is its *proof*, its limiting the allowing at same time true species & its adaptation to classification & affinities its extension' (my italics).[50] And later the same year (1838) he wrote: 'Seeing what Von Buch (Humboldt) G.St. Hilaire, & Lamarck have written I pretend to no originality of *idea* — (though *I arrived at them quite independently* & have used them since) the line of proof & reducing facts to law only merit if merit there be in following work' (my italics).[51] This claim to originality is rather surprising, considering that he had known Lamarck's work since his time in Edinburgh and von Humboldt's since his last year in Cambridge.

However this may be, as he started out to work on evolution, he realised that Lamarck had made important contributions to this subject, but in the 'Historical Sketch' we may read:

Lamarck was the first man whose conclusions on the subject

excited much attention. This justly-celebrated naturalist first published his views in 1801; he much enlarged them in 1809 for his 'Philosophie Zoologique', and subsequently, in 1815, in the Introduction to his 'Hist. Nat. des Animaux sans Vertébres'. In these works he upholds the doctrine that all species, including man, are descended from other species. He first did the eminent service of arousing attention to the probability of all change in the organic, as well as in the inorganic world, being the result of law, and not of miraculous interposition. Lamarck seems to have been chiefly led to his conclusion on the gradual change of species, by the difficulty of distinguishing species and varieties, by the almost perfect gradation of forms in certain groups, and by the analogy of domestic productions. With respect to the means of modification, he attributed something to the direct action of the physical conditions of life, something to the crossing of already existing forms, and much to use and disuse, that is, to the effect of habit. To this latter agency he seems to attribute all the beautiful adaptations in nature . . . But he likewise believed in a law of progressive development; and as all the forms of life thus tend to progress, in order to account for the existence at the present day of simple productions, he maintains that such forms are now spontaneously generated.[52]

Thus a very sympathetic presentation, and correct except for the effect of 'the direct action of the physical conditions of life'. And further, apart from the clause concerning 'progressive development', the views advanced by Lamarck coincided with some supported by Darwin.

In this light Darwin's assertion in a footnote on the same page becomes completely incomprehensible: 'It is curious how largely my grandfather, Dr. Erasmus Darwin, anticipated the views and erroneous grounds of opinion of Lamarck in his "Zoonomia" . . . published in 1794.' But surely, the only 'erroneous grounds of opinion' that Darwin could ascribe to Lamarck would be those concerning progressive evolution and spontaneous generation. Erasmus Darwin thought that ' "all vegetables and animals now existing were originally derived from the smallest microscopic ones, formed by spontaneous vitality" in primeval oceans'.[53] Thus far it might be said that he believed in progressive evolution and in spontaneous generation. But Darwin envisaged a similar course of evolution; although he later rejected progressive evolution, he had once written: 'The simplest cannot help becoming more complicated; and if we look to first origin, there must be progress.'[54] At any rate his grandfather never specifically advocated a 'law of progressive development', so in this respect he did not anticipate Lamarck.

Darwin knew that 'spontaneous generation' was a touchy topic, from a scientific, and perhaps even from a religious point of view. Twice he broached the problem in his notebooks; in 1838 he wrote: 'In my speculations, must not go back to first stock of all animals, but merely to classes where types exist, for if so, it will be necessary to show how the first eye is formed . . . which is impossible.'[55] And in 1839 he observed: 'My theory leaves quite untouched the question of spontaneous generation.'[56] In fact, he never declared publicly his belief that life had arisen from inorganic substances; he ended *On the Origin of Species* with the words:

> There is grandeur in this view of life, with its several powers, having been originally breathed by the Creator into a few forms or into one; and that, whilst this planet has gone cycling on according to the fixed law of gravity, from so simple a beginning endless forms most beautiful and most wonderful have been, and are being evolved.[57]

But if Darwin possibly remained ambiguous on this problem he ought as an agnostic at least to respect the standpoint adopted by Erasmus Darwin and Lamarck, in so far as it is a logical step to take for anyone believing that evolution has been governed by 'secondary laws'. It therefore seems that his attack on his grandfather is unmotivated, and it rather reveals that his apparently appreciative review of Lamarck does not correspond to his true opinion.

When we turn to Darwin's correspondence this suspicion is corroborated. In 1844, a few years after he had considered Lamarck a 'lofty genius', his opinion had changed conspicuously; thus he wrote to Hooker: 'Heaven forfend me from Lamarck nonsense of a "tendency to progression", "adaptation from the slow willing of animals", &c.! But the conclusions *I am led to are not widely different from his*; though the means of change are wholly so' (My italics).[58] And later he wrote to the same correspondent: 'With respect to books on this subject, I do not know of any systematical ones, except Lamarck's, which is veritable rubbish.'[59]

In 1859 Darwin sent proofs to Lyell asking for comments. Among these we find the following one:

> In the first place . . . it cannot surely be said that the most

eminent naturalists have rejected the view of the mutability of species? You do not mean to ignore G.St. Hilaire and Lamarck. As to the latter, you may say, that in regard to animals you substitute natural selection for volition to a certain considerable extent, but in his theory of the changes of plants he could not introduce volition; he may, no doubt, have laid an undue comparative stress on changes in physical conditions, and too little on those of contending organisms. He at least was for *the universal mutability of species* and for *a genealogical link between the first and the present*. The men of his school also appealed to domestic varieties. (Do you mean *living* naturalists?). (My italics, except for the last ones)[60]

Here we see Lyell acknowledging Lamarck as the founder of the theory on the *reality* of evolution and of the theory on the *history* of evolution, allotting to Darwin the merit of having submitted a theory on the *mechanism* of evolution which, in his view, to a certain extent is but a modification of Lamarck's.

In Darwin's answer we may read: 'The omission of "living" before eminent naturalists was a dreadful blunder.'[61] And the 'blunder' was corrected in the proofs. But even the corrected question: 'Why, it may be asked have all the most eminent living naturalists and geologists rejected this view of the mutability of species?',[62] is a distortion of the truth, as confided to his notebook, and acknowledged in the 'Historical Sketch'. Incidentally, Darwin ended his letter to Lyell in the following way: 'P.S. — You often allude to Lamarck's work; I do not know what you think about it, but it appeared to me extremely poor; I got not a fact or *idea* from it' (My italics).[63]

The discussion was resumed in 1863 when Lyell published his *The Geological Evidences of the Antiquity of Men*. In this context Lyell wrote to Darwin:

As to Lamarck I find that Grove, who has been reading him, is wonderfully struck with his book. I remember that it was the conclusion he came to about man that fortified me thirty years ago against the great impression which his arguments at first made on my mind, all the greater because Constant Prévost, a pupil of Cuvier's forty years ago, told me his conviction 'that Cuvier thought species not real, but that science could not advance without assuming that they were so'. When I came to the conclusion that after all Lamarck was going to be shown to be right, that we must 'go the whole orang', *I re-read his book, and remember-ing when it was written, I felt I had done him injustice*.

Even as to man's gradual acquisition of more and more ideas, and then of speech slowly as the ideas multiplied, and then his persecution of the beings most nearly allied and competing with him — *all this is very Darwinian*.

The substitution of the variety-making power for 'volition', 'muscular action', &c. (and in plants even volition was not called in) is in this respect *only a change of names*. Call a new variety a new creation, one may say of the former as of the latter, what you say when you observe that the creationist explains nothing, and only affirms 'it is so because it is so'.

Lamarck's belief in the slow changes in the organic and inorganic world in the year 1800, *was surely above the standard of his times*, and he was right about *progression* in the main, though *you* have vastly advanced that doctrine. (My italics)[64]

In Darwin's answer we may read: 'As for Lamarck, as you have such a man as Grove with you, you are triumphant; not that I can alter my opinion that to me it was an absolutely useless book. Perhaps this was owing to my *always searching books for facts*' (My italics).[65]

It seems to me that Darwin's statements are completely unjustified. Lamarck was a professional biologist, in charge of the department of invertebrate zoology at the most outstanding museum of natural history at the time. He had studied thousands and thousands of specimens, discovered a great number of new species, and laid the foundations to the present classification of the kingdom Animalia. All his observations were summarised in the two works mentioned above (*Philosophie Zoologique* and *Histoire Naturelle des Animaux sans Vertèbres*). Without slighting the factual experience which Darwin had acquired on his journey and through his zoological and botanical studies at Down, it cannot be disputed that of the two Lamarck was the one possessing the most extensive and systematic knowledge of biological facts, and he shared his insight with the readers of his works. But aside from that he also communicated ideas, great ideas, and Darwin knew of them and used them in his own work.

But Lamarck's facts were *not* of the kind which Darwin could appreciate. One might say that he was more interested in ecology than in systematics, and his scrutiny of the literature therefore resulted in a rather unsystematic compilation of anecdotes on natural lore. In a letter to Hooker he admitted this himself: 'I am a complete millionaire in odd and curious little facts'.[66] And above all, the facts he looked for were such as could corroborate his own theory, nothing else. On the premises suggested here Darwin's assertions become subjectively, if not objectively understandable.

Much discussion has been devoted to the question of whether or not Lamarck is a precursor to Darwin. In general those who want to further the case of Lamarck have asserted that he is indeed a precursor, whereas Darwin's supporters have rejected this.[67] This is an ironical situation, at least if the definitions given above are accepted. For Lamarck was neither neglected nor forgotten, he was famous all over Europe,[68] for his work on the invertebrates and his views on evolution; in fact, these two aspects are inseparable. This does not mean that his theories were generally accepted, but they were *known*, and of course known by Darwin. And therefore we cannot but acknowledge that, against Darwin's protest, but in agreement with Lyell's opinion, Darwin was Lamarck's epigone with respect to the theory on the reality of evolution and the theory on the history of evolution, nothing more, nothing less. Darwin had precursors with respect to his theory on the mechanism of evolution, but Lamarck was not among them. So in no respect was he Darwin's precursor.

4

The Macromutationists

Si l'homme s'était borné à recueillir des faits, les sciences ne seraient qu'une nomenclature stérile, et jamais il n'eût connu les grandes lois de la nature. C'est en comparant les faits entre eux, en saissant leurs rapports, et en remontant ainsi à des phénomènes de plus en plus étendus, qu'il est enfin parvenu à reconnaître ces lois, toujours empreintes dans leurs effets les plus variés.[1]

Pierre Simon Laplace

Les objets et les faits observés appartiennent à la nature; les conséquences, les raisonnemens, les théories en un mot, sont des actes humains, des produits de notre intelligence. Ils participent necessairement de notre foiblesse, des bornes de nos moyens.[2]

J.-B. de Lamarck

What can we call a person who advocated evolution in the half century between Lamarck and Darwin (1809–59), without invoking natural selection?

It turns out that, among the major figures in this category we find, with one exception, well-accomplished scientists in the fields of comparative morphology and embryology, and the exception, Robert Chambers, was familiar with this kind of work. And it further turns out that all of them made use of their knowledge in endorsing the same theory on the mechanism of evolution, the epigenetic macromutation theory of evolution. I shall therefore call these persons 'Macromutationists'. Among the Macromutationists we may list Etienne Geoffroy Saint-Hilaire, Karl Ernst von Baer, Richard Owen and Robert Chambers. Geoffroy Saint-Hilaire and Richard Owen, and the pupils of the former, are often called 'Transcendentalists', usually in a deprecatory way which suggests that they were metaphysicians. I shall investigate the justification of this estimation in a special section. Another question of interest in the present context is the phenomenon of ontogenetic recapitulation which will also be discussed below.

TRANSCENDENTALISM

What does 'Transcendentalism' mean? Consulting the dictionary we
get the following information:

> **1. a.** any system of philosophy . . . holding that the key to reality
> lies in the critical examination of reason. **b.** any system of
> philosophy . . . that emphasizes intuition as a means to
> knowledge or the importance of the search for the divine. **2.**
> Vague philosophical speculation . . .[3]

Clearly, the concept is rather ambiguous, but since today the
Transcendentalists are usually considered the most extravagant
speculators in the history of biology, it seems that it is the second
definition given here that is implied. But the situation is completely
reversed if we turn to the first definitions, at least if we disregard
'the search for the divine', which clearly is a metaphysical
endeavour. For I am sure that everybody will agree that the 'critical
examination of reason' is the foremost duty of people engaged in
intellectual activities, and it is not a disgrace, but rather a necessity
to apply one's intuition in this context.

Who were the Transcendentalists, and were they metaphysicians,
and if not, what did they stand for? The Transcendentalists were in
general comparative morphologists. In Germany, where they were
also called *Naturphilosophen*, the most important names were Karl
Friedrich Kielmeyer, Lorentz Oken, Johann Friedrich Meckel and
Julius Victor Carus. But, typically for this country, they were joined
by poets and philosophers like Johann Wolfgang von Goethe, Johann
Gottfried von Herder, and Friedrich Wilhelm Joseph von Schelling.
During the early years of the last century Schelling was even
regarded as the spiritual leader of the Transcendentalists. In France
we find the Transcendentalists Etienne Geoffroy Saint-Hilaire and
his successors, Antoine Etienne Reynard Augustin Serres, Marie-
Jules-César Savigny and Jean-Victor Audouin. Ostensively, there
was only one Transcendentalist in England, namely Richard Owen.
I suppose the reason is that no other morphologist was so despised
as to attract the abuse involved in the word.

In fact, the transcendentalist approach has been adopted by many
comparative morphologists all over the world, with reservation, of
course, for the excesses committed by some of the pioneers. I
venture to suggest that it is difficult to get a proper perspective on
the Transcendentalists from present-day work. Fortunately there is a

63

contemporaneous discussion of this topic, written by Isidore Geoffroy Saint-Hilaire,[4] the son of Etienne. This review is to some
extent an apology for his father, but I nevertheless believe that the
views forwarded are essentially correct.

The author begins by outlining three approaches to science, the
elementary, represented by Cuvier, the *transcendental*, represented
by Schelling, and the *scientific*, represented by Etienne Geoffroy
Saint-Hilaire.

The view of Cuvier, the one which brought him in opposition to
Lamarck and Geoffroy Saint-Hilaire, was that speculation of any
kind is anathema in science; to observe, to describe, to name and to
classify is all that a true scientist is allowed to do. This extreme
Empiricist or Positivist standpoint was defended with reference to
'the fundamental axiom of the positive sciences', which asserts that
all experience shows that man-made theories are falsified time and
again, and that therefore well-sustained facts are the only lasting
acquisitions of the human intellect. Notwithstanding the apparent
correctness of Cuvier's axiom, his attitude is basically false. He
forgot (i) that observations, descriptions, namings and classifications cannot be made without preconceived theories on many levels
of abstraction, and (ii) that facts may lose their relevance, but if they
do not, then, whenever a theory is falsified, a new theory must
account for all empirical knowledge, including the facts which were
found to falsify the previously ruling theory. Hence the new theory
is better, being closer to the truth than the old one. There is thus a
parallelism between the growth in human knowledge and the evolution of life, as envisaged by Darwin; there is a 'struggle for
existence' among the theories which ensures the 'survival of the
fittest'.[5]

Nevertheless, if today we can see that Cuvier was wrong, I still
have a certain understanding and sympathy for his view. For the
speculations which were published around the turn of the century,
including some committed by Lamarck and Geoffroy Saint-Hilaire,
were abominable. To protest against them was not to be reactionary.

The other extreme is represented by Schelling whose ideas on
Naturphilosophie have been summarised in the following way:
'Nature is not to be understood only from the perspective of
empirical observation and scientific theory; it is rather a reality of
its own which speculative or intellectual intuition has to interpret.
Such an interpretation discloses that nature is a universal organism
endowed with a world soul, as Plato taught.'[6]

Schelling's intuition clearly brought him far beyond the bounds of the empirical world; his Transcendentalism was of the metaphysical kind. He further assumed a parallelism between the human intellect and Nature. According to Isidore Geoffroy Saint-Hilaire he claimed that 'Nature must be the visible spirit, like the spirit the invisible Nature',[7] and therefore we think the same way as God has created the world. Our thought is almost an interior creation. Hence: 'To philosophize about Nature means to create Nature.'[8] Therefore, all that is required to understand Nature is to sit down and think logically and deductively from true premises reached through intuition. As the notions thus arrived at by necessity are true, empirical observations clearly lose all interest. Of course, one might from time to time throw a glance at Nature to check that it follows the proper laws, but that is about all.

Evidently, Schelling was a kind of Cartesian Rationalist — if not of the critical type — who believed that the truth can be reached by intellectual efforts alone. He was not, however, a biologist, and that can explain some of his excesses. In fact, it appears that although initially some of the German biologists followed his lead and indulged in wild speculations, most of them soon became much more sober in their activities.

The one who adopted the proper middle road was Etienne Geoffroy Saint-Hilaire. He said: 'Observation and analysis are indispensable, but they do not suffice: reasoning and synthesis also have their rights. Let us apply our senses to observation, as much and as well as possible, but also, after the observation, the *most noble faculties* which we possess, *our judgement and our comparative sagacity.*'[9] He was thus in no respect opposed to Cuvier's empirical work, he only thought it incomplete, because Cuvier objected to the synthesis, but he was entirely opposed to the metaphysical approach of Schelling.

The younger Geoffroy Saint-Hilaire has given his father's position in a very illuminating way:

These *preconceived* ideas may usefully guide the search for facts; but they should not lead us to give up this search: observation alone can give the ideas right of existence in science. This is the true spirit of Geoffroy Saint-Hilaire's doctrine, and it is through that he completely dissociates himself from the German philosophers of Nature. Like them, he often conceives *a priori*, but he demonstrates *a posteriori*.[10]

As I see it, the standpoint here advocated is that generalisations, which may be pure guesswork, should direct scientific research, the aim of which is to test the generalisations. But this conforms to the message propounded for nearly half-a-century by Karl Popper;[11] if Geoffroy Saint-Hilaire had lived today I think we might have called him a Popperian. As it is perhaps we should call Popper a Saint-Hilairian?

Geoffroy Saint-Hilaire carefully avoided to use the word 'transcendental' of his father's epistemology. But Serres called one of his works *Anatomie Transcendante*, and therefore he evidently did not consider the adjective deprecatory. Indeed, we may accept that he and his master, and several of the German comparative morphologists, were Transcendentalists in the non-metaphysical meaning of the word, implying that they searched for generalisations — laws — beyond the immediate sense data, generalisations which can be reached only through intuitive guessing.

I have here defended the transcendentalists on the basis of a document which may not be impartial. For that reason I shall quote another source, written during the second decade of our century:

Here we touch the kernel of *Naturphilosophie* — the search for rational laws which are active in Nature, the discontent with merely empirical laws . . . Geoffroy . . . alone brought to clear consciousness the principles on which pure morphology could be based: the Germans were transcendental philosophers first, and morphologists after.[12]

This evaluation is perhaps less flattering than the one presented above, but the general idea is the same.

Admittedly, even the most critical and careful among the Transcendentalists, like Geoffroy Saint-Hilaire and Owen, did go too far in their generalisations. Yet, we should not forget that they were pioneers, and after all, many of their ideas are still acknowledged by the dwindling breed of comparative morphologists. That some of their notions, for instance 'the unity of plan' or 'the archetype' are rejected by current adherents to the micromutation theory on the mechanism of evolution is natural enough, for they do not fit with their theory. However, this need not necessarily mean that the comparative morphologists are wrong.

I have written this little digression on Transcendentalism because we are here facing another example among many of misrepresentations in the history of biology. There were 'madmen' among the Transcendentalists, but on the whole they were not inferior to their empiricist opponents, and basically they were right. Furthermore, we should recall that their insight into morphology, and particularly into morphogenesis, naturally led them to propound the epigenetic macromutation theory of evolution.

As a postscript to this section I would like to point to the statement from Lamarck's previously unpublished manuscripts quoted at the head of this chapter. Here Lamarck expresses a view similar to the one defended by Geoffroy Saint-Hilaire. It is perhaps no coincidence that the latter was, apparently, the only person at the Museum to treat Lamarck decently, and that both of them were on fighting terms with Cuvier.

ONTOGENETIC RECAPITULATION

The idea of ontogenetic recapitulation dates back to a speech given by Kielmayer in Tübingen, 1793. Here he stated:

Since the distribution of forces in the series of organisations follows the same order as the distribution in the various stages of development in the same individual it may be inferred that the force through which development is realized in the latter, that is, the reproductive force, follows the same laws as those through which the series of organisations on the earth came into existence.[13]

The succession of organisations mentioned here may be taken to represent the 'Chain of Beings', and Kielmayer thus states that individual organisms during their development follow this sequence. This is an interesting idea, and the statement gains further importance because it claims that the *forces* responsible for ontogenesis have been involved also in phylogenesis, it thus refers to morphogenetic *mechanisms*.

This phenomenon of ontogenetic recapitulation must have had great appeal, for it was adopted by many authors: among these were Meckel, who wrote: 'The development of the individual organism obeys the same laws as the development of the whole animal series; that is to say the higher animal, in its gradual evolution, essentially passes through the permanent organic stages which lie below it.'[14] This statement, representing the so-called 'Meckel–Serres law', clearly asserts that the embryo passes through stages corresponding to the *adults* of lower forms. As we shall discuss in a separate

67

section, this notion was contested in 1828 by von Baer, who from his own studies concluded that embryos of higher forms pass through a succession of stages corresponding to a passage from the general to the specific, i.e. from the superior to the inferior taxa to which they belong.

If one accepts the notion of evolution, the von Baerian onto-genetic recapitulation immediately acquires a particular significance as a mechanism of evolution. For to anyone acquainted with von Baer's view it is evident that evolutionary innovation must depend upon changes in ontogenetic development, and it follows that such changes at times may entail one-step modifications of adult form, corresponding, for instance, to the origin of a new phylum, class or order. In other words, the adherents to von Baer must adopt the epigenetic macromutation theory of evolution.

Before Haeckel seized upon the notion of recapitulation, Fritz Müller had published his book *Für Darwin* (1864), in which he conceived that evolutionary change may occur in two different ways: 'Descendants . . . reach a new goal, either by deviating sooner or later whilst still on the way towards the form of their parents, or by passing along this course without deviation, but then instead of standing still advancing still further.'[15] Fritz Müller thus accepted both the mechanisms implied by von Baer's theory, deviation and terminal modification, and this, of course, is the correct solution, but he missed the point that terminal modification may sometimes involve an abbreviation of ontogenesis.

When Haeckel adopted the theory of evolution he realised the importance of recapitulation, and formulated his *Biogenetische Grundgesetz*, the 'Biogenetic Law'. Which kind of recapitulation did he allow for, the Meckel–Serres or the von Baer variant? As a Darwinian Micromutationist he had little choice. Yet, the former kind of recapitulation leads to quite baroque consequences, for instance that the human child represents the adult form of an ancestor. For this reason Darwin, and still more Haeckel, had to rely upon various secondary mechanisms to ensure agreement between theory and reality.

It may be said that the theory of evolution brought *life* into the idea of 'recapitulation'. However, whereas this entailed almost insurmountable difficulties for the Micromutationists, it was a great gain for the Macromutationists, a rather convincing corroboration of the theory they uphold.

ETIENNE GEOFFROY SAINT-HILAIRE (1772–1844)

Geoffroy Saint-Hilaire was appointed professor of vertebrate zoology at the Musée d'Histoire Naturelle in 1793, at the same time as Lamarck started his career as an invertebrate zoologist. His work as the Museum was interrupted during the years 1798–1801, when he joined Napoleon's expedition in Egypt. There Geoffroy Saint-Hilaire had the possibility to do research and make very valuable collections for the Museum. Later, in 1808, he was sent by Napoleon on a mission to Spain and Portugal.[16]

As we have seen, the classificatory work required by his new position in a few years turned Lamarck into an Evolutionist, advocating a *Philosophie Zoologique*. Similarly, the comparative studies assumed by Geoffroy Saint-Hilaire led him to conceive of a *Philosophie Anatomique*, which asserts another general biological principle, the 'unity of type', which so much facilitates the comparison between animals belonging to the several higher taxa.

Geoffroy Saint-Hilaire called himself a disciple of Lamarck. Yet, if he accepted Lamarck's theory on the reality of evolution, he rejected his theory on the mechanism of evolution. Publicly he began the discussion of evolutionary questions in 1825, but his most outspoken statements on this topic were published in the following decade, after the death of Lamarck.

Was this postponement due to consideration for Lamarck, or was he simply scared of challenging the ruling orthodoxy? The former alternative is quite plausible in view of what he wrote at one occasion:

. . . when one considers to turn the sciences back in a progressive direction, one must accept the inconveniences of a difficult position. One must inevitably speak to the public about what it ignores, that which it has not yet in any way grasped, and one risks to be judged with extreme severity. Nevertheless, this fear has never stopped an innovator who is at the same time conscientious and convinced. In this respect, one may refer to the progressive faculties and the instinctive needs of the human spirit. Yet, it is devotion and courage rather than prudence which direct the zeal.[17]

Geoffroy Saint-Hilaire's theory of evolution asserts that living organisms are adapted to their environment (*le milieu ambiant*). The latter is composed of many elements, each of which normally remains constant, and therefore the 'species' will prevail unchanged for extended periods of time. However, if a change occurs in any of the elements, then the organisms will follow suit and accommodate to the altered conditions. Hence, the principal feature of this theory is that living beings adapt themselves to their environment, and thus the latter becomes the driving force in evolution. In this respect Geoffroy Saint-Hilaire's theory coincides with Lamarck's and with the one later submitted by Darwin.

By failing to distinguish between progressive and divergent (adaptive) evolution, this new theory is a step backwards compared to Lamarck's, but with respect to the mechanism of interaction between organism and environment an important novelty is introduced. For Geoffroy Saint-Hilaire submits that changes in the environment may affect the *development* of those organisms which happen to prevail in the particular environment.

After mentioning some examples of this kind of interaction, not very persuasive in the context, the author proceeds to state that there are two different kinds of factors to study in the embryonic organisation: (i) those related to the 'essence of the germ' and (ii) those which arise from the intervention of the environment. Having allowed for the transformation of living organisms, it is suggested that the course of ontogenesis is determined by either of these sets of factors, the latter being those responsible for evolution through adaptation. This theory is thus *the first epigenetic theory of evolution*. In this respect Geoffroy Saint-Hilaire's theory is superior to Lamarck's and Darwin's, both of which imply that it is the concordance between the adult organisms and the environment which directs the course of evolution.

The empirical evidence advanced in favour of this theory consisted of various observations on changes occurring during normal ontogenesis and on monstrosities, spontaneous or experimentally provoked. For an adherent of the epigenetic theory of evolution these examples are relevant, but they hardly suffice to convince sceptics. And in any case, they do not expose the mechanisms which are involved in evolution. Geoffroy Saint-Hilaire's theory is not a micromutation theory, so he could not, like Lamarck and Darwin, protect himself from demands of demonstration by reference to the minuteness of the individual steps and the slowness of the process. Instead he proposed that the reason why we do not see evolution taking place around us is that the environment does not change at present.

Geoffroy Saint-Hilaire wrote of Lamarck:

He was ingenious in putting down principles drawn from deliberate ideas of causality, but less so in his choice of particular proofs, when he advanced a large number of facts, which seemed to him to establish that the actions and the habits of the animals led at length to modifications in their organisation.[18]

On this point Geoffroy Saint-Hilaire was not more successful than Lamarck; when discussing the external forces involved in evolutionary transformations, all he had to say was that the respiratory milieu is of utmost importance, through its influence on all parts of the organism. It is in this context we get the famous statement, often quoted:

It is evidently not through an insensible change that the lower oviparous animals have given rise to the higher degree of organisation represented by the birds. A possible incident, quite slight as regards its initial extent, but of an immeasurable importance as to its effects (this incident, which I shall not even attempt to characterise, has happened in one of the reptiles), has sufficed for the evolution of all the parts of the body constituting the avian type.[19]

Here, I confess, a modern Macromutationist must protest, surely many important and independent changes are required to pass from a reptile to a bird.

In contrast to Lamarck, Geoffroy Saint-Hilaire accepted the necessary implication of a theory of evolution: '. . . the animals living today descend, through a succession of generations and without interruptions, from the extinct animals from the antediluvian world.'[20] Isodore Geoffroy Saint-Hilaire claimed that this was the first time the implication of the fossil record was correctly stated.

If we accept the claim made by his son, then Geoffroy Saint-Hilaire had what amounts to a rather correct epistemological approach to science. The general idea behind his anatomical philosophy ought to be acceptable to comparative morphologists in general, but when it comes to details, it must be admitted that he permitted his speculations to run amok. Theoretically Cuvier may have been on the wrong side of the fence in the controversy between him and Geoffroy Saint-Hilaire, which was running in the French Academy in the early 1830s, but his criticism was justified. This dispute has attracted particular attention because it was followed with great interest by the ageing Goethe.[21]

Etienne Geoffroy Saint-Hilaire has contributed little to the furtherance of evolutionary thought, his ideas were too vague and his evidence too meagre. Yet, it cannot be contested that he was the founder of the epigenetic theory of evolution.

Of Geoffroy Saint-Hilaire Darwin wrote that he '. . . seems to have relied chiefly on the conditions of life, or the *monde ambiant* as the cause of change. He was cautious in drawing conclusions, and did not believe that existing species are now undergoing modification'.[22] Darwin did not, apparently, realise that the essential point in the theory was its being an epigenetic macromutation theory. As we shall see, Darwin relied as much on the 'monde ambiant' as the cause of change, and with respect to the continuous operation of evolution in nature it must be admitted that it is a matter which has not been directly demonstrated so far, except for very trivial instances.

KARL ERNST VON BAER (1792–1876)

Von Baer was born into a German noble family living in Estonia, then part of the Russian Empire. He began his studies on comparative embryology in Würzberg, and continued them in Königsberg, where he was appointed professor. In 1834 he accepted to become academician at Saint Petersburg, and although he continued to be active in many fields, he never again made any outstanding contributions to science.

In the course of his studies von Baer was led to formulate his famous four laws of embryonic development, published in 1828 in *Ueber Entwickelungsgeschichte der Thiere Beobachtung und Reflexion*:

(1) *The general features of a major group of animals are formed earlier in the embryo than the special ones . . .*

(2) *The less general form relations are successively formed from the more general ones, until finally the most special arises . . .*

(3) *Instead of passing through the other particular forms, the embryo of a particular animal form deviates more and more from them.*

(4) *Basically the embryo of a higher animal is thus never similar to another animal form, but only to its embryo.*[23]

The fourth law is a rejection of the embryonic recapitulation of adult forms implied by Meckel–Serres' law. According to von Baer the early embryo does not resemble the adults of lower forms, but rather their embryos. In this law he thus allows for recapitulation of embryonic form, but this is in fact a contradiction of the first three laws. For according to the latter the embryo passes through stages corresponding for a succession of subordinate taxa, say, Craniata, Vertebrata, Gnathostomata . . . Tetrapoda . . . Amniota . . . Mammalia . . . Carnivora . . . Felidae, etc., whereas the fourth law literally states that the mammalian embryo passes through stages corresponding to embryos of fishes, amphibians, reptiles, etc.

Elsewhere he claims that all which is common to the embryos of his four basic types (radiate, e.g. echinoderms; segmented, e.g. annelids; compact, e.g. molluscs; vertebrate) is the early spherical embryo, the blastula. From this stage on they diverge as stated in the third law. In fact, this assertion is not generally valid; thus, for instance, in yolk-rich amniote eggs the spherical stage has been obliterated.

If von Baer had worked with insects rather than with vertebrates, it is rather unlikely that he would have come upon his laws, for whenever metamorphosis occurs during ontogenesis, it is quite difficult to apply his laws. It should also be pointed out that the generalisation does not hold for all characters, but only for those that are causally involved in the epigenetic processes. To illustrate this point it may be mentioned that if von Baer's laws had general validity, feathers should be formed in the bird embryo at the time when the avian body plan prevails in the embryo. As a matter of fact, the feathers are formed at a much later ontogenetic stage.[24]

This interpretation of ontogenetic development, published in his epoch-making work, so highly abstract and unconventional, is a testimony of von Baer's geniality. As we have discussed above, a believer in evolution ought immediately to realise that von Baer's teaching contains the clue to the mechanism of evolutionary change: 'The phylogenetic succession of adults is the product of successive ontogenies. Ontogeny does not recapitulate Phylogeny; it creates it.'[25]

Did von Baer believe in evolution? In his treatise from 1828 he affirmed his disbelief by deriding the theory ruling at the time, Lamarckism, yet without mentioning its author. However, in 1833 he gave a lecture which was reprinted in 1864 in the first volume of his *Reden gehalten in wissenschaftlichen Versammlungen*. In the preface to this work we find a very curious statement:

Although the general content of this lecture had remained very actual to me, since it still now belongs to the convictions which I have acquired through the study of nature, the details were yet lost from my memory. When re-reading this talk after a long time, in preparation for the new edition, I was therefore surprised that the view on the transmutation of organic forms in the course of time and in the succession of generations is here definitely stated, but within circumscribed limits, approximately such as I still now hold to be validated . . . In spite of this I do not by any means want to make claims on the priority to the so-called Darwinian theory. Rather, every scientist, who, like myself has lived for many years, knows that formerly the question about the constancy or the variability of species often has been discussed, and that frequently the most audacious hypotheses were constructed on this topic. Among the older natural scientists there must be few who have not read Lamarck's *Philosophie Zoologique*.[26]

So von Baer had completely forgotten that he, 25 years before Darwin, had expressed his belief in the theory on the reality of evolution! And although he was familiar with the work of Lamarck, he is nevertheless seen to associate the name of Darwin with this theory.

In the lecture proper we can find the following passage:

From this it evidently follows that all modifications caused by *chance* or by some sudden external influence, *cannot in the slightest way change* the body type in the offspring. *Only deviation occurring in the autogenesis of an organism affects the reproduction*, and we see here the most remarkable confirmation of the statement made previously, that ontogenesis is nothing but a continuation of the autogenesis or the growth.[27]

Thus, von Baer rejects the inheritance of acquired characters and suggests that modifications in the organisms arise from changes in the ontogenetic development, in this way advancing the epigenetic macromutation theory at almost the same time as Geoffroy Saint-Hilaire. For this is the next step he makes, hesitatingly it must be admitted:

So far the question remains unsettled whether the various forms which we are accustomed to regard as separate species may not have arisen through gradual transformation from one to another, and only appear to be originally different to us because our experience is too short to recognise the entire extent of change.[28]

But von Baer puts down certain limits to evolution: '. . . it might seem permitted to imagine that antilope, sheep and goat, which are related in so many ways, have evolved from a common ancestor, but on the other hand I cannot see any probability supporting that all animals have evolved from each other through transmutation'[29] and '. . . a transformation of certain original forms of animals in the successive series of generations has very probably occurred, but only to a *limited extent*, the complete extinction of many types is certain and the gradual, rather than simultaneous appearance of others is equally certain'.[30] This statement is astounding, for it is surely one consequence of von Baer's laws that the transformation from one major taxon to another within the taxon Craniata may arise through epigenetic modifications during the early embryonic development. Von Baer clearly did not himself realise the far-reaching consequences of his own work.

As we have seen, von Baer himself admitted that he had forgotten his youthful adventure with Evolutionism. This is also shown by a letter Huxley received from him in 1860:

You have written a review of Mr. Darwin's work, of which I have found just some fragments in a German Journal . . . Being very much interested in the ideas of Mr. Darwin, on which I have lectured in public and on which I might perhaps print something — you would render me a great service if you would forward to me what you have written on these ideas.

I have stated the same ideas as Mr. Darwin on the transformation of types or the origin of species. But I rely merely on zoogeography.[31]

This is a most surprising confession, von Baer being an Evolutionist, but supporting his conviction on biogeographical data rather than on embryological ones.

The above citation is found in a letter from Huxley to Darwin, whose reaction was: 'If you write to Von Baer, for heaven's sake tell him that we should think one nod of approbation on our side, of the greatest value; and if he does write anything, beg him to send us a copy, for I would try and get it translated and published . . .

to touch up Agassiz.'[32]

Indeed, von Baer did write about Darwin's work, but it was not 'a nod of approbation', rather a vicious attack in an article called *Ueber Darwins Lehre* from 1876. Here he writes:

> In my view a scientist cannot disclaim the transformation or the descent of the various forms from each other, even though a general transmutation definitely has not been demonstrated, simply because as a scientist he may not believe in miracles, that is, the suspension of the natural laws, for his task is just to search for the natural laws: what lies beyond them does not exist for him. It seems to me that for this reason he may not assume a repeated interference by the Omnipotence.[33]

> [He continues:] Although I cannot disclaim the transformation, I do not hesitate to contradict vigorously the *mechanism* imagined by Darwin. In order to state something about this, I must emphatically point out . . . that the so-called Darwinism or Darwin's hypothesis is nothing but an attempt to give a specific explanation of the transformation, and that the belief in the transmutation prevailed a long time before Darwin, but always without any detailed explanation of the phenomenon . . .

> I think that Darwin's teaching is wrong already in its first foundation, in so far as it allows for the origination of the differences between the organisms with reference to the small variations which exist between parents and some of their progeny. These variations are only shifting imperfections in the reproduction, and if they are not complete monstrosities, they will return to the basic form during the following generations. (My italics)[34]

It appears that von Baer did not consider Lamarck's theory as an attempt to explain the mechanism of evolution. However, like almost all of Darwin's critics he rejected the mechanism proposed by Darwin, involving the accumulation of micromutations.

So far we can follow von Baer. But he goes on:

> Above all we must oppose that Darwin considers the entire history of the organisms to be simply the result of material influences, not as a development. To us it seems evident that the gradual formation of the organisms to higher forms and finally to man was a development, an advance towards a goal, which one may nevertheless imagine to be relative rather than absolute.

76

If I consider the gradual appearance of the various animal forms as a development, that is, as a process which leads to a definite goal, then it also seems understandable, and even necessary that the present is different from the past, and that in past times a greater productive power prevailed than today.[35]

Here we find that, like Asa Gray, von Baer could not imagine evolution without design and purpose, and, like Lyell and Wallace, he had special doubts with respect to the origin of man. His suggestion that the productive power of Nature was greater in the past is correct in so far as the origin of the higher taxa dates from the distant past.

Next von Baer gives a correct description of epigenesis:

Let us choose a higher animal form, since this passes through a larger sequence of changes. Initially the latter are very numerous, the singular forms follow quickly and deviate rapidly from one another. Some parts even appear and disappear again, having only the purpose to serve as substratum for other permanent parts, others function indeed during the entire embryonic development, but no longer. Already very early all the essential parts are present, in the subsequent development some of them grow stronger, and finally a point is reached where the transformation has not quite come to an end, but where only so much new material is deposited as corresponds to what is dissolved and removed through the vital process.[36]

This is used as an attack on the 'recent Darwinians', one of whom was Haeckel, who advertised the biogenetic law:

The recent Darwinians claim that during the formation of a higher organism the development of each individual goes quickly through the forms of their ancestors, or as they express themselves, the ontogeny is a brief recapitulation of the phylogeny . . . To me this statement does not seem founded, since the development of an individual does not pass through the animal series [die Thierreihe], but passes from the general characters of a major group to the more and more special ones.[37]

With respect to the validity of the biogenetic law he has the following to say:

In the development of a particular animal form, and in a series
of forms, which are supposed to have evolved from each other,
certain similarities, if not conformities may, and do actually
occur, since a development may also be distinguished in the
sequence in which the animal forms may be arranged. It is
evident that the fishes came before the amphibians and the
reptiles, and these before the birds and the mammals. However,
among the invertebrates the sequence is not so regular.[38]

Here von Baer clearly states the parallelism between ontogenesis and
classification. His observation also bears out the point made above,
namely, that if he had worked with invertebrates, he would probably
not have come upon his laws.

We have seen that von Baer wanted purpose in evolution. But he,
like so many others, realised that Darwin's theory involves purpose
because it involves adaptation:

It is above all this elimination of every purpose which has brought
about the quite extraordinary renown of the Darwinian hypothesis. It is the more remarkable that he still has not been able
quite to avoid the purposiveness. He merely tacks it behind the
doctrines of inheritance and adaptation . . . This purposiveness
shows through still more immediately and obviously in the adaptation, which forms an essential part of the Darwinian hypothesis.
The adaptation is nothing but the striving towards the utilization
of the prevailing conditions for the support of life . . . In fact, the
synthesis is shrewd, for the inheritance confers similarity, and
adaptation dissimilarity to the offspring. Thus, with these two
words unlimited variability is easily created, since a scale for the
inheritance and the adaptation is nowhere to be found.[39]

We are not left in doubt about von Baer's view on the mechanism
of evolution:

But . . . if these wholly purposeless, but still efficient slight
variations apparently are unacceptable, although the transmutation still may be conceived as possible, then we must ask in which
form it may be imagined? I answer unconditionally: as a saltatory
process in which the development is somewhat changed, while
the ensuing result is substantially modified.[40]

I have here quoted von Baer in detail in order to refute another of the perversions in the history of biology; namely, that von Baer was an anti-Evolutionist. It is not possible in every case to quote such misrepresentations, but in the present case I shall make an exception, because the sinner is a most outstanding contributor to the history of biology, Arthur D. Lovejoy.

Lovejoy has written:

The discourse *Über Darwin's Lehre* is mainly a serious and earnest effort to confute evolutionism [sic!], partly by already trite arguments intended to show that the internal structural similarities between organisms of different classes are not evidences of community of descent.[41]

As we have seen, this is not correct, von Baer accepted that evolution had indeed taken place, proposing that the epigenetic macromutation theory could explain much, if not all of evolution. But he was an anti-Darwinian, and for anyone who falsely equates Evolutionism and Darwinism, he must of course have been an anti-Evolutionist.

It is further stated:

The fourth law, for example, which is oftenest quoted, *might, when taken apart from its context, seem to be only another denial, not of recapitulation as such, but simply of recapitulation of adult forms*, for it runs: 'the embryo of a higher form of animal never resembles a lower form of animal, but only its embryonic form'. The text makes clear, however, that this last clause does not imply that embryos tell us anything whatever as to the class or order from which they are descended. For the fourth law is conceived by von Baer simply as a corollary of the first: 'that the form which is the most general (*das Allgemeinste*) in a large group of animals is earlier in the embryo than the more specific form (*das Besondere*)'. In other words, the order in which the larval and foetal forms follow one another is not in any degree determined by or correspondent to the temporal order in phylogeny of any other kinds of organisms, and the gradual transition from the first of those forms to the last of them is not a transition from an older to a later type, but a transition from a *logically* more 'general' and indefinite type to a logically more determinate and specific type. (The first italics are mine)[42]

What nonsense! It is true that the fourth law to some extent contradicts the first ones, but it is not true that 'the general' and 'the specific' represent 'logical' types. The vertebrate archetype or body plan is something very material, present in every early vertebrate embryo in the form of a notochord, surrounded beneath by the primordial gut, at the sides by the segmented mesoderm and on the top by the neural tube, swollen more or less extensively at the anterior end. And this archetype *always* forms before fins, limbs, teeth, beaks or trunks or any of the many other features which distinguish the taxa to which the embryo belongs. Not being an Evolutionist when he wrote the work discussed here, von Baer could not see that the laws he formulated represent a recapitulation of evolution. In fact, the several taxa represented by the successive embryonic, or rather, ontogenetic stages represent the order in which the taxa arose in the course of evolution. Although he later accepted evolution, his aversion towards the notion of recapitulation seems to have been so strong that he never came to realise that his own work implied a kind of recapitulation, 'von Baerian recapitulation',[43] but as we have seen above, Herbert Spencer did that in his *Principles of Biology* from 1864.

Except for Geoffroy Saint-Hilaire, it appears that all the supporters of the epigenetic macromutation theory of evolution were inspired by von Baer's embryological studies. As we have seen, he himself adopted this theory, even at a very early time. Is therefore von Baer one of the founders of this theory? He himself did not make this claim, and rightly so, I think. For his early advocacy went unnoticed, and was forgotten by himself, and when belatedly he made public his adherence to the macromutation theory, it had already been advertised by several others.

RICHARD OWEN (1804–1892)

Richard Owen was not an outsider. Born into a middle-class family, he became apprentice to a surgeon and apothecary at the age of 16, and in 1824 he began studies at Edinburgh University. He was introduced to George Cuvier when the latter visited England in 1830 and repaid the visit in 1831; he became professor of comparative anatomy at St Bartholomew's in 1834, Hunterian professor at the College of Surgeons in 1837, and superintendent of the Natural History Department of the British Museum in 1856.[44]

Owen, 'the British Cuvier', made many important contributions to comparative anatomy and enjoyed a great reputation in the international scientific community. He was heaped with honours, and was intimately acquainted with the highest levels of the English 'Establishment'.

Soon after his return to England Darwin met Owen and they co-operated in preparing *The Zoology of the Voyage of HMS Beagle*, in which work Owen was responsible for dealing with the fossil mammals. There are two references to Owen in Darwin's first notebook on the transmutation of species from 1837. The first one states: 'Mr Owen suggested to me, that the production of monsters . . . which follow certain laws according to species, present an analogy to production of species.'[45] I should guess that for the majority of my readers, including biologists, this statement appears to be nothing more than a curiosity. But in reality it is something much more important — it is a confession by the young Owen to the (five years) younger Darwin that *he believed in Geoffroy Saint-Hilaire's epigenetic theory of evolution.* Thus, at a time when Darwin was looking for support of his suspicions, and years before he confided his secret beliefs to Joseph Hooker, Owen was rather open about his views, at least in private.

The other reference says: 'Curious paper by M. Serres on Molluscous animals representing foetuses of Vertebrata etc . . . Owen says nonsense.'[46] This shows that Owen rejected the combination of the theories of recapitulation and unity of plan which, in the hands of the supporters of Geoffroy Saint-Hilaire, might at times have had consequences that seemed rather fantastic.

When Darwin wrote about Richard Owen in the 'Historical Sketch' he was in high spirits; nowhere else does his irony reach such levels:

Professor Owen, in 1849 . . . wrote as follows: — 'The archetypical idea was manifested in the flesh under diverse such modifications, upon this planet, long prior to the existence of those animal species that actually exemplify it. To what natural laws or secondary causes the orderly succession and progression of such organic phenomena may have been committed, we, as yet, are ignorant.'[47]

I suppose Darwin was sufficiently acquainted with current terminology to make the following interpretation, as stated in modern terms: members of the present higher taxa (phyla, classes, etc.) different from, but ancestors to those living today, have lived long ago on this planet. The mechanisms responsible for this evolution and progress are unknown. If so, then Darwin's following comments become incomprehensible. He writes:

> In his Address . . . in 1858, he speaks . . . of 'the axiom of the continuous operation of creative power, or of the ordained becoming of living things'. Farther on . . . after referring to geographical distribution, he adds, 'These phenomena shake our confidence in the conclusion that the Apteryx of New Zealand and the Red Grouse of England were distinct creations in and for those islands respectively. Always, also, it may be well to bear in mind that by the word "creation" the zoologist means a "process he knows not what" '. He amplifies this idea by adding, that when such cases as that of the Red Grouse are 'enumerated by the zoologist as evidence of distinct creation of the bird in and for such islands, he chiefly expresses that he knows not how the Red Grouse came to be there, and there exclusively; signifying also, by this mode of expressing such ignorance, his belief that both the bird and the islands owed their origin to a great first Creative Cause'. If we interpret these sentences given in the same Address, one by the other, it appears that this eminent philosopher felt in 1858 his confidence shaken that the Apteryx and the Red Grouse first appeared in their respective homes, 'he knew not how', or by some process 'he knew not what' . . .[48]

Perspicuity was not the main quality of Owen's statements, so Darwin's irony is justified, particularly if we do not recall how scared he had been himself publicly to state his view on evolution and how willingly he confessed our ignorance when that suited his argument. Nevertheless, it is evident that as early as 1849, significantly five years after the publication of Chambers' *Vestiges of the Natural History of Creation*, Owen was prepared to divulge as his opinion that a process of evolution might have been responsible for the origin of the living world. But he had to be careful, he had his prestige to guard, and besides, unlike Darwin, he was not economically independent. In a letter from 1848 he wrote:

> As I do not know the secondary cause by which it may have pleased the Creator to introduce organized species into this planet, I have never expressed orally or in print an opinion on the subject. Whenever in the course of special investigations I have met with phenomena bearing upon the hypothetical secondary

cause to which you allude, I have pointed out such bearing incidentally; but the hypothesis itself, 'transmutation of specific characters', which is always coupled with the idea of a specific direction — viz. *upwards* — has not been the subject of any express writing or discourse of mine.[49]

We have seen that Owen advocated Geoffroy Saint-Hilaire's theory of evolution in 1837. But he was also acquainted with von Baer's work, which became known in England through two articles by Martin Barry in *Edinburgh New Philosophical Journal* (1836–7) and through the translation of Johannes Müller's *Handbuch der Physiologie des Menschen* (1838–42). Barry's articles were read by William B. Carpenter, who discussed von Baer's theory in his *Principles of General and Comparative Physiology* (1839) and by Owen, who incorporated it in his lectures at the Royal College of Surgeons in 1837. And in his *Lectures on the Comparative Anatomy and Physiology of the Invertebrate Animals* (1843) he advocated the notion that development is a process of divergence from common forms. Owing to these various works von Baer's ideas were known to Chambers, Spencer and Darwin, influencing their thinking to varying degrees.[50] Given this background, it is surprising to read the following statement made by Huxley: 'My translation of "Fragments relating to Philosophical Zoology", selected from the Works of K.E. Von Baer, was published in "Scientific Memoirs" for February and May 1853. Up to that time, I believe, von Baer's ideas were hardly known outside Germany.'[51]

We may get an idea of Owen's attitude towards evolution from his reaction to *Vestiges of the Natural History of Creation*. Having received a copy of the book outlining a theory of evolution based on von Baerian notions he wrote to the anonymous author:

Sir, — I beg to offer you my best thanks for the copy of your work entitled 'Vestiges of the Natural History of Creation', which I have perused with the pleasure and the profit that could not fail to be imparted by a summary of the evidences from all the Natural Sciences bearing upon the origin of all Nature, by one who is evidently familiar with the principles of so extensive a range of human knowledge. It is to be presumed that no true searcher after truth can have a prejudiced dislike to conclusions based upon adequate evidence, and the discovery of the general secondary causes concerned in the production of organized beings upon this planet would not only be received with pleasure, but is probably the *chief end* which the best anatomists and physiologists have in view. (My italics)[52]

These are not the words of an anti-Evolutionist. In fact, when he was requested from various sides to join the chorus against Chamber's book, he did not comply. The simplest explanation of this fact is that he could go a long way with the anonymous author. On a few points he had reservations. Thus, for instance, he did not believe in reports on spontaneous generation as willingly as Chambers, and he could not accept that man had evolved from a monkey.

In 1851 Owen and Carpenter, adopting an idea proposed by Agassiz, began to apply von Baer's conceptions on the interpretation of palaeontological data, showing that just like in ontogenetic development the fossil history of animal life testifies to progress and divergence from general to special forms.[53]

And then 1859 arrived, and with that the publication of *On the Origin of Species*. Shortly afterwards, Darwin wrote to Owen:

> You made a remark in our conversation something to the effect that my book could not probably be true as it attempted to explain so much. I can only answer that this might be objected to any view embracing two or three classes of facts . . . I should be a dolt not to value *your* scientific opinion very highly. If my views are *in the main* correct, whatever value [they] may possess in pushing on science will now depend very little on me, but on *the verdict pronounced by eminent men in science*. (The last italics are mine)[54]

And Owen's verdict came as a long, anonymous review in *The Edinburgh Review*. In this we may read:

> The origin of species is the question of questions in Zoology; the supreme problem which the most untiring of our original labourers, the clearest zoological thinkers, and the most successful generalisers, have never lost sight of, whilst they have approached it with due reverence. We have a right to expect that the mind proposing to treat of, and assuming to have solved, the problem, should show its equality to the task. The signs of such intellectual power we look for *in clearness of expression*, and *in the absence of all ambiguous or unmeaning terms*. Now, the present work is occupied by arguments, beliefs, and speculations

on the origin of species, in which, as it seems to us, the fundamental mistake is committed, of *confounding the questions, of species being the result of a secondary cause or law,* and *of the nature of that creative law.* (My italics)[55]

Owen is frank about the weaknesses in Darwin's work; many of Darwin's supporters were aware of shortcomings, even if they informed him (Darwin) in less blunt terms. And above all, Owen saw right away that Darwin was unable to distinguish between the theory on the reality of evolution and his own theory on the mechanism of evolution.

Owen continued:

The principles, based on rigorous and extensive observation, which have been established since the time of Cuvier, and have tended to impress upon the minds of the most exact reasoners in biology the conviction of a constantly operating secondary creational law, are the following: — The law of irrelative or vegetative repetition, referred to at p. 437 of Mr. Darwin's work; the law of unity of plan or relations to an archetype; the analogies of transitory embryonal stages in a higher animal to the matured forms of lower animals; the phenomenon of parthenogenesis; a certain parallelism in the laws governing the succession of forms throughout time and space; the progressive departure from type, or from the more generalised to more specialised structures, exemplified in the series of species from their first introduction to the existing forms. In his last published work Professor Owen does not hesitate to state 'that perhaps the most important and significant result of palaeontological research has been the establishment of the axiom of *the continuous operation of the ordained becoming of living things'.* The italics are the author's. As to his own opinions regarding the nature or mode of that 'continuous creative operation', the Professor is silent.[56]

Evidently Owen did not conceal his being an Evolutionist. He is not attacking Darwin for being an Evolutionist, but for having advanced a theory which by necessity must be unacceptable for people with profound knowledge in morphology and embryology. Note, however, that Owen apparently ascribes Geoffroy Saint-Hilaire's ideas to Cuvier, and that he misinterprets von Baer.

Owen then continued:

Mr. Darwin rarely refers to the writings of his predecessors, from whom, rather than from the phenomena of the distribution of the inhabitants of South America, he might be supposed to have derived his ideas as to the origin of species. When he does allude to them [without mentioning their names], their expositions on the subject are inadequately represented. Every one studying the pages of Lamarck's original chapters . . . will see how much weight he gives to inherent constitutional adaptability, to hereditary influences, and to the operation of long lapses of time on successive generations, in the course of transmuting a species. *The common notion of Lamarck's philosophy*, drawn from the tirades which a too figurative style of illustrating the reciprocal influence of innate tendencies and outward influences have drawn upon the blind philosopher, *is incorrect and unjust*. (My italics)[57]

That Owen's reproach is correct and just is suggested by the fact that similar objections were made by Darwin's friend Charles Lyell.

Owen also spotted Darwin's notorious illustration of the power of natural selection:

'In North America the black bear was seen by Hearne swimming for hours with widely open mouth, thus catching, *like a whale*, insects in the water. Even in so extreme a case as this, if the supply of insects were constant, and if better adapted competitors did not already exist in the country, *I can see no difficulty in a race of bears being rendered, by natural selection, more and more aquatic in their structure and habits, with larger and larger mouths, till a creature was produced as monstrous as a whale.*'

If the ursine species had not been restricted to northern latitudes, we might have surmised this to have been one of the facts connected with 'the distribution of the inhabitants of South America', which seemed to Mr. Darwin, when naturalist on board H.M.S Beagle, 'to throw some light on the origin of species'. But the close resemblance of the style, and of the tone and frame of mind which could see no difficulty in the adequacy of the above-cited circumstances of 'external conditions, of habit, of volition', to change a bear into a whale, to those exemplified in the 'Philosophie Zoologique', point strongly to the writings of Lamarck as the true suggestor of Mr. Darwin's views of animated nature. We look, however, in vain for any instance of hypothetical transmutation in Lamarck so gross as the one above cited . . .

Vague and general as is the illustration based upon Hearne's remark, it is made still more vague [indeed, void of sense] in a later reprint of the volume 'On the Origin of Species'. It now reads, 'In North America the black bear was seen by Hearne swimming for hours with widely opened mouth, thus catching, almost like a whale, insects in the water'. (My italics)[58]

It appears that Lyell also commented upon Darwin's grotesque bear-whale transformation, for Darwin wrote to him in September 1860: 'Observe, that in my wretched Polar Bear [sic!] case, *I do show the first step* by which conversion into a whale "would be easy", "would offer no difficulty"!!'[59] And so did William H. Harvey, Hooker's friend, who was answered by Darwin as follows: 'The bear case has been well laughed at, and disingenuously distorted by some into my saying that a bear could be converted into a whale. As it offended persons, I struck it out in the second edition; but I still maintain that there is no special difficulty in a bear's mouth being enlarged to any degree useful to its changing habits.'[60]

In fact, Darwin never quite forgot this illuminating example of natural selection in action, for as late as in 1881 he wrote: 'This sentence was omitted in the subsequent edition, owing to the advice of Prof. Owen, *as it was liable to be misinterpreted*; but I have always regretted that I followed this advice, *for I still think the view quite reasonable*'[61] (my italics). But it was not re-inserted in later editions.

Owen went on:

Lasting and fruitful conclusions have, indeed, hitherto been based only on the possession of knowledge; now we are called upon to accept the hypothesis on the plea of want of knowledge. The geological record, it is averred, is so imperfect! But what human record is not? Especially must the record of past organisms be much less perfect than of present ones. We freely admit it. But when Mr. Darwin, in reference to the absence of the intermediate fossil forms required by his hypothesis . . . the countless hosts of transitional links which, on 'natural selection', must certainly have existed at one period or another in the world's history — when Mr. Darwin exclaims what may be, or what may not be, the forms yet forthcoming out of the graveyards of strata, we would reply, that *our only ground for prophesying of what may come, is by analogy of what has come to light* . . .

Mr. Darwin asks, 'How is it that varieties, which I have called incipient species, become ultimately good and distinct species?' To which we rejoin with the question: — Do they become good and distinct species? Is there any one instance proved by observed facts of such transmutation? We have searched the volume in vain for such. (My italics)[62]

As a morphologist Owen was well aware that a micromutation theory cannot explain organic evolution, macromutations must be invoked to account for many evolutionary changes. Hence he must reject the 'homoeopathic form of the transmutation hypothesis'[63] submitted by Darwin, and with that the role of natural selection as the creator of variation. That does not imply that he denied the occurrence of natural selection, only it had a different function. His views on this point were not clearly stated in the review, but at least he wrote:

The individuals of species least adapted to bear [the never-ending mutation of geographical and climatal conditions on the Earth's surface] and incapable of modifying their organisation in harmony therewith, have perished. Extinction, therefore, on this hypothesis, is due to the want of self-adjusting, self-modifying power in the individuals of the species.[64]

In this way he makes selection the agent of the progressive evolution, the occurrence of which he believed to be disclosed by the fossil record. It may seem a weak point in a theory proclaiming ordained evolution that the latter should involve an endless series of mistakes which had to be eliminated. However, the stand taken by Owen does not involve any logical flaw: God might have chosen this policy in spite of or perhaps *because* of his omniscience. Owen's theory as well as Darwin's attempted to account for the several empirical facts which suggest that evolution has taken place; the participation of God is a completely metaphysical question which Owen could not prove, and Darwin not disprove.

Owen's review was not a friendly one, and it touched upon the essential weaknesses in Darwin's theory; he, and many others besides, including Darwin's friends, were shrewd enough to look through the verbiage and detect the flaws in the argument. Darwin was much concerned about the review. In a letter to Huxley he complains about the 'misrepresentations', writing: '. . . he says we are called on to accept the hypothesis on the plea of ignorance, whereas I think I could not have made it clearer that I admit the imperfection of the Geological Record as a great *difficulty*[65] (my italics). I am afraid that Owen was right here, for great difficulties usually imply refutation.

We shall end this discussion of the relation between Owen and Darwin by returning to the 'Historical Sketch'. In continuation of the passages already quoted Darwin writes:

When the first edition of [*On the Origin of Species*] was published, I was so completely deceived . . . by such expressions as 'the continuous operation of creative power', that I included Professor Owen with other palaeontologists as being firmly convinced of the immutability of species; but it appears . . . that this was on my part a preposterous error. In the last edition of this work I inferred . . . from a passage beginning with the words 'no doubt the type-form', &c. . . . that Professor Owen admitted that natural selection may have done something in the formation of new species; but this it appears . . . is inaccurate and without evidence. I also gave some extracts from a correspondence between Professor Owen and the Editor of the 'London Review', from which it appeared manifest to the Editor as well as to myself, that Professor Owen claimed to have promulgated the theory of natural selection before I had done so; and I expressed my surprise and satisfaction at this announcement; but as far as it is possible to understand certain recently published passages . . . I have either partially or wholly again fallen into error . . . As far as the mere enunciation of the principle of natural selection is concerned, it is quite immaterial whether or not Professor Owen preceded me, for both of us, as shown in this historical sketch, were long ago preceded by Dr. Wells and Mr. Matthews [sic!].[66]

One comment before we look into the correspondence mentioned by Darwin: must the expression 'the continuous operation of creative power' imply the immutability of species?

In 1866 the first volume of Owen's *On the Anatomy of Vertebrates* was examined in *The London Review*. The writer quoted the following passage:

The actual presence, therefore, of small species of animals in countries where larger species of the same natural families formerly existed, *is not the consequence of any gradual diminu-*

tion of the size of such species, but is the result of circumstances which may be illustrated by the fable of the 'Oak and the Reed'; the smaller and feebler animals have bent and accommodated themselves to changes which have destroyed the larger species. They have fared better in the 'battle' of life. (My italics)

The phrase emphasised here shows clearly how Owen dissociates himself from any kind of Darwinian natural selection, without therefore rejecting the notion of the 'struggle for existence'. Nevertheless the reviewer, who did not understand the subject better than Darwin, asked '. . . if this was not actually an admission of the Darwinian theory'.[67]

Owen replied:

If your readers will refer to the IVth volume of *Zool. Trans.*, 'Memoir on Diornis' (Feb., 1850) — the theory of the extinction and conservation of species.

In that exposition of my theory . . . I speak of those faring better in 'the contest which, as a living organism, the individual of each species has to maintain against the surrounding agencies'; . . . in the elementary work of 1866, I use the brief expression 'in the battle of life'. That is all the difference.[68]

All previous advocates of natural selection, except Patrick Matthew, had ascribed to it an intraspecific sifting action serving to keep the members of the species in an optimal state of adaptation. Matthew and Darwin added to this normalising selection a separate function, directive selection, which permitted natural selection to pass beyond the bonds of the species limits. But to Owen the 'battle for life' is interspecific, leading to progressive evolution, a phenomenon the existence of which was refuted by Darwin. So Wells and Matthews were not precursors of Owen, and I am afraid that if Darwin could not see this point then he had indeed 'wholly fallen in error'. He was willing to sacrifice his claim on priority to snub Owen, but it was all in vain.

Considering what we know of Owen's stand with respect to evolution, stated privately to Darwin in 1837, and repeated often in writing, in careful wording to be sure, it is nothing but incredible that Darwin could write in 1859: '. . . all the most eminent palaeontologists, namely Cuvier, *Owen*, Agassiz, Barrande, Falconer, E. Forbes, &c., and all our greatest geologists, as Lyell, Murchison, Sedgwick, &c., have unanimously, often vehemently, maintained the immutability of species' (my italics).[69] In spite of the distinguished company, Owen complained, and in later editions of *On the Origin of Species* his name was deleted.

By including Owen among various outspoken anti-Evolutionists Darwin shows that: (i) he made no distinction between Lamarck's theory on the reality of evolution and theories on the mechanism of evolution; and (ii) he acknowledged only one theory on the mechanism of evolution, his own. Hence, those who did not believe in Darwinism must perforce believe in Creation. This is logic, but based on premises which have no merit for their upholder. But it seems that the only other possible explanation of Darwin's statement spells dishonesty.

Owen and Huxley were involved in fights on several occasions, primarily, but not exclusively on the question of evolution and Darwinism. As a consequence of the prevailing image of Huxley as Darwin's noble guardian, and as part of the Darwinian myth, it is currently assumed that Owen was constantly defeated in these encounters. Adrian Desmond has recently published a book dealing with these schisms in which it is shown that the views of Owen generally turned out to be correct.[70]

The picture we have of Richard Owen has been painted by Darwinians, and according to them he was arrogant and scheming, and exceedingly zealous in guarding his prestige. No doubt there is some truth in this — nobody who has read his contribution to *The Edinburgh Review*, while accepting Buffon's maxim, 'Le style, c'est l'homme même',[71] can ever be a great admirer of Owen.

For many years Owen believed in a theory of evolution, based on the views of Geoffroy Saint-Hilaire and von Baer, a theory coinciding to a considerable extent with those professed by Chambers and Mivart. He was hesitant to speak out on this topic, but once Darwin had broken the ice he stated his views clearly enough to earn a place among the founders of the macromutation theory.

ROBERT CHAMBERS (1802–1871)

In 1844 a book was published anonymously in London under the title *Vestiges of the Natural History of Creation*.[72] This book is an ambitious attempt to outline the history of the universe and, in particular, our planet. It deals with astronomy, geology, physics, chemistry, palaeontology, botany, zoology and even anthropology and linguistics. Based on the evidence of the fossil record and the fundamental unity of organisation on which the classification of plants and animals is based, the author professes the belief that the organic world, including man, has arisen through a process of evolution originating in the distant past. From this point of departure the conclusion had to be the same as that reached by Lamarck, namely, that the evolution had been progressive:

> The idea, then, which I form of the progress of organic life upon our earth . . . is, *that the simplest and most primitive type, under a law to which that of like-production is subordinate, gave birth to the type next above it, that this again produced the next higher, and so on to the very highest*, the stages of advance being in all cases very small — namely, from one species only to another; so that the phenomenon has always been of a simple and modest character.[73]

The book was a great success with the reading public, indeed, its reception was better than the one bestowed upon Darwin's book 15 years later.

As might be expected, the author did not master all the subjects covered with equal skill. He was well versed in geology and palaeontology, but his biology was poor. And this was demonstrated in particular when he attempted to establish the relation between various animal groups. Some of his observations on this topic were quite shrewd, but some were appalling. Many of his mistakes have been quoted, I shall mention only one example: 'The penguin, in its fin-like wings, and the posterior position of the feet, points to a more probable origin for this class in the fishes.'[74] Today this suggestion sounds ridiculous, but it seems to have been unavoidable that the early speculations on evolution should go astray. And Chambers' particular example was in the air, so to speak, for Darwin was at some time thinking along the same lines: '?We need think that fish and penguins really pass into each other.'[75]

The reaction from the Establishment, clerical as well as scientific, was violent; and a number of savage reviews appeared in the periodical literature. The author took the criticism *ad notam*, introduced corrections in the subsequent editions, and even wrote *Explanations: A Sequel to Vestiges of the Natural History of Creation*.

Among the severest critics were Huxley, who in 1854 reviewed a new edition of the book. He later wrote:

As for the 'Vestiges', I confess that the book simply irritated me by the prodigious ignorance and thoroughly unscientific habit of mind manifested by the writer. If it had any influence on me at all, it set me against Evolution; and the only review I ever have qualms of conscience about, on the ground of needless savagery, is one I wrote on the 'Vestiges' while under that influence.[76]

At the time Darwin prepared *On the Origin of Species* for publication 'evolution' spelt 'Vestiges', and it was probably unavoidable to mention this book. In fact, it was the only work on evolution mentioned in the first edition of *On the Origin of Species*, where in the introduction Darwin wrote:

The author of the 'Vestiges of Creation' would, I presume, say that, after a certain unknown number of generations, some bird had given birth to a woodpecker, and some plant to the misseltoe, and that these had been produced perfect as we now see them; but this assumption seems to me to be no explanation, for it leaves the case of the coadaptations of organic beings to each other and to their physical conditions of life, untouched and unexplained.[77]

Evidently, Darwin's main objection was the theory being a macromutation theory, permitting the evolution to pass in one step from one species to another one.

In later editions Chambers was transferred to the 'Historical Sketch'. Here Darwin went into further detail:

The 'Vestiges of Creation' appeared in 1844. In the tenth and much improved edition . . . the anonymous author says . . .: — The proposition determined on after much consideration is, that the several series of animated beings, from the simplest and oldest up to the highest and most recent, are, under the providence of God, the results, *first*, of an impulse which has been imparted to the forms of life, advancing them, in definite times, by generation, through grades of organization . . . these grades being few in number . . . *second*, of another impulse connected with the vital forces, tending, in the course of genera-tions, to modify organic structures in accordance with external circumstances . . . The author apparently believes that organisa-tion progresses by sudden leaps, but that the effects produced by the conditions of life are gradual. He argues with much force on *general grounds* that species are not immutable productions. But

I cannot see how the two supposed 'impulses' account in a scientific sense for the numerous and beautiful coadaptations which we see throughout nature . . . The work, from its powerful and brilliant style, though displaying in the earlier editions little accurate knowledge and a great want of scientific caution, immediately had very wide circulation. In my opinion it has done excellent service in this country in calling attention to the subject, in removing prejudice, and in thus preparing the ground for the reception of analogous views. (The last italics are mine)[78]

Darwin's dissatisfaction is unjustified, for here is what he wrote himself: 'Such considerations as these incline me to lay less weight on the direct action of the surrounding conditions, than on a tendency to vary, due to causes of which we are quite ignorant.'[79] Surely, there is no decisive difference between 'impulse' and 'tendency'.

As to the last clause, Darwin undoubtedly was right, the author of *Vestiges of the Natural History of Creation* was indeed Darwin's 'John the Baptist'. For many years after the appearance of the book, the origin of life was subject to public and, we may presume, private discussions in England. In spite of all attacks, the book continued to appear in new and revised editions; people bought it and read it. The general public was well acquainted with the idea of evolution when Darwin's book was finally published. And by that time the opponents had wasted most of their bile, some had even accepted the theory.

Who was the mysterious 'Mr. Vestiges', and why had he chosen anonymity? People guessed, among the candidates were Albert, the Prince Consort, and Charles Darwin. In a letter to Hooker in 1845 Darwin wrote: 'Did you hear Forbes, when here, giving the rather curious evidence (from a similarity in error) that Chambers must be the author of the *Vestiges*'?[80] That the author was Robert Chambers was officially acknowledged in the last edition of the book, in 1883, 13 years after the death of the author.

Robert Chambers was a self-made man. He and his brother William started a bookshop, which was soon enlarged with a printing shop and made into a publishing firm. And Robert Chambers became an author, supplying much of the material printed and published by his brother. In 1832 *Chambers' Edinburgh Journal* was launched, bringing popular articles on science to the people. In this way he became interested in science in general and after some time arose the ambition to write a book on the natural history of the creation of the universe and the living world.

In order to have the privacy required to keep his enterprise secret, he moved to nearby Saint Andrews. Was this step really necessary? In perspective it is difficult to understand Chambers' anxiety, for as we have seen, the idea of evolution was not new, Lamarck's work was known all over Europe; many authors had dealt with the problem. But there was much opposition to such ideas in English academic circles, presumably because of the clerical supervision of the universities. Additionally, Chambers was not economically independent, and a bad reputation might bring harm to his business. In fact, Chambers had an experience suggesting that the choice of anonymity was well advised. Thus, the mere rumour that he was the author of *Vestiges of the Natural History of Creation* sufficed to force through his withdrawal as candidate for the post of Lord Provost in Edinburgh.[81]

Darwin's survey of Chambers' theory suggests it is a modification of Lamarck's, as it makes a distinction between progressive and divergent adaptive evolution. I have been unable to find this idea clearly stated in any of the editions available to me, but it is probable that Chambers would have been influenced by Lamarck. One might expect therefore that Chambers would pay tribute to the great pioneer, but this was hardly the case:

Early in this century, M. Lamarck, a naturalist of the highest character, suggested an hypothesis of organic progress which deservedly incurred much ridicule, although it contained a glimmer of the truth. He surmised, and endeavoured, with a great deal of ingenuity, to prove, that one being advanced in the course of generations to another, in consequence merely of its experience of wants calling for the exercise of its faculties in a particular direction, by which exercise new developments of organs took place, ending in variations sufficient to constitute a new species . . . Now it is possible that wants and the exercise of faculties have entered in some manner into the production of the phenomena which we have been considering; but certainly not in the way suggested by Lamarck, whose whole notion is obviously so inadequate to account for the rise of the organic kingdoms, that we can only place it with pity among the follies of the wise.[82]

Evidently, Chambers had little esteem for Lamarck's work. He correctly dissociates himself from Lamarck's faulty theory on the mechanism of evolution involving the inheritance of acquired characters, but he is fair enough to admit Lamarck's handicap with respect to factual knowledge:

> Had the laws of organic development [ontogenesis] been known in his time, his theory might have been of a more imposing kind. It is upon these that the present hypothesis is mainly founded. I take existing natural means, and shew them to have been capable of producing all the existing organisms, with the simple and easily conceivable aid of a higher generative law, which we perhaps still see operating upon a limited scale.[83]

Apparently, Chambers did not see that as an explanation of progressive evolution his 'higher generative law' is not a great advance compared to Lamarck's 'la pouvoir de la vie'.

It is seen that Chambers envisaged evolutionary changes to involve modifications of the embryonic development. In the first edition he did not divulge his source of inspiration, but later he wrote:

> First surmised by the illustrious Harvey, afterwards illustrated by Hunter in his wondrous collection at the Royal College of Surgeons, finally advanced to mature conclusions by Tiedemann, St. Hilaire, and Serres, embryotic development is now a science. Its primary positions are — 1. that the embryos of all animals are not distinguishably different from each other; and 2. that those of all animals pass through a series of phases of development, each of which is the type or analogue of the *permanent* configuration of tribes inferior to it in the scale. (My italics)[84]

I think that we must make a reservation with respect to the word 'all' appearing in both statements. Also, it is seen that the second statement is a version of Meckel–Serres' law which later became associated with the name of Haeckel.

In his works on comparative vertebrate embryology, von Baer had strongly emphasised that the notion of adult recapitulation is wrong, embryos do not recapitulate the permanent or adult stages of lower forms, but rather, if not exactly, their embryonic stages. But Chambers was acquainted with von Baer's work and corrected his error, although without quoting his source, for later he writes:

> It has been seen that, in the reproduction of the higher animals, the new being passes through stages in which it is successively

Figure 3: Robert Chambers' attempt to illustrate the origin of some vertebrate forms through modification of the embryonic development

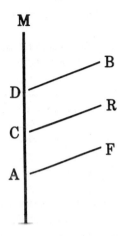

See text for further details. After R. Chambers, *Vestiges of the Natural History of Creation* (1969).

fish-like and reptile-like. But the resemblance is not to the adult fish or the adult reptile, but to the fish and reptile at a certain point in their foetal progress; this holds true with regard to the vascular, nervous, and other systems alike . . . This may be illustrated by a simple diagram [see Figure 3].

The foetus of all the four classes may be supposed to advance in the identical condition to the point A. The fish there diverges and passes along a line apart, and peculiar to itself, to its mature state at F. The reptile, bird and mammal, go on together to C, where the reptile diverges in like manner, and advances by itself to R. The bird diverges at D, and goes on to B. The mammal then goes forward in a straight line to the highest point of organization at M. This diagram shews only the main ramifications; but the reader must suppose minor ones, representing the subordinate differences of orders, tribes, families, genera, &c., if he wishes to extend his views to the whole varieties of being in the animal kingdom. Limiting ourselves at present to the outline afforded by this diagram, it is apparent that the only thing required for an advance from one type to another in the generative process is that, for example, the fish embryo should not diverge at A, but go on to C before it diverges, in which case the progeny will be, not a fish, but a reptile. To protract the *straightforward part of a gestation over a small space* — and from species to species the space would be small indeed — is all that is necessary.[85]

Incidentally, this quotation suggests that Spencer may have been inspired by Chambers. The latter summarised his view in the following way:

The whole train of animated beings, from the simplest and oldest, up to the highest and most recent, are, then, to be regarded as a series of *advances of the principle of development*, which have depended upon external physical circumstances, to which the resulting animals are appropriate.[86]

It is obvious that Chambers' theory is no different from the one advanced by Etienne Geoffroy Saint-Hilaire; he even later specifies, in partial agreement with the latter, that '. . . air and light are possibly amongst the principal agencies . . . which operated in educing the various forms of being'.[87]

It is easy to find errors and mistakes in Chambers' work, even in the later and corrected versions, but this is a feature common to all works on evolution in the nineteenth century, and perhaps even today. Indeed, Chambers cannot claim much originality for he was strongly influenced by Lamarck, Etienne Geoffroy Saint-Hilaire, von Baer and other biologists. All the same we must admit that he, almost as early as Owen, realised that evolutionary change must be explained by an epigenetic macromutations theory of evolution. In doing so he showed more biological commonsense than Darwin and his successors.

I shall end this survey of Chambers' contribution to evolutionary thought with the following assertion, published in England in 1878, at a time when almost everybody had lost belief in Darwin's natural selection, and many were converted to the macromutation theory advocated by Chambers, Owen and Mivart:

Hardly any advance has since been made on Chambers' general arguments, which at the time they appeared would have been accepted as convincing, but for theological truculence and scientific timidity. And Chambers himself only gave unity to thoughts already in wide circulation . . . Chambers was not a scientific expert, nor altogether an original thinker, but he had studied scientific literature to better purpose than any professor . . . The considerations that now recommend evolution to popular audiences are no other than those urged in the 'Vestiges'.[88]

THE NON-PRECURSORS

The first to appreciate the bearing of the facts of embryology on the problem of evolution was, of course, Darwin, and the realization that they had such a bearing was his own discovery.[89]

Gavin de Beer

The persons dealt with in this chapter had written about evolution before Darwin. To be sure, Owen had been overcautious when he stated his views in public, so Darwin might with some justification pretend that he was unaware of Owen's stand. But we know that Owen had communicated it to Darwin as early as 1837, and I therefore think that Owen deserves to be included in this group of 'non-precursors'.

These people were successors to Lamarck as far as the theory on the reality of evolution is concerned, but they were not precursors to Darwin, for they did not operate with natural selection. Rather, inspired directly or indirectly by Geoffroy Saint-Hilaire and von Baer, Owen and Chambers advocated the epigenetic macromutation theory of evolution, without, however, making any further contributions to it. This is typical of all the supporters of this theory; in spite of its impressive age of more than 150 years, the theory is still largely undeveloped. The reason for this is to a large extent the fact that it has been rejected by the majority of the biological community, but in part it is due to lack of initiative. As we shall see, there is no lack of empirical data of relevance for the elaboration of the macromutation theory.

5

Charles Darwin (1809–1882)

What now are we to say to these several facts? . . . These several facts accord
well with my theory.[1]

Charles Darwin

In short, Darwin muddled into genius and greatness like a true Englishman.[2]

William Irvine

In our time, when so many worry about the negative sides of
capitalism, it is consoling to contemplate that Darwin and his work
display one of its positive consequences, intellectual freedom. Complete freedom of expression requires complete economic
independence. Darwin's mother and wife were of the Wedgwood
family, owners of the famous porcelain pottery, and his father,
Robert Darwin, was a successful and wealthy provincial physician.
This pedigree made it possible for Darwin to support himself and his
family without ever holding a salaried employment.

He began university studies, medicine in Edinburgh and afterwards theology in Cambridge, where he took the degree of Bachelor
of arts.

His great chance came when in 1831 he was offered to join the
crew of HMS *Beagle*, which was to circumnavigate the world,
mainly for cartographical purposes. As a naturalist Darwin was
evidently a self-made man, whose principal training occurred during
this voyage where he had time to read, to think, and to make a
wealth of observations on geology, palaeontology, biogeography,
botany and zoology.

Upon his return he soon found himself married with his cousin
Emma, with whom he had ten children, of whom seven reached
adulthood. After a few years in London, the family moved to the
now world-famous house in Down, where Darwin assumed the
existence of a landed gentleman-scholar, an outsider to the academic
Establishment. His work was severely handicapped by chronic
illness, of which he wrote to Hooker in 1845: 'I believe I have not
had one whole day, or rather night, without my stomach having been
greatly disordered, during the last three years, and most days great

100

prostration of strength . . . many of my friends, I believe, think me a hypochondriac.'[3] The last point, of great concern to Darwin, was due to the fact that various doctors, including his own father, could not diagnose his disease; most of the specialists were inclined to believe that neurotic disorder lay behind the somatic symptoms.

Some years ago a rather plausible solution was suggested to Darwin's suffering, *Chaga's Disease*, caused by a microorganism, *Trypanosoma cruzi*, the chief vector of which is a large South American bloodsucking bug, *Triatoma infestans*. On 26 March 1835, as Darwin spent the night in a village in the Argentinian province of Mendoza, he was attacked by this bug. The trypanosoma invades various tissues of the body of the victim, giving rise to symptoms similar to those that troubled Darwin.[4]

Although his bad health interfered, he nevertheless went to London several times every year, to pay visit to his brother Erasmus and to his friends, and to clubs and learned societies. So even though Darwin lived a secluded life, he was not quite isolated. However, his best contact with the outside world was through his correspondence, part of which has been published in five large volumes. A new and even more comprehensive collection of his correspondence is now under preparation; the first volume has already been published.

Darwin was not an Evolutionist when he was on board the *Beagle*, but he had made observations, notably in continental South America and on the Galapagos Islands, which seemed to contradict the orthodox view. However, Darwin was not ready merely to accept the fact that evolution had occurred, he wanted to understand how it had happened, he wanted to know the *mechanism* of evolution. In July 1837 he started his notebooks on the transmission of species, but it was to take a long time before he could start to work in this project, for first he had to deal with the material collected on the journey with the *Beagle*, and when that was finished, he started to work on the systematics of barnacles, a task which took him eight years, ending in 1854. He did, however, commit his theory to sheets of writing paper in the 'Sketch' of 1842, and an extended version, the 'Essay', was prepared in 1844. In that year *Vestiges of the Natural History of Creation* entered the scene, and the treatment it received made a deep impression upon Darwin. He remained silent for years, confiding only in Hooker. The story about the happenings which prompted Darwin to write and publish *On the Origin of Species* is told elsewhere in this book (see pp. 210–21).

Darwin's earlier work had created for him a good reputation as a scientist, but this book made him world-famous. It was translated into many different languages, and during the rest of his life a never-ending stream of distinctions were bestowed upon him. However, working part-time because of his health, Darwin went on writing books, on botany, on domesticated animals and plants, on the descent of man, on the activities of earthworms and the small biography of his grandfather Erasmus Darwin, etc., altogether some 20 books.

Darwin found time for one more activity: the management of his fortune. Both his father and his father-in-law contributed to the household of the young Darwin couple; they began with a yearly income of about £1,200. This was more than they needed, so Darwin could begin to make investments, and these, as well as the income, went on increasing as the years went by. He also made some money from his literary activities. Thus during his lifetime he had an income of about £2,800 on the various editions of *On the Origin of Species*.[5] In the last year of his life the household expenses were £1,159; this includes a staff of five women and three men, costing altogether £367. In 1879 he could make a yearly allowance to each of his sons, by then aged between 30 and 40 years, of £829. The amounts given here can be seen in their true perspective when it is known that Huxley was paid a salary of £400 as a professor, and that the Civil Service Pension which Darwin helped to procure for Wallace was £200. The estate left by Darwin was evaluated at £282,000 which is the equivalent of about £10 million today.

When he died Darwin was generally acknowledged as the 'Newton of Biology', so it was only natural that he should come to rest in Westminster Abbey.[6]

ON THE ORIGIN OF SPECIES BY MEANS OF NATURAL SELECTION OR THE PRESERVATION OF FAVOURED RACES IN THE STRUGGLE FOR LIFE

As we have seen, Darwin's first work on evolution, going usually under the name of *On the Origin of Species* or *The Origin*, has repeatedly been compared to Newton's *Principia Mathematica*. In the present context it is unavoidable to subject this work to a very careful scrutiny in order to establish whether this claim can be substantiated.

Several objections may be raised against this project. The most obvious is perhaps that Darwin is indeed the 'Newton of Biology' and hence his work is raised beyond the evaluation of self-appointed critics.

Others may say: we know that Darwin was a muddled thinker, and that his main work is crammed with misunderstandings, contradictions, wild speculations and transparent *ad hoc* hypotheses, but his basic idea is correct, and therein lies his greatness. To this assertion two questions may be asked. First: would Newton be held in the same esteem if, although fundamentally correct, *Principia Mathematica* was known to be crammed with misunderstandings, contradictions, etc.? Second: is Darwin's basic idea correct, has his particular notion on the mechanism of evolution survived to the present day? If not, the above objection is invalid.

Another reservation may be: Darwin wrote several books on evolution, and therefore it is unfair to judge him solely on this single work. Yet, Darwin himself considered *On the Origin of Species* to be his most important work, and next to the journal from the voyage with *Beagle*, it is considered the most readable of his books. And since it would be impossible to go through all the books written by Darwin, I shall consider that even this objection is refuted.

Some may say, indeed have said: it is true that the ideas advanced by Darwin were not too original, partly they were even erroneous, and his way of presenting them may be anything but flawless, but his is the merit to have convinced the world that evolution has taken place. It has happened before in the history of science that a theory advanced by one person is rejected or ignored in his lifetime, only to be accepted later through the efforts of somebody else. However, what is honoured by the scientific community is originality, not publicity. Darwin did a great service to biology by ensuring that Lamarck's theories on evolution were generally accepted, but this fact does not make him a genius, a 'Newton of Biology'.

In this chapter I shall use the sixth edition of *On the Origin of Species* as the basis of my evaluation. This was the last edition attended by Darwin, and contains all the corrections he wanted to make to his work. I shall largely discuss the chapters one by one as they follow in the book; in some instances I may collect material from more than one chapter in the same section.

'Variation under Domestication'

His own observations on the distribution of animals in nature, together with Lyell's discussion of Lamarck in *Principles of Geology* and perhaps his grandfather's work, were unquestionably the sources of inspiration for Darwin's adopting the theory on the reality of evolution, Lamarck's creation. His theory on the mechanism of evolution may also be traced to two sources, observations on domesticated plants and animals, which indicate how variations arise, and Malthus' book *An Essay on the Principle of Population*, which suggested to Darwin a mechanism for the survival of some of the variations. It was therefore quite natural that Darwin's first chapter was called 'Variation under Domestication'.

In a section called 'Causes of Variation' Darwin begins by observing that domestic plants and animals vary much more than wild ones, a state of affairs which cannot be contested. If it is accepted that the existence of variability is a matter (i) of the spontaneous origination of variations and (ii) of their survival, then the difference observed may be explained with reference to either of these factors. It is rather unlikely, if not impossible, that a spontaneous process is affected by the external conditions. It would therefore seem natural, especially for a believer in a theory in which survival is the most important agent, to explain the difference between domestic and wild organisms as a consequence of the differential survival of the spontaneous variations. This hypothesis seems to be eminently corroborated, for in nature most variations, all but the advantageous ones, must become eliminated according to Darwin's theory. In contrast, the domestic organisms are under constant surveillance, so almost every perceptible variation will be observed, and its survival is dictated wholly by the breeder's whims. As is well known, this circumstance entails the survival of many variations which were doomed to succumb under natural conditions.

Such a simple explanation did not appeal to Darwin; rather, he assumed that domesticated organisms actually vary more than wild ones, the reason being the differences in their living conditions. It seems that Darwin made a bad choice, and as it takes more words to advocate a wrong than a right case, he engaged himself in a long and tedious discussion of the means and the effects of the environment. We shall not delve into this question; suffice it to observe that none of the examples illustrating the effect of the environment is very convincing. The *facts* quoted by Darwin in this context rather tend to show that variations, even extensive ones, may arise spontaneously in one out of many organisms living under closely similar conditions.

Darwin's next section deals with 'Effects of Habit and of the Use or Disuse of Parts: Correlated Variation: Inheritance'.

Darwin begins:

Changed habits produce an inherited effect, as in the period of the flowering of plants when transported from one climate to another. With animals the increased use or disuse of parts has had a more marked influence; thus I find in the domestic duck that the bones of the wing weigh less and the bones of the legs more, in proportion to the whole skeleton, than do the same bones in the wild-duck; and this change may be safely attributed to the domestic duck flying much less, and walking more, than its wild parents . . . Not one of our domestic animals can be named which has not in some country drooping ears; and the view which has been suggested that the drooping is due to the disuse of the muscles of the car, from the animals being seldom much alarmed, seems probable.[7]

Here, Darwin is pronouncing views which coincide completely with those of Lamarck. And the question which we must ask is this: are these changes inherited? It is too bad that Darwin, who loved to make small experiments, did not come upon the idea to put an egg laid by a tame duck in the nest of a wild one, or *vice versa*, and see what happened! As regards the drooping ears: is it really true that this feature occurs in all species of domestic mammals, and is it probable that one species is less alarmed in one, and a second species in another country?

Darwin mentions several striking instances of correlated variations:

Important changes [and even unimportant ones] in the embryo or larva will probably entail changes in the mature animal. In monstrosities, the correlations between quite distinct parts are very curious . . . Hairless dogs have imperfect teeth: long-haired and coarse-haired animals are apt to have . . . long or many horns; pigeons with feathered feet have skin between their outer toes; pigeons with short beaks have small feet, and those with long beaks large feet. Hence if man goes on selecting, and thus augmenting, any peculiarity, he will almost certainly modify unintentionally other parts of the structure, owing to the mysterious laws of correlation.[8]

The addition in brackets is intended to emphasise the pheno-menon of 'epigenetic amplification'; a variation, imperceptible in an embryo whose length is measured in millimetres, may be substantial in the adult, even if its relative length is unchanged. The specific examples mentioned by Darwin are very interesting: the first three show that when keratinisation is interfered with, it will have repercussions in all structures containing keratin; and the last two apparently, and surprisingly, that the growth of the keratinous beak and the ossified bones of the feet are controlled in part by the same agent.

As concerns inheritance we find Darwin stressing its importance for evolutionary change: 'Any variation which is not inherited is unimportant for us';[9] but he also states: 'The laws governing inheritance are for the most part unknown.'[10] When Darwin prepared the edition from which this quotation is taken, some of the laws governing inheritance were in fact known. A few years earlier Mendel had published his epoch-making observations and reflections demonstrating that inheritance is particulate and not blending, as commonly presumed at the time. We cannot blame Darwin that Mendel's work was unknown to him, it was ignored even by people acquainted with it. However, many facts known at the time, also by Darwin, demonstrated beyond any possible doubt that inheritance cannot be blending.

In association with the discussion on inheritance Darwin unexpectedly takes up a new topic:

Having alluded to the subject of reversion, I may here refer to a statement often made by naturalists — namely, that our domestic varieties, when run wild, gradually but invariably revert in character to their aboriginal stocks. Hence it has been argued that no deductions can be drawn from domestic races to species in a state of nature. I have in vain endeavoured to discover on what decisive facts the above statement has so often and so boldly been made. There would be great difficulty in proving its truth: we may safely conclude that very many of the most strongly marked domestic varieties could not possibly live in a wild state. In many cases we do not know what the original stock was, and so could not tell whether or not nearly perfect reversion had ensued . . .

If it could be shown that our domestic varieties manifested a strong tendency to reversion, — that is, to lose their acquired characters, whilst kept under the same conditions, and whilst kept in a considerable body, so that free intercrossing might check, by blending together, any slight deviations in their structure, in such case, I grant that we could deduce nothing from domestic varieties in regard to species. But there is not a shadow of evidence in favour of this view.[11]

Arguing against reversion Darwin first observes that some domestic forms cannot live unprotected by man. But to them the term 'when run wild' does not apply, and therefore neither the statement about reversion. And second, would it not suffice to observe those cases where the original stock is known, at least approximately? In any case I am convinced that the advocates of reversion would hardly assert that it might be 'nearly perfect'.

Thus, in Darwin's view it holds that if reversion is a common phenomenon, then observations on domesticated plants and animals have no bearing on what is going on in nature. And, since an essential part of his argument concerning the mechanism of evolution would be lost if this was true, he argues against reversion. One is therefore astonished to read the following when some pages later he discusses observations made on his beloved pigeons:

I then crossed one of the mongrel barb-fantails with a mongrel barb-spot, and they produced a bird of as beautiful a blue colour, with the white loins, double black wing-bar, and barred and white-edged tail feathers, as any wild rock-pigeon! We can understand these facts, on *the well-known principle of reversion to ancestral characters*, if all the domestic breeds are descended from the rock-pigeon. (My italics)[12]

Now that he needs the phenomenon of reversion in support of his argument, he seems to have forgotten his earlier distrust.

Darwin further gives examples showing that in plants as well as in animals, new races may arise spontaneously, but concludes:

We cannot suppose that *all* the breeds were suddenly produced as perfect and as useful as we now see them; indeed, in many cases, we know that this has not been their history. The key is man's power of accumulative selection: *nature gives successive variations*; man adds them up in certain directions useful to him. *In this sense he may be said to have made for himself useful breeds*. (My italics)[13]

It seems to me that this quotation clearly demonstrates that the variations are *spontaneous creations of Nature*. Man may wish to ensure the *survival* of certain forms to the detriment of some others,

and the initial step required for this end is to isolate the desired variation through *inbreeding*. One may indeed say that in doing so he
undertakes a *selection*, and that he thereby *makes* a new breed, as
long as one is aware of the exact and restricted implication of these
words.

Darwin admitted that variations range from minute to extensive,
but he had a special axe to grind: he believed that all major evolutionary advances represent the accumulation of innumerable small
changes: individual variations. And therefore he writes:

> If selection consisted merely in separating some very distinct
> variety, and breeding from it, the principle would be so obvious
> as hardly to be worth notice; but its importance consists in the
> great effect produced by the accumulation in one direction,
> during successive generations, of differences absolutely
> inappreciable by an uneducated eye — differences which I for one
> have vainly attempted to appreciate.[14]

One may or may not accept this assertion, but one thing is
absolutely certain, if it is correct that the change which can be
accumulated in each generation is 'inappreciable', then the process
must be extremely slow, taking several generations of *breeders* to
get appreciable results. Clearly, Darwin must have forgotten what
he wrote half a page before: 'The great power of this principle of
selection is not hypothetical. It is certain that several of our eminent
breeders have, *even within a single lifetime, modified to a large
extent* their breeds of cattle and sheep.' (my italics)[15]

Darwin, like many others before him, realised that the observations made by the breeders of animals and plants have direct bearing
on the mechanism of evolution. Most of what he wrote on this
subject in the first chapter is correct, but he made three mistakes:
he claimed that the external conditions affect the variability of living
organisms; that inheritance is blending; and that major changes
accomplished by the breeders arise through the accumulation of
minute variations.

As I have tried to show, the evidence available to him did not
support these premises. Darwin always considered his greatest
contribution to evolutionary thought to be his collection of facts —
supporting the notion of evolution in general, and his own ideas in
particular. However as early as this first chapter we learn about the
way Darwin handled his facts; when they did not fit his views he
ignored them or tried to explain them away.

With the rise of Mendelian genetics, Darwin's two first premises have long been falsified. As far as the third is concerned, it has in some cases been possible to obtain major changes through gradual accumulation. However, it holds for plants as well as for animals that the major innovations are the effects of one or a few mutations.

'Variation under Nature'

The range of variation displayed by living organisms is enormous. But for Darwin evolution involved the transformation of one species to another one, so the only really important variation to him was that which occurred within the confines of a species. All further variation was supposed to arise through accumulation of such intraspecific variation. As a consequence the discussion in the second chapter concerns only the variation prevailing in varieties, subspecies, species and genera.

Much of the discussion actually deals with the difficulties facing the systematists when they have to decide whether a certain group of organisms form a species or a taxon of lower rank. Thus Darwin writes:

> No one definition [of the term 'species'] has satisfied all naturalists; yet every naturalist knows vaguely what he means when he speaks of a species. Generally the term includes the unknown element of a distinct act of creation. The term 'variety' is almost equally difficult to define; but here community of descent is almost univerally implied, *though it can rarely be proved*. (My italics)[16]

This confession is extremely perplexing, considering that Darwin's purported aim was to *prove* that species and even higher categories originated through 'community of descent'.

Darwin continues: 'We have also what are called monstrosities; but they *grade into varieties*. By a monstrosity I presume is meant some considerable deviation of structure, generally *injurious*, or *not useful* to the species'[17] (my italics). It is evident that, without interruption, Darwin jumped from dealing with the actually established variation in nature to discuss a mechanism of variation, sports or macromutations. And according to him, when they occur in Nature they invariably give rise to monsters, injurious or at least not useful. Considering Darwin's belief in the purgatory effect of natural

109

selection, no 'monsters' should exist in Nature. Therefore it would have been much more logical to begin the statement: 'We do not have', but then of course their 'grading into varieties' would be irrelevant.

Behind Darwin's reasoning there is a premise which I shall challenge: monsters do not exist in Nature. Is not the elephant a monster, as well as the giraffe, the porcupine, *Apteryx*, the wingless bird, the octopus and the praying mantis, just to mention a few cases. Everything depends on the way we use the word, but it is true, of course, that for anyone who believes that survival depends only on victory in the struggle for existence, it must be difficult to accept the survival of monsters. As we shall see, the situation is changed radically, when isolation is accepted as an important factor for survival.

After this Darwin goes on:

The many slight differences which appear in the offspring from the same parents . . . are of the highest importance for us, for they are often inherited . . . and they thus afford materials for natural selection to act on and accumulate . . . These individual differences generally affect what naturalists consider unimportant parts; but I could show by a long catalogue of facts, that parts which must be called important . . . sometimes vary in the individuals of the same species . . . It would never have been expected that the *branching of the main nerves* close to the great central ganglion of an insect would have been *variable in the same species* . . . [Sir J. Lubbock] . . . has also shown that the *muscles* in the larvae of certain insects are *far from uniform*. (My italics)[18]

I do not think that these examples from his 'long catalogue of facts' are very convincing; truly, the nervous and muscular system as such are 'important parts', but nothing suggests that the variation quoted by Darwin is anything but trivial without any functional significance. And therefore I think that the following accusation against potential opponents, when inverted, may be raised against himself: 'Authors sometimes argue in a circle when they state that important organs never vary; for these same authors practically rank those parts as important . . . which do not vary; and, under this point of view, no instance will ever be found of an important part varying.'[19]

In this chapter Darwin also describes the phenomenon

of dominance:

> . . . the most flourishing, or, as they may be called, the *dominant*
> species, — [are] those which range widely, are the most diffused
> in their own country, and are the most numerous in individuals
> . . . One of the higher plants may be said to be dominant if it be
> more numerous in individuals and more widely diffused than the
> other plants of the same country, which live under nearly the
> same conditions. A plant of this kind is not the less dominant
> beause some conferva inhabiting the water or some parasitic
> fungus is infinitely more numerous in individuals, and more
> widely diffused. But if the conferva or parasitic fungus exceeds
> its allies in the above respects, *it will then be dominant within its
> own class.* (My italics)[20]

This quotation demonstrates how well Darwin understood
ecological relationships. Otherwise there is little to say about the
second chapter except that we learn little on the topic of 'Variation
under Nature'.

'Struggle for Existence'

After some preliminaries Darwin writes: 'I should premise that I use
this term [the "struggle for existence"] in a large and metaphorical
sense including dependence of one being on another, and including
(which is more important) not only the life of the individual, but
success in leaving progeny.'[21] He goes on to exemplify: 'Two
canine animals, in a time of dearth, may be truly said to struggle
with each other which shall get food and live.'[22] The expression 'in
a time of dearth', is most unfortunate, as it seems to suggest that the
struggle for life is occasional. In fact, the premise which Darwin had
borrowed from Malthus implies that the environment is always
sated; hence the dearth is permanent, and so is the struggle for life.
    Darwin is completely right when he writes: 'The mistletoe is
dependent on the apple and a few other trees, but can only in a far-
fetched sense be said to struggle with these trees, for, if too many
of these parasites grow in the same tree, it languishes and dies.'[23]
Predator and prey, parasite and host are dependent upon each other,
but they do not compete, and therefore they are not involved in a
mutual struggle for existence.
    Darwin goes on:

As the species of the same genus usually have, though by no means invariably, much similarity in habits and constitution, and always in structure, the struggle will generally be more severe between them, if they come into competition with each other, than between the species of distinct genera.[24]

This is a vague formulation of the 'Axiom of Competitive Exclusion', according to which two taxa cannot share the same ecological niche. For if one of the taxa is dominant relative to the other one, the members of the latter must succumb, and the taxon become extinguished. And if none of the taxa is dominant, the organisms may live peacefully together in adjacent niches, neither of them can prevail over the other one. Dominance may obtain between the members of taxa of widely varying rank, but even a variety of a species may be dominant *vis-à-vis* another variety of the same species. However, the likelihood that dominance prevails must increase with the taxonomic distance, and therefore it is not true that the struggle is severest between species of the same genera, and still less between members of the same species. This, I believe, is borne out by many examples where Darwin discusses the success of plants and animals which have been transported by man to a new geographical location. Darwin mentions this situation:

Hence we can see that when a plant or animal is placed in a new country amongst new competitors, the conditions of its life will generally be changed in an essential manner, although the climate may be exactly the same as in its former home. If the average numbers are to increase in its new home, *we should have to modify it in a different way* to what we should have to do in its native country; for we should have to give it some advantage over a different set of competitors or enemies. (My italics)[25]

When Darwin writes 'we should have to modify', one gets the impression that we are dealing with domestic organisms. But as these in general are protected from 'competitors or enemies', this interpretation is obviously wrong. But in that case Darwin is wrong, for we do not modify wild animals and plants, and these would have no chance to establish themselves unless they were dominant at the outset.

'Natural Selection; or the Survival of the Fittest'

This chapter is probably the most important in Darwin's book. First, of course, because he here presents his own theory, but also because he there puts down all the elements of the ecological theory of evolution.

Darwin poses the questions:

> Can it . . . be thought *improbable*, seeing that variations useful to man have undoubtedly occurred, that other variations useful in some way to each being in the great and complex battle of life, should occur in the course of many successive generations? If such do occur, can we doubt (remembering that many more individuals are born than can possibly survive) that individuals having any advantage, however slight, over others, would have the best chance of surviving and of procreating their kind? On the other hand, we may feel sure that any variation in the least degree injurious would be rigidly destroyed. This *preservation* of favourable individual differences and variations, and the *destruction* of those which are injurious, I have called Natural Selection, or the Survival of the Fittest. *Variations neither useful nor injurious would not be affected by natural selection.* (My italics)[26]

Darwin here gives a clear and unambiguous presentation of his particular theory of evolution. We may notice that neutral characters were no difficulty to Darwin, but they are a great problem for some of his present-day successors.

Darwin writes: '*Unless* [profitable variations] *occur, natural selection can do nothing.* Under the term of "variations", it must never be forgotten that *mere individual differences* are included'[27] (my italics). It is certainly a mistake, and a contradiction of an earlier quotation, that 'profitable' variations are necessary for natural selection to become engaged. All the same, if variations are missing, natural selection is impotent, a circumstance which may menace the credibility of his theory. In the fifth edition Darwin therefore adds the sentence dealing with 'individual differences'; since these are sure to be present whenever individuals prevail, the potency of Darwin's agent is restored.

We have seen that natural selection functions by ensuring the preservation among randomly arising minute variations of those which through accumulation will gradually improve functions useful

113

to the organism in question. Since the usefulness of most functions depends upon the environment, it follows that the outcome of the activity of natural selection will be an adjustment between organism and environment, that is, the organism becomes adapted. This raises the question: can an organism live in an environment without being adapted to it? An affirmative answer to this question is a challenge to commonsense in general and to past and current biological thought in particular. If the answer is no, then two alternative interpretations are possible: (i) When various animals and plants live side by side, then they live in, and are adapted to the same environment. In this case adaptation is a rather crude adjustment between organism and environment. (ii) If Darwin's theory is correct, then the properties of every taxon, from the kingdom and to the lowest subspecific level, is determined through adaptation to their particular environment. The second alternative has some interesting implications. Thus, members of the same species, living far apart, must have the same environment, whereas their closest neighbours live in a different environment.

As envisaged by Darwin the organisms must continuously adjust themselves to the slightest environmental changes. This phenomenon clearly presupposes the presence of the variations required for the adapation. And it is obvious that if this does not obtain, then 'adaptation' loses its sense. One more consequence: adaptations must imply a unique correlation between organism and environment, which involves that the organism actually is isolated and protected from competition from other organisms. Apparently, the phenomenon of adaptation involves a contradiction of the struggle for life, at least the interspecific variation allowed for by Darwin, if not by his latter-day adherents.

Are the consequences outlined above compatible with reality? We shall turn to Darwin for an answer:

No country can be named in which all the native inhabitants are now so perfectly adapted to each other and to the physical conditions under which they live, that none of them could be still better adapted or improved; for in all countries, the natives have been so far conquered by naturalized productions, that they have allowed some foreigners to take firm possession of the land. And as foreigners have thus in every country beaten some of the natives, we may safely conclude that the natives might have been modified with advantage, so as to have better resisted the intruders.[28]

The concept of 'adaptation' may still be saved for we may assert that the intruders are adapted to the natives + the common environment, whereas the natives are adapted to the common environment, but not to the intruders. Nevertheless, I think that Darwin's statement shows that evolution is more than adaptation, it is also progress. Darwin forgot what he had written about dominant species.

Darwin then touches a very important problem:

> It may be well here to remark that with all beings there must be much fortuitous destruction, which can have little or no influence on the course of natural selection. For instance a vast number of eggs or seeds are annually devoured, and these could be modified through natural selection only if they varied in some manner which protected them from their enemies. Yet many of these eggs or seeds would perhaps, if not destroyed, have yielded individuals better adapted to their conditions of life than any of those which happened to survive. So again a vast number of mature animals and plants, whether or not they be the best adapted to their conditions, must be annually destroyed by accidental causes, which would not be in the least degree mitigated by certain changes of structure or constitution which would in other ways be beneficial to the species. But let the destruction of the adults be ever so heavy, if the number which can exist in any district be not *wholly kept down* by such causes, — or again let the destruction of eggs or seeds be so great that only a hundredth or a thousandth part are developed, — yet of those which do survive, the best adapted individuals, supposing that there is any variability in a favourable direction, will tend to propagate their kind in larger numbers than the less well adapted. If the numbers be *wholly kept down* by the causes just indicated, as will often have been the case, natural selection will be powerless in certain beneficial directions; but this is no valid objection to its efficiency at other times and in other ways; for we are far from having any reason to suppose that many species ever undergo modification and improvement at the same time in the same area. (My italics)[29]

By 'fortuitous destruction' Darwin means elimination before the individual has had the possiblity to hold their own in the competition for reproduction. And that must apply not only to eggs and seeds, but also to the young ones until they have reached maturity. So Darwin was right: the overwhelming part of the elimination which we think of as the struggle for existence is random and has nothing to do with natural selection. Darwin uses twice the expression 'wholly kept down'; in the first instance it seems to mean 'completely eliminated', but I fail to see that this interpretation will make sense the second time.

Darwin was not sure that his readers had really grasped the manner in which natural selection works. One might expect that he would use some of his 'facts' to improve upon this situation, but instead he chose the following expedient:

> In order to make it clear how, as I believe, natural selection acts, I must beg permission to give one or two *imaginary* illustrations. Let us take the case of a wolf, which preys on various animals, securing some by craft, some by strength, and some by fleetness; and let us suppose that the fleetest prey, a deer for instance, had from any change in the country *increased* in numbers, or that other prey had decreased in numbers, during that season of the year when the wolf was hardest pressed for food. Under such circumstances the swiftest and slimmest wolves would have the best chances of surviving, and so be preserved or selected, — provided always that they retained strength to master their prey at this or some other period of the year, when they were compelled to prey on other animals. *I can see no more reason to doubt that this would be the result*, than that man should be able to improve the fleetness of his greyhounds by careful and methodical selection. (My italics)[30]

I fail to see that an increase in the number of prey, fleet or not, can lead to the wolf being hard pressed for food. But in any case, those deer which happened to be caught would be the least fleet, and the result would be that predator and prey would evolve in parallel. And since there would always be individual differences in fleetness, the wolves and the deer would become engaged in an endless race for swiftness, from which the wolves at least gained nothing.

In the discussion of circumstances favouring the action of natural selection Darwin writes:

> Isolation, also, is an important element in the modification of species through natural selection . . . Moritz Wagner has lately published an interesting essay on this subject, and has shown that the service rendered by *isolation in preventing crosses between newly-formed varieties* is probably greater even than I supposed.

But . . . I can by no means agree with this naturalist, that migration and isolation are necessary elements for the formation of new species. The importance of isolation is likewise great in *preventing*, after any physical change in the conditions . . . *the immigration of better adapted organisms* . . . *If,* however, *an isolated area may be very small* . . . the total number of the inhabitants will be small; and this *will retard the production of new species through natural selection,* by decreasing the chances of favourable variations arising. (My italics)[31]

Just as in domestication, inbreeding is important in Nature for the preservation of new variations. Moritz Wagner saw this; Darwin accepted it and then again rejected it. Next, Darwin describes with great clarity that the survivors are not always the fittest; in random isolation the less fit may happily abide. Why was this fact never incorporated in a maxim? Darwin further asserts that the production of new species through natural selection is proportional to the number of individuals. This is a completely unfounded assertion; the probability of *new variations arising* may well be proportional to this number, but not necessarily their survival. The *empirical facts* show clearly that this is favoured by isolation; Darwin knew that very well from his knowledge of the Galapagos Islands.

Darwin goes on:

The mere lapse of time by itself does nothing, either for or against natural selection. I state this because it has been erroneously asserted that the element of time has been assumed by me to play an all-important part in modifying species, as if *all* the forms of life were necessarily undergoing change through some innate law. Lapse of time is only so far important, and its importance in this respect is great, that it gives a better chance of beneficial variations arising, and of their being selected, accumulated, and fixed . . .

If we turn to nature to test the truth of these remarks, and look at any small isolated area, such as an oceanic island, although the number of species inhabiting it is small . . . yet, of these a very large proportion are endemic, — that is, have been *produced* there, and nowhere else in the world. Hence an oceanic island *at first sight seems to have been highly favourable for the production of new species.* But we may thus deceive ourselves, for to ascertain whether a small isolated area, or a large open area like a

117

continent, has been most favourable for the production of new organic forms, we ought to make the comparison within equal times; and this we are incapable of doing. (My italics)[32]

Darwin's charge against his critics is somewhat obscure, for whatever mechanism lies behind evolutionary change, it seems likely that there will be a relatively direct correlation between time and change, and it is difficult to see any other way in which time may be involved. But it is completely incomprehensible that he must go to an oceanic island to test this notion. And what he finds is, as we have seen, that the isolation prevailing there is *favourable* for evolutionary innovation. But this he really does not want to find, and therefore he must resort to an *ad hoc* hypothesis to explain away the disturbing reality. And this expedient is time: he must assume the oceanic islands to be much older than the continents to explain the observed facts. However, as he knows this to be untrue, he does not say so, but observes that the point he went out to test really cannot be tested at all.

In a section called 'The Probable Effects of the Action of Natural Selection through Divergence of Character and Extinction, on the Descendants of a Common Ancestor', Darwin presents his famous, often reproduced, 'phylogenetic' diagram (Figure 4). There would be no reason to discuss it here, were it not for the repeated claims that Darwin, through this figure and the accompanying discussion, founded the theoretical basis of phylogenetic systematics.

We have already seen that we owe to Lamarck the idea that phylogenetic classification should be possible, and also the distinction between divergent and progressive evolution. Influenced by Lamarck and by von Baer, Spencer was later able to state the complete correspondence between ontogenetic and phylogenetic recapitulation. Although Spencer may not himself have asserted this, perhaps not even realised it, this parallelism implies that the superior taxa correspond to a reality existing in Nature, thus they are more than plain conventions.

Darwin rejected Lamarck's ideas from the outset, and Spencer's views were not published when he prepared the first edition of *On the Origin of Species*, but from 1864 he had access to an essentially correct outline of the implication of phylogenetic classification. As we have seen, Spencer's work did not make much impression upon Darwin, so when he set out to interpret his diagram, the discussion was based completely on the ruling Linnaean systematics. As realised already by Lamarck, the latter is based on a number of

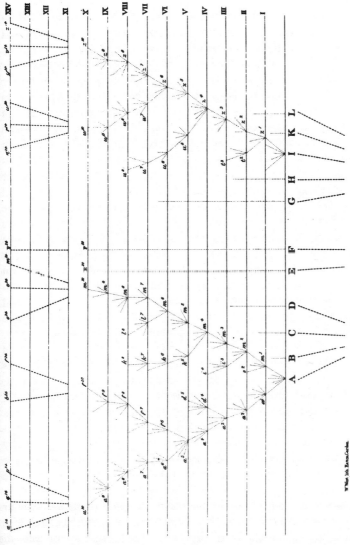

Figure 4: Charles Darwin's renowned attempt to account for the course of evolution through classification

See text for further details. From C. Darwin, *On the Origin of Species* (1966).

conventions which are incompatible with phylogenetic classification. Of these conventions only one needs be mentioned here, namely, that the *only taxon which has any correspondence to things existing in nature is the species.* Under these circumstances what existed in the past was species, and these evolved through divergence to new species. As the number of the latter became too large for easy survey, it was necessary to include the species in genera, the genera in families, the families in orders, etc. However, the various superior taxa are nothing but collections of species, established merely for convenience; they do not represent anything but the personal discretion of the person undertaking the classification.

This way of interpretation runs counter to the actual course of evolution, and it is therefore not surprising that it leads to insurmountable logical difficulties. However, there are still many Systematists, bound by the Linnaean conventions, who do not consider the Linnaean species concept inadequate.[33] I believe that this is why there are yet people ready to celebrate Darwin as the founder of phylogenetic systematics.

The next topic is 'On the Degree to which Organisation tends to advance', that is, 'progressive evolution'. Darwin writes:

> Natural selection acts exclusively by the preservation and accumulation of variations, which are beneficial under the organic and inorganic conditions to which each creature is exposed *at all periods of life.* The ultimate result is that *each creature* tends to *become more and more improved* in relation to its conditions. This improvement *inevitably* leads to *the gradual advancement* of the organisation of *the greater number* of living beings throughout the world. (My italics)[34]

Darwin is right, of course; the inevitable result of natural selection is progressive evolution. However, this is not because natural selection creates new and better organisms, but because it eliminates the ancient and inferior ones, for elimination is all it can accomplish.

Yet, now Darwin was caught in a trap, for he knew enough biology to realise that evolution has not always been progressive. He wrote:

> But here we enter on a very intricate subject, for naturalists have not defined to each other's satisfaction what is meant by an advance in organisation . . .

If we take as the standard of high organisation, the amount of differentiation and specialisation of the several organs in each being when adult (and this will include the advancement of the brain for intellectual purposes), natural selection clearly leads towards this standard: for all physiologists admit that the specialisation of organs, inasmuch as in this state they perform their functions better, is an advantage to each being; and hence the accumulation of variations tending towards specialisation is within the scope of natural selection. On the other hand . . . it is quite possible for natural selection gradually to fit a being to a situation in which several organs would be superfluous or useless: in such cases there would be retrogression in the scale of organisation.[35]

The reason for Darwin's uneasiness is that he had only one mechanism at his disposal to account for the mechanism of evolution: natural selection. And whereas this agent may easily explain evolutionary progress, it is not so certain that it can also ensure retrogressive evolution. This problem has remained a difficulty for Darwin's followers to the present day.

But Darwin at least made an attempt to submit an explanation:

But it may be objected that if *all* organic beings thus tend to rise in the scale, how is it that throughout the world a multitude of the lowest forms still exist; and how is it that in each great class some forms are far more highly developed than others? Why have not the more highly developed forms everywhere supplanted and exterminated the lower? Lamarck, who believed in an innate and inevitable tendency towards perfection in all organic beings, seems to have felt this difficulty so strongly, that he was led to suppose that new and simple forms are continually being produced by spontaneous generation . . . On our theory the continued existence of lowly organisms offers no difficulty; for natural selection, or the survival of the fittest, *does not necessarily include progressive development* — it only takes advantage of such variations as arise and are beneficial to each creature under its complex relations of life. And it may be asked *what advantage*, as far as we can see, *would it be* to an infusorian animalcule — to an intestinal worm — or even to an earth-worm, *to be highly organised*. If it were no advantage, these forms would be left, by natural selection, *unimproved or but little improved*, and *might remain for indefinite ages in their present lowly condition*. And geology tells us that some of the lowest forms . . . have remained for an enormous period in nearly their present state. But to *suppose that most* of the many *now existing low forms have not in the least advanced* since the first dawn of life would be extremely rash; for every naturalist who has dissected some of the beings now ranked as *very low* in the scale, must have been struck with their *really wondrous and beautiful organisation*. (My italics)[36]

I shall not comment further upon these seemingly contradictory statements. We have already discussed Lamarck's views and we therefore know that Darwin misinterprets him. In fact, Lamarck had, unknowingly perhaps, solved the problem which troubled Darwin so much. For Lamarck operated with two kinds of evolution, divergent and progressive, respectively. The divergent taxa subsist in isolation and in side branches to the lineages of progressive evolution. This is a logical solution to the problem, in contrast to Darwin's, for the assertion that it is of no advantage to lower organisms to evolve towards higher levels in the hierarchy implies that they never could evolve. If living organisms did not have an *innate* tendency towards the creation of the multitude of organisms which have existed since the origin of life, there would have been no evolution. But that this evolution to a significant extent has been progressive, *is solely due to Darwin's natural selection.*

If the quoted statements rather unsatisfactorily account for the existence of low organisms we need not be worried, for we only have to read on to get a correct explanation of the existence of low forms, an explanation which makes the preceding quotation non-sensical. Darwin writes:

Although organisation, on the whole, may have advanced and be still advancing throughout the world, yet the scale will always present many degrees of perfection; for the high advancement of certain whole classes, or of certain members of each class, does not at all necessarily lead to the extinction *of those groups with which they do not enter into close competition.* In some cases, as we shall hereafter see, lowly organised forms appear to have been preserved to the present day, from inhabiting *confined* or *peculiar* stations, where they have been subjected to less severe competition. (My italics)[37]

If we take the words 'confined' and 'peculiar' to represent 'random' and 'non-random' isolation, respectively, then Darwin in this little citation gives a complete account of the ecological mechanisms responsible for the survival of non-dominant forms. And now we also get an explanation of the fact that the several primitive organisms remained unchanged to the present day, namely, that 'variations or individual differences of a favourable nature may never have arisen for natural selection to act on and accumulate'.[38] If we disregard the 'micromutational' wording, this explanation appears to be correct.

'Laws of Variation'

Darwin starts this chapter with a famous and often quoted statement: 'I have hitherto sometimes spoken as if the variations . . . were due to chance. This, of course, is a wholly incorrect expression, but it serves to acknowledge plainly our ignorance of the cause of each particular variation.'[39] Darwin here confuses two phenomena: (i) where and when a particular variation arises, is wholly a matter of chance; (ii) however, the nature of the potential variations is strictly restrained by the organisation of the organisms in question and may broadly be said to be directed by macromolecular and epigenetic laws. The mechanism proposed by Darwin to explain the origin of evolutionary innovation, involving the accumulation of individual differences prevailing mainly at the adult stage, seemingly circumvents the need to take epigenetic laws into account. However, he was aware that there are some laws which regulate the pattern of change in living organisms. These he called the 'laws of variation'.

The first part of the chapter does not deal with this topic, but with the influence of the external conditions and the effect of use and disuse. In this context Darwin writes:

In some cases we might *easily* put down to disuse modifications of structure which are *wholly*, or *mainly*, due to natural selection. Mr. Wollaston has discovered the remarkable fact that 200 beetles, out of the 550 species . . . inhabiting Madeira, are so far deficient in wings that they cannot fly . . . Several facts, — namely, that beetles in many parts of the world are frequently blown to sea and perish; that the beetles in Madeira . . . lie much

concealed, *until the wind lulls* and the sun shines; that the proportion of wingless beetles is larger on the exposed Desertas than in
Madeira itself; and especially the extraordinary fact . . . that
certain large groups of beetles, elsewhere excessively numerous,
which *absolutely require the use of their wings, are here almost
entirely absent*; — these several considerations make me believe
that the wingless condition of so many Madeira beetles is *mainly*
due to the action of natural selection, *combined probably with
disuse*. For during many successive generations each individual
beetle which flew least, either from its wings having been *ever
so little less perfectly developed* or *from indolent habit*, will have
had the best chance of surviving from not being blown out to sea;
and, on the other hand, those beetles which most readily took to
flight would oftenest have been blown to sea, and thus destroyed.
(My italics)[40]

Let it be noticed first that if the beetles lie low when the wind is
blowing, then natural selection cannot influence the wing size.
Second, if beetles which *absolutely* require the use of wings cannot
survive on Madeira, then the proposed mechanism seems rather
dubious. Third, if the beetles survive because of their indolent
habits, then it is the latter, and not the wing size which will be
affected by natural selection.

But Darwin goes on:

The insects in Madeira which are not ground-feeders, and which
. . . must habitually use their wings to gain their subsistence,
have . . . their wings *not at all reduced, but even enlarged. This
is quite compatible with the action of natural selection*. For when
a new insect first arrived on the island, *the tendency of natural
selection to enlarge or to reduce the wings, would depend upon
whether a greater number of individuals were saved by successfully battling with the winds, or by giving up the attempt and
rarely or never flying*. As with mariners shipwrecked near a
coast, it would have been better for the good swimmers if they
had been able to swim still further, whereas it would have been
better for the bad swimmers if they had not been able to swim at
all and had stuck to the wreck. (My italics)[41]

I believe it is quite evident that those beetles which battled with the
winds would have their wings reduced, while those which gave up
the attempt would have their wings unchanged. But Darwin could

not carry this simple logical argument to the end, and therefore arrived at the opposite result. One further marvels at the superb explanatory power of Darwin's theory; whether the wings are reduced or enlarged is quite immaterial, natural selection can explain every possible change.

We now come to the main subject: 'Correlated Variation'. Darwin writes:

> I mean by [correlated variation] that the whole organisation is so tied together during its growth and development, that when slight variations in any one part occur, and are accumulated through natural selection, other parts become modified. This is a very important subject, most imperfectly understood, and no doubt wholly different classes of facts may be here easily confounded together.[42]

Nothing could be more true. Darwin mentions several observations, some of which are correct and very illuminating, and some irrelevant.

We must, however, leave this subject and pass on to 'Compensation and Economy of Growth'. Here we read the following statement:

> The elder Geoffroy and Goethe propounded, at about the same time their law of compensation or balancement of growth; or, as Goethe expressed it, 'in order to spend on one side, nature is forced to economise on the other side' . . . With species in a state of nature it can hardly be maintained that the law is of universal application; but many good observers, more especially botanists, believe in its truth. I will not, however, here give any instances, for I see hardly any way of distinguishing between the effects, on the one hand, of a part being largely developed through natural selection and another and adjoining part being reduced by this same process or by disuse, and, on the other hand, the actual withdrawal of nutriment from one part owing to the excess of growth in another and adjoining part.
>
> I suspect, also, that some of the cases of compensation which have been advanced, and likewise some other facts, may be merged under a more general principle, namely, that natural selection is continuously trying to economise every part of the organisation. If under changed conditions of life a structure, before useful, becomes less useful, its diminution will be

favoured, for it will profit the individual not to have its nutriment wasted in buildig up an useless structure . . .

Thus, as I believe, natural selection will tend in the long run to reduce any part of the organisation, as soon as it becomes, through changed habits, superfluous, without by any means causing some other part to be largely developed in a corresponding degree. And, conversely, that natural selection may perfectly well succeed in largely developing an organ without requiring as a necessary compensation the reduction of some adjoining part.[43]

So the epigenetic laws may be reduced to, and even superseded by natural selection!

Darwin goes on discussing the laws of variation for another 14 pages, but as he does not deal with any epigenetic topics we shall go on to the next chapter.

'Difficulties of the Theory'

Even in the first edition Darwin had a chapter dealing with the difficulties of his theory. It begins like this:

Long before the reader has arrived at this part of my work, a crowd of difficulties will have occurred to him. Some of them are *so serious that to this day I can hardly reflect on them without being in some degree staggered*; but, to the best of my judgement, *the greater number are only apparent*, and *those that are real* are not, I think, *fatal* to the theory. (My italics)[44]

Darwin's admirer's, then and now, have praised him for the honesty and candour he thus displayed. I am not so sure that this attitude is justified. If a theory has too many 'difficulties' it should not be published, but rejected; indeed, I believe this is the procedure adopted by most scientists. It is possible, of course, that increased knowledge may show that facts once thought to be embarrassing are not after all. If we find this to be the case with Darwin's difficulties, then he is completely vindicated; if not, then the theory was falsified at the outset. This is the question we shall try to answer here.

Darwin goes on:

These difficulties and objections may be classed under the

following heads: — First, why, if species have descended from other species by fine gradations, do we not everywhere see innumerable transitional forms? Why is not all nature in confusion, instead of the species being, as we see them, *well defined*?

Secondly, is it possible that an animal having, for instance, the structure and habits of a bat, could have been formed by the modification of some other animal with widely-different habits and structure? Can we believe that natural selection could produce, on the one hand, an organ of trifling importance, such as the tail of a giraffe, which *serves as a fly-flapper*, and, on the other hand, an organ as wonderful as the eye?

Thirdly, can instincts be acquired and modified through natural selection? What shall we say to the instinct which leads the bee to make cells, and which has practically anticipated the discoveries of profound mathematicians?

Fourthly, how can we account for species, when crossed, being sterile and producing sterile offspring, whereas, when varieties are crossed, their fertility is unimpaired?

The two first heads will here be discussed; some miscellaneous objections in the following chapter: Instinct and Hybridism in the two succeeding chapters. (My italics)[45]

Darwin begins the discussion in this way:

As natural selection acts solely by the preservation of profitable modifications, each new form will tend in a fully-stocked country to take the place of, and finally to exterminate, its own less improved parent-form and other less-favoured forms with which it comes into competition. *Thus extinction and natural selection go hand in hand.* Hence, if we look at each species as descended from some unknown form, both the parent and all the transitional varieties will generally have been exterminated by the very process of the formation and perfection of the new form. (My italics)[46]

Apart from the wording, this statement is a perfectly correct account of progressive evolution. I like in particular the emphasised sentence, for in fact elimination is all that natural selection can accomplish.

Upon this follows a lengthy discussion of the first difficulty facing his micromutation theory, the absence of traditional forms. The argument goes back and forth until a length Darwin decides to elucidate the problem by means of an example:

> For any form existing in lesser numbers would . . . run a greater
> chance of being exterminated than one existing in large numbers;
> and in *this particular case* the intermediate form would be
> eminently liable to the inroads of closely-allied forms existing on
> both sides of it. But it is a far more important consideration, that
> during the process of further modification, by which two varieties
> are supposed to be converted and perfected into two distinct
> species, the two which exist in larger numbers, from inhabiting
> larger areas, will have a great advantage over the intermediate
> variety, which exists in smaller numbers in a narrow and
> intermediate zone. For forms existing in larger numbers will have
> a better chance, within any given period, of presenting further
> favourable variations for natural selection to seize on, than will
> the rarer forms which exist in lesser numbers . . . I may illustrate
> what I mean by *supposing* three varieties of sheep to be kept, one
> adapted to an extensive mountainous region; a second to a
> comparatively narrow, hilly tract; and a third to the wide plains
> at the base; and that the *inhabitants* are all trying with equal
> *steadiness* and *skill* to improve their stocks by selection; the
> chances in this case will be strongly in favour of the holders on
> the mountains or on the plains, improving their breeds more
> quickly than the small holders on the intermediate narrow, hilly
> tract; and consequently the improved mountain or plain breed
> will soon take the place of the less improved hill breed; and *thus*
> the two breeds, which originally existed in greater numbers, will
> come into close contact with each other, without the interposition
> of the supplanted, intermediate hill-variety. (My italics)[47]

Darwin envisages three varieties of sheep, each adapted to their
particular environment. The numerical inferiority of the
intermediate form has nothing to do with the fact that it is
intermediate, but depends solely on its occupying a 'narrow, hilly
tract'. But it would seem that if the two other varieties were going
to displace the intermediate one, then natural selection would have
to adapt them to the 'hilly tract', which on the given premises seems
to imply that evolution would have to be reversed.

As to the 'steady and skillful inhabitants' mentioned in the above
quotation, this expression seems to refer to the *owners* of the sheep,
but if this is so, then the outcome proposed by Darwin would hardly
come true; we may presume that the owners of the hill breed would

know to defend their right of property. If, perchance, Darwin is here alluding to the sheep, then his wording is more Lamarckian than anything Lamarck ever wrote.

The next section concerns 'Organs of extreme Perfection and Complication'. Darwin once wrote in a letter: 'The eye to this day gives me a cold shudder, but when I think of the fine known gradations, my reason tells me I ought to conquer my cold shudder.'[48] The reason for Darwin's apprehension was that many had pointed out that among all the 'adaptations' encountered in the animal kingdom there is one which less than any other lends itself to the micromutation interpretation: the vertebrate — and the cephalopod — eye. And therefore Darwin felt obliged to account for origination of the eye in this section:

> To suppose that the eye with all its inimitable contrivances . . . could have been formed by natural selection, seems, I freely confess, absurd in the highest degree. When it was first said that the sun stood still and the world turned round, the common sense of mankind declared the doctrine false; but the old saying of *Vox populi, vox Dei* . . . cannot be trusted in science. *Reason* tells me, that if numerous gradations from a simple and imperfect eye to one complex and perfect can be shown to exist, each grade being *useful* to its possessor, as is *certainly* the case; if further, the eye ever varies and the variations be inherited, as is likewise *certainly* the case; and if such variations should be useful to *any* animal under changing conditions of life, then the difficulty of believing that a perfect and complex eye could be formed by natural selection, though *insuperable by our imagination*, should not be considered as subversive of the theory . . .
>
> To arrive, however, at a just conclusion regarding the formation of the eye, with all its marvellous yet not absolutely perfect characters, *it is indispensable that the reason should conquer the imagination; but I have felt the difficulty far too keenly to be surprised at others hesitating to extend the principle of natural selection to so startling a length.* (My italics, except for the Latin words)[49]

In this quotation I have excluded all the empirical evidence which Darwin mobilised to support his stand. This seems justified not the least because each of the 'fine gradations' discussed by him is separated from the nearest ones by steps which are larger than anything a Macromutationist would ever insist on. And I do not think

129

that his 'facts' ever convinced any of his opponents, which are dismissed as 'vox populi', as opposed to his own 'vox Dei'. In fact, I am not sure he convinced himself; the circumstance that he, contrary to habit, repeatedly appeals to reason seems to suggest this.

Darwin was aware that he had not yet provided support for his micromutation theory, so he continues in the next section dealing with *Modes of Transition*:

> If it could be demonstrated that any complex organ existed, which could not possibly have been formed by numerous, successive, slight modifications, then *my* theory would absolutely break down. *But I can find out no such case*. No doubt many organs exist of which we do not know the transitional grades, more especially if we look to much-isolated species, round which, according to the theory, *there has been much extinction*. Or again, if we take an organ common to all the members of a class, for in this latter case the organ must have been originally formed at a remote period, since which all the many members of the class have been developed; and in order to discover the early transitional grades through which the organ has passed, we should have to look to very ancient ancestral forms, *long since become extinct*.
>
> *We should be extremely cautious in concluding that an organ could not have been formed by transitional gradations of some kind*. (My italics)[50]

The evolutionary changes which according to Darwin's critics cannot be accounted for by the accumulation of micromutations are of two kinds, some occurring in the very early development, and some happening during later developmental stages, even after hatching or birth. The former we shall neglect in the present case except by pointing out that they obviously cannot be explained by Darwin's accumulation theory. As far as the other modifications are concerned, it must be admitted that theoretically the transition from an insectivore's forelimb to a bat's wing may occur through 'numerous, successive, slight modifications'. However, this can be done only if we refrain from the demand, inevitably dictated by the theory of natural selection, namely, that each stage in the succession must be useful to the organism. It was an easy match for Darwin's critics to see that this and other examples imply the breakdown of Darwin's theory, since *at the intermediate stages the forelimbs can be used neither for walking nor for flying*. Worse is, of course, that none of the 'facts' which Darwin had collected lend any support whatsoever to his micromutation theory — all he could do was to account for the missing evidence by reference to extinction. But this implies that the available evidence cannot be used to test the theory, which means either that the theory is false or that it is metaphysical. However, we may agree with Darwin that we shall always be cautious in our conclusions, and therefore we may wonder why he was anything but cautious in his conclusions about the validity of his theory on natural selection.

In the following section Darwin discusses 'Special Difficulties of the Theory of Natural Selection' and concludes:

[i] Finally then, although in many cases it is most difficult even to conjecture by what transitions organs have arrived at their present state; [ii] yet, considering how small the proportion of living and known forms is to the extinct and unknown, [iii] I have been astonished *how rarely an organ can be named, towards which no transitional grade is known to lead.* [iv] It certainly is true, that *new organs appearing as if created for some special purpose, rarely or never appear in any being;* — as indeed is shown by that old, but somewhat exaggerated, canon in natural history of 'Natura non facit saltum'. We meet with this admission in the writings of almost every experienced naturalist; or as Milne Edwards has well expressed it, Nature is prodigal in variety, but niggard in innovation. Why, on the *theory of Creation*, should there be so much variety and so little real novelty? Why should all the parts and organs of many independent beings, each supposed to have been separately created for its proper place in nature, be so commonly linked together by graduated steps? Why should not Nature take a sudden leap from structure to structure? On the theory of natural selection, we can clearly understand why she should not; for natural selection acts only by taking advantage of slight successive variations; she can never take a great and sudden leap, but must advance by short and *sure*, though slow steps. (My italics)[51]

Some comments: (i) If it is in many cases difficult to *conjecture* the transitions, it must be even more difficult to *observe* them, and (ii) this situation is surely worsened by the fact that the proportion of living and known forms is small compared to those extinct and unknown. On these premises it is false to assert that (iii) only rarely are transitions unknown. It is further asserted that (iv) 'new organs appearing as if created for some special purpose, rarely or never appear in any being'. This statement must be analysed in several steps. First, according to Darwin's theory natural selection will ensure the utility of the various organs found in living organisms. As usefulness implies purposefulness, the several organs are, if not created, then at least made for some special purpose. Second, if organs are used for a particular purpose, we may in general expect that they appear to be made for that purpose. Third, since Darwin could hardly deny that *new* organs arise from time to time, it appears that this statement is refuted by his own theory in combination with known empirical facts.

But as we read on, we discover that Darwin's assertion does not mean what it appears to do, but rather that macromutations are rare or non-existent. If statements (i) and (ii) are correct, and if macromutations are vastly less frequent than micromutations, then they should 'rarely . . . appear in any being'; neither Darwin nor anybody else is entitled to use the word 'never' in the present context. So Darwin's claim with respect to new purposeful organs cannot be supported by any evidence, and that may be the reason why he relied on an 'old canon', an otherwise unusual expedient in science, where emphasis is put on empirical observations and logical reasoning. Under any circumstances it is obvious that he could not use Milne Edward's statement in support of his micromutation theory.

As to Darwin's three questions, I propose the following answers: Why not? Any observation can be made compatible with a theory of Creation. Why not? Even the Creator may use a good device more than once. Yes, why not, indeed? Darwin's arguments against this possibility are postulates, unfounded by any evidence.

Next we are going to deal with 'Organs of Little Importance, as affected by Natural Selection'. We read:

As natural selection acts by life and death, — by the survival of the fittest, and by the destruction of the less well-fitted individuals, — I have sometimes felt great difficulty in understanding the origin or formation of parts of little importance; almost as great, though of a very different kind, as in the case of the most perfect and complex organs . . .

The tail of the giraffe looks like an artificially constructed fly-flapper; and it seems at first incredible that this could have been *adapted* for *its present purpose* by successive slight modifications each better and better fitted, *for so trifling an object as to drive away flies*; yet we should pause before being too positive even in this case, for we know that the distribution and existence of cattle and other animals in South America absolutely depend on their power of resisting the attacks of insects: so that individuals which could by any means defend themselves from these small enemies, would be able to range into new pastures and thus gain a great advantage. *It is not that the larger quadrupeds are actually destroyed* (except in some rare cases) by flies, but they are incessantly harrassed and their strength reduced, so that they are more subject to disease, or not so well enabled in *a coming dearth* to search for food, or to escape from beasts of prey . . .

A well-developed tail having been formed in an aquatic animal, it might subsequently come to be worked in for all sorts of purposes, — as a fly-flapper, an organ of prehension, or as an aid in turning, as in the case of the dog, *though the aid in this latter respect must be slight, for the hare, with hardly any tail, can double still more quickly.* (My italics)[52]

The general assertion that plants and animals are purposeful organisms may be well-substantiated, and yet, when it comes to ascribe purpose to any single attribute, then one is easily led astray towards ridicule. Darwin shows it here, and the same has been demonstrated by many of his successors. As concerns the fly-flapper, with which the giraffe has been outfitted by natural selection, I am rather astounded that it was not made so long as to reach all parts of the body, that surely would aid the giraffe in the search for food in a coming dearth.

The last section in this chapter is called 'Utilitarian Doctrine, how far true: Beauty, how acquired'. Darwin expresses his wish

. . . to say a few words on the protest lately made by some naturalists, against the utilitarian doctrine that *every detail of structure has been produced for the good of its possessor* . . . I fully admit that many structures *are now of no direct use to their possessors, and may never have been of any use to their progenitors* . . . *No doubt the definite action of changed conditions, and the various causes of modifications,* lately specified, have all produced an effect, *probably a great effect, independently of any advantage thus gained.* But a still more important consideration is that the chief part of the organisation of every living creature is due to *inheritance*; and consequently, though each being assuredly is well fitted for its place in nature,

CHARLES DARWIN

many structures have now no very close and direct relation to present habits of life. Thus, we can hardly believe that the webbed feet of the upland goose or of the frigate-bird are of special use to these birds; we cannot believe that the similar bones in the arm of the monkey, in the fore-leg of the horse, in the wing of the bat, and in the flipper of the seal, are of special use to these animals. We may safely attribute these structures to inheritance. But webbed feet no doubt were as useful to the progenitor of the upland goose and of the frigate-bird, as they now are to the most aquatic of living birds. So we may believe that the progenitor of the seal did not possess a flipper, but a foot with five toes fitted for walking or grasping; and we may further venture to believe that the several bones in the limbs of the monkey, horse, and bat, were originally developed, on the principle of utility, probably through the reduction of more numerous bones in the fin of some ancient fish-like progenitor of the whole class. It is scarcely possible to decide how much allowance ought to be made for such causes of change, as the definite action of external conditions, so-called spontaneous variations, and the complex laws of growth; but with these *important exceptions*, we may conclude that the structure of every living creature either now is, or was formerly, of some direct or indirect use to its possessor. (My italics)[53]

The utilitarian doctrine is the essential basis of Darwin's theory, for natural selection can preserve merely what is useful in the struggle for life. *Only on this premise is it permissible to make any inferences as to the purpose of any structure in living organisms, the expedient adopted by Darwin and his successors. If there are exceptions to this principle, and important ones at that, the game is lost.* To state that a structure is not, and may never have been of any use seems to be a falsification of the theory of natural selection. So Darwin sets out to save his theory by submitting the claim that an attribute may originate 'independently of any advantage gained'. He seems to forget, however, that on his own premises it will be lost as a consequence of disuse. Therefore, when this additional Darwinian principle is adopted, it follows that *all structures found in living organisms must be useful*. So Darwin is disowning himself, when he admits that many structures are of no use. All that he would be entitled to claim is that it may well be difficult to discover the purpose of a particular character, but that is another matter. In fact, it is a remarkable circumstance that Darwin does not mention use and disuse in the present context; is it because that would make the

134

whole discussion void of sense? However this may be, we may conclude that on Darwin's premises the tail of the giraffe is useful, if not necessarily as a 'fly-flapper' or 'as an aid in turning'. And the same holds true for the webbed feet of the upland goose and the frigate-bird.

We have now only one point left to discuss in Darwin's present chapter. Darwin writes in an often quoted statement:

Natural selection tends only to make each organic being as perfect as, or slightly more perfect than, the other inhabitants of the same country with which it comes into competition. And we see that this is the standard of perfection attained under nature. The endemic productions of New Zealand, for instance, are perfect one compared with another; but they are now rapidly yielding before the advancing legions of plants and animals introduced from Europe. Natural selection will not produce absolute perfection, nor do we always meet, as far as we can judge, with this high standard under nature.[54]

This quotation shows the embarrassment which follows from the fact that Darwin refuted the occurrence of progressive evolution. For how could any organism ever have ascended above the lowest forms of life, if no organism could rise above its neighbours?

Furthermore, it follows from the ecological theory on the mechanism of evolution that living organisms survive either because they are dominant, or because they are isolated, randomly or non-randomly, as the case may be. This holds for the organisms in New Zealand as well as elsewhere on our planet. However, the former subsist in random isolation *vis-à-vis* the latter, and if some of the invaders can occupy the same niches as the endemic forms, and happen to be dominant, they may cause the extinction of their competitors.

Darwin's next chapter is called 'Miscellaneous Objections to the Theory of Natural Selection'. It is mainly a rejoinder to St George Mivart's book *On the Genesis of Species*, and it will be dealt with in a later context.

'Instinct'

We have seen above that the third difficulty worrying Darwin was whether instincts 'can be acquired through natural selection'. A

whole chapter was devoted to this question, in which Darwin
discusses the instincts of the cuckoo, of slave-making ants, of the
hive-bee, and of neuter and sterile ants.

As to the first topic he writes:

> It is supposed by some naturalists that the more immediate cause
> of the instinct of the cuckoo is, that she lays her eggs, not daily,
> but at intervals of two or three days; so that, if she were to make
> her own nest and sit on her own eggs, those first laid would have
> to be left for some time unincubated, or there would be eggs and
> young birds of different ages in the same nest. If this were the
> case, the process of lying and hatching might be inconveniently
> long, more especially as she migrates at a very early period; and
> the first hatched young would probably have to be fed by the male
> alone.[55]

Is not this to put the cart before the horse? Surely, natural selection
would never permit such an inconvenient situation to arise in the first
instance; rather, the pattern of egg laying must be an adjustment to
the cuckoo's parasitic habits. But no, for Darwin continues: 'But the
American cuckoo is in this predicament; *for she makes her own nest,
and has eggs and young successively hatched*, all at the *same* time
[sic!].'[56] What a declaration of incompetence on behalf of natural
selection!

And yet, we distinguish a faint ray of light:

> New let us *suppose* that the ancient progenitor of our European
> cuckoo had the habits of the American cuckoo, and that she
> *occasionally* laid an egg in another bird's nest. If the old bird
> profited by this occasional habit through being enabled to migrate
> earlier or through any other cause; or if the young were made
> more vigorous by advantage being taken of the mistaken instinct
> of another species than when reared by their own mother,
> encumbered as she could hardly fail to be by having eggs and
> young of different ages at the same time; then the old birds or the
> fostered young would gain an advantage. And analogy would lead
> us to *believe*, that the young thus reared would be apt to follow
> by inheritance the *occasional and aberrant habit* of their mother,
> and in their turn would be apt to lay their eggs in other birds's
> nests, and thus be more successful in rearing their young. By a
> continued process of this nature, I *believe* that the strange instinct
> of our cuckoo has been generated. (My italics)[57]

It is not difficult to understand why Darwin was so concerned about instincts and natural selection; here surely was an instance where the micromutation theory has all chances. Thus the cuckoos might begin by cheating once every fifth year, working down the scale to one egg every year. They might then try twice every year, etc., until in the end they deposed all their eggs in foreign nests and could dispense with nest building on their own behalf.

Still, it would be nice to have an intermediate stage between Europe and America, for it is difficult to understand how the 'encumbered' American cuckoo manages in the struggle for life. Luckily

. . . we have learned something about three Australian species, which lay their eggs in other bird's nests. The chief points to be referred to are three: first, that the common cuckoo, with rare exceptions, lays only one egg in a nest . . . Secondly, that the eggs are remarkably small   That the small size of the egg is a real case of adaptation we may infer from the fact of the non-parasitic American cuckoo laying full-sized eggs. Thirdly, that the young cuckoo, soon after birth, has the instinct, the strength, and a properly shaped back for ejecting its foster-brothers, which then perish from cold and hunger. This has been boldly called a beneficient arrangement, in order that the young cuckoo may get sufficient food, and that its foster-brothers may perish before they had acquired much feeling!

Turning now to the Australian species; though these birds generally lay only one egg in a nest, it is not rare to find two and even three eggs in the same nest.[58]

In a parasitising species like the cuckoo it would seem an obvious advantage to lay one egg in each nest, thereby ensuring better exploitation of the foster parents and avoidance of competition between members of the same brood. It appears that natural selection has accomplished this in Europe, but not in Australia.

As regards egg size we next learn:

In the [Australian] Bronze cuckoo the eggs vary greatly in size . . . Now if it had been of an advantage to this species to have laid eggs even smaller than those now laid, so as to have deceived certain foster-parents, or, as is more probable, to have been hatched within a shorter period . . . then *there is no difficulty in believing* that a race or species might have been formed which

137

CHARLES DARWIN

would have laid smaller and smaller eggs; for these would have
been more safely hatched and reared . . . The eggs . . . vary . .
to an extraordinary degree in colour; so that in this respect, as
well as in size, natural selection might have secured and fixed *an*
advantageous variation. (My italics)[59]

Here again we learn that natural selection can accomplish what ever
is needed, but it appears that what is advantageous on one continent
may not be so on a second. Indeed, it seems that in Australia there
are no particularly advantageous variations with respect to either
size or colour.

Concerning the third point, the ejection instinct, Darwin
writes:

In the case of the European cuckoo, the offspring of the foster
parents are commonly ejected from the nest . . . a young cuckoo
. . . was actually seen, whilst still blind and not able even to hold
up its own head, in the act of ejecting its foster-brothers . . . With
respect to the means by which this strange and odious instinct was
acquired, if it were of great importance for the young cuckoo, as
is probably the case, to receive as much food as possible soon
after birth, *I can see no special difficulty in its having gradually
acquired*, during successive generations, the blind desire, the
strength, and structure necessary for the work of ejection; for
those young cuckoos which had such habits and structure best
developed would be the most securely reared. The first step
towards the acquisition of the proper instinct might have been
mere unintentional restlessness on the part of the young bird
when somewhat advanced in age and strength; the habit having
been afterwards improved, *and transmitted to an earlier age.
can see no more difficulty* in this, than in the unhatched young of
other birds acquiring the instinct to break through their own
shells. (My italics)[60]

But surely, the latter habit could not possibly have been
'gradually acquired, during successive generations'. And the same
holds, it seems, with respect to the ejection instinct; one cannot eject
arbitrary fractions of a 'foster-brother'. And once the faculty to deal
with a whole one had been gained, there is no reason to believe that
the young cuckoo would stop when the first one was got rid of. And
therefore Darwin had to use his imagination again, suggesting that
'unintentional restlessness' might be accumulated and telescoped
back into the newly hatched bird. No evidence exists in support of

138

the latter mechanism, it is pure speculation, and in any case, how can accumulated restlessness lead to the ejection instinct, and especially to changes in anatomical structure. Furthermore, one wonders if it would not have been of advantage to the Australian cuckoo to eject its nest mates, for in that case it would have involved 'no special difficulty in its having gradually acquired, etc'. I realise, of course, that the circumstance that more than one egg is sometimes laid in the same nest might entail losses to the own species initially, but natural selection should be able to ensure that the young cuckoos could tell the difference between their own kin and their 'foster-brothers'.

I have here dealt with only one of the four examples, but the argumentation employed is so similar that it is unnecessary to discuss the remaining ones. The only comment to be made here is that the habit of the European cuckoo no doubt is so advantageous that it would be favoured by natural selection once acquired. There is nothing wrong about natural selection, but it is evident that in spite of Darwin's heroic attempts to save it, his micromutation theory cannot explain the state prevailing in the world of cuckoos.

In the present quotations, and many more times throughout his book, Darwin assures us that *he* can see no difficulty in *believing* that Nature conforms to his theory. It is true that all our knowledge is belief in the last instance, but nevertheless there is a distinction between scientific knowledge and 'belief' in the common sense of the word. The former is based on a mixture of logical reasoning and critical evaluation of empirical data. It was when his contemporaries adopted this approach that *they found great difficulties in believing that Darwin's theory conveys a realistic interpretation of Nature.*

'Hybridism'

Darwin's fourth difficulty concerns hybridism, a question dealt with in a separate chapter which begins thus:

> The view commonly entertained by naturalists is that species, when intercrossed, have been specially endowed with sterility, in order to prevent their confusion. This view certainly seems at first highly probable, for species living together could hardly have been kept distinct had they been capable of freely crossing. The subject is in many ways important for us, more especially as *the sterility of species* when first crossed, and that of their hybrid

offspring, *cannot have been acquired*, as I shall show, *by the preservation of successive profitable degrees of sterility. It is an incidental result of differences in the reproductive systems of the parent-species*. (My italics)[61]

The answer to the question is thus given in the first paragraph, and although the formulation is somewhat ambiguous (perhaps prudent is a better characterisation), it is clear nevertheless that Darwin's micromutation theory cannot account for the sterility usually prevailing between species, even when these are closely related. I suppose nobody will object to my classifying a mutation leading to sterility between two species as a macromutation. If so, it follows that in this case at least we find the macromutation theory endorsed by Darwin.

There was one particular reason why the question of interspecific sterility was so important to Darwin. Certain naturalists, among them his friend Huxley, admitted that the breeders had obtained forms of plants and animals so different that they would have been classed as belonging to different species and genera had they been wild. However, in almost every case it turns out that within each domesticated species the several races are interfertile; thus they do not represent new species on the infertility criterion. Therefore, so argued some critics, the observations on domesticated organisms teach us nothing about evolution. Yet, the correlation between taxonomic affinity and interfertility is not as clear-cut as stated in Darwin's question. Darwin knew this and discussed it at great length in the present chapter. It is crammed with facts, and even if many of these are irrelevant in the context, and some of the arguments unacceptable, the conclusions advanced are nevertheless correct.

In principle there are two possible species criteria: (i) Distinctions may be made on the basis of overt differences in form, pattern and behaviour. When such differences reach a certain level, they are considered to define different species, below this level they specify subspecies, races, etc. (ii) Species may be defined on the sterility criterion. Evidently the second cannot be generally employed, if for no other reason than because taxonomists usually work with preserved specimens.

Darwin pointed out '. . . that the degree of fertility, both of first crosses and hybrids, graduates from zero to perfect fertility'.[62] So the two criteria do not always coincide. It is evident, however, that whereas a large measure of subjectivity may be involved in the first species criterion, sterility, in principle at least, constitutes an absolute criterion. Therefore there is a tendency to let the latter prevail whenever disagreement obtains. This is noted by Darwin: 'Kölreuter makes the rule universal . . . for in ten cases in which he found two forms, considered by most authors as distinct species, quite fertile together, he unhesitatingly ranks them as varieties'[63] and '. . . if two forms hitherto reputed to be varieties be found in any degree sterile together, they are at once ranked by most naturalists as species'.[64] Darwin is therefore right in his conclusion that 'neither sterility nor fertility affords any certain distinction between species and varieties'.[65]

Darwin next turns to the important question about the mechanism through which sterility is acquired. He writes:

At one time it appeared to me probable, as it has to others, that the sterility of first crosses and of hybrids might have been slowly acquired through the natural selection of slightly lessened degrees of fertility which, like any other variation, spontaneously appeared in certain individuals of one variety when crossed with those of another variety. For it would clearly be advantageous to two varieties or incipient species, *if they could be kept from blending*, on the same principle that, when man is selecting at the same time two varieties, *it is necessary that he should keep them separate* . . .

But he who will take the trouble to reflect on the steps by which this first degree of sterility could be increased through natural selection to that high degree which is common with so many species . . . will find the subject extraordinarily complex. *After mature reflection it seems to me that this could not have been effected through natural selection* . . .

But it would be superfluous to discuss this question in detail; for *with plants we have conclusive evidence that the sterility of crossed species must be due to some principle, quite independent of natural selection.* (My italics)[66]

Alfred Wallace was 'more Darwinian than Darwin himself' in the sense that, except for the evolution of man, he did not allow for any other evolutionary agent than natural selection. And therefore he could not accept the impotency of natural selection with respect to the establishment of interspecific sterility. In 1868 several letters were exchanged between Darwin and Wallace concerning this question; even Darwin's son George was involved.[67] Agreement was never obtained, but it is worth noticing the following statement made by Wallace: 'If Natural Selection can *not* do this, how do specie ever arise, except when a variety is isolated?'[68] I believe tha present-day biologists would answer Wallace: 'They don't,' for it i now generally accepted that isolation is a prerequisite for divergen evolution. Thus, Wallace had the correct answer within reacl without knowing it.

On the question of hybridism Darwin is seen to argue logicall and correctly — against his own theory, and *for* the macromutatio theory. I for one find his reasoning much more satisfactory unde these conditions than when he adopts the opposite stand.

'On the Imperfection of the Geological Record' and 'On the Geological Succession of Organic Beings'

Darwin devoted two chapters to the relevance of palaeontologica data for the study of evolution. To Darwin, as to any upholder o the micromutation theory, the fossil record is defective in so far a it in no case has demonstrated evolution through the accumulatio of micromutations. Darwin was completely aware of this and h therefore dedicated the first of these chapters to bringing together a the reasons he thought responsible for the lack of conformatio between Nature and Darwinism. His arguments are summarised i the following way:

> I have attempted to show that the geological record is extremel imperfect; that only a small portion of the globe has bee geologically explored with care; that only certain classes c organic beings have been largely preserved in a fossil state; tha the number both of specimens and of species, preserved in ou museums, is absolutely as nothing compared with the number c generations which must have passed away even during a singl formation; that, owing to subsidence being almost necessary fc the accumulation of deposits rich in fossil species of many kind and thick enough to outlast future degradation, great intervals c time must have elapsed between most of our successive forma tions; that there has probably been more extinction during th periods of subsidence, and more variation during the periods c elevation, and during the latter the record will have been lea: perfectly kept; that each single formation has not been continu ously deposited; that the duration of each formation is, probably short compared with the average duration of specific forms; tha

migration has played an important part in the first appearance of new forms in any one area and formation; that widely ranging species are those which have varied most frequently, and have oftenest given rise to new species; that varieties have at first been local; and lastly, although each species *must* have passed through numerous transitional stages, it is probable that the periods, during which each underwent modification, though many and long as measured by years, have been short in comparison with the periods during which each remained in an unchanged condition. These causes, taken conjointly, will to *a large extent* explain why — though we do find many links — we do not find interminable varieties, connecting together *all* extinct and existing forms by the finest graduated steps. It should also be constantly borne in mind that any linking variety between two forms, which might be found, would be ranked, unless the whole chain could be perfectly restored, as a new and distinct species; for it is not pretended that we have any sure criterion by which species and varieties can be discriminated. (My italics)[69]

Some comments: (i) We do not ask for varieties connecting '*all* extinct and existing forms by the finest graduated steps'. A few instances would be convincing, and *one* single case would be reassuring — but none was ever found. (ii) I think that the situation is much more complicated than Darwin allows. Since the fossil record consists of petrified hard parts, for instance animal shells and skeletons, it follows that many features have been lost which otherwise are specific characteristics. Furthermore, in many cases it may be difficult to distinguish between large and small animals, representing adults of different species, and old and young individuals of the same species.

Be this as it may, should not this lengthy series of reasons convince the hardest critic? It seems not, for several of them were unfair enough to point out that here Darwin was arguing from ignorance; among these were, as we have already seen, Richard Owen.

Darwin comments:

Mr. Hopkins . . . states . . . that, 'I argue in favour of my views from the extreme imperfection of the Geological Record', and says this is the first time in the History of Science he has ever heard of ignorance being adduced as an argument. But I repeatedly admit, in the most emphatic language which I can see, that the imperfect evidence which Geology offers in regard to transitorial forms *is most strongly opposed to my views*. Surely there is *a wide difference* in fully admitting an objection, and then in *endeavouring to show that it is not so strong as it at first appears*, and in Mr. Hopkins' assertion that I found my argument on the Objection. (My italics)[70]

Is there really such a wide difference? Is it not rather that the fossil record constitutes a refutation of Darwin's micromutation theory, which he refuses to accept by advancing a number of *ad hoc* hypotheses? Darwin fully realised the necessity of this expedient, for he writes: 'He who rejects this view of the imperfection of the geological record, *will rightly reject the whole theory*. For he may ask in vain where are the numberless transitional links which *must* formerly have connected the closely allied or representative species, found in the successive stages of the same great formation?' (My italics).[71] What Darwin did not seem to realise is that if the macromutation theory is correct, then the fossil record will forever be 'extremely imperfect' from the Darwinian point of view. The palaeontological evidence clearly suggests the macromutation theory to be correct, and yet, owing to Darwin's *ad hoc* hypothesis it remains useless for the adherents to the macromutation theory.

There are some points in Darwin's chapter which require further comment.

He writes: 'But I do not pretend that I should *ever* have suspected how poor was the record in the best preserved geological sections, had not *the absence of innumerable transitional links* between the species which lived at the commencement and close of each formation, *pressed so hardly on my theory*' (my italics).[72] Here we have another example of the workings of 'the Darwinian method', asserted to be based on empiricist principles. In fact, some empiricists claim to use empirical data for the construction of theories. If this approach is valid then, obviously, the theories thus derived must be correct too, and further data should therefore be affirmative. If this situation does not obtain there are only two possibilities: either the inductive empiricist method is wrong or the data are unreliable. This second possibility was the one adopted by Darwin.

Darwin continues his methodological discussion: 'But we continually overrate the perfection of the geological record, and *falsely infer*, because certain genera or families have not been found beneath a certain stage, that they did not exist before that stage. In all cases positive palaeontological evidence may be implicitly trusted; *negative evidence is worthless*, as experience has so often shown' (my italics).[73] It is indeed true that lack of evidence cannot be used to falsify Darwin's theory, but Darwin seems to forget that it cannot be used to verify it either.

The circumstances listed by Darwin imply that the fossil evidence does not support the micromutation theories, neither Lamarck's nor Darwin's. On the other hand, it constitutes a rather convincing vindication of Lamarck's theory on the reality of evolution.

In the second chapter Darwin discusses several points of great interest, for example, rarity:

> I may repeat what I published in 1845, namely, that to admit that species generally become rare before they become extinct — to feel no surprise at the rarity of a species, and yet to marvel greatly when the species ceases to exist, is much the same as to admit that sickness in the individual is the forerunner of death — to feel no surprise at sickness, but, when the sick man dies, to wonder and to suspect he died by some deed of violence.[74]

It is rather a truism that rarity is a 'forerunner' to extinction, but Darwin should have pointed out that extinction is not a *necessary* consequence of rarity. The various 'living fossils', some of which were known to Darwin, e.g. fishes like *Latimeria* and the lungfishes, the reptile *Sphenodon* and the egg-laying mammals *Ornithorhyncus* and *Echidna*, are quite rare, and yet they have survived, in some instances for hundreds of millions of years. Their survival is a consequence of their isolation.

This point is made in a following page where Darwin once more neatly outlines the three possibilities for survival implied by the ecological theory of evolution:

> But it must often have happened that *a new species belonging to some one group has seized on the place occupied by a species belonging to a distinct group, and thus have caused its extermination* . . . But whether it be species belonging to the same or to a distinct class, which have yielded their places to other modified and improved species, *a few of the sufferers may often be preserved for a long time, from being fitted to some peculiar line of life, or from inhabiting some distant and isolated station, where they will have escaped severe competition.* (My italics)[75]

But very soon we return to a less sophisticated view:

We have seen . . . that the degree of differentiation and specialisation of the parts in organic beings, when arrived at maturity, is the best standard, as yet suggested, of their degree of perfection or highness. We have also seen that, as the specialisation of parts is an advantage to each being, so natural selection will tend to render the organisation of each being more specialised and perfect, *and in this sense higher*; not but that it may leave many creatures with simple and unimproved structures fitted for simple conditions of life, and in some cases it will even degrade or simplify the organisation, yet leaving such degraded beings better fitted for their new walks of life. In another and more general manner, new species become superior to their predecessors; for they have to beat in the struggle for life all the older forms, with which they come into close competition. We may therefore conclude that if under a nearly similar climate the eocene inhabitants of the world could be put into competition with the existing inhabitants, the former would be beaten and exterminated by the latter, as would the secondary by the eocene, and the palaeozoic by the secondary forms. So that by this fundamental test of victory in the battle for life, as well as by the standard of the *specialisation* of organs, modern forms ought, on the theory of natural selection, to stand higher than ancient forms. Is this the case? A large majority of palaeontologists would answer in the affirmative; and it seems that this answer must be admitted as true, though difficult of proof.

It is no valid objection to this conclusion, that certain Brachiopods have been but slightly modified from an extremely remote geological epoch; and that certain land and fresh-water shells have remained nearly the same, from the time when . . . they first appeared. *It is not an insuperable difficulty* that Foraminifera have not . . . progressed in organisation since even the Laurentian epoch; for some organisms would have to remain fitted for simple conditions of life, and what could be better fitted for this end than the lowly organised Protozoa? Such objections as the above would be fatal to *my* view, if it included advance in organisation as a necessary contingent . . . When advanced up to any given point, *there is no necessity, on the theory of natural selection, for their further continued progress*. (My italics)[76]

Let us first observe that Darwin again outlines a scenario illustrating the process of progressive evolution. The word 'specialisation' is unfortunate in the given context, 'perfection' is much better. And this, that is, progress, is the evident and necessary outcome of natural selection. Although Darwin had mentioned it a few pages earlier, he did not see that this process concerns solely dominant forms. There are other forms which survive in isolation, but as isolation spells avoidance of participation in the struggle for life, then such organisms can permit themselves to undergo degradation if that otherwise furthers their prospect of survival.

'Geographical Distribution'

Darwin devotes two chapters to the topic of geographical distribution. There is very little to criticise in these chapters, which shows partly that Darwin was well acquainted with the subject, and partly that the several empirical facts do not concern the alternative macromutations–micromutations; thus Darwin was not forced to defend his theory against refutatory evidence.

He discusses 'Single Centres of supposed Creation':

Undoubtedly there are many cases of extreme difficulty in understanding how the same species could possibly have migrated from some one point to the several distant and isolated points, where now found. Nevertheless the simplicity of the view that each species was first produced within a single region captivates the mind. He who rejects it, rejects the *vera causa* of ordinary generation with subsequent migration, and calls in the agency of a miracle. It is universally admitted, that in most cases the area inhabited by a species is continuous; and that when a plant or animal inhabits two points so distant from each other, or with an interval of such a nature, that the space could not have been easily passed over by migration, the fact is given as something remarkable and exceptional.[77]

It is perhaps not so common that the same species is found in 'several distant and isolated points'; rather, what we observe is that species belonging to the same genus or some other supraspecific taxon may live in regions separated by enormous areas distinguished by the absence of their congeners. For Darwin this state of affairs may be explained in two ways: (i) the organisms in question were created *in loco* by a supernatural power or (ii) the organisms had their origin in one of the places and subsequently somehow were

147

dispersed and ended up in the observed locations. There is, however, a third possibility, namely, that the characters which are used to unite the organisms in the same genus, etc., have originated independently on two or more occasions. This phenomenon is called *convergence*; and it cannot be excluded *a priori*. It serves to complicate the work of biologists studying evolution, and all means should be deployed to expose such cases. Yet, on the principle of parsimony the Evolutionist must argue on the assumption that convergence may be disregarded or corrected for.

In adopting the second alternative Darwin apparently accepts that the organisms are ecologically isolated from those inhabiting the intermediate space, and hence that these are dominant *vis-à-vis* the isolated ones. This means that the organisms must have come to their present locations through exceptional means of dispersal. Darwin was fascinated by this problem, and made several experiments to demonstrate that seeds and fresh-water snails can survive the exposure to salt water for many days, and that dry earth sticking to the feet of birds may contain seeds of various kinds, etc. Some people have ridiculed Darwin for these efforts, presumably because the notion behind them involves random dispersal. Randomness is never appreciated, because the implication is non-predictability. Personally I am convinced that there are instances in Nature which cannot be explained otherwise than by the mechanism envisaged by Darwin: *random dispersal has occurred on many occasions*. Nevertheless, I grant the critics of Darwin on this point that he overlooked another mechanism, much more likely than his own. This we shall understand when we consider the topic 'Dispersal during the Glacial Period'.

Darwin writes:

The identity of many plants and animals, on mountain-summits, separated from each other by hundreds of miles of lowlands, where Alpine species could not possibly exist, is one of the most striking cases known of the same species living at distant points, without the apparent possibility of their having migrated from one point to the other. It is indeed a remarkable fact to see so many plants of the same species living on the snowy regions of the Alps or Pyrenees, and in the extreme northern parts of Europe; but it is far more remarkable, that the plants on the White Mountains, in the United States of America, are all the same with those of Labrador, and nearly all the same . . . with those on the loftiest mountains of Europe . . .

The former influence of the glacial climate on the distribution of the inhabitants of Europe, as explained by Edward Forbes, is substantially as follows . . . As the cold came on, and as each more southern zone became fitted for the inhabitants of the north, these would take the places of the former inhabitants of the temperate regions. The latter, at the same time, would travel further and further southward . . . The mountains would become covered with snow and ice, and their former Alpine inhabitants would descend to the plains. By the time that the cold had reached its maximum, we should have an arctic fauna and flora, covering the central parts of Europe, as far south as the Alps and Pyrenees, and even stretching into Spain. The now temperate regions of the United States would likewise be covered by arctic plants and animals and these would be nearly the same with those of Europe; for the present circumpolar inhabitants, which we suppose to have everywhere travelled southward, are remarkably uniform round the world.

As the warmth returned, the arctic forms would retreat northward, closely followed up in their retreat by the productions of the more temperate regions. And as the snow melted from the bases of the mountains, the arctic forms would seize on the cleared and thawed ground, always ascending, as the warmth increased and the snow still further disappeared, higher and higher, whilst their brethren were pursuing their northern journey. Hence, when the warmth had fully returned, the same species, which had lately lived together on the European and North American lowlands, would again be found in the arctic regions of the Old and New Worlds, and on many isolated mountain-summits far distant from each other.[78]

I do not know if present-day biogeographers will accept every detail of this interpretation, but in the salient points I suppose it still holds. Under any circumstances Darwin's many words can be replaced by the following: the present arctic and alpine organisms once were ubiquitous in Europe and Northern America, but after the glaciation they were in most regions replaced by dominant organisms entering from the South. As we have seen, this explanation was not Darwin's, but Edward Forbes'. Too bad that Darwin did not see that many of his 'remarkable and exceptional' distributions can be explained in an analogous way, that is, the forms now located in distant and isolated stations once occupied even the intermediate area, from which they have later been excluded by dominant

CHARLES DARWIN

species. Neither Darwin nor most of his followers had imagination enough to apply this principle; it has been left for Croizat and the present-day adherents to his theory of vicariance to do that.[79]

'Mutual Affinities of Organic Beings: Morphology: Embryology: Rudimentary Organs'

If it is accepted that the mechanism of evolution comprises both epigenetic and ecological aspects, and if it is further acknowledged that natural selection cannot affect the epigenetic processes going on inside the living organisms, except by ensuring their survival, then it follows that the discussion in Darwin's book up to now has concerned mainly the ecological aspects of evolution. In his first two chapters, in the one on the 'Laws of Variation', and superficially in other chapters, epigenetic problems are touched upon, but, as appears from the heading, it is in this chapter, the last but one, that we are going to deal with embryology, the science concerned with the mechanisms through which living organisms are created.

Darwin must have realised the importance of this subject, for shortly after the publication of *On the Origin of Species* he wrote to Hooker: 'Embryology is my pet bit in my book, and confound my friends, not one has noticed this to me.'[80] In spite of this insight, Darwin was not going to devote a whole chapter to this topic; rather, he included it in a chapter that might as well have been called 'Miscellanea', dealing with classification, morphology, embryology and rudimentary organs (sic!). The problem of classification is also discussed in Darwin's Chapters IV and XI.

He begins the chapter thus:

From the most remote period in the history of the world organic beings have been found to resemble each other in descending degrees, so that they can be classed in groups under groups . . .

Expressions such as that famous one by Linnaeus, which we often meet with in a more or less concealed form, namely, that the characters do not make the genus, but that the genus gives the characters, seem to imply that some deeper bond is included in our classification than mere resemblance. I believe that this is the case, and that community of descent — the one known cause of close similarity in organic beings — is the bond, which though observed by various degrees of modification, is *partially* revealed to us by our classifications. (My italics)[81]

It seems unfortunate that Darwin should refer to Linnaeus here; it may well be that his view implies a kind of bond, but surely a rather metaphysical one. I believe that an Evolutionist ought to adopt the opposite stand, that is, that the several characters 'make' or 'give' or rather, *define* the various taxa. We have seen that Lamarck boldly stated that our classifications of plants and animals ought to outline *the course* taken by Nature in creating the living beings. Like Lamarck, Darwin thought that the Linnaean classification only partially fulfils this purpose; on this point he is absolutely correct, Linnaean systematics is not phylogenetic.

Darwin goes on:

> It might have been thought . . . that those parts of the structure which determined the habits of life, and the general place of each being in the economy of nature, would be of very high import-ance in classification. Nothing can be more false. No one regards the external similarity of a mouse to a shrew, of a dugong to a whale, of a whale to a fish, as of any importance. These resem-blances, though so intimately connected with the whole life of the being, are ranked as merely 'adaptive or analogical characters' . . . It may even be given as a general rule, that the less any part of the organisation is concerned with special habits, the more important it becomes for classification.[82]

We have seen that so far as the ecological aspect of evolution is concerned, the main target is survival, usually resulting from isola-tion. And since this isolation most often involves a change of habits, it follows that variations allowing for such changes have a very great survival value. They are therefore apt to be preserved whenever they arise; this circumstance implies that the same, or a similar variation may occur in several different taxa. It is thus possible to furnish an empirical basis for Darwin's generalisation. And therefore we do not appreciate reading some pages further on: 'As we find organs of high physiological importance — those which serve to preserve life under the most diverse conditions of existence — *are generally the most constant*, we attach especial value to them; but if these same organs, in another group or section of a group, are found to differ much, we at once value them less in our classification' (my italics).[83]

Darwin writes: 'We can see why characters derived from the embryo should be of equal importance with those derived from the adult, for a natural classification of course includes all ages. But it is by no means obvious, on the ordinary view, why the structure of the embryo should be more important for this purpose than that of the adult, which alone plays its full part in the economy of nature.'[84] According to the 'ordinary view', which seems to coincide with Darwin's theory, it is primarily the adults which are involved in the 'struggle for existence', and therefore natural selection should be particularly concerned with the 'adaptation' of adult characters. That the opposite is true is not obvious and requires a special exposition, but it would lead too far to discuss this point here.

Darwin devotes five pages to the subject of morphology. He begins:

> We have seen that the members of the same class, *independently of their habits of life*, resemble each other in the general plan of their organisation. This resemblance is often expressed by the term 'unity of type'; or by saying that the several parts and organs in the different species of the class are homologous . . . What can be more curious than that the hand of a man, formed for grasping, that of a mole for digging, the leg of the horse, the paddle of the porpoise, and the wing of a bat, should all be constructed on the same pattern, and should include similar bones, in the same relative positions? . . .
>
> Geoffroy St. Hilaire has strongly insisted on the high importance of relative position or connexion in homologous parts; they may differ to almost any extent in form and size, and yet remain connected together in the same invariable order. We never find, for instance, the bones of the arm and fore-arm, or of the thigh and leg, transposed. Hence the same names can be given to the homologous bones in widely different animals . . .
>
> Nothing can be more hopeless than to attempt to explain this similarity of pattern in members of the same class, *by utility or by the doctrine of final causes* . . . On the ordinary view of the independent creation of each being, we can only say that so it is; — that it has pleased the Creator to construct all the animals and plants in each great class on a uniform plan; but this is not a scientific explanation. (My italics)[85]

Darwin mentions that it is hopeless to explain it by utility, but his theory on natural selection in fact depends on this expedient. He would therefore seem to be in a bothersome predicament, but as usual he finds a way out:

The explanation is to a large extent simple on the theory of the selection of successive slight modifications, — each modification being *profitable* [i.e. useful] in some way to the modified form, but often affecting by correlation other parts of the organisation. In changes of this nature, *there will be little or no tendency to alter the original pattern*, or to transpose the parts. The bones of a limb might be shortened and flattened to any extent, becoming at the same time enveloped in thick membrane, so as to serve as a fin; or a webbed hand might have all its bones, or certain bones, lengthened to any extent, with the membrane connecting them increased, so as to serve as a wing; yet *all these modifications would not tend to alter the framework of the bones or the relative connexion of the parts. If we suppose that an early progenitor —* the archetype as it may be called — of *all mammals, birds, and reptiles, had its limbs constructed on the existing general pattern, for whatever purpose they served, we can at once perceive the plain signification of the homologous construction of the limbs throughout the class.* (My italics)[86]

Darwin is right; once limbs of the tetrapod pattern exist it is relatively easy to envisage how the various modifications arose, even if not quite as easy, perhaps, as Darwin implied. But the real problem is surely the origin of the tetrapod limb in the first place; by premising this Darwin shuns the issue — and not for the first time. The limb and and its various modifications are the outcome of epigenetic processes taking place in the embryo. At birth the forelimbs of man, the mole, the horse, the porpoise, if not the bat, already have the form typical of their species, and this state of affairs may generally be traced back to the very early stages of development.

Then we come to Darwin's 'pet bit', 'Development and Embryology'. We must begin with a citation from an earlier chapter:

Agassiz and several other highly competent judges insist that ancient animals resemble to a certain extent the embryos of recent animals belonging to the same classes; and that the geological succession of extinct forms is nearly parallel with the embryological development of existing forms. This view *accords admirably well* with our theory. In a future chapter I shall attempt to show that *the adult differs from its embryo, owing to variations having supervened at a not early age*, and having been inherited at a corresponding age. This process, whilst it leaves the embryo almost unaltered, *continually adds*, in the course of successive generations, *more and more difference to the adult*. Thus the embryo comes to be left as a sort of picture, preserved by nature, of the former and less modified condition of the species. *This view may be true, and yet may never be capable of proof*. Seeing, for instance, that the oldest known mammals, reptiles and fishes strictly belong to their proper classes, though some of these old forms are in a slight degree less distinct from each other than are the typical members of the same group at the present day, it would be in vain to look for animals having the common embryological character of the Vertebrata, until beds rich in fossils are discovered far beneath the lowest Cambrian strata — a discovery of which the chance is small. (My italics)[87]

Darwin apparently expects to find an adult form corresponding to a tail bud embryo or an early larva. But as these contain no ossified parts they would have left no traces, had they ever existed. Evidently he is here advocating the theory of recapitulation known as 'Meckel–Serres Law'. Why is Darwin suggesting that this view may not be proved? This question may be answered if we turn to the first edition, in which the beginning of the above quotation reads as follows:

Agassiz insists that ancient animals resemble to a certain extent the embryos of recent animals of the same classes; or that the geological succession of extinct forms is in some degree parallel to the embryological development of recent forms. *I must follow Pictet and Huxley in thinking that the truth of this doctrine is very far from proved. Yet I fully expect to see it hereafter confirmed, at least in regard to subordinate groups, which have branched from each other within comparatively recent times*. (My italics)[88]

I suspect that if Pictet and Huxley thought the truth of the doctrine 'very far from proved', the implication must be that they, presumably from acquaintance with von Baer's work, realised that Meckel–Serres law is false. However, in the fifth edition Pictet and Huxley were dismissed — all that remained of Darwin's doubts concerned the possible testability of his view.

In the section we are dealing with now Darwin writes:

It has already been stated that various parts in the same individual which are exactly alike during an early embryonic period, become widely different and serve for widely different purposes in the adult state. So again it has been shown that generally the embryos of the most distinct species belonging to the same class are closely similar, but become, when fully developed, widely dissimilar. A better proof of this latter fact cannot be given than the statement by Von Baer that 'the embryos of mammalia, of birds, lizards, and snakes, probably also of chelonia, are in their earliest stages exceedingly like one another, both as a whole and in the mode of development of their parts; so much so, in fact, that we can often distinguish the embryos only by their size. In my possession are two little embryos in spirit, whose names I have omitted to attach, and at present I am quite unable to say to what class they belong. They may be lizards or small birds, or very young mammalia, so complete is the similarity in the mode of formation of the head and trunk in these animals. The extremities, however, are still absent in these embryos. But even if they had existed in the earliest stage of their development we should learn nothing, for the feet of lizards and mammals, the wings and feet of birds, no less than the hands and feet of man, all arise from the same fundamental form.[89]

This little anecdote, wrongly attributed to Agassiz in the early editions, is used by Darwin to illustrate the point that embryos at an early stage are very similar, becoming gradually different. However, von Baer's criticism of Meckel–Serres' law is not mentioned. This circumstance motivates a closer study of Darwin's position towards the ideas of von Baer.

We may thus observe that in the first edition von Baer is not mentioned at all, but in the sixth edition his name occurs three times, one of which is in the above citation. Speaking about the advance in organisation which may be expected as a consequence of natural selection, Darwin writes in an earlier chapter:

It might be thought that the amount of change which the various parts and organs pass through in their development from the embryo to maturity would suffice as a standard of comparison; but there are cases, as with certain parasitic crustaceans, in which several parts of the structure become less perfect, so that the mature animal cannot be called higher than its larva. Von Baer's standard seems the most widely applicable and the best, namely, the amount of differentiation of the parts of the same organic being, *in the adult state as I should be inclined to add*, and their specialisation for different functions. (My italics)[90]

The third time is in a discussion of progress. Here we may read: 'To attempt to compare members of distinct types in *the scale of highness* seems hopeless; who will decide whether a cuttle-fish be higher than a bee — that insect which the great von Baer believed to be "in fact more highly organised than a fish, although upon another type"?' (my italics).[91]

Thus, Darwin uses von Baer to help refute the notion of progressive evolution, nothing more. Considering the importance of embryogenesis for evolution — Darwin's own assertion — it is most surprising that he did not adopt the ideas of von Baer, who was then considered the most outstanding embryologist in Europe. The obvious explanation, namely, that Darwin was unfamiliar with this part of von Baer's work, turns out to be wrong. For in the 'Sketch' from 1842 Darwin writes:

> This general unity of type in great groups of organisms . . . displays itself in a most striking manner in the stages through which the foetus passes. In early stage, the wing of bat, hoof, hand, paddle are not to be distinguished. At a still earlier stage there is no difference between fish, bird, etc., and mammal . . . It is not true that one passes through the form of a lower group, though no doubt fish more nearly related to foetal state.[92]

And in the 'Essay' from 1844 he wrote:

> . . . it has often been asserted that the higher animal in each class passes through the state of a lower animal; for instance, that the mammal amongst the vertebrata passes through the state of a fish: but Müller denies this, and affirms that the young mammal is at no time a fish, as does Owen assert that the embryonic jelly-fish is at no time a polyp, but that mammal and fish, jelly-fish and polyp pass through the same state; the mammal and jelly-fish being only further developed or changed.[93]

Here there is no ambiguity, in both cases Darwin is clearly stating the view advanced by von Baer. Incidentally, in the latter quotation we learn who were his most important sources of information on von Baer's work, Johannes Müller and Richard Owen.

Yet, it is one thing to quote an author, another to believe him. And a few pages later we find the following passage in the 'Essay':

It follows strictly from the above reasoning only that the embryos of . . . existing vertebrata resemble more closely the embryo of the parent-stock of this great class than do full-grown existing Vertebrata resemble their full-grown parent-stock. But it may be argued with much probability that in the earliest and simplest conditions of things the parent and embryo must have resembled each other, and that the passage of any animal through embryonic states in its growth is entirely due to subsequent variations affecting *only* the more mature periods of life. If so, the embryos of the existing vertebrata will shadow forth the full-grown structure of some of those forms of this great class which existed at the earlier periods of the earth's history: and accordingly, *animals with a fish-like structure ought to have preceded birds and mammals* . . . This order of precedence in time in some of these cases is believed to hold good; but I think our evidence is so exceedingly incomplete regarding the number and kinds of organisms which have existed during all, especially the earlier, periods of the earth's history, that I should put no stress on this accordance, even if it held truer than it probably does in our present state of knowledge. (The last italics are mine)[94]

Darwin here once more tries to vindicate the theory of embryonic recapitulation of adult ancestral form. Yet, his conclusion concerning the succession of vertebrates cannot be based on facts, for *it is not possible to observe the full-grown structure of a fish in any avian and mammalian embryo*. It is thus evident that as early as 1844 Darwin was inclined to reject von Baer's theory in favour of Meckel–Serres' law, in defiance of the authorities.

For what reason did Darwin assume his rebellious stand? As we have seen, it was von Baer's views which inspired the Macromutationists Owen and Chambers, probably also Carpenter and Huxley, and possibly, indirectly, even Mivart, to adopt the idea that the major evolutionary changes are the result of modifications of the embryonic development. Darwin turned down this theory because it inevitably implies the existence of macromutations, and adopted instead Meckel–Serres' law, according to which he thought he could explain evolution as an accumulation of terminal changes modifying the adult body. Thus, when Darwin thought embryology to be one of his strongest trumps he was arguing on the basis of a theory rejected by many of the outstanding biologists at the time. And he did not consider that embryonic recapitulation of adult forms really is of no help to a theory which is based on terminal modifications.

157

Darwin goes on to explain embryological observations:

How, then, can we explain these several facts in embryology, — namely, the very general, though not universal, difference in structure between the embryo and the adult; — the various parts in the same individual embryo, which ultimately become very unlike and serve for diverse purposes, being at an early period of growth alike; — the common, but not invariable, resemblance between the embryos or larvae of the most distinct species in the same class; — the embryo often retaining whilst within the egg or womb, structures which are of no service to it, either at that or at a later period of life; on the other hand larvae, which have to provide for their own wants, being perfectly adapted to the surrounding conditions; — and lastly the fact of certain larvae standing higher in the scale of organisation than the mature animal into which they are developed? I believe that *all* these facts can be explained, as follows.

It is commonly assumed, perhaps from monstrosities affecting the embryo at a very early period, that slight variations or individual differences necessarily appear at an equally early period. We have little evidence on this lead, but what we have certainly points the other way . . . We see this plainly in our own children; we cannot tell whether a child will be tall or short, or what its precise features will be. The question is not, at what period of life each variation may have been caused, but at what period the effects are displayed. The cause may have acted, and I believe often has acted, on one or both parents before the act of generation. It deserves notice that it is of no importance to a very young animal, as long as it remains in its mother's womb or in the egg, or as long as it is nourished and protected by its parent, whether most of its characters are acquired a little earlier or later in life. It would not signify, for instance, to a bird which obtained its food by having a much-curved beak whether or not whilst young it possessed a beak of this shape, as long as it was fed by its parents. (My italics)[95]

It is very ambitious to try to account for such a variety of phenomena under one heading. The explanation offered seems to be that as long as organisms are not engaged in the battle for life they need not and cannot undergo any change. But in that case all organisms ought to hatch as undifferentiated lumps of cells, undergoing only subsequently the differentiation required for assuming the struggle for existence. Evidently, in his enthusiasm for the micromutation theory, Darwin strays from the point. As we know, it is determined at a very early stage whether the developing individual is going to be, say, a reptile, a bird or a mammal, and also its belonging to various subordinate taxa within those mentioned. The change from one of these several taxa to another cannot be achieved through terminal modifications, but only through changes in the course of early ontogenetic development.

We may agree with Darwin that variations, whether slight or large, which for causal reasons occur during the terminal ontogenetic phases, cannot possibly prevail in any earlier ontogenetic stage. It might be advantageous to the young bird to hatch with 'a much-curved beak', or to the mammal to reach adult size in the mother's womb, and yet no selection process in the world could accomplish such things. Nature has its course, ruled by laws, and one of these is that many form changes occur as the result of differential growth, with the emphasis on *differential* before, and *growth* after hatching or birth.

We may now end the discussion of 'Darwin and embryology', but it is still necessary to deal with the relationship between the views of von Baer and those of Darwin. We have seen that an adherent to the micromutation theory must for logical reasons reject von Baer's theory and adopt Meckel–Serres theory of recapitulation. Darwin understood this, and so did his champion Haeckel. The difference between them was that the latter knew so much morphology and embryology that he realised that very often there is no evidence of any recapitulation. To account for this difference between theory and reality Haeckel did not hesitate to introduce some ridiculous, but deceptive *ad hoc* hypotheses.

It may not be generally realised today that to choose Darwin implies the rejection of von Baer, and *vice versa*. But this view was clearly stated by Lovejoy:

But if [the laws of von Baer] . . . were correct, the argument from embryonic recapitulation, which had seemed to Darwin 'second to none' among the evidences of organic evolution, and to Haeckel, LeConte, and many others the most impressive and most cogent of all, had been exploded — and expoded thirty years before the publication of the *Origin of Species* . . .

If he *had* read and pondered von Baer's book, he might possibly have given up the embryonic–recapitulation argument as one of the proofs of organic evolution — or much more probably

159

have merely modified it. If he had done either of these things, his successors would doubtless have done the same. But as he neither abandoned nor amended it, that argument in its original form held its place in biology for almost a century.[96]

I am sure that if Darwin had not only read and pondered, but also understood von Baer's views, he would have given up the micromutation theory, as did all the others who had reached this point.

An outstanding embryologist, Jane Oppenheimer, who considers it 'an embryological enigma' that Darwin did not understand the implications of von Baer's comparative embryology, has written:

Although it is fruitless, it is nonetheless fascinating to speculate what direction embryology [Evolutionism?] might have followed had Darwin in the *Origin of Species* placed less emphasis on Agassiz' conclusions and more on von Baer's. And it is tempting to wonder whether he might not have better understood the contributions of von Baer, and have become more convinced of the cogency and significance of his criticisms of the old recapitulation theories, had he read his works in the original more easily, or more frequently, or more comprehendingly. In 1881, the year before he died, he still did not even own von Baer's works . . .

Darwin may have believed, as he said he did, that his embryological considerations were vital to the successful development of his concepts of natural history. But what he accepted from von Baer to further them was drawn from von Baer's reflections more than from his observations. What von Baer described that was new Darwin mainly ignored. *The power of von Baer's ideas was sufficiently strong that these could eventually triumph, no matter how they were treated by the more revisionistic apostles of Darwin.* (My italics)[97]

I endorse every word with one reservation. As a good empiricist Jane Oppenheimer believes that von Baer's greatness lies in the observations he made. But surely, everybody can fix and section some chicken embryos and look at them in the microscope. It holds for von Baer's work, as it holds for all great contributions to science, that it is *new ideas* which ensure the major advances in knowledge and understanding.

Darwin has confessed: 'I have steadily endeavoured to keep my mind free so as to give up any hypothesis, however much beloved (and I cannot resist forming one on every subject), as soon as facts are shown to be opposed to it.'[98] We shall never know the validity of this statement, for we do not know how many false theories were rejected by Darwin. But it is not generally true, time upon time Darwin did not hesitate to explain away embarrassing facts by means of *ad hoc* hypotheses. In the present case Darwin faced two ways to explain the course of events occurring during ontogenesis. One of these, von Baer's interpretation, had been adopted by the leading morphologists at the time, mostly of course by the younger generation. This option is easy to understand, for anybody even slightly acquainted with embryology knows that no miniatures of adult fishes, amphibians, or reptiles, not to speak of sea urchins and snails, are found in the mammalian embryo. But since von Baer's views did not conform with his micromutation theory, Darwin did not hesitate to reject them and adopt the second alternative, the obsolete Meckel–Serres' theory of adult recapitulation. This is an illustration of Darwin's respect for empirical facts when these contradicted a 'beloved' hypothesis of his.

'Recapitulation and Conclusion'

We have now reached the last chapter in Darwin's book. I shall concentrate on his conclusion and especially on the changes Darwin made therein in the course of the editions for which he was himself responsible.

In the first edition we read:

> I have now recapitulated the chief facts and considerations which have thoroughly convinced me that species have changed, and are still slowly changing by the preservation and accumulation of successive slight favourable variations.[99]

In the sixth edition he writes:

> I have now recapitulated the facts and considerations which have thoroughly convinced me that species have been modified, during a long course of descent. This has been effected chiefly through the natural selection of numerous successive, slight, favourable variations; aided in an important manner by the inherited effects of use and disuse of parts; and in an unimportant manner, that is

161

in relation to adaptive structures, whether past or present, by the direct action of external conditions, and by variations which seem to us in our ignorance to arise spontaneously. It appears that I formerly underrated the frequency and value of these latter forms of variation, as leading to permanent modification of structure independently of natural selection. But as my conclusions have lately been much misrepresented, and it has been stated that I attribute the modification of species exclusively to natural selection, I may be permitted to remark that in the first edition of this work, and subsequently, I placed in a most conspicuous position — namely, at the close of the Introduction — the following words: 'I am convinced that natural selection has been the main but not the exclusive means of modification'. This has been of no avail. Great is the power of steady misrepresentation; but the history of science shows that fortunately this power does not long endure.

It can hardly be supposed that a false theory would explain, in so satisfactory a manner as does the theory of natural selection, the several large classes of facts above specified. It has recently been objected that this is an unsafe method of arguing; but it is a method used in judging of the common events of life, and has often been used by the greatest natural philosophers. The undulatory theory of light has thus been arrived at; and the belief in the revolution of the earth on its own axis was until lately supported by hardly any direct evidence. It is no valid objection that science as yet throws no light on the far higher problem of the essence or origin of life. Who can explain what is the essence of the attraction of gravity? No one now objects to following out the results consequent on this unknown element of attraction; notwithstanding that Leibnitz [sic!] formerly accused Newton of introducing 'occult qualities and miracles into philosophy'.

I see no good reason why the views given in this volume should shock the religious feelings of any one. It is satisfactory, as showing how transient such impressions are, to remember that the greatest discovery ever made by man, namely, the law of the attraction of gravity, was also attacked by Liebnitz, 'as subversive of natural, and inferentially of revealed, religion'. A celebrated author and divine has written to me that 'he has gradually learnt to see that it is just as noble a conception of the Deity to believe that He created a few original forms capable of self-development into other and needful forms, as to believe that He required a fresh act of creation to supply the voids caused by the action of His laws'.[100]

This extended apology comprises three parts, an outline of the mechanisms involved in evolution, a defence of his method, and a reconciliatory move towards his religious adversaries. The outline is formally very unsatisfactory; when it is scrutinised at close quarters it appears to make the following statements:

(a) 'change of species is effected mainly by the accumulation of spontaneous [slight] variations';
(b) 'aided by the inherited effects of use and disuse (important), and of direct action (unimportant)';
(c) 'as well as by spontaneous [large] variations (unimportant)';
(d) 'I formerly underrated these last variations';
(e) 'I still think them unimportant (statement (c))'.[101]

However this may be, we notice that in the final conclusion Darwin includes four mechanisms: Darwinian natural selection, Lamarckian use and disuse, Buffonian action of the external conditions, and macromutations. He even admits that he may have underrated the importance of this last mechanism, presumably in order to placate Huxley and others of his critics. Yet, it must be emphasised that earlier in this chapter he had written: 'As natural selection acts *solely* by accumulating slight, successive, favourable variations, it can produce no great or sudden modifications; it can act only by short and slow steps. Hence the canon of "Natura non facit saltum", *which every fresh addition to our knowledge tends to confirm*, is on this theory intelligible' (my italics).[102]
And to make sure that he had not really changed his view as to the significance of macromutations he writes three pages after the general conclusion quoted above: 'Under a scientific point of view, and as leading to further investigation, but little advantage is gained by believing that new forms are suddenly developed in an inexplicable manner from old and widely different forms, over the old belief in the creation of species from the dust of the earth.'[103]
Certainly, Darwin's acknowledgement of macromutations as a fourth mechanism of evolution was *not* based on conviction. Anyway, he might admit that other mechanisms than his own are involved in evolution, but that could not save him from criticism of the mechanism he suggested to be the most important of all. In the defence of his method Darwin is ambiguous; which theories explain which facts? None of the evidence collected by Darwin supports his

micromutation theory, but much of it is in agreement with Lamarck's theory on the reality of evolution. But worst of all: he ignores refuting evidence and that is indeed 'an unsafe method of arguing'.

Even in the first edition, and almost unchanged in the successive ones we find Darwin trying to disarm his critics:

> Although I am fully convinced of *the truth* of the views given in this volume under the form of an abstract, I by no means expect to convince *experienced naturalists whose mind are stocked with a multitude of facts all viewed*, during a long course of years, *from a point of view directly opposite to mine. It is to easy to hide our ignorance under such expressions as the 'plan of creation', 'unity of design', &c., and to think that we give an explanation when we only restate a fact. Any one whose disposition leads him to attach more weight to unexplained difficulties than to the explanation of a certain number of facts will certainly reject my theory*. A few naturalists, endowed with much flexibility of mind, and who have already begun to doubt *the immutability of species*, may be influenced by this volume; but I look with confidence to the future, to young and rising naturalists, who will be able to view both sides of the question with impartiality. Whoever is led to believe that *species are mutable* will do good service by conscientiously expressing his conviction; for only thus can the load of prejudice by which this subject is overwhelmed be removed. (My italics)[104]

It is realy surprising that anybody dared to criticise Darwin after this onslaught! But in fact, he missed the point. Very few criticised Darwin's advocacy of the mutability of the species, but many realised that his micromutation theory does not work.

I shall end this review with a note of Darwinian optimism which, regrettably, I do not share:

> As all the living forms of life are the lineal descendants of those which lived long before the Cambrian epoch, we may feel certain that the ordinary succession by generation has never once been broken, and that no cataclysm has desolated the whole world. Hence we may look with some confidence to a secure future of great length. And as natural selection works solely by and for the

good of each being, all corporeal and mental endowments will tend to progress towards perfection.[105]

THE NEWTON OF BIOLOGY

From a few examples and particulars (with the addition of common notions and perhaps of some portion of the received opinions which have been most popular) they flew at once to the most general conclusions, or first principles of science. Taking the truth of these as fixed and immovable, they proceeded by means of intermediate propositions to educe and prove from them the inferior conclusions; and out of these they framed the art. After that, if any new particulars and examples repugnant to their dogmas were mooted and adduced, either they subtly molded them into their systems by distinctions and explanations of their rules, or else coarsely got rid of them by exceptions; while to such particulars as were not repugnant they laboured to assign causes in conformity with those of their principles.[106]

Francis Bacon

[On the Origin of Species is] a mass of facts crushed and pounded into shape, rather than held together by the ordinary medium of an obvious logical bond.[107]

T.H. Huxley

. . . two of Darwin's chief virtues were ones not usually praised in a scientist: jumping to conclusions which go well beyond the evidence available; and maintaining his faith in his position regardless of the valid arguments that could be brought against it.[108]

Walter F. Cannon

The picture which emerges from the preceding analysis of *On the Origin of Species* cannot be described as ambiguous: Darwin may have been an excellent collector of facts, but as a thinker he was confused and inconsistent, and much less original than he thought himself. This is a conclusion which has been reached by many others than the two authors quoted above. I admit that it is easy to find enthusiastic adulations of Darwin's greatness as a thinker, but I venture to affirm that this is a relatively recent phenomenon; when we go back to Darwin's own times, there were very few besides Wallace, Haeckel and Huxley who considered Darwin the equal of Newton.

Why is it that we are less critical today than were his contemporaries? Can it be that we have accepted that Darwin was wrong in detail, but that the correct theory, 'the modern synthesis', is a revision of Darwin's theory, the same way as Einstein's theory has been said to include Newton's theory as an approximation? If this really is true then it may explain the prevailing forbearance towards

Darwin. But if it is false then we face a completely different situation. The stand taken here is that Darwin's theory is false, not because it operates with natural selection as an evolutionary agent, but because it is a micromutation theory. And since this also holds for the current theory, it follows that almost all the criticism which was raised against Darwin's theory is valid also for its successor.

Darwin's theory on the mechanism of evolution concerns the survival in the struggle for life of varieties occurring in various living beings. The theory thus deals partly with phenomena going on outside and between different organisms — the struggle, and partly with events occurring inside individual organisms — the variations. It would seem an obvious premise that no single theory can take into account two kinds of phenomena as distinct as these. And since Darwin's theory so clearly deals with events occurring outside the living organisms he might very well have premised the existence of the variations necessary for the occurrence of evolution. Since he was not necessarily required to account for any particular case of evolution, he might have done so without any detailed discussion about the nature of variations and their cause. If he had adopted this attitude he might have avoided making a mistake similar to that committed by Buffon, namely, the assertion that evolutionary variation is imposed upon the organisms by their environment.

Without entering into detail it would nevertheless be necessary to deal with one property of the variations, namely, their effect. A most reasonable stand would be that variations may be deleterious or beneficial, and large or slight. Of the four possible combinations of these properties, two might be neglected immediately, for natural selection would ensure the elimination of all deleterious variations, including Darwin's 'monsters'. But Darwin also rejected the contribution to evolution of large beneficial variations. His objections to these were: (i) they occur less frequently in nature than under domestication; (ii) when they occur they are likely to be lost through lack of inbreeding; (iii) the changes occurring during ontogenesis are gradual, not sudden; and (iv) the adaptation of organisms cannot be accounted for.[109]

We have already discussed the first two points and found that the chance of *survival* is considerably slighter in nature than under domestication, but this is easily compensated for by time. The third argument is either irrelevant or false, for in fact embryos develop from one major taxon to another — large changes indeed. And the fourth argument is anti-Darwinian, all variations but those spelling adaptations will be eliminated. The reason why Darwin rejected beneficial macromutations was that he had greater ambitions on behalf of his mechanism of natural selection; it was not enough that it ensures the survival of variations created by 'internal forces' residing within the various organisms, it must itself *create* the evolutionary innovations. Under these circumstances the variations themselves must be slight and insignificant as regards their effect; only through the accumulation by natural selection of such micromutations are large-scale changes possible in evolution.

With this option Darwin remained within the realm of Lyellian gradualism, but he paid a high price: (i) The individual variations with which he works are mostly quantitative; as pointed out by his critics they cannot account for *qualitative* evolutionary innovations. (ii) They cannot either explain the incipient stages of structures which in principle represent quantitative changes. (iii) They cannot explain many transitions which are known to have taken place. (iv) They imply transitions between adult forms, but embryology teaches us that most transitions occur in the embryo. (v) They do not agree with the fossil record. Furthermore, (vi) if natural selection is going to be the creative agent in evolution, then it follows that the necessary variation always prevails. A selection theory requires high frequency of variations, and this is a characteristic of slight variations, the large ones are rare. So if 'selection pressure' is driving evolution, then the corresponding variation must consist of micromutations. Yet, although his theory thus implies the constant availability of variations, Darwin had to admit that many facts rather indicate the frequent absence of the necessary variation.

Darwin believed that he was open-minded to the falsifying evidence constituted by empirical facts, but he was not. By 1842 when he wrote the 'Sketch' Darwin had opted for the micromutation theory; he may often have doubted its validity, particularly in the face of an almost unanimous macromutationist criticism, but he never abandoned it. Presumably he was a captive of his triumph.

In his autobiography Darwin wrote: 'Some of my critics have said, "Oh, he is a good observer, but he has no power of reasoning!" I do not think that this can be true, for the "Origin of Species" is one long argument from the beginning to the end, and it has convinced not a few able men.'[110] Darwin's evaluation of his work is true, but in a very particular sense: it is one long argument trying to convince the reader of the validity of the micromutation theory in spite of the fact that all available empirical evidence speaks against it. Darwin's collection of facts, whether real or imagined, might corroborate Lamarck's theory on the reality of evolution, but he never found any data supporting the micromutation theory. Bacon's characterisation of the ancient philosophers, quoted at the head of this section, excellently describes the Darwinian method.

6

The Two Evolutionists

Toutes ces recherches [pratiques] terminées, on essaye d'en déduire les conséquences, et peu à peu la philosophie de la science s'établit, se rectifie et se
perfectionne.

C'est par cette voie seule que l'intelligence humaine peut acquérir les
connaisances les plus vastes, les plus solides et les mieux liées entre elles, dans
quelque science que ce soit; et c'est uniquement par cette méthode d'analyse que
toutes les sciences font de véritables progrès et que les objets qui s'y rapportent
ne sont jamais confondus, et peuvent être connus parfaitement.[1]

J.-B. de Lamarck

I worked on true Baconian principles, and without any theory collected facts on
a wholesale scale, more especially with respect to domesticated productions, by
printed enquiries, by conversation with skilful breeders and gardeners, and by
extensive reading.[2]

Charles Darwin

Ever since the Renaissance the Western European world of learning
has been influenced by two different philosophies, Empiricism and
Rationalism. The first, developed by Francis Bacon, stresses the
importance of empirical observations for the advancement of
knowledge; conversely, René Descartes, the founder of Rationalism, put the weight on critical logical thinking. Empiricism early
gained foothold in England, presumably because it fit so well with
the practically-minded British spirit. Rationalism was long predominant in France, but towards the end of the eighteenth century
Empiricism became the great fashion. It went so far that Condillac
considered happy the man who lived in a time that furnished him
with so many facts that he did not have to use his imagination.[3]

The reasons for this change may be many, perhaps the thinking
was at times neither critical nor logical enough, but surely the great
strides made by British scientists and engineers were also an efficient cause. In France Georges Cuvier was the leading advocate of
Empiricism, and we have already seen how this role brought him in
conflict with Lamarck and with Etienne Geoffroy Saint-Hilaire, both
of whom defended the role of creative thinking in science.
Empiricism won the day, and has dominated the scene for more than
50 years. Under these conditions it is understandable that Cuvier's,

and later Darwin's low opinion of Lamarck's contribution to biology has prevailed to the present day.

Darwin himself repeatedly stressed his Empiricist faith and his inductive approach, and this assertion has been accepted quite uncritically by most people. It may be presumed that this has contributed to the fact that, in contrast to Lamarck, he is still held in high esteem.

Yet, is the traditional view on the relative merits of the two philosophical schools correct, and furthermore, is the evaluation of the respective approaches of Lamarck and Darwin correct? These two questions are discussed in the following section.

A COMPARISON

Karl Popper claims that he has killed Inductivism–Positivism–Empiricism.[4] He has written elsewhere:

> The advance of science is not due to the fact that more and more perceptual experiences accumulate in the course of time. Nor is it due to the fact that we are making ever better use of our senses. Out of uninterpreted sense-experiences sciences cannot be distilled, no matter how industriously we gather and sort them. Bold ideas, unjustified anticipations, and speculative thought, are our only means for interpreting nature: our only organon, our only instrument, for grasping her.[5]

This assertion, which according to Popper represents his 'critical rationalism',[6] rather appears to be a vindication of Lamarck's view, quoted above, that it is through the rational treatment of our observations that we reach understanding. As we have seen, as long as he could support his ideas on empirical data, as in his two theories of evolution, Lamarck's thinking is irreproachable. However, when he endeavoured to establish a theory on the mechanism of evolution the facts were missing. And consequently he became a *philosophe* a Rationalist, but not a critical one. If this was his only contribution to science, his current reputation would be justified.

Surely, Lamarck was more of a Popperian than Darwin, a circumstance which perhaps may account for his achievements. But in those pre-Popperian times Lamarck was an outsider, and he knew it:

. . . I have not been able to keep silent about what my studies have led me to discover. Thus I have found myself involved in a controversy which time, rather than reason may properly terminate; for now I have hardly any other judges than the party whose precepts I combat; the party which has on its side the advantage of the opinion.[7]

Darwin was also aware of the fact that progress in science implies creative thinking. Yet, he believed that admitting this publicly would weaken his position, so statements like the following ones were made only in private: 'How odd it is that anyone should not see that all observation must be for or against some view if it is to be of any service!'[8] and '. . . no man could be a good observer unless he was an active theorizer'.[9] In a similar vein he wrote in one of his early letters to Wallace: 'I am extremely glad to hear that you are attending to distribution in accordance with theoretical ideas. I am a firm believer that without speculation there is no good and original observation.'[10]

An anonymous referee of the manuscript of the present book has written: 'My own interpretation of Lamarck's works is that they are obscure, often imprecise and sometimes contradictory.' There is no doubt a certain measure of truth in this statement, for from an epistemological point of view there is much to criticise in Lamarck's work. However, the present scrutiny of Darwin's master work ought to show that he does not fare better. And considering that Darwin was sixty-five years his junior, I believe that this comparison turns out to the advantage of Lamarck.

THE THEORY MAKERS

La postérité vous honorera![11]

Corneille de Lamarck

Lamarck and Darwin were both theory makers. This is a very special breed of people, excellently characterised by Darwin in the following way in a letter to his son Horace:

I have been speculating last night . . . what makes a man a discoverer of undiscovered things, and a most perplexing problem it is. Many men who are very clever — much cleverer than the discoverers — never originate anything. As far as I can conjecture the art consists in habitually scarching for the causes and meaning of *everything* that occurs. (My italics)[12]

I have emphasised 'everything' because neither Lamarck nor Darwin showed any inhibitions as concerns the fields of knowledge for which they tried to account. This may be the theory maker's strength, but since all theories are conjecture, it implies the risk that there is an inverse relation between the ambition and the quality of his endeavours. Cuvier was not all wrong, much of what Lamarck thought out probably is not worth the paper on which it was printed, even when measured with contemporaneous standards. But in the world of theory making bad theories are so common that they do not count, only good ones do.

We have seen that on this account Lamarck made three contributions to evolutionary thought: he founded the theories on the reality and the history of evolution; he further made a sensible, if crude attempt to establish a phylogenetic classification of kingdom Animalia; and lastly he made an important contribution to the ecological theory on the mechanism of evolution by distinguishing two kinds of evolution, progressive and divergent, respectively.

Darwin's contribution to evolutionary thought is a mechanism, natural selection, which may account for Lamarck's progressive evolution. As is well known, he also contributed decisively to the general acceptance of the theory on the reality of evolution, Lamarck's first theory of evolution.

If the present evaluation of the achievements of these two scientists is correct, then there is clearly a disproportion between their contributions and their reputations. This is one aspect of the Darwinian myth.

7

The Friends

I saw more of Lyell than of any other man both before and after my marriage.
I became very intimate with Hooker, who has been one of my best friends throughout life.
I . . . became intimate with Huxley . . . He has been a most kind friend to me and would always take any trouble for me.[1]

Charles Darwin

Although all the men who stood closest to Darwin, who were most in sympathy with him — Hooker, Wallace [?], Huxley, Gray, Falconer, and Lyell — sought to persuade him that the formative or creative claims he made for Natural Selection were extravagant, Darwin remained adamant.[2]

Arthur Keith

Among Darwin's many acquaintances three stand out as the *friends*, Charles Lyell, Joseph Hooker and Thomas Huxley. These three prominent scientists, a geologist, a botanist and a zoologist, firmly settled in the English 'Establishment' of science, stood by Darwin whenever difficulties arose, and advertised his teaching wherever opportunities prevailed. It would seem obvious that these three men were convinced adherents to Darwin's theory. Those acquainted with the history of evolutionary thought know that they were not. To most people this must sound incredible, but it is true. In the following pages I shall substantiate this assertion.

CHARLES LYELL (1797–1875)

Charles Lyell was the son of a wealthy Scottish land-owner, renowned as a botanist and a translator of works of Dante. As a boy he was greatly interested in natural history; at Oxford he became interested in geology, the subject to which he was to devote his life. He was later called to the Bar, and practised law for two years, and for some years he was professor of geology at King's College. Apart from these short spells he was, as a man of independent means, free to pursue full time his geological studies. During these he travelled a lot, in England, Europe and North America. His work, which includes the famous *Principles of Geology*, won him great fame; he was undisputedly the leading geologist in Europe in the middle of the last century.[3]

In order to understand Lyell's position in geology and his influence on Darwin, we must return to the *Scala Naturae*, this hypothetical ordering of all living beings in an descending scale of complexity. This ladder is to some extent reproduced by the fossil record, where the primitive organisms appear in the lower, supposedly earlier strata, whereas the higher organisms first are found in the more recent deposits. However, the palaeontological evidence embodies three elements embarrassing to Christian orthodoxy: (i) It is unlikely that the fossil-bearing sediments can have been deposited during the short time allowed for by the Bible; (ii) it is possible to distinguish a number of separate strata, each characterised by its chemical composition and its organic remains; and (iii) many of the organisms found as fossils are now extinct.

In order to compromise between dogma and empirical evidence the theory of Catastrophism was launched. According to this hypothesis the living world arose through a sequence of catastrophes causing multiple extinctions, the Noachian deluge being the last of these. Each catastrophe was followed by a creative contribution on the part of God, the succession of organisms thus arising being progressive with respect to organisation and complexity. Seemingly it had pleased God to improve upon his work each time an opportunity was offered. The theory of Catastrophism was therefore also known as 'Progressionism'.

This theory was ruling during the last part of the eighteenth and the first part of the nineteenth century. Yet, dissenting voices were raised, directed primarily against the weak point of Catastrophism the time factor. An opposing theory, Uniformitarianism or Gradualism, was first published by James Hutton in 1788. In Hutton's view no catastrophes were required to account for the changes suffered by our planet; rather, they had been caused by the same forces as those active today, frost, wind and running water plus, of course, the internal heat of the earth. This theory does not attempt to explain the succession of geological strata or the phenomenon of extinction; these questions were neglected, to some extent justified by the reigning state of knowledge. On the other hand, by implication the theory refutes Biblical notions about the age of the planet; hundreds of millions of years would be required to shape it by the forces allowed for by Uniformitarianism.

Hutton's ideas went largely unnoticed, but were resumed forty years later by Charles Lyell in his *Principles of Geology*. Times had changed, now Uniformitarianism was accepted by many scientists with acclaim. The gist of Lyell's theory has been stated with the words: 'the thing that is, is the thing that has been, and shall be.'[4] It is evident that this view does not allow for the evolution of life, whether progressive or not. However, since the times of Hutton, palaeontological knowledge had advanced conspicuously, many finds supporting the notion of progressive evolution espoused by the Catastrophists. The validity of this refuting evidence was questioned by Lyell with reference to the imperfection of the fossil record. Lyell's, or perhaps Hutton's theory might well account correctly for the inorganic world and yet be invalid in the realm of life, the laws governing the latter being indisputably different and much more complex than those ruling in lifeless Nature.

Evolution turned into an issue for Lyell when he came to know Lamarck. In 1827 he himself described how:

> I devoured Lamarck *en voyage* . . . and with . . . pleasure. His theories delighted me more than any novel I ever read, and much in the same way, for they address themselves to the imagination, at least of geologists who know the mighty inferences which would be deducible were they established by observations. But though I admire even his flights, and feel none of the *odium theologicum* which some modern writers in this country have visited him with, I confess I read him rather as I hear an advocate on the wrong side, to know what can be made of the case in good hands. I am glad he has been courageous enough and logical enough to admit that his argument, if pushed as far as it must go, if worth anything, would prove that men may have come from the Ourang-Outang. But after all, what changes species may really undergo! How impossible it will be to distinguish and lay down a line, beyond which some of the so-called extinct species have never passed into recent ones. That the earth is quite as old as he supposes, has long been my creed.[5]

Lyell was fascinated by Lamarck's ideas, but could not accept them. Yet, he felt them important enough to devote much space to their rejection in the second volume of *Principles of Geology*, published 1832. This was where Darwin met with Lamarck the second time, and however much 'the distribution of the inhabitants of South America' may have perplexed him, we cannot doubt that Lyell's opinion must have acted as a curb on the budding Evolutionist on board the *Beagle*.

Darwin met Lyell upon his return to England, and communicated to him his various geological observations, among them his theory on the formation of coral reefs, which Lyell generously consented to be better than his own views on the topic. Lyell helped Darwin in many ways, above all by introducing him into the scientific circles of London. They never became intimate friends, during most of his life Darwin preserved an attitude of admiration and reverence towards Lyell, his senior by twelve years and his master in matters of geology.

As we have seen, when Darwin had the leisure needed to survey all his observations, he came to realise that the facts in support of evolution were overwhelming; he had to part company with Lyell. But he softened the blow by adopting two of Lyell's notions, Gradualism and refutation of progressive evolution. We have already discussed the fatal consequences of these options.

When, in 1856, Lyell first heard of Darwin's ideas on evolution, his views on the subject had not changed, for he wrote in a letter at that time: 'When Huxley, Hooker, and Wollaston were at Darwin's last week, they (all four of them) ran a tilt against species farther I believe than they are deliberately prepared to go . . . I cannot easily see how they can go so far, and not embrace the whole *Lamarckian doctrine*'. (My italics)[6]

In 1859, while Darwin's book was in the printer's office, Lyell was President of the Geological Section at the British Association for Advancement of Science meeting in Aberdeen, and in his Presidential address he said:

> On this difficult and mysterious subject a work will very shortly appear by Mr. Charles Darwin . . . [who] has been led to the conclusion that those powers of nature which give rise to races and permanent varieties in animals and plants, are the same as those which in much longer periods produce species, and in a still longer series of ages give rise to differences of generic rank. He appears to me to have succeeded by his investigations and reasonings in throwing a flood of light on many classes of phenomena . . . for which no other hypothesis has been able, or has even attempted to account.[7]

Did any other scientific book ever get so forceful advance publicity? Could Lyell go so far out in support of Darwin without committing himself? Darwin at least was optimistic, for he wrote to Lyell:

> . . . you have . . . given me [intense] pleasure by the manner you have noticed my species work. Nothing could be more satisfactory to me, and I thank you for myself, and even more for the subject's sake, as I know well that the sentence will make many fairly consider the subject, instead of ridiculing it. Although your *previously* felt doubts on the immutability of species, may have more influence in converting you (if you be converted) than my book; yet as I regard your verdict as far more important in my own eyes, and I believe in the eyes of the world than of any other dozen men, I am naturally very anxious about it . . . not that I shall be disappointed if you are not converted; for *I remember the long years it took me to come round*; but I shall be most deeply delighted if you do come round, especially if I have a fair share in the conversion, I shall then feel that my carrier is run, and care little whether I ever am good for anything again in this life. (My italics)[8]

Lyell was indeed exposed to a heavy pressure. While he was busy reading the proofs of *On the Origin of Species*, Darwin wrote to him:

> I hope that you will read all, whether dull . . . or not, for I am convinced there is not a sentence which has not a bearing on the whole argument . . . I have, as Murray says, corrected so heavily, as almost to have re-written it; but yet I fear it is poorly written. Parts are intricate; and I do not think that even you could make them quite clear. Do not, I beg, be in a hurry in committing yourself (like so many naturalists) to go a certain length and no further; for I am deeply convinced that it is absolutely necessary to go the whole vast length, or stick to the creation of each separate species . . . Remember that *your verdict* will probably have more influence than *my book* in deciding whether such views as I hold will be *admitted or rejected at present*; in the future I cannot doubt about their admittance. (My italics)[9]

Lyell's verdict was hardly what Darwin had hoped, for in spite of his public support Lyell was not in the slightest converted; indeed, he had many and grave objections to make. First, to Lyell the main issue was Creation *or* Evolution, and he knew who had first espoused the latter alternative to the world of science. And

177

therefore, much to Darwin's vexation, Lyell regarded Darwin's work as a modified, although improved, version of Lamarck's theory. We have already touched upon this question, and we shall return to it later.

Second, the two theories of evolution he was acquainted with, Lamarck's and Darwin's, were both micromutation theories, suggesting that all evolutionary changes could occur through the accumulation of minute modifications. Lyell realised that this suggestion meets with insurmountable difficulties, especially with respect to the origin of man. In particular he clearly saw, like most of Darwin's critics and not a few of his supporters, that natural selection does not account for the *origin* of variations; that something more is needed to explain biological evolution. Exactly how he stated his views, we do not know, for his letter is not preserved, but in the answer Darwin wrote:

> I have reflected a good deal on what you say on the necessity of continued intervention of *creative power*. I cannot see this necessity; and its admission, I think, *would make the theory of Natural Selection valueless. Grant a simple Archetypal creature*, like the Mud-fish or Lepidosiren, with five senses and some vestige of mind, and *I believe natural selection will account for the production of every vertebrate animal*. (My italics)[10]

From this quotation one may get the impression that Lyell was advocating a metaphysical explanation of the origin of life. This is not necessarily the case, for Darwin thought, at certain periods at least, that no other 'creative power' than natural selection was required to account for the mechanism of evolution.

I do believe that Lyell more willingly than the other members of the quartet of friends allowed for the possible interference by God, but nevertheless from statements made in other contexts it appears that his opposition to evolution was primarily based on practical and logical reasons — not on religious reasons. This is shown, for instance, by the fact that as early as 1836 Lyell wrote in a letter to John Herschel:

> In regard to the origination of new species, I am very glad to find that you think it probable that it may be carried on through the intervention of intermediate causes. *I left this rather to be inferred, not thinking it worth while to offend a certain class of persons* by embodying in words what would only be a

speculation. (My italics)[11]

One may possibly conclude that Lyell was a considerate, or perhaps rather a cautious person, and one may even suspect that he was 'slippery' to a certain extent, for by making this admission he seems to 'embrace the whole Lamarckian doctrine'.

Third, Lyell was not particularly convinced by Darwin's book. In October 1859 he wrote to Darwin:

I have just finished your volume and right glad I am that I did my best with Hooker to persuade you to publish it without waiting for a time which probably could never have arrived, though you lived till the age of a hundred, when you had prepared all your facts on which you ground so many grand generalizations.

It is a splendid case of close reasoning . . . the condensation immense, *too great perhaps for the uninitiated*, but an effective and important *preliminary* statement, which will admit, even before your detailed *proofs* appear, of *some occasional useful exemplifications* . . .

I mean that, when, as I fully expect, a new edition is soon called for, you may here and there insert *an actual case to relieve the vast number of abstract propositions*. So far as I am concerned, I am so well prepared to take your statements of facts for granted, that I do not think the 'pièces justificatives' when published will make much difference, and I have long seen most clearly that if any concession is made, all that you claim in your concluding pages will follow. It is this which has made me so long hesitate, always feeling that the case of Man and his races, and of other animals, and that of plants is one and the same, and that if a 'vera causa' be admitted for one, instead of a purely unknown and imaginary one, such as the word 'Creation', all the consequences must follow. (My italics)[12]

From the outset Darwin had intended as his particular task the compilation of facts *proving* his own theory, and it may be supposed that he had let his friends into this design. It ought to have been a great disappointment to be told that none of his 'detailed proofs' had yet appeared, and that he should 'insert an actual case'. But Lyell was right: Darwin had promised to demonstrate that evolution occurs through natural selection, and this he did not do, neither in the first nor in any of the succeeding corrected editions of *On the Origin of Species*. He might have made a good case for the theory

179

on the reality of evolution, but that did not suffice for Lyell.

Darwin did not react to this serious blow, but rather concentrated on Lyell's criticism of his facts. Lyell had written:

The want of peculiar birds in Madeira is a greater difficulty than seemed to me allowed for. *I could cite passages where you show that variations are superinduced from the new circumstances of new colonists, which would require some Madeira birds*, like those of the Galapagos, *to be peculiar*. There has been ample time. (My italics)[13]

Lyell could draw logical conclusions from given premises! Darwin answered: 'You are right, there is a screw out here; *I thought no one would have detected it*; I blundered in omitting a discussion, which I have written out in full' (my italics).[14] In later editions Darwin made some changes in the pertinent text, but he never inserted the discussion mentioned in the letter to Lyell.[15]

In 1863 the strife was assumed again, in connection with the publication of Lyell's *The Geological Evidences of the Antiquity of Man with Remarks on the Theories of the Origin of Species by Variation*, in which it had been expected and hoped that he would publicly announce his belief in the theory on the reality of evolution, if not in Darwinism.

As we have seen, Lyell was initially opposed both to Progressionism and to Evolutionism. Realising that palaeontological evidence did in fact support a progressive course of life, he had rejected these notions by reference to the incompleteness of the fossil record. In 1863 he began the discussion of evolution with a presentation of Lamarckism. On this topic he writes:

While, in 1832, I argued against Lamarck's doctrine of the *gradual* transmutation of one species into another, I agreed with him in believing that the system of changes now in progress in the organic world would afford, *when fully understood*, a complete key to the interpretation of all the vicissitudes of the living creation in past ages. I contended against the doctrine, then very popular, of the sudden destruction of vast multitudes of species, and the abrupt ushering into the world of new batches of plants and animals . . .

The *only* point on which I doubted was, whether the force might not be *intermittent* instead of being, as Lamarck supposed, in *ceaseless operation*. Might not the births of new species, like the deaths of old ones, be sudden? . . . In that case, I imagined that although the first appearance of a new form might be as abrupt as the disappearance of an old one, yet naturalists might never yet have witnessed the first entrance on the stage of a large and conspicuous animal or plant. (My italics)[16]

As it appears, Lyell is here arguing against Lamarck's micromutation theory in favour of a macromutation theory. Lyell continues:

It may now be useful to offer some remarks on the very different reception which the twin branches of Lamarck's development theory, namely, *progression* and *transmutation*, have met with, and to enquire into the causes of the popularity of the one, and the great unpopularity of the other. We usually test the value of a scientific hypothesis by the number and variety of the phenomena of which it offers a fair or plausible explanation. If transmutation, when thus tested, has decidedly the advantage over progression, and yet is comparatively in disfavour, we may reasonably suspect that its reception is retarded, not so much by its own inherent demerits, as by some apprehended consequences which it is supposed to involve, and which run counter to our preconceived opinions. (My italics)[17]

Lyell then discusses the evidence which in the intervening years had accumulated in favour of Progressionism. He concludes:

. . . I regard [the theory now under consideration] not only as a useful, but rather . . . as an indispensable hypothesis, and one which . . . will never be overthrown.

It may be thought almost paradoxical that writers who are most in favour of transmutation (Mr. C. Darwin and Dr. J. Hooker, for example) are nevertheless among those who are most cautious, and one would say timid, in their mode of espousing the doctrine of progression; while, on the other hand, the most zealous advocates of progression are oftener than not very vehement opponents of transmutation. We might have anticipated a contrary leaning on the part of both, for to what does the theory of progression point? It supposes a gradual elevation in grade of the vertebrate type, in the course of ages, from the most simple ichthyic form to . . . the human race — this last thus appearing as an integral part of the same continuous series of acts of development, one link in the same chain, the crowning operation as it were of one and the same series of manifestations of *creative power*. (My italics)[18]

Once more one is impressed by the reasoning power of Lyell. Both systematics and palaeontology testify to the phenomenon of progress, so if there has been evolution, there has been progressive evolution.

Lyell continues to discuss transmutation, beginning with Robert Chambers:

The anonymous author of 'The Vestiges of Creation' published in 1844 a treatise, written in a clear and attractive style, *which made the English public familiar with the leading views of Lamarck on transmutation and progression*, but brought no new facts or original line of argument to support those views, or to combat the principal objections which the scientific world entertained against them.

No decided step in this direction was made until the publication in 1858 of two papers, one by Mr. Darwin and another by Mr. Wallace, followed in 1859 by Mr. Darwin's celebrated work. (My italics)[19]

In the following survey of the theory of natural selection we find a most astonishing passage:

If one variety, *being in other respects just equal to its competitors*, happens to be more prolific, some of its offspring will stand a greater chance of being among those which will escape destruction, and their descendants, being in like manner very fertile, will continue to multiply at the expense of all less prolific varieties. (My italics)[20]

The theory of natural selection is based on differential survival or, what amounts to the same thing, *differential elimination*. What Lyell asserts in the quoted statement is the principle of *differential reproduction*, no part of Darwin's theory, but the one on which the current theory of evolution — Neo-Mendelism — is based.

Further on we read:

Every naturalist admits that there is a general tendency in animals and plants to vary; but *it is usually taken for granted, though we have no means of proving the assumption to be true, that there*

182

are certain limits beyond which each species cannot pass under any circumstances, or in any number of generations. Mr. Darwin and Mr. Wallace say that the opposite hypothesis, which assumes that every species is capable of varying indefinitely from its original type, is not a whit more arbitrary, and has this manifest claim to be preferred, that it will account for a multitude of phenomena which the ordinary theory is incapable of explaining. (My italics)[21]

Lyell then goes on to discuss the various facts marshalled by Darwin and by Hooker in favour of evolution, without pointing out that this evidence does not necessarily support the Darwinian micromutation theory.

After observing: 'Hitherto, no rival hypothesis has been proposed as a substitute for the doctrine of transmutation; for "independent creation", as it is often termed, or the direct intervention of the Supreme Cause, must simply be considered as an avowal that we deem the question to lie beyond the domain of science',[22] Lyell then discusses various objections to the 'transmutation hypothesis'. Yet, at no place did he openly declare himself an adherent of evolution in general, and still less of the micromutation theory of Lamarck and Darwin, which, in his view, does not afford a satisfactory explanation of the mechanism of evolution. Still, he writes: 'Yet we ought by no means to undervalue the importance of the step which will have been made, should it ever become highly probable that the past changes of the organic world have been brought about by the *subordinate* agency of such causes as "Variation" and "Natural Selection" ' (My italics).[23]

Darwin wrote to Hooker:

He has shown great skill in picking out salient points in the argument for change of species; but I am deeply disappointed (I do not mean personally) to find that his timidity prevents him giving any judgement . . . From all my communications with him I must ever think that he has really entirely lost faith in the immutability of species; and yet one of his strongest sentences is nearly as follows: 'If it should *ever* be rendered highly probable that species change by variation and natural selection', &c. &c. I had hoped he would have guided the public as far as his own belief went . . . No doubt the public or a part may be induced to think that, as he gives to us a larger space than to Lamarck, he must think there is something in our view.[24]

From this letter it appears that Darwin envisaged that acceptance of the theory on the reality of evolution implied acceptance of his own theory. But this was not Lyell's opinion, and when Darwin complained to him, his answer was:

I *cannot go Huxley's length in thinking that natural selection and variation account for so much* [sic!], and not so far as you, if I take some passages of your book separately.

I think the old 'creation' is almost as much required as ever, but of course it takes a new form if Lamarck's views improved by yours are adopted. (My italics)[25]

From his publications it is indeed very difficult to know exactly where Lyell stood. He was somewhat more frank in his correspondence; thus, in a letter from 1860 he wrote:

I confess that Agassiz's last work drove me far over into Darwin's camp, or the Lamarckian view, for when he attributed the original [sic] of every race of man to an independent starting point, or act of creation, and not satisfied with that, created whole 'nations' at a time, every individual out of 'earth, air, and water' as Hooker styles it, the miracles really became to me so much in the way of S. Antonio of Padua, or that Spanish saint whose name I forget, that I could not help thinking Lamarck must be right.[26]

And in 1863 he wrote to Hooker:

[Darwin] seems much disappointed that I do not go farther with him, or do not speak out more. I can only say that I have spoken out to the full extent of my present convictions, and even beyond my state of *feeling* as to man's unbroken descent from the brutes, and I feel I am half converting not a few who were in arms against Darwin . . .

I don't care what people have been expecting as to the extent to which I may go with Darwin, but I certainly do not wish to be inconsistent with myself. Though, as I have been gradually changing my opinion, I do not want to insist on others going round at once. When I read again certain chapters of the 'Principles', I am always in danger of shaking some of my confidence in the new doctrine, but am brought back again on reconsidering such essays as Darwin's, Wallace's and yours. I see too many difficulties to be in the danger of many new converts who outrun their teacher in faith.[27]

I believe we may interpret these citations to the effect that Lyell was willing, albeit reluctantly, to accept Lamarck's first and second theory of evolution, without thereby accepting Darwin's theory of natural selection. If this is correct, then he really went very far for old acquaintance's sake in the quotation made above.

Lyell's book also upset Darwin for another reason — the generous space denoted to Lamarck:

> Lastly, you refer repeatedly to my view as a modification of Lamarck's doctrine of development and progression. If this is your deliberate opinion there is nothing to be said, but it does not seem so to me. Plato, Buffon, my grandfather before Lamarck, and others, propounded the *obvious* view that if species were not created separately they must have descended from other species, and *I can see nothing else in common between the 'Origin' and Lamarck*. I believe this way of putting the case is very injurious to its acceptance, *as it implies necessary progression*, and closely connect Wallace's and my views with what I consider, after two deliberate readings, as a wretched book, and one from which (*I well remember my surprise*) I gained nothing. But I know you rank it higher, which is curious, as it did not in the least shake your belief. (My italics, except for the first ones)[28]

Here we see Darwin carrying a false argumentation, either on purpose because he wants to debase Lamarck's contribution, or else because he confounds the issue. For it is *obvious* that *if* 'species were not created separately they must have descended from other species', but it is not so *obvious* that *they were not created separately*: as we know, this assertion is the main premise in Lamarck's theory on the reality of evolution.

In 1867–8 Lyell published the tenth edition of his *Principles of Geology*, in which we may read: '*Was Lamarck right*, assuming *progressive development* to be true, in supposing that the changes of the organic world may have been effected by the gradual and insensible modification of older pre-existing forms? Mr. Darwin, *without absolutely proving this*, has made it appear in the highest degree *probable*' (my italics).[29] From the italics it seems that this declaration ought to be received with mixed feelings by Darwin, and yet the rejoicing was great in the Darwinian camp because, it was declared, Lyell had now given up his opposition to evolution.

To celebrate the event, Wallace wrote an article in *The Quarterly Review*, in which we find the following statement:

The history of science hardly presents so striking an instance of youthfulness of mind in advanced life as is shown by this abandonment of opinions so long held and so powerfully advocated; and if we bear in mind the extreme caution, combined with the ardent love of truth which characterize every work which our author has produced, we shall be convinced that so great a change was not decided without long and anxious deliberation, and that the views now adopted must indeed be supported by arguments of overwhelming force. *If for no other reason than that Sir Charles Lyell in his tenth edition has adopted it, the theory of Mr. Darwin deserves an attentive and respectful consideration from every earnest seeker after truth.* (My italics)[30]

Had Lyell now become a convert to Darwinism? To elucidate this question I shall quote two letters written in 1868. The first was addressed to the Duke of Argyll:

I objected in my 'Antiquity of Man' to what I there called the deification of natural selection, which I consider as a law or force *quite subordinate* to that variety-making or creative power to which all the wonders of the organic world must be referred. I cannot believe that Darwin or Wallace can mean to dispense with that *mind* of which you speak as directing the forces of nature. *They in fact admit that we know nothing of the power which gives rise to variation* in form, colour, structure or instinct. (My italics)[31]

The second letter was written to Ernst Haeckel:

I have to thank you for your kindness in sending me a copy of your important work on the 'History of Creation', and especially for the chapter entitled 'On Lyell and Darwin'. Most of the zoologists forget that anything was written between the time of Lamarck and the publication of our friend's 'Origin of Species'.

I am therefore obliged to you for pointing out how clearly I advocated a law of continuity even in the organic world, so far as possible without adopting Lamarck's theory of transmutation
. . .

But while I taught that as often as certain forms of animals and plants disappeared, for reasons quite intelligible to us, others took their place by virtue of a causation which was beyond our comprehension; it remained for Darwin to accumulate proof that there is no break between incoming and outgoing species, that they are the work of evolution, and not of special creation . . .

I had certainly prepared the way in this country, in six editions of my work before the 'Vestiges of Creation' appeared in 1842 [sic!], for the reception of Darwin's *gradual* and *insensible* evolution of species, and I am very glad you noticed this. (My italics)[32]

The first letter clearly shows that Lyell did not consider the mechanism proposed by Darwin sufficient to explain the process of evolution, the word 'mind' even suggests the involvement of metaphysical agents. In the second letter he seems to acclaim Darwinism, but as opposed to 'special creation'. It thus appears that nobody ever suggested a theory on the mechanism of evolution acceptable to Lyell, and therefore he remained hesitant and doubtful on this point. Indeed, Lyell was not 'in a hurry to commit himself', he never became a convinced Darwinian.

Delving into the history of evolution, one becomes acquainted with many persons contrasting in several respects. In particular, one encounters more or less sympathetic people. I feel that Erasmus Darwin, Lamarck and Chambers belong to the first category, and among the friends Lyell unquestionably does. He possessed some of the characteristics with which we outsiders associate the English gentleman: his treatment of Lamarck shows that to him fairness comes before friendship, and his treatment of Darwin the importance he attached to freedom of expression.

JOSEPH DALTON HOOKER (1817–1911)

Joseph Hooker was born to become a prince in the realm of botany. His father, William Jackson Hooker, was professor of botany at the University of Glasgow, and later director of Kew Gardens, the botanical garden in London. Twenty-two years old, Hooker left England on board HMS *Erebus*, bound for Australia, New Zealand, Tasmania and the Antarctic. During four years he made large collections which were the foundation for floras composed and edited in later years. Another long voyage was made to India in 1847–50. Hooker first became assistant to his father at Kew and later he took over the directorship, being by then the leading botanist in Europe. He died 94 years old, a greatly honoured man.[33]

Hooker met Darwin shortly before he embarked on his first voyage, and when he returned a friendship was established between the two globe-trotters which, I believe, was singularly harmonious, as demonstrated not the least by the scores of letters they exchanged during most of 40 years. Hooker was a systematist and bio-geographer; in the first respect he was Darwin's master, in the second they could co-operate on more equal terms. No one else was so much charged by Darwin with questions and problems, in letters and during numerous visits to Down, but in spite of the enormity of his own work load Hooker always had time for Darwin. Darwin felt a great indebtedness to Hooker, and for good reason, for 'without Hooker's aid Darwin's great work would hardly have been carried out on the botanical side'.[34] But Hooker was also interested in more theoretical problems, particularly the 'species question', and on such topics it may be surmised that Darwin was the mentor. The perfect match between them is beautifully illustrated by the fact that Hooker felt indebted as much as Darwin: '. . . I at any rate always left with the feeling that I had imparted nothing and carried away more than I could stagger under.'[35]

It is an indication of the intimacy of their friendship that Darwin as early as 1844 revealed his most secret thoughts on evolution to Hooker: '. . . I determined to collect blindly every sort of fact, which could bear any way on what are species. I have read heaps of . . . books, and have never ceased collecting facts. At last gleams of light have come, and I am almost convinced (*quite contrary to the opinion I started with*) that species are not (it is like confessing a murder) immutable' (My italics).[36]

The topic is almost absent from the correspondence until the mid-1850s, when Lyell and Huxley also joined the band of conspirators. From letters we realise that Hooker objected to various aspects of the theory; certainly, he was not an easily converted proselyte. He wrote himself: '. . . I was aware of Darwin's views *fourteen years* before I adopted them, and I have done so *solely* and *entirely* from an independent study of plants themselves.'[37] But he did accept the theory on the reality of evolution in 1858, and in the Introduction to his *Flora Tasmanica* he committed himself, almost simultaneously with the appearance of Darwin's *On the Origin of Species*.

Some time after receiving a complementary copy of Darwin's book Hooker wrote:

I have not yet got half through the book, not from want of will, but of time — for it is the very hardest book to read to full profit that I ever tried; it is so cram-full of matter and reasoning. I am all the more glad that you have published in this form, for the [planned] 3 vols., unprefaced by this, would have choked any Naturalist of the XIX century and certainly have softened my brain in the operation of assimilating their contents. I am perfectly *tired* of marvelling at the wonderful amount of *facts* you have brought to bear, and your skill in marshalling them and throwing them on the enemy. It is also *extremely clear* as far as I have gone, but *very hard to fully appreciate*. (My italics)[38]

But later Hooker's critical spirit was aroused, so he wrote:

You certainly make a hobby of Nat. Selection and probably ride it too hard — that is a necessity of your case. If *improvement* of the *creation by variation doctrine* is *conceivable*, it will be *unburdening your theory of Natural Selection*, which at first sight seems overstrained; i.e. to account for *too much*. I think too that some of your difficulties which you override by Nat. Selection may give way before other explanations. (My italics, except for the last ones)[39]

Hooker went on brooding on the problem, writing in March 1862 to Darwin:

I cannot conceive what you say, that climate could have effected even such a single character as a hooked seed. You know I have a morbid horror of two laws in nature for obtaining the same end; hence I incline to attribute the smallest variation to the inherent tendency to vary; a principle wholly independent of physical conditions — but whose effects on the race are absolutely dependent on physical conditions for their *conservation*.

Huxley is rather disposed to think you have overlooked '*Saltus*', but I am not sure that he is right. Saltus quoad *individual*, is not saltus quoad *species*. (The first italics are mine)[40]

It seems that the view adopted here is very simple: variations arise spontaneously and are selected, i.e. survive, according to their usefulness under the given environmental conditions. The last paragraph is included to show that Hooker was opposed to macromutations, apparently because he did not see that an individual undergoing 'saltus' may give rise to a new species through inbreeding.

Later in the year Hooker repeated his criticism against natural selection, as we may see from Darwin's answer:

> But the part of your letter which fairly pitched me head over heels with astonishment, is that where you state that *every single difference which we see might have occurred without any selection. I do and have always fully agreed*; but you have got right round the subject, and viewed it from an entirely opposite and new side, and when you took me there I was astounded. When I say I agree, I must make the proviso, that under your view, as now, each form long remains adapted to certain fixed conditions, and that the conditions of life are in the long run changeable; and second, which is more important, that each individual form is a self-fertilizing hermaphrodite, so that each hair-breadth variation is not lost by intercrossing. Your manner of putting the case would be even more striking than it is if the mind could grapple with such numbers — it is grappling with eternity — think of each of a thousand seeds bringing forth its plant, and then each a thousand. A globe stretching to the furthest fixed star would very soon be covered. I cannot even grapple with the idea, even with races of dogs, cattle, pigeons, or fowls; and here all admit and see the accurate strictness of your illustration.
>
> *Such men as you and Lyell thinking I make too much of a Deus of Natural Selection is a conclusive argument against me.* (My italics)[41]

We should indeed like to know Hooker's illustration, for to me the text between the two italicised statements indicates that Darwin hardly grasped Hooker's view. In fact, the words make no sense unless the reference to the 'fixed star' implies that in the absence of natural selection there is no elimination of plants and animals. But this is wrong, elimination does not imply selection, since it may be random and thus non-selective.

One understands Darwin when he wrote a few days later to Hooker:

> I hardly know why I am a little sorry, but my present work is leading me to *believe rather more in the direct action of physical conditions*. I presume I regret it, because it lessens the glory of

Natural Selection, and is so confoundly doubtful. Perhaps *I shall change again* when I get all my *facts* under one point of view, and a pretty hard job this will be. (My italics)[42]

But worse was to come; in a Presidential Address in 1868 Hooker was to discuss *the fact that Darwin's theory had failed.* Darwin commented:

I am glad to hear that you are going to touch on the statement that *the belief in Natural Selection is passing away.* I do not suppose that even the *Athenaeum* would pretend that the belief in the common descent of species is passing away, and *this is the more important point.* This now almost universal belief in the evolution (somehow) of species, I think may be fairly attributed in large part to the *Origin* . . .

If you argue about the non-acceptance of *Natural Selection*, it seems to me a very striking fact that the *Newtonian theory of gravitation*, which seems to everyone now so certain and plain, was rejected by a man so extraordinarily able as Leibnitz. The *truth* will not penetrate a preoccupied mind. (My italics)[43]

For a moment, Darwin seems to acquiesce to the role as the prompter of the triumph of Lamarck's theory on the reality of evolution, but, feeling perhaps uneasy about this modest contribution to science, he turns around and transforms himself into Newton, and Hooker to an 'extraordinarily able', but 'preoccupied', Leibniz.

Like most of Darwin's opponents Hooker thus objected to natural selection in that it does not account for the origin of variation. In suggesting that variations occur independently of selection it would seem that he would be advocating the existence of macromutations, but as we have seen above, he did not do that. That a botanist should take this stand is rather surprising, for macromutations are not uncommon in the vegetable kingdom, a fact which was known also to Darwin.

In 1860 Hooker wrote to his friend William Harvey: '. . . seven of the ablest men of this day (and a host of smaller fry) pronounced Darwin's book to be the most remarkable of its generation, and, though *not conclusive as to its own ultimate views*, to have thrown the doctrine of original creation of *species* to the winds — this is my view of the question' (first italics mine).[44] Thus, *in Hooker's view Darwin's main contribution was not his own theory, but that he caused the general abandonment of the theory of Creation.*

Darwin once wrote to Hooker: 'Talk of fame, honour, pleasure, wealth, all are dirt compared with affection; and this is a doctrine with which, I know, from your letter, that you will agree with from the bottom of your heart.'[45]

In my view there is not much to envy in Darwin's life, but there is one *great* thing, his friendship with Hooker. Joseph Hooker was a very fine man, honest, fair, helpful and considerate.

THOMAS HENRY HUXLEY (1825–1895)

Although the son of a schoolteacher, Huxley received very little formal instruction. Working on his own, he studied philosophy, languages, natural sciences and history, thus preparing for the Matriculation Examination at London University. After two years apprenticeship with practising physicians, Huxley obtained a Free Scholarship at the Charing Cross Hospital and Medical College in 1842. As he finished his studies in 1846 he entered the Medical Service of the Navy, being soon appointed assistant-surgeon on HMS *Rattlesnake*, which in December that year left England bound for the southern hemisphere. The voyage lasted four years, during which Huxley took up the study of zoology. His work was greatly appreciated, and soon after his return he became a Fellow of the Royal Society and was awarded the Royal Medal.

In 1854 he became Naturalist under the Geological Survey, and began lecturing at various institutions, among others the School of Mines in Jermyn Street. Here he remained until his retirement in 1885. Huxley published a large number of important observations in natural history, mostly in comparative anatomy, the evaluation of which may be testified by the many honours bestowed upon him. Yet, as long as Owen was alive, and Huxley survived him by only three years, he was not the leading anatomist in Europe. This may in part be explained by the fact that Huxley did not confine himself to natural science, but wrote treatises on philosophy, ethics, etc. In intellectual acuity and scholarship he was the most outstanding in the quartet of friends.[46]

We have seen above that in 1856 Huxley was running 'a tilt against the species' at Down. This does not mean that he believed in evolution; although he was more easily converted than Hooker, it seems that only in 1859 did he become an Evolutionist and the never failing champion of Darwin.

Before we discuss his views on Darwinism, we may first consider his attitude towards Lamarck, the founder of evolutionary thought. In his essay *On the Reception of the 'Origin of Species'* from 1888 he writes:

> With respect to the 'Philosophie Zoologique', it is no reproach to Lamarck to say that the discussion of the Species question in that work, whatever might be said for it in 1809, was miserably below the level of knowledge of half a century later . . . To any biologist whose studies had carried him beyond mere species-mongering in 1850, one-half of Lamarck's arguments were obsolete and the other half erroneous, or defective, *in virtue of omitting to deal with the various classes of evidence which had been brought to light since his time* . . . I do not think that any impartial judge who reads the 'Philosophie Zoologique' now . . . will be disposed to allot to Lamarck a much higher place in the establishment of biological evolution than that which Bacon assigns to himself in relation to physical science generally, — *buccinator tantum* [just a trumpeter, i.e. all bleat, no wool]. (First italics mine)[47]

This quotation is remarkable, for it suggests a lack of understanding of theoretical issues in Huxley, which, to put it mildly, is quite unexpected; in particular it seems unfair to reproach Lamarck for omitting evidence 'brought to life since his time'. Furthermore, Huxley was clearly unaware of Lyell's opinion that the theory on the reality of evolution was the creation of Lamarck. His work was rejected *in toto* because his theory on the mechanisms of evolution was wrong.

In another context, in 1859, he had written: 'Since Lamarck's time, almost all competent naturalists have left speculations on the origin of species to such dreamers as the author of the "Vestiges", by whose well-intentioned efforts the Lamarckian theory received its final condemnation in the minds of all sound thinkers.'[48] It will be recalled that Chambers specifically rejected Lamarck's theory on the mechanism of evolution, proposing an alternative. Owen realised in 1844 that the latter was the epigenetic theory which he himself had adopted, the one which, as we shall see, Huxley himself advocated in 1860. These two quotations, and some to follow, suggest that Huxley's views on the topic of evolutionary theory were rather confused.

Huxley's treatment of Lamarck at these occasions is ruthless and unfair and, worst of all, it is at variance with the view he saw fit to

193

express in private correspondence. Thus, in 1882 he wrote in a letter: 'I am not likely to take a low view of Darwin's position in the history of science, but *I am disposed to think that Buffon and Lamarck would run him hard in both genius and fertility.* In breadth of view and in extent of knowledge these two men were giants, though *we are apt to forget their services. Von Baer was another man of the same stamp*' (my italics).[49]

In the essay mentioned above, Huxley writes of Lyell: 'On the other hand, Lyell, up to that time a pillar of the anti-transmutationists . . . declared himself a Darwinian, though not without putting in a serious *caveat*. Nevertheless, he was a tower of strength, and his courageous stand for *truth* as against consistency, did him infinite honour' (the last italics are mine).[50] Later we may read: '. . . from the concluding paragraph, Whewell evidently imagines that by "creation" Lyell means a preternatural intervention of the Deity; whereas the letter to Herschel [p. 178] shows that, in his own mind, Lyell meant natural causation.'[51]

Of Owen he writes: 'Neither did it help me to be told by an eminent anatomist that species had succeeded one another in time, in virtue of "a continuously operative creational law". That seemed to me to be no more than saying that species had succeeded one another, in the form of a vote-catching resolution, with "law" to please the man of science, and "creational" to draw the orthodox.'[52]

This is not an objective and fair presentation, in particular since Lyell to the end remained sceptical of Darwin's theory and Owen adhered to a theory similar to the one advocated by Huxley. Surely, either Lyell's 'creation' and Owen's 'creational law' were synonyms, or else Lyell's concept was more metaphysical than Owen's. If Huxley really was ignorant on this point, then he was not qualified for writing the essay.

There are no interesting references to evolution in the early correspondence between Huxley and Darwin, but in October 1859 Darwin writes to Huxley: 'I shall be *intensely* curious to hear what effect the book produces on you. I know that there will be much in it which you will object to, and I do not doubt many errors. I am very far from expecting to convert you to many of my heresies; but if, on the whole, you and two or three others think I am on the right road, I shall not care what the mob of naturalists think.'[53]

When Huxley had received Darwin's book he wrote a letter in which we may read:

Since I read Von Baer's essays, nine years ago, no work on Natural History Science I have met with has made so great an impression upon me, and I do most heartily thank you for the great store of new views you have given me. Nothing, I think, can be better than *the tone of the book, it impresses those who know nothing about the subject.* As for your doctrine, I am prepared to go to the stake, if requisite, *in support of Chapter IX,* and *most parts* of Chapters X., XI., XII., and Chapter XIII. contains *much* that is most admirable, but on one or two points I enter a *caveat* until I can see further into all sides of the question.

As to the first four chapters, *I agree thoroughly and fully with all the principles laid down in them.* I think you have demonstrated a *true* cause for the production of species, and have thrown the *onus probandi*, that species did not arise in the way you suppose, on your adversaries . . .

The *only* objections that have occurred to me are, 1st that *you have loaded yourself with an unnecessary difficulty* in adopting *Natura non facit saltum* so unreservedly . . . And 2nd, it is not clear to me why, if continual physical conditions are of so little moment as you suppose, variation should occur at all. (My italics, except for the Latin expressions)

This was a rather reserved acclamation, the only chapter he could defend wholeheartedly being the one on the imperfection of the fossil record. And the first objection was a serious one, showing Huxley to be a Macromutationist.

Yet, in spite of this he had already at this moment made up his mind that he was going to be Darwin's partisan, for the letter continued:

I trust you will not allow yourself to be in any way disgusted or annoyed by the considerable abuse and misrepresentation which, unless I greatly mistake, is in store for you. Depend upon it you have earned the lasting gratitude of all thoughtful men. And as to the curs which will bark and yelp, you must recollect that some of your friends, at any rate, are endowed with an amount of combativeness which (though you have often and justly rebuked it) may stand you in good stead.

I am sharpening up my claws and beak in readiness.[54]

Huxley wrote a short review in *The Times* in 1859, and in 1860 he published a long essay in which he accounted for his personal views. In particular, he discussed two well-known cases of large-scale inheritable mutations which arise spontaneously, the Ancon sheep and hexadactyly in humans. We shall here deal only with what he wrote about the first example:

It appears that one Seth Wright . . . in Massachusetts, possessed a flock of fifteen ewes and a ram of the ordinary kind. In the year 1791, one of the ewes presented her owner with a male lamb, differing, for no assignable reason, from its parents by a proportionally long body and short bandy legs, whence it was unable to emulate its relatives in those sportive leaps over the neighbours' fences, in which they were in the habit of indulging, much to the good farmer's vexation . . .

Two circumstances are well worthy of remark . . . the variety appears to have arisen in full force, and, as it were, *per saltum*; a wide and definite difference appearing, at once, between the Ancon ram and the ordinary sheep . . . it [is not] possible to point out any obvious reason for the appearance of the variety. Doubtless there were determining causes for [this] as for all other phaenomena; but they do not appear, and we can be tolerably certain that what are ordinarily understood as changes in physical conditions, as in climate, in food, or the like, did not take place and had nothing to do with the matter. *It was no case of what is commonly called adaptation to circumstances*; but, to use a conveniently erroneous phrase, the variations arose spontaneously. The fruitless search after final causes leads their pursuers a long way; but even those hardy teleologists, who are ready to break through all the laws of physics in chase of their favourite will-ó-the-wisp, may be puzzled to discover what purpose could be attained by the stunted legs of Seth Wright's lamb . . .

Varieties then arise we know not why; and it is more than probable that *the majority of varieties have arisen in this 'spontaneous' manner*, though we are, of course, far from denying that they may be traced, in some cases, to distinct external influences . . . But however they may have arisen, what especially interests us at present is, to remark that, once in existence, many varieties obey the fundamental law of reproduction that like tends to produce like; and their offspring exemplify it by tending to exhibit the same deviation from the parental stock as themselves . . .

If a variation which approaches the nature of a monstrosity [hexadactyly] can strive thus forcibly to reproduce itself, it is not wonderful that less aberrant modifications should tend to be preserved even more strongly; and the history of the Ancon sheep is, in this respect, particularly instructive. With the 'cuteness' characteristic of their nation, the neighbours of the Massachusetts farmer imagined it would be an excellent thing if all his sheep were imbued with the stay-at-home tendencies enforced by Nature upon the newly-arrived ram; and they advised Wright to kill the old patriarch of his fold, and install the Ancon ram in his place. The results justified their sagacious anticipations . . . The young lambs were almost always either pure Ancons, or pure ordinary sheep. But when sufficient Ancon sheep were obtained to interbreed with one another, it was found that the offspring was always pure Ancon . . . Here, then, is a remarkable and well-established instance, not only of *a very distinct race being established* per saltum, *but of that race breeding 'true' at once, and showing no mixed forms, even when crossed with another breed*. (My italics, except for the Latin expressions)[55]

Later in the same review Huxley writes:

There is *no fault* to be found with *Mr. Darwin's method*, then; but it is another question whether *he has fulfilled all the conditions imposed by that method. Is it satisfactorily proved*, in fact, *that species may be originated by selection? that there is such a thing as natural selection? that none of the phaenomena exhibited by species are inconsistent with the origin of species in this way?*
. . .

After much consideration, and with assuredly *no bias against* Mr. Darwin's views, it is our *clear conviction* that, *as the evidence stands*, it is *not absolutely proven* that a group of animals, having all the characters exhibited by species in Nature, *has ever been originated by selection*, whether artificial or natural. (My italics)[56]

Part of Huxley's opposition refers to the fact that he regarded infertility between members of different species an absolute species criterion, a question we have already dealt with, but the other part was, as we have seen here, based on his belief in macromutations. Indeed, one may sympathise with Darwin when he wrote to Lyell: 'There is a *brilliant* review by Huxley, with capital hits, but I do not know that he much advances the subject.'[57]

Later that year Darwin wrote to Huxley:

> I entirely agree with you, that the difficulties on my notions are terrific, yet having seen what all the Reviews have said against me, I have far more confidence in the *general* truth of the doctrine than I formerly had. Another thing gives me confidence, viz. that some who went half an inch with me now go further, and some who were bitterly opposed are now less bitterly opposed. And this makes me feel a *little disappointed that you are not inclined to think the general view* in some slight degree *more probable than you did at first.* This I consider rather ominous. *Otherwise* I should be more contended with your degree of belief. I can pretty plainly see that, if my view is ever to be generally adopted, *it will be by young men growing up and replacing the old workers*, and then young ones finding that they can group facts and search out new lines of investigation better on the notion of *descent*, than on that of *creation.* (My italics, except for the first ones)[58]

As usual Darwin could not distinguish between Lamarck's on the reality of evolution and his theory on the mechanism of evolution. Huxley did not reject evolution, but he could not accept that it had taken place *via* Darwinian micromutations. It is amusing to see that Huxley, who was by then 35 years of age, is brushed aside in favour of 'young men growing up'.

In fact, as a man with deep insight in morphology, Huxley could not but embrace the epigenetic macromutation theory advocated in England by Chambers, Owen and Mivart, the theory inspired by the work of Geoffroy Saint-Hilaire and von Baer. Huxley was well acquainted with the embryological treatises of the latter which he had translated into English. It is remarkable, therefore, that in his essay *Evolution in Biology*[59] from 1878 he discusses embryonic recapitulation with reference to Meckel; apparently, but unbelievably, like Darwin he did not understand the implications of von Baer's views.

However this may be, that Huxley did not believe in Darwin's natural selection was illustrated in a striking fashion in 1880, when *On the Origin of Species* was going to celebrate its 21st anniversary. Huxley took the opportunity to lecture at the Royal Institution on 'The Coming of Age of the Origin of Species', in which *'Natural Selection' was not once mentioned.* He even stated:

History warns us, however, that it is the customary fate of new truths to begin as heresies and to end as superstitions; and as matters now stand, it is hardly rash to anticipate that, in another twenty years, the new generation, educated under the influences of the present day, *will be in danger of accepting the main doctrines of the 'Origin of Species', with as little reflection, and it may be with as little justification, as so many of our contemporaries, twenty years ago, rejected them.*[60]

On the same occasion he asserted 'that the essence of the scientific spirit is criticism', and his declaration on Darwinism might therefore be taken as an expression of his concern for the progress of science. However, knowing his own stand *vis-à-vis* Darwin's theory one might expect that he was looking forward to have it replaced sooner or later by one in better agreement with his own views.

Darwin wrote to thank him, and he answered: 'I hope you do not imagine because I had *nothing* to say about ''Natural Selection'', that *I am at all weak of faith on that article* . . . But *the first thing seems to me to be to drive the fact of evolution into people's heads*; when that is once safe, the rest will come easy' (my italics).[61] At this time Huxley knew, as well as Hooker and Darwin, that the theory on the reality of evolution had won the day; it was quite generally accepted, even by those who formerly had objected to it for religious reasons. Darwin's own contribution, however, had been rejected with equal unanimity, because its shortcomings were so glaring. Huxley was not honest at this occasion, probably because we would not hurt Darwin's feelings.

Anyhow, Darwin was not fooled, for he wrote: 'I saw your motive for not alluding to Natural Selection, and quite agreed in my mind to its wisdom. But at the same time *it occurred to me that you might be giving it up*, and that anyhow you could not safely allude to it *without various 'provisos'* too long to give in a lecture' (my italics).[62] There is one mistake in Darwin's letter, Huxley could not give up natural selection, for he had never believed in it.

In his essay *On the Reception of the 'Origin of Species'*, included in *The Life and Letters of Charles Darwin* Huxley on several occasions underscores the Newtonian myth, for instance, the '. . . theory of the origin of the forms of life peopling our globe, with which Darwin's name is bound up as closely as that of Newton with the theory of gravitation'.[63] He goes on to describe how his uncertainties about the problem of evolution withered under the influence of Darwin's theory: '. . . with any and every critical doubt which

199

my sceptical ingenuity could suggest, the *Darwinian hypothesis* remained incomparably more probable than the *creation hypothesis*' (my italics). And he continues:

> The result has been that complete *volte-face* of the whole scientific world, which must seem so surprising to the present generation. I do not mean to say that all the leaders of biological science have avowed themselves *Darwinians*; but I do not think that there is a single zoologist, or botanist, or palaeontologist, among the multitude of active workers of this generation, who is other than an evolutionist, profoundly influenced by Darwin's views. (My italics)[64]

Like Darwin Huxley was well able to 'wriggle'; in the last two quotations we see that he first identifies Lamarck's theory of evolution with Darwin's theory on natural selection, and next makes a clear distinction between them.

Huxley was in many respects a very fine person; thus, as a true liberal he devoted much of his time to humanitarian purposes. But on the topic of evolution, the one where his combativity came most to the fore, he assumed an attitude which euphemistically may be called 'ambiguous'. In the case of Owen this might be explained by professional rivalry, but why did he attack such innocuous and defenceless persons as Chambers and Mivart (Chapter 9) so fiercely? Although he is usually considered to have been 'Darwin's bulldog', the preceding quotations show quite convincingly that he could only come out wholeheartedly in the defence of Darwin when he equated 'Darwinism' with Lamarck's theory on the reality of evolution.

THE THREE MUSKETEERS

> I remember thinking, above a year ago, that if ever I lived to see Lyell, yourself, and Huxley come round, partly by my book, and partly by their own reflections, I should feel that the subject is safe, and all the world might rail, but that ultimately the theory of Natural Selection . . . would prevail. Nothing will ever convince me that three such men, with so much diversified knowledge, and so well accustomed to search for truth, could err greatly.[65]
>
> Charles Darwin

> Again, you misquote and misunderstand Huxley, who is a complete convert. Prof. Asa Gray and Dr. Hooker, the two first botanists of Europe and America, are converts. And Lyell, the first geologist living, who has all his life written against such conclusions as Darwin arrives at, is a convert and is about to declare or already has declared his conversion.[66]
>
> Alfred Russel Wallace

Old J.E. Gray, at the British museum, attacked me in fine style: 'You have just reproduced Lamarck's doctrine, and nothing else, and here Lyell and others have been attacking him for twenty years, and because *you* (with a sneer and laugh) say the very same thing, they are all coming round; it is the most ridiculous inconsistency, &c. &c.[67]

Charles Darwin

And if [Lyell,] Hooker or Huxley resisted conversion, it was not because of religious prejudice but only because of reservations about its scientific validity. Only amateurs who did not know enough to have such reservations were uninhibited in their enthusiasm. Such amateur enthusiasms, however, have a notoriously high mortality rate.[68]

Gertrude Himmelfarb

Darwin never experienced that his friends 'came round' to his theory of natural selection. Apparently, in spite of the many discussions on the species problem which had taken place at Down, the friends were only vaguely aware of his ideas, for their reactions on seeing either the proofs or the printed book were clearly disappointment and reservation.

Lyell set out to make a lot of detailed criticism, asking for evidence corroborating the theory. And when he finally admitted the possibility of organic evolution, he still implied agents other than natural selection. Following his own notions he became in the end a Lamarckian, but not a Darwinian. As a botanist and as a very kind man, Hooker had less to criticise and initially he was even exuberant in his praise. However, from the beginning he had doubts about natural selection, and he ended by publicly acknowledging that natural selection was 'passing away'. Yet, he had become convinced of the truth of the theory on the reality of evolution. Huxley was reserved at the outset, and very soon declared himself a believer in the epigenetic theory of evolution which most supporters and critics advocated. To him, indeed, natural selection had 'passed away' before 'coming of age'. This situation is very difficult to reconcile with the generally accepted idea that the three friends were fighting for Darwin's theory against ignorance and prejudice in the religious and intellectual circles of Victorian England. Certainly, it raises a number of points which need to be disentangled. For one thing, did not each of them know exactly where the others stood? Apparently not:

The anomalous situation was made more anomalous by the circumstance that each of these confidants — Lyell, Hooker and Huxley — suspected the others of believing more than he himself

did, and more than in fact they did. While Lyell was firmly denying Sedgwick's charge that he was a crypto-evolutionist, he was
warning others that Hooker and Huxley were getting more deeply
implicated than they knew. Hooker, on the other hand, knowing
his own reservations, assumed Huxley to be the true believer;
while Huxley, dramatically conscious of his own scepticism,
thought that Hooker was 'capable de tout' in the way of
evolution.[69]

On this background it appears that the common idea concerning
the contribution of the friends must be a misunderstanding. It is
hardly possible that they ever advocated Darwin's theory; publicly,
they defended his right to be heard, and the two of them, Hooker
and Huxley, even advocated Lamarck's theory of evolution in the
belief, or conveying the impression at least, that it was Darwin's
creation. In public meetings, not the least at the historical meeting
in Oxford 1860, where Hooker and Huxley crossed words with
Bishop Samuel Wilberforce, and behind closed doors, in clubs and
committee rooms, they could, and did use all their influence to
further the cause of Darwin. Yet, while praising Darwin, Lyell and
Hooker always preserved a sense of proportion; it was only Huxley,
and Darwin himself, who compared *On the Origin of Species* with
Newton's *Principia Mathematica*.

Peter J. Vorzimmer has asserted:

> Strangely enough, in spite of all the modifications in his evolu-
> tionary thought after 1859, Darwin never accepted a suggestion
> resulting in any signigicant change in his theory from his personal
> friends of the 'inner circle' of Darwinians. Instead, he made his
> greatest revision under the influence of his severest critics
> (Agassiz, Pouchet, Jenkin, and Mivart).[70]

This is not an easy question to settle, because the objections made
by his supporters mostly coincide with those of his critics. It is true
and natural that he devoted most space to those who had most
forcefully criticised his work, but he did what he could to placate
his partisans, introducing an extra 'Creator' to please Asa Gray and
'the survival of the fittest' upon the insistence of Wallace.

But the greatest admission made by Darwin was when he
accepted that variation may arise independently of natural selection
that is, by macromutations. By this amendment he adjusted his
theory to the view upheld by Huxley and many others among his

202

critics. Nobody appears to have realised the consequences of this concession, fatal to Darwin's micromutation theory. I would be much surprised if Darwin himself grasped the consequences, but even if he had, his hands were bound; a revision would ruin his lifework. But making the admission was bad enough, so he made sure to reject it at several places in the text, lest anybody should believe it was seriously meant.

The outcome of Darwin's efforts to comply with his critics was that '. . . of the 3,878 sentences in the first edition, nearly 3,000, about 75 per cent, were rewritten from one to five times each. Over 1,500 sentences were added, and of the original sentences plus these, nearly 325 were dropped. Of the original and added sentences there are nearly 7,500 variants of all kinds'.[71]

The ambiguity involved in the conduct of Darwin's friends as partisans of Darwin goes *crescendo* from Lyell to Huxley. What were the underlying motives? Did they do it out of sympathy for their good friend, so haunted by disease? Is their behaviour, otherwise unusual in academic circles, to be explained by the fact that Darwin in no case was felt a professional challenge? I cannot imagine that any of them, knowing Darwin's intellectual limitations, would believe in 1859 that he was later to supersede them all, becoming the most celebrated biologist in history. Or did they, except Lyell, accept the confusion between 'Lamarckism' and Darwinism as '. . . a false excuse for not having acknowledged earlier what had long been perfectly obvious to laymen like Chambers or Spencer'?[72] We do not know, and I do not think we shall ever know.

8

The Supporters

Some of my critics declare that I am more Darwinian that Darwin himself, and in this, I admit, they are not far wrong.[1]

Alfred Russel Wallace

Under the circumstances I suppose I do your theory more good here, by bespeaking for it a fair and favourable consideration, and by standing non-committed as to its full conclusions, than I should if I announced myself a convert; nor could I say the latter, with truth.[2]

Asa Gray

Die Selectionstheorie Darwins bedarf zu ihrer vollen Gültigkeit keine weiteren Beweise.[3]

Ernst Haeckel

Darwin's book was heavily criticised from many sides, partly because it advertised the theory on the reality of evolution, partly because Darwin's theory was found inadequate for its intended purpose. Among those upholding the latter point of view we find several of the persons who supported Darwin in the public debate which followed the publication of *On the Origin of Species*. The most noteworthy example in this group is Asa Gray. There were also some who accepted Darwinism without reservations; I am not sure that among these there are any outstanding Anglophone biologists, but we find some Germans — particularly Ernst Haeckel. It is an ironic state of affairs that we can place Darwin's co-discoverer, Alfred Wallace, in no other group than the present one.

ALFRED RUSSEL WALLACE (1823–1913)

Wallace is the next member in our series of outsiders. Born into a middle-class family with dwindling resources, he got his only formal training during six years spent in a provincial grammar school. At the age of thirteen he left school and became apprenticed to his older brother who worked as a surveyor. He was 18 years old when he bought his first book on botany and somewhat later he began to collect flowers for a herbarium. He read many books on travel and natural history, particularly while for a year he worked as a schoolmaster at Leicester. Among the books he read were Alexander von Humboldt's *Personal Narrative of Travels in South America* and Darwin's *Voyage of the 'Beagle'*, Malthus' *Essay on the Principle of Population*, Lyell's *Principles of Geology* and Chambers' *Vestiges of the Natural History of Creation*.[4]

During this time he became the friend of Henry Walter Bates, amateur entomologist, from whom Wallace learned some zoology. The travel books tempted the lust for adventure, and Wallace persuaded Bates to go with him to South America. In 1848 they left England, 'to make for ourselves a collection of objects, dispose of the duplicates in London to pay expenses,, and gather *facts . . . toward solving the problem of the origin of species*'.[5]

The third part of the programme was Wallace's particular project, and the inspiration was Robert Chambers' book. Wallace did not possess either the prejudice — or, to some extent — the knowledge of detail which caused most Fellows of established science to abuse *Vestiges of the Natural History of Creation* and its anonymous author, so therefore he could appreciate the central message of the book: evolution of life. This was many years later acknowledged by Wallace:

> Ever since I had read the *Vestiges of Creation* before going to the Amazon, I continued at frequent intervals to ponder on the great secret of the actual steps by which each new species had been produced, with all its special adaptations to the conditions of its existence . . . I myself believed that [each species] was a direct modification of the preexisting species through the ordinary process of generation as had been argued in the *Vestiges of Creation*.[6]

On this point Wallace differs from Darwin, who had written both his 'Sketch' and his 'Essay' by the time Chambers' book appeared. Wallace's return to England in 1852 was most dramatic and unfortunate, the ship carrying him back caught fire, and most of his valuable collections and journals were lost. However, he did not despair, in 1854 he started a new expedition, this time to the Malay Archipelago, present-day Indonesia, residing there until 1862. During his stay he continued to ponder on the 'species question', and in 1855 his views were published in *Annals and Magazine of Natural History* in a paper entitled 'On the Law Which Has Regulated the Introduction of New Species'. At the end of the first section

Wallace writes:

> The great increase of our knowledge within the last twenty years, both of the present and past history of the organic world, has accumulated a body of facts which should afford a sufficient foundation for a comprehensive law embracing and explaining them all, and giving a direction to new researchers. *It is about ten years since the idea of such a law suggested itself to the writer of this essay, and he has since taken every opportunity of testing it by all the newly-ascertained facts with which he has become acquainted*, or has been able to observe himself. These have all served to convince him of the correctness of his hypothesis. Fully to enter into such a subject would occupy much space, and it is only in consequence of some views having been lately promulgated, he believes, in a wrong direction, that he now ventures to present his ideas to the public, with only such obvious illustrations of the arguments and results as occur to him in a place far removed from all means of reference and exact information.

After this the new law is presented in the following ten propositions:

GEOGRAPHY

1. Large groups, such as classes and orders, are generally spread over the whole earth, while smaller ones, such as families and genera, are frequently confined to one portion, often to a very limited district.

2. In widely distributed families the genera are often limited in range; in widely distributed genera, well marked groups of species are peculiar to each geographical district.

3. When a group is confined to one district, and is rich in species, it is almost invariably the case that the most closely allied species are found in the same locality or in closely adjoining localities, and that therefore the natural sequence of the species by affinity is also geographical.

4. In countries of a similar climate, but separated by a wide sea or lofty mountains, the families, genera and species of the one are often represented by closely allied families, genera and species peculiar to the other.

GEOLOGY

5. The distribution of the organic world in time is very similar to its present distribution in space.

6. Most of the larger and some small groups extend through several geological periods.

7. In each period, however, there are peculiar groups, found nowhere else, and extending through one or several formations.

8. Species of one genus, or genera of one family occurring in the same geological time, are more closely allied than those separated in time.

9. As generally in geography no species or genus occurs in two very distant localities without being also found in intermediate places, so in geology the life of a species or genus has not been interrupted. In other words, no group or species has come into existence twice.

10. The following law may be deduced from these facts: — *Every species has come into existence coincident both in space and time with a pre-existing closely allied species.* (The first italics are mine)[7]

The rest of the article attempts to show that various kinds of empirical observations are in agreement with this law, but not with the 'Theory of Polarity' advanced shortly before by Edward Forbes, and which Wallace considered to be 'in a wrong direction'.

Before we discuss Wallace's contribution, let us first observe that in his copy of the journal Darwin wrote in the margin opposite proposition 8: 'Can this be followed.'[8] Darwin's question is warranted, the existence of 'living fossils' shows that the statement is not absolutely valid. The same objection may be made against proposition 9, as exemplified by the fact that we nowhere find, say, intermediate forms between the lungfishes living in Australia, Africa and South America. But the several instances which may be found to contradict these statements are undoubtedly exceptions; in most cases Wallace's generalisations have been confirmed by empirical observations.

What is the message of Wallace's paper? With hindsight the answer is obvious, it is a declaration of adherence to the authenticity of biological evolution. Although, through the works of Lyell and Chambers, Wallace was well acquainted with the fact that this theory was the creation of Lamarck, there is no mention of Lamarck in the text. Still more remarkable is the circumstance that the 'Creation–Evolution' issue is nowhere clearly stated.

The theory advanced by Wallace is eclectic. Like Darwin he followed Lyell in presuming the process of evolution to be gradual and, allowing for certain exceptions, he accepted the notion of progressive evolution, possibly under the influence of Chambers. The result, a micromutation theory allowing for progressive evolution, evidently comes close to Lamarck's first theory; no wonder, therefore, that Wallace could write in his notebook: 'Many of Lamarck's views are untenable and it is easy to controvert them but not so the simple question of a species being produced in time from a closely allied distinct species.'[9]

The paper was quite short, Wallace declared himself that it '. . . *is, of course, only the announcement of the theory, not its development. I have prepared the plan and written portions of an extensive work embracing the subject in all its bearings and endeavoring to prove what in the paper I have only indicated.*'[10]

Some people were able to read between the lines, in particular Lyell, who was highly impressed by the *arguments* and the *facts* mobilised in favour of evolution. Although Darwin himself considered the compilation of facts being his particular merit, it appears that Wallace was Darwin's superior in marshalling evidence in support of an argument. This, at least, was asserted by Lyell several years later when he wrote to Wallace: 'I have been reading over again your paper published in 1855 . . . passages of which I intend to quote, not in reference to your priority of publication, but simply because *there are some points laid down more clearly than I can find in the work of Darwin itself, in regard to the bearing of the geological and zoological evidence on geographic distribution and the origin of species.*'[11]

In fact, Wallace's paper must have made a deep impression on Lyell, for shortly after its appearance in September 1855 he '. . . opened his own species notebooks, with Wallace's name at the top of the first page of text'.[12] Lyell became so engaged in the problem that in the spring of 1856 he felt the need to discuss it with Darwin. As they met on 16 April, Darwin told Lyell about his theory on natural selection, and they discussed Wallace's paper.

Knowing this we can understand Lyell's advice to Darwin about writing down his views, to avoid being forestalled; Lyell realised that Wallace was at Darwin's heels. As appears from his summary of Wallace's paper, Darwin was not equally perspicacious:

185 Wallace's paper: Law of Geograph. Distrib Nothing very new — 186 His general summary 'Every species has come into existence coincident in time and space with pre-existing species' — *Uses my simile of tree. It seems all creation with him* — alludes to Galapagos 189 on even adjoining species being closest — (*It is all creation* but why does (is) his law hold good, *he puts facts in striking point of view* — 194 *argues against our supposed geological perfect knowledge* [sic!] — Explains rudimentary organs on same idea (I should state *put generation* for *creation* and I quite agree). (My italics)[13]

Darwin's lack of sensitivity towards other people's ideas has never, I think, been exposed more blatantly than here: Wallace was no threat at all, not because he had failed to produce a *mechanism of evolution*, but because he was a *Creationist*. But apparently Darwin came to realise that he had to heed Lyell's warning and at last it happened: '1856 May 14th Began by Lyell's advice writing Species Sketch.'[14]

On the initiative of Wallace a correspondence began between him and Darwin; as so often, only letters from Darwin are preserved. In the first letter he wrote:

Moor Park, May 1st, 1857

My Dear Sir, — I am much obliged for your letter of October 10th, from Celebes, received a few days ago; in a laborious undertaking, sympathy is a valuable and real encouragement. By your letter and even still more by your paper in the Annals . . . I can plainly see that we have thought much alike and to a certain extent have come to similar conclusions. In regard to the Paper in the Annals, I agree to the truth of almost every word of your paper; and I dare say that you will agree with me that it is very rare to find oneself agreeing pretty closely with any theoretical paper . . . This summer will make the 20th year (!) since I opened my first note-book, on the question how and in what way do species and varieties differ from each other. I am now preparing my work for publication.[15]

Since Darwin did not believe in Creation, this letter must be taken to imply that when at length it was written, Darwin had finally come to realise that Wallace was an Evolutionist, and hence a potential rival. Whether Lyell or Wallace's letter had most contributed to the conversion, we shall never know. Yet, Wallace had not suggested a mechanism of evolution, so Darwin could write in a letter later that year:

> Though agreeing with you on your conclusions in that paper, I believe I go much further than you; but it is too long a subject to enter on my speculative notions . . .
>
> You ask whether I shall discuss 'man'. I think I shall avoid the whole subject, as so surrounded with prejudices; though I fully admit that it is the highest and most interesting problem for the naturalist. My work, on which I have now been at work more or less for twenty years, will not fix or settle anything; but I hope it will aid by giving a large collection of facts, with one defined end.[16]

Wallace mentions in his 1855 paper that he had been working with the problem of evolution for about ten years — that is since 1845, the year following the composition of Darwin's 'Essay'. Wallace cannot have made his comment on time in order to ensure any kind of priority, for he did not know that anybody else was working on the same problem. The situation is different as far as Darwin is concerned; the circumstance that he in both letters mentioned his 20-year engagement may have been intended to convince Wallace about his own priority. If this is true, then he was unbelievably successful.

The next dispatch from Wallace, sent from Ternate on 9 March 1858, contained the paper 'On the Tendency of Varieties to Depart Indefinitely from the Original Type'. In this essay was outlined a mechanism of evolution, according to which '. . . we have *progression and continued divergence* deduced from the general laws which regulate the existence of animals in a state of nature, and from the undisputed fact that varieties do frequently occur'.[17] Briefly told, independently of Darwin, Wallace had conceived the theory of natural selection.

The paper naturally came upon Darwin '. . . like a thunderbolt from a cloudless sky',[18] and gave rise to what is probably the most dramatic incident in the history of biology, at least in the last century. However, before we can deal with this event we must make a detour and discuss the 'Principle of Divergence'. In his autobiography Darwin writes:

> But at that time [1844] I overlooked one problem of great importance; and it is astonishing to me, except on the principle of Columbus and his egg, how I could have overlooked it and its

solution. This problem is the tendency in organic beings descended from the same stock to diverge in character as they become modified. That they have diverged greatly is obvious from the manner in which species of all kinds can be classed under genera, genera under families, families under sub-orders, and so forth; and I can remember the very spot in the road, whilst in my carriage, when to my joy the solution occurred to me; and this was long after I had come to Down. The solution, as I believe, is that the modified offspring of all dominant and increasing forms tend to become adapted to many and highly diversified places in the economy of nature.[19]

This confession is most astounding. For, as we have seen, it was known to Darwin that, according to Lamarck, it is possible to distinguish two kinds of evolution, progressive and divergent (adaptive), respectively. And although natural selection is eminently suited to explain progressive evolution, Darwin repeatedly dissociated himself from this phenomenon, for the reason that evolution has not always been progressive. Rather, he insisted that natural selection works by ensuring the adaptation of living organisms to their environment, and if this assertion is adopted, then it follows that either there is only one environment on our planet or else evolution has been divergent. Since the first inference is evidently false, it follows on Darwin's own premises that his mechanism cannot account for anything but divergent evolution. However this may be, according to Darwin's own admission he could not explain this phenomenon in 1844, and yet, in 1876, when he wrote the autobiography, he knew the correct answer.

In 1909, Darwin's 'Essay of 1844' was published. The editor, his son Francis, for reasons incomprehensible except, perhaps, on the basis of what follows here, openly opposed his father by declaring that the mechanism of divergent evolution was stated in the essay.[20] However, the statements advanced to support this view are rather unconvincing, so I think that we must accept Darwin's own version. Under these circumstances it becomes of great historical interest to know *when* the solution to the problem occurred to Darwin, an event about which we know only that it took place 'long after I had come to Down'. Darwin's devoted advocate, Gavin de Beer, has suggested that Darwin solved the problem in 1852, but the following account does not corroborate this assertion.[21]

In recent years some authors have more or less independently set forth the startling supposition that Darwin found the solution in late

May or early June 1858, and that he found it in Wallace's Ternate paper.[22] This accusation is so serious that it cannot be ignored in the present context, so let us take a look at what actually happened during the stipulated period of time.

We have seen that upon the instigation of Lyell Darwin began to write a short account of his views in May 1856, but he soon realised that he could not carry through this undertaking, to convince his readers he had to present his views in detail; in a 'big species book' planned to carry the name *Natural Selection*.[23] From Darwin's diary the progress of the work may be followed, thus the following notation is found under 31 March 1857: 'Finished Ch. 6 Nat: Selection'.[24]

The distressing information in the journal is found a year later: ' ''April 14th Discussion on large genera & small & on Divergence & Correcting Ch. 6 (Moor Park) finished June 12th & Bee Cells'' . . . A more personal item for 1858 recorded that Darwin had stayed from April 20 to May 4 at Moor Park, a hydrotherapy establishment in Surrey . . . A letter to Joseph Hooker . . . two days after his return to Down from Moor Park enclosed the manuscript on species in large, as opposed to small genera.'[25] This shows that between 6 May and 12 June Darwin could concentrate on 'Divergence & correcting Ch. 6', an undertaking which he seemingly had begun in Moor Park. It is important to observe that nobody asserts that Darwin received the letter from Wallace while still at Moor Park, or during the early days of May, so we may conclude that if the entry is correct, the revision of Chapter 6 was started on Darwin's own initiative.

As it turned out, the revisions made in May–June 1858 were extensive, amounting almost to a doubling of the original chapter, and much of it was concerned with divergence, a topic which seems to have been dealt with in one page in the original manuscript.[26] That particular page is missing, but the available evidence suggests that its contents must have been similar to that found in a letter to Asa Gray written in September 1857. In this letter we may read:

> One other principle, which may be called the principle of divergence, plays, I believe, an important part in the origin of species . . . Now every single organic being, by propagating rapidly, may be said to be striving its utmost to increase in numbers. *So it will be with the offspring of any species after it has broken into varieties, or sub-species, or true species.* And it follows, I think, from the foregoing facts, that the varying off-

spring of each species will try (only a few will succeed) to seize on as many and as diverse places in the economy of nature as possible. Each new variety or species when formed will generally take the place of, and so exterminate its less well-fitted parent. This, I believe, to be the origin of the classification or arrangement of all organic beings at all times. (My italics)[27]

This quotation, as revised by Darwin, forms part of the joint publication by Darwin and Wallace in the *Journal of the Linnean Society* in August 1858, and it is assumed to have been included to vindicate Darwin's priority as concerns the problem of divergent evolution.[28] However, the emphasised statement shows that he had not achieved this goal at the time, for what he explains is the survival of the new forms through ecological isolation, *once they have arisen*, without accounting for their origination in the first place. In fact, if each new species exterminates the parent species then the basis for divergent evolution seems to be lacking.

Returning now to the Ternate paper, I shall begin by listing the headings of its various sections, as found in the version published by Brackman, to show that the two men were indeed thinking along similar lines:

Instability of Varieties supposed to prove the Permanent Distinctness of Species.
The Struggle for Existence.
The Law of Population of Species.
The Abundance or Rarity of a Species Dependent upon its more or less Perfect Adaptation to the Conditions of Existence.
Useful Variations will tend to Increase; Useless or Hurtful Variations to Diminish.
Superior Varieties will ultimately Extirpate the Original Species.
The Partial Reversion of Domesticated Varieties explained.
Lamarck's Hypothesis very Different from that now Advanced.
Conclusion.[29]

It is interesting to observe that these striking 'Darwinian' headlines are missing in the original issue of the *Journal of the Linnaean Society*, as well as in the 1908 and the 1958 memorial editions of the Darwin–Wallace papers.[30] However this may be, it cannot be doubted that an article dealing with such matters must have upset Darwin, but the question is: Did it contain anything that could clarify his notions on the question of divergent evolution? The closest approach made by Wallace towards this problem seems to be the following:

> Granted, therefore, a 'tendency' to reproduce the original type of the species, still the variety must ever remain preponderant in numbers, and under adverse physical conditions *again alone survive*. But this new, improved, and populous race might itself, in the course of time, give rise to new varieties, exhibiting several diverging modifications of form, any of which, tending to increase the facilities for preserving existence, must, by the same general law, in their turn become predominant.[31]

Honestly, as far as the mechanism of divergent evolution is concerned, I fail to see that Darwin can have benefited from this statement. At any rate, Darwin's opportunity to establish his priority occurred on 1 July 1858. We know that what was published at that occasion had been written down by Darwin before he received the Ternate paper, so we can acquit him of plagiarism as far as the Darwin–Wallace joint contribution is concerned. This does not exclude that Darwin was affected by Wallace's 1855 paper, it may indeed have induced the revision undertaken in the spring of 1858. There is, for instance, some rather convincing evidence in support of the view that Darwin's famous phylogenetic diagram is inspired by Wallace's paper.[32]

But if we concentrate on Darwin's view on the question of divergence, we find the following statement in the manuscript revised in May–June 1858:

> Now in nature, I cannot doubt, that an analogous principle, not liable to caprice, is steadily at work, through a widely different agency; & that varieties of the same species, & species of the same genus, family or order are all, more or less, subjected to this influence. For in any country, a far greater number of individuals descended from the same parents can be supported, when greatly modified in different ways, in habits constitution & structure, so as to fill as many places, as possible, in the polity of nature, than when not at all or only slightly modified.[33]

We have seen above that in September 1857 Darwin explained divergent evolution on the assumption that once they had arisen, new varieties survive through ecological isolation. It seems that Darwin's views had not changed in 1858, and apparently he did not realise that ecological isolation presupposes the possession of particular capabilities not shared by the members of the ancestral taxon. This requirement evidently cannot be accomplished by natural selection, which can only ensure 'adaptation' to the prevailing environmental conditions. The only solution to the problem of taxonomic divergence therefore is either antecedent macromutations allowing for ecological isolation or else random isolation. It is a fair claim that Darwin never grasped this point, and therefore it seems justified to contend that he did not solve the problem of divergent evolution.

Let us now turn to the dramatic events during the early summer of 1858. Sometime in June Lyell received a letter:

Down, 18th

My dear Lyell,

Some year or two ago you recommended me to read a paper by Wallace in the 'Annals', which had interested you and, as I was writing to him, I knew this would please him much, so I told him. He has to-day sent me the enclosed, and asked me to forward it to you. It seems to me well worth reading. Your words have come true with a vengeance — that I should be forestalled . . . I never saw a more striking coincidence; if Wallace had my MS. sketch written out in 1842, he could not have made a better short abstract! . . . Please return me the MS., which he does not say he wishes me to publish, but I shall, of course, *at once write and offer to send to any journal.* So all my originality, whatever it may amount to, will be smashed, though my book, if it will ever have any value, will not be deteriorated; as all the labour consists in the application of the theory. (My italics)[34]

It will be observed that the letter is not properly dated, and this, unfortunately, was a bad habit of Darwin's. This has had the consequence that if the addressee did not complete the dating, the editor of Darwin's letters (Francis Darwin) found it necessary to try to figure out the day the letter was written. In the present case we find the addition (June 1858).

This date, 18 June 1858, has for almost a century been accepted without dissent as the day on which Wallace's letter arrived at Down. But as already mentioned, in recent years the official story has been challenged from various quarters. First, a letter was discovered, sent from Ternate the same day (9 March) as the one to Darwin, the envelope of which shows that it arrived at Leicester on 3 June.[35] This letter was marked 'via *Southampton*' by Wallace, which was the route taken by 'heavy mail'; according to the schedule it reached London on 2 June. If it had gone by train via Marseille it might have reached London on 28 May. In fact, according to the official time tables, this letter ought to have arrived in London on 20 May, so it seems to have been unduly delayed on its way. Therefore, the possibility cannot be excluded that the letter to Darwin arrived in London in the middle of the month, and that the '18th' in Darwin's letter was indeed '18th May'.[36] If this is true, Darwin may have known the contents of Wallace's Ternate paper when he was working on 'Divergence & correcting Ch. 6'. But this would not have helped him much; as we have seen, there is no solution to the problem of divergence in either Wallace's or Darwin's manuscript. That Darwin may have realised this himself is suggested by the following footnote in the revised manuscript: 'June 1858 I doubt whether I have got intermediate links yet clear.'[37] So it seems that the explanation of divergent evolution which he published in the first edition of On the Origin of Species dawned upon him when he prepared this work for publication.

With this background I see three possibilities to account for the letter to Lyell: (i) Darwin may have received Wallace's letter on 18 June. This is possible, if unlikely, but it corresponds to the mood of the letter. (ii) He may have received Wallace's letter on 3 or 4 June, and brooded upon the consequences for two weeks before he announced his calamity. This implies that he deliberately lied to Lyell about the day of arrival, and in that case he would hardly have forgotten to write 'June' at the head of the letter. (iii) He may have received Wallace's letter on 18 May, writing the letter to Lyell the same day. Having calmed down, he may have decided not to mail the letter immediately. In that case the letter may have been posted 18 June.

Although it is supported by the Postal Service records, I shall exclude the second possibility; in consequence this survey suggests that the letter was written either on 18 May or 18 June, and that it was sent to Lyell around 18 June. In spite of the measure of improbability it implies, I think that the second date is preferable. This conclusion is supported by a letter which Darwin wrote to Lyell the following week. As we are going to return to this letter, I shall here quote only two clauses which were *deleted* when the letter was published by Francis Darwin: '. . . I should not have sent off *your letter* without further reflection, for I am at present quite upset, but write now to get subject for time out of mind. But I confess it never did occur to me, as it might, that Wallace could have made any use of *your letter* . . .' (my italics); 'I do not in the least believe that he originated his views from anything which I wrote to him.'[38]

From these excerpts it appears that Darwin had calmed down; as we shall see later, to the extent even that he had conceived the plan that should save his priority. The present quotations are made partly because they support the suggestion that the first letter was written a week earlier, rather than more than a month earlier. Besides they are interesting because they represent answers to suggestions or questions made by Lyell. In the first quotation the expression 'your letter' occurs twice, the first time clearly referring to Darwin's own letter. J.L. Brooks, who published the deleted parts of the letter, discusses the possibility that the second time the expression refers to a letter from Lyell to Wallace. But since there is no evidence in support of this interpretation, I believe that 'your letter' is again Darwin's letter. If that is true, then one may wonder in which way Wallace could have made use of it. Perhaps this confusion indicates that Darwin still was somewhat upset. The second clause suggests that Lyell suspected Darwin might have been too indiscreet in his correspondence; as we have seen, Darwin anxiously avoided giving away any of his ideas.

It will be realised that it is impossible at the moment to settle the issue between Darwin and Wallace. And the reason for this is not only that the published Darwin correspondence has been censured, but worse still that almost every letter sent to Darwin during the period 1855–8 seems to have been disposed of. Several of those who have studied this period of Darwin's life have come to the conclusion that 'somebody cleaned up the file', and the suspicion is strongly focused on Francis Darwin, who edited Darwin's correspondence, and who could not satisfactorily account for the missing letters.[39] Should this be true, then one must of course presume that there was something to hide. However this may be, we must acquit Darwin of the accusation that he filched the solution to the problem of divergent evolution from Wallace, for the simple reason that the latter had not solved the problem.

We may now return to the letter from Darwin to Lyell on 25 June:

. . . There is nothing in Wallace's sketch which is not written out much fuller in my sketch, copied out in 1844, and read by Hooker some dozen years ago. About a year ago I sent a short sketch, of which I have a copy, of my views . . . to Asa Gray, so that I could most truly say and prove that I take nothing from Wallace. I should be extremely glad now to publish a sketch of my general views in about a dozen pages or so; but I cannot persuade myself that I can do so honourably. Wallace says nothing about publication, and I enclose his letter. But as I had not intended to publish any sketch, can I do so honourably, because Wallace has sent me an outline of his doctrine? I would far rather burn my whole book, than that he or any other man should think that I had behaved in a paltry spirit. Do you not think his having sent me this sketch ties my hands.[40]

To Hooker he wrote a few days later:

I am quite prostrated, and can do nothing, but I send Wallace, and the abstract of my letter to Asa Gray, which gives most imperfectly only the means of change, and does not touch on reasons for believing that species do change. I dare say all is too late. I hardly care about it. But you are too generous to sacrifice so much time and kindness. It is most generous, most kind. I send my sketch of 1844 solely that you may see by your own handwriting that you did read it. I really cannot bear to look at it. Do not waste much time. It is miserable in me to care at all about priority.

The table of contents will show you what it is.

I would make a similar, but shorter and more accurate sketch for the 'Linnean Journal'.

I will do anything. God bless you, my dear kind friend. I can write no more.[41]

Fortunately, Darwin had understanding and influential friends, and within two weeks a joint publication by Darwin and Wallace was communicated to the Linnaean Society by Lyell and Hooker. In a prefatory letter they wrote, referring to 'Mr. Wallace's Essay':

So highly did Mr Darwin appreciate the value of the views therein set forth, that he proposed, in a letter to Sir Charles Lyell, *to obtain Mr Wallace's consent to allow the Essay to be published* as soon as possible. Of this step we highly approved, provided Mr Darwin did not withhold from the public, as he *was strongly inclined to do* (in favour of Mr Wallace), the memoir which he had himself written on the same subject, and which, as before stated, one of us had perused in 1844, and the contents of which we had both of us been privy to for *many* years. On representing this to Mr Darwin, he gave us permission to make what use we thought proper of his memoirs, etc.; and in adopting our present course . . . we have explained to him that we are not solely considering the relative claims to priority of himself and his friend, but the interests of science generally. (My italics)[42]

This letter is a masterpiece of deception! (i) The first emphasised statement suggests, and has been interpreted by some authors to imply that Wallace had consented to the presentation in the Linnaean Society; this was plainly impossible since mail normally took ten weeks between Dutch East India and Europe at that time. (ii) Being familiar with the behaviour befitting an English gentleman, and realising that Wallace clearly wanted to have his work published, Darwin had no choice: he had to waive his claim to priority. Of course, the situation would change completely if it was not he himself, but his friends who decided that he could go to press together with Wallace. (iii) One of the friends had indeed seen the 'Essay of 1844', but the other had not heard about the 'species question' before April 1856, two years before. And 'two' is not equal to 'many' in ordinary language. (iv) Finally, I find it necessary to react to the word 'friend' for several reasons, but mainly because they had never met.

Darwin proposed the material which might save his priority, an extract of an essay never meant for publication plus abstracts of a letter. But such material is not normally published in scientific periodicals, and certainly, it would not do to have the paper called *On the Tendency of Varieties to Depart Indefinitely from the Original Type* by Alfred Russel Wallace, followed by *Excerpts Proving that the Priority to the Theory of Natural Selection belongs to Charles Darwin* by Charles Darwin. So the friend struck a questionable compromise, they made a joint paper:

On the Tendency of Species to form Varieties; and on the Perpetuation of Varieties and Species by Natural Means of Selection. By Charles Darwin, Esq., FRS, FLS, & FGS, and Alfred Wallace, Esq. Communicated by Sir Charles Lyell, FRS, FLS, and J.D. Hooker, Esq., MD, VPRS, FLS, &c.

Alphabetically the succession of authors may be defensible, but otherwise one might expect that a complete paper ought to precede some unfinished abstracts. Furthermore, the title, presumably composed by Hooker, could hardly have been satisfactory to Wallace, since it seems to convey notions contrary to his own.

In their zeal to save Darwin's priority, his friends ignored the
rules of decency.

This was not an occasion of 'mutual nobility', nor was it 'a monu-
ment to the natural generosity of both the great biologists', as is
so often claimed. It was clearly not mutual because Wallace's
paper was read without his knowledge or consent, and he knew
nothing about it until October. Nor does it seem to have been
particularly noble. However just Darwin's claim to priority, he
was a gainer, not a loser, from the decision. Wallace had no
opportunity to be either noble or generous.[43]

Indeed, '. . . that Wallace was not consulted on the matter and
was presented with a *fait accompli* with no real opportunity to
protest — he never saw page proofs nor heard of the resolutions of
the matter until his paper was *in print*, nor was his original paper
returned — is a black mark on the characters of Darwin, Hooker and
Lyell. Darwin's halfhearted pleas that he would take a back seat to
Wallace cannot be taken seriously'.[44] I agree, and yet I think worse
things have happened in the history of science. After all, the
behaviour of Darwin and his friends shows that the notion of 'fair
play' applied, even when the opponent was a person so utterly
insignificant as Wallace was in 1858.

Once the excitement had abated, Wallace was duly informed by
Hooker and Darwin. In this context we find the following in a letter
to Hooker:

Your letter to Wallace seems to me perfect, quite clear and most
courteous. I do not think it could possibly be improved, and I
have to-day forwarded it with a letter of my own. I always
thought it very possible that I might be forestalled, but I fancied
that I had a grand enough soul not to care; but I found myself
mistaken and punished; I had, however, quite resigned myself,
and had written *half a letter* to Wallace to give up all priority to
him, and should certainly not have changed had it not been for
Lyell's and your quite extraordinary kindness. I assure you I feel
it, and shall not forget it. I am *more* than satisfied at what took
place at the Linnean Society. I had thought that your letter[?] and
mine to Asa Gray *were to be only an appendix to Wallace's
paper*. (The first and last italics mine)[45]

[And to Lyell he wrote:] . . . I do not think that Wallace can think my conduct unfair in allowing you and Hooker to do whatever *you* thought fair. I certainly was a little annoyed to lose all priority, but had resigned myself to my fate. (My italics)[46]

The letters from Hooker and Darwin can hardly have conveyed to Wallace the motive behind the meeting in the Linnean Society, for he wrote to his mother in October 1858:

I have received letters from Mr. Darwin and Dr. Hooker, two of the most eminent naturalists in England, which has highly gratified me. I sent Mr. Darwin an essay on a subject on which he is now writing a great work. He showed it to Dr. Hooker and Sir C. Lyell, *who thought so highly of it that they immediately read it before the Linnean Society*. This assures me the acquaintance and assistance of these eminent men on my return home. (My italics)[47]

Under these circumstances it is understandable that Wallace readily accepted the way the friends had handled the 'Wallace affair'. Darwin wrote to him in January 1859: 'I was extremely much pleased at receiving three days ago your letter to me and that to Dr. Hooker. Permit me to say how heartily I admire the spirit in which they are written. Though I had *absolutely nothing whatever* to do in leading Lyell and Hooker to what they thought a fair course of action, yet I naturally could not but feel anxious to hear what your impression would be' (my italics).[48]

One can understand Darwin's relief. He returned to the question in a letter in April 1859:

P.S. You cannot tell how I admire your spirit, in the manner in which you have taken all that was done about publishing all our papers. *I had actually written a letter to you*, stating that I would not publish anything before you had published. *I had not sent that letter to the post when I received one from Lyell and Hooker*, urging me to send some MS. to them, and *to allow them to act as they thought fair and honestly to both of us*; and I did so. (My italics)[49]

So the half letter had been ready for mailing.

Wallace was never told about the stir caused by his 1858 paper, so he learned about it only when Darwin's *Life and Letters* was published. At that occasion he wrote to Francis Darwin: 'Many thanks for the copy of your father's "Life and Letters", which I shall read with very great interest . . . I was not aware before that your father had been so distressed — or rather disturbed — by my sending him my essay from Ternate, and I am very glad to feel that his exaggerated sense of honour was quite needless so far as I was concerned.'[50]

Darwin sent a copy of *On the Origin of Species* to Wallace, asking for comments. In Darwin's answer to these we read:

Your letter has pleased me very much, and I most completely agree with you on the parts which are strongest and which are weakest. The imperfection of the Geological Record is, as you say, the weakest of all; but yet I am pleased to find that there are almost more geological converts than of pursuers of other branches of natural science . . . I think geologists are more *easily converted* than simple naturalists, because more accustomed to reasoning . . . you must let me say how I admire the generous manner in which you speak of my book. *Most persons would in your position have felt some envy or jealousy.* (My italics)[51]

But then Wallace was also mentioned in Darwin's book — three times. In the Introduction we read:

I have more especially been induced to [publish this Abstract], as Mr. Wallace . . . has arrived at *almost exactly* the same general conclusions that I have on the origin of species. (My italics)[52]

And in the chapter on biogeography Darwin wrote: This view of the relation of species in one region to those in another, does not differ much (by substituting the word variety for species [?]) from that lately advanced in an ingenious paper by Mr. Wallace, in which he concludes, that 'every species has come into existence coincident both in space and time with a pre-existing closely allied species'. And I know *from correspondence*, that *this coincidence he attributes to generation with modification* (My italics)[53]

It is quite surprising that Darwin needed Wallace's personal interpretation to understand what he aimed at. Lyell was not wavering on this point, and he said so to Darwin. Wallace is mentioned a third time with reference to his biogeographical work in the Malay Archipelago. One understands that Darwin later regretted 'not having (by inadvertence) mentioned Wallace towards the close of the book in the summary, not that any one had noticed this to me'.[54] The inadvertence was remedied in later editions of the book.

Thomas Sims, Wallace's brother-in-law, did not appreciate the way Wallace was treated by Darwin, and complained about it in a letter to Wallace, who answered:

> Now for Mr. Darwin's book. *You quite misunderstand Mr. D.'s statement in the preface and his sentiments.* I have, of course, been in correspondence with him since I first sent him my little essay. His conduct has been most liberal and *disinterested*. I think anyone who reads the Linnean Society papers and his book will see it. I do back him up in his whole round of conclusions and look upon him as the *Newton of Natural History*. (The first and second italics are mine)[55]

Indeed, '. . . in Wallace [Darwin] happened to have a man of that rare natural magnanimity for whom priority meant little; Charles Darwin had already worked on the matter and had already hit on the solution: what more was there to be said?'[56]

On the occasion of a critical review by Janet, Wallace wrote to Darwin in 1866:

> . . . I see that he considers your weak point to be that you do not see that 'thought and direction are essential to the action of Natural Selection' . . . Now, I think this arises almost entirely from your choice of the term 'Natural Selection' and so constantly comparing it in its effects to Man's Selection, and also your so frequently personifying nature as 'selecting', as 'preferring', as 'seeking only the good of the species', etc., etc. To the few this is *as clear as daylight*, and beautifully suggestive, but to many it is evidently a stumbling-block. I wish, therefore, to suggest to you the possibility of entirely avoiding this source of misconception . . . in any future editions of the *Origin*, and I think it may be done without difficulty and very effectively by adopting Spencer's term . . . viz., 'survival of the fittest'.
>
> The term is the plain expression of the fact; Natural Selection is a metaphorical expression of it, and to a certain degree indirect and incorrect, since, even personifying Nature, *she does not so much select special variations as exterminate the most unfavourable ones* . . .
>
> I find you use the term 'Natural Selection' in two senses: (1)

for the simple preservation of favourable and rejection of unfavourable variations, in which case it is equivalent to 'survival of the fittest'; and (2) for the effect or change produced by this preservation . . .

There is another objection made by Janet . . . It is that the chances are almost infinite against the particular kind of variation required being coincident with each change of external conditions, to enable an animal to become modified by Natural Selection in harmony with such changed conditions; especially when we consider that, to have produced the almost infinite modifications of organic beings, this coincidence must have taken place an almost infinite number of times.

Now, it seems to me that you have yourself led to this objection being made, by so often stating the case *too strongly against yourself*. For example . . . you ask if it is 'improbable that useful variations should sometimes occur in the course of thousands of generations'; and . . . you say, 'unless profitable variations do occur, Natural Selection can do nothing'. Now, such expressions have given your opponents the advantage of assuming that favourable variations are rare accidents, or may even for long periods never occur at all, and thus Janet's argument would appear to many to have great force. I think it would be better to do away with all such qualifying expressions, and constantly maintain (what I certainly believe to be the fact) *that variations of every kind are always occurring in every part of every species, and therefore that favourable variations are always ready when wanted.* You have, I am sure, abundant materials to *prove* this. (My italics)[57]

Evidently, Wallace accused Darwin of taking an anti-Darwinian stand! And Darwin had to defend his terminology:

I have been much interested by your letter, which is *as clear as daylight. I fully agree* with all that you say on the advantages of H. Spencer's excellent expression of 'the survival of the fittest'. This, however, had *not occurred to me* till reading your letter. It is, however, a great objection to this term that it cannot be used as a substantive governing a verb; and that this is a real objection I infer from H. Spencer continually using the words Natural Selection. I formerly thought . . . that it was a great advantage to bring into connection natural and artificial selection; this indeed led me to use a term in common, and I still think it some advantage. I wish I had received your letter two months ago, for I would have worked in 'the survival', etc., often in the new edition of the *Origin* . . . The term Natural Selection has now been so largely used abroad and at home that I doubt whether it could be given up, and with all its faults I should be sorry to see the attempt made . . . As for M. Janet, he is a metaphysician, and such gentlemen are so *acute* that I think they often misunderstand common folk. Your criticism on the double sense in which I have used Natural Selection is new to me and *unanswerable*; but my blunder has done no harm, for I *do not belive that any one, excepting you, has ever observed it*. Again, I *agree* that I have said too much about 'favourable variations', but I am inclined to think that you put the opposite side too strongly: if every part of every being varied, I do not think we should see the same end or object gained by such wonderfully diversified means. (My italics)[58]

Wallace was also correcting Darwin's sloppy wording and reasoning, for he was logical enough to see that unless the variations are large enough and frequent enough it has no sense to invoke natural selection as an evolutionary agent, and even then it could only work by elimination.

In spite of his objection Darwin adopted Wallace's suggestion to the extent that in later editions of *On the Origin of Species*, he wrote: 'This preservation of favourable individual differences and variations, and the destruction of those which are injurious, *I* have called Natural Selection, or the Survival of the Fittest' (my italics).[59]

In fact, as he averred himself on several occasions, Wallace differed from Darwin on various points. Thus he rejected the disreputed Lamarckian inheritance of acquired characteristics, in his view the theory of natural selection could and should explain evolution without recourse to the theory of Lamarck. Furthermore, he clearly saw that one of the most important implications of the theory is that evolution has been progressive, since elimination of the inferior spells survival of the superior. Yet, he did not insist that evolution had always been progressive, in particular he asserted in his book *Darwinism* (1890) that '. . . extinction on an enormous scale has again and again stopped all progress in certain directions, and has often compelled a fresh start in development from some comparatively low and imperfect type'.[60] Clearly Wallace became a Catastrophist! And even on this point he was logical, for the one who believes in the power of natural selection to adapt living organisms to their conditions cannot account for the fact that extinction has occurred, except on the assumption that events have occurred which eliminated the preconditions for their existence.

The most important topic upon which he differed from Darwin was the evolution of the human mind. Darwin envisaged a gradual advance in the mental and moral characteristics from the lower mammals over the primates and 'savages' to civilised man. Wallace, from his logical vantage point, could see that certain mathematical, musical, artistic and other mental faculties could not possibly have arisen through natural selection, for the simple reason that, as amply evidenced by history, their possession had at no time been an asset in the struggle for existence. And therefore he concluded: 'The special faculties we have been discussing clearly point to the existence in man of something which he has not derived from his animal progenitors — something which we may best refer to as being of a spiritual essence or nature, capable of progressive development under favourable conditions.'[61] In fact, he thought

> . . . that there are at least three stages in the development of the organic world when some new cause or power must necessarily have come into action.
>
> The first stage is the change from inorganic to organic, when the earliest vegetable cell, or the living protoplasm out of which it arose, first appeared . . .
>
> The next stage is still more marvellous, still more completely beyond all possibility of explanation by matter, its laws and forces. It is the introduction of sensation or consciousness, constituting the fundamental distinction between the animal and vegetable kingdoms . . .
>
> The third stage is . . . the existence in man of a number of his most characteristic and noblest faculties, those which raise him furthest above the brutes . . .
>
> These three distinct stages of progress from the inorganic world of matter and motion up to man, point clearly to an unseen universe — to a *world of spirit, to which the world of matter is altogether subordinate.* (My italics)[62]

On reading this one sympathises with Darwin. If Wallace thought that evolution by natural selection had to be supplemented by metaphysical forces, then it is difficult to see the difference between his view and the stand adopted by Lyell, who could not accept the origin of man through evolution.

Wallace had stated his opinion in 1869 in a review of the tenth edition of Lyell's *Principles of Geology*. In this context Darwin wrote to Wallace:

I have been wonderfully interested by your article, and I think Lyell will be much gratified by it . . . Your exposition of Natural Selection seems to me inimitably good; there never lived a better *expounder* than you. I was also much pleased at your discussing the difference between *our* views and Lamarck's. One sometimes sees the odious expression, 'Justice to myself compels me to say', &c., but you are the only man I ever heard of who persistently does himself an injustice, and never demands justice. Indeed, *you ought in the review to have alluded to your paper in the 'Linnean Journal'*, and I feel sure all our friends will agree in this . . . I presume that your remarks on Man are those to which you alluded in your note. *If you had not told me I should have thought that they had been added by some one else.* As you expected I differ grievously from you, and I am very sorry for it. I can see no necessity for calling in an additional and proximate cause in regard to man. (My italics)[63]

Lyell, of course, was highly appreciative of Wallace's version of Darwinism. He wrote to Darwin in 1869:

I quite *agree with you* that Wallace's sketch of natural selection is admirable. I wrote to tell him so after I had read the article, and . . . reminded him that as to the origin of man's intellectual and moral nature I had allowed in my first edition that its introduction was a real *innovation*, interrupting the uniform course of the causation previously at work on the earth . . . In other words, as I feel that *progressive development or evolution* cannot be entirely explained by natural selection, I rather hail Wallace's suggestion that there may be a Supreme Will and Power which may not abdicate its functions of interference, but may guide the forces and laws of Nature . . .

At the same time I told Wallace that I thought his arguments, as to the hand, the voice, the beauty and the symmetry, the naked skin, and other attributes of man, implying a preparation for his subsequent development, might easily be controverted . . .

In reply to this . . . Wallace said: 'It seems to me that if we once admit the necessity of *any action* beyond "natural selection" in developing man, we have no reason whatever for confining that action to his brain. On the mere doctrine of chances, it seems to me in the highest degree improbable that so many points of structure all tending to favour his mental development should concur in man, and in man alone of all animals. If the *erect posture*, the freedom of the *anterior* limbs for *purposes of locomotion*, the *powerful* and *opposable* thumb, the naked skin, and *the great symmetry of force*, the *perfect organs of speech*, and his mental faculties, *calculation of numbers, ideas of symmetry*, of *justice*, of *abstract reasoning*, of *the infinite*, of *a future state*, and many others, cannot be shown to be each and all *useful* to man in the very lowest state of civilisation, how are we to explain their coexistence in him alone of the whole series of organized beings? (The first two italics are mine)[64]

Surely Wallace was right that all these features cannot be explained by natural selection. To solve this dilemma he ought to have adopted the solution suggested by most of Darwin's critics, macromutations. Indeed, as we have seen, the option chosen by him was unacceptable even to Lyell. On this point his logical sense deserted him; to Darwin, his friends, his supporters and critics alike the salient feature of the theory of natural selection was its attempt to explain evolution without the interference of supernatural forces. From this point of view Wallace's version of Darwinism was a step backwards beyond Lamarckism.

How can we explain Wallace's 'treason' to the cause of 'Darwinism'? Wallace was an extremely gullible person as soon as he moved out of the realm of science. He believed in Mesmerism, spiritism, phrenology and other more or less metaphysical creeds and thus he was unlikely to feel any reluctance towards appeals to a 'world of spirit' when trying to account for the process of biological evolution. Wallace might in many respects be 'more Darwinian than Darwin himself', but the fact remains that he *did not believe in the theory advanced by Darwin*.

What would have happened if Wallace had had his paper published without the interference of Darwin and his friends? Presumably it would have been neglected as much as his 1855 paper, because it would not have been backed up by the pillars of the scientific Establishment. Butler wrote: 'No one who has not a strong social position should ever advance a new theory, unless a life of hard fighting is part of what he lays himself out for.'[65] And surely, Wallace lacked a strong social position as much as a fighting spirit. But there is another point to make: an article never has the same impact as a book. If Wallace's 1858 article had discouraged Darwin:

'. . . we might possibly still have had the Origin of Species though a somewhat different book by a very different author'.[66] Yet, if Wallace had included his metaphysical speculations it would hardly have succeeded; what people wanted and what they got from Darwin was a theory explaining the origin of life on a materialist basis.

In the history of evolutionary thought Wallace is a leading figure, and he is also one of the most sympathetic ones. His modesty, and his magnanimity towards Darwin is unequalled; in many respects he was the nobler person of the two. However, even though he made what I believe to be valuable contributions to biogeography, it is still as a co-author with Darwin in 1858 that he attracts interest today. In this respect Wallace stands in debt to Darwin.

ASA GRAY (1810–1888)

Asa Gray was Fisher Professor of Natural History at Harvard University. He published several important works on botany, and ranks among the most outstanding American botanists.

Darwin had met Gray at Kew Gardens, and in 1855 he wrote him a letter making inquiries on some botanical topics; later, in 1857 Darwin sent him the famous letter which was to prove his priority *vis-à-vis* Wallace. In this letter he wrote:

To talk of climate or Lamarckian habit producing such adaptations to other organic beings is futile. This difficulty I believe I have surmounted . . .

Selection acts *only* by the accumulation of very slight or *greater* variations, *caused by external conditions, or* by the *mere fact* that in generation *the child is not absolutely similar to its parent* . . .

In nature we have some *slight* variations, occasionally in all parts: and I think it can be shown that *a change in the conditions of existence* is the *main cause of the child not exactly resembling its parents*; and in nature, *geology* shows us what changes *have taken place*, and *are taking place* . . .

Now take the case of a country undergoing some change; this will tend *to cause some of its inhabitants to vary slightly; not but what I believe most beings vary at all times enough for selection to act on.* Some of its inhabitants will be exterminated, and the remainder will be exposed to the mutual action of a different set of inhabitants, which I believe to be more important to the life of

229

each being than mere climate. (My italics, except for *slight*)[67]

From this letter it seems that Darwin was exaggerating when claiming to have surmounted 'Lamarckian habit'. Upon receiving this confusing text Gray understandably asked for further information, and in his answer Darwin wrote: 'I may just mention, in order that you may believe that I have *some* foundation for my views, that Hooker had read my MS., and though he at first demurred to my main point, he has since told me that further reflection and new facts have made him a convert.'[68]

In November 1859 Darwin sent Gray *On the Origin of Species*, in which he asked to have Gray's opinion, and added: '. . . you will excuse my conceit in telling you that Lyell highly approves of the *two Geological chapters* . . . He is nearly a convert to my views' (my italics).[69]

Gray complied, and wrote:

The *best part*, I think, is the *whole, i.e.* its *plan* and *treatment*, the vast amount of facts and acute inferences handled *as if* you had a perfect mastery of them . . .

Then your candour is worth everything to your cause. It is refreshing to find a person with a new theory who frankly confesses that he finds difficulties, *insurmountable*, at least for the present . . .

The moment I understood your premises, I felt sure you had a real foundation to hold on. Well, if one admits your premises, I do not see how he is to stop short of your conclusions, as a *probable hypothesis at least* . . .

Well, what seems to be the weakest point in the book is the attempt to account for the formation of organs, the making of eyes, &c., by natural selection. Some of this reads quite *Lamarckian*. (My italics, except for those in the first paragraph)[70]

Thus, once more reluctance towards Darwin's original contribution, natural selection. However, Gray announced that he would write a review of the book, and Darwin answered:

I quite think a review from a man, who is not an *entire* convert, if fair and moderately favourable, is in all respects the *best* kind of review. *About the weak points I agree.* The eye to this day gives me a cold shudder; but when I think of the fine *known* gradations, my *reason* tells me I ought to conquer the cold shudder . . .

P.S. — I feel pretty sure . . . that if you . . . keep the subject of the origin of species before your mind, you will go further and further in *your belief.* (My italics)[71]

And when he saw Gray's review in September 1860, Darwin was extremely pleased:

You will be weary of my praise, but it does strike me as quite admirably argued, and so well and pleasantly written. Your many metaphors are inimitably good. I said in a former letter that you were a lawyer, but I made a gross mistake, I am sure you are a poet. No, by jove, I will tell you what you are, a hybrid, a complex cross of lawyer, poet, naturalist and theologian: 'Was there ever such a monster seen before?'[72]

But Darwin was not at all satisfied with Gray's attitude. He never could understand that people in general, and friends and supporters in particular, could be so prejudiced as to have any hesitations at all with respect to his glorious theory. And being insistent on winning proselytes, he tried to combat Gray's 'narrow-mindedness' through persuasion, so two weeks later he wrote: 'I yet hope and almost believe, that the time will come when you will go further, in believing *a very large amount* of modification of species, than you did at first or do now. Can you tell me whether you *believe further or more firmly* than you did at first? I should really like to know this. I can perceive in my immense correspondence with Lyell, who objected to much at first, that he has, perhaps *unconsciously to himself, converted himself very much* during the last six months, and I think this is the case *even* with Hooker' (my italics).[73] As we see here, *in Darwin's view conversion to belief in Darwinism may occur in small steps, just like Darwinian evolution proper.*

In fact, Gray was a religious man, and therefore he was much concerned whether Darwin's theory implied outright atheism, or whether it was compatible with pantheism. He came to the following conclusion:

Since natural science deals only with secondary or natural causes, the scientific terms of a theory of derivation of species . . . must needs be the same to the theist as to the atheist. The difference appears only when the inquiry is carried up to the question of primary cause — a question which belongs to philosopy. [And therefore] . . . the adoption of a derivate hypothesis, and of Darwin's particular hypothesis . . . would leave the doctrines of final causes, utility, and special design, just as they were before.[74]

But Gray could not leave it at that, he wanted to prove that Darwin's theory was theistic, reasoning as follows:

If . . . he anywhere maintains that the natural causes through which species are diversified operate without an ordaining and directing intelligence, and that the orderly arrangements and admirable adaptations we see all around us are fortuitous or blind, undesigned results — that the eye, though it came to see, was not designed for seeing, nor the hand for handling — then, we suppose, he is justly chargeable with denying, and very needlessly denying, all design in organic Nature; otherwise, we suppose not.[75]

Here we see how the religious zeal gets the upper hand; Darwin maintained that the variations proper are fortuitous, but that natural selection ensures the accumulation of those that are useful under the given conditions. Natural selection is not ordaining, but it is certainly directing, and if the results are not designed, they are surely purposeful.

Gray did not give up his stand, but went on publishing articles in which he argued that natural selection is not inconsistent with theism; he even advocated 'Evolutionary Teleology'. But Darwin could not accept that variation is directed, and for years he discussed the question of design in his correspondence with Gray, without ever reaching a compromise.

However, it appears that gradually Darwin '. . . began to see that what he considered to be misinterpretations were, in effect, softening the blow of evolutionism and, paradoxically, gaining him adherents'.[76]

In his various publications Darwin often expressed himself ambiguously, so it was no problem to find support for theistic views. However, Darwin's personal view did not change, as we may see from his autobiography: 'We can no longer argue that, for instance, the beautiful hinge of a bivalve shell must have been made by an intelligent being, like the hinge of a door by man. There seems to be no more design in the variability of organic beings and in the action of natural selection, than in the course which the wind blow. Everying in nature is the result of fixed laws.'[77]

ERNST HEINRICH HAECKEL (1834–1919)

In England Wallace, in the United States Asa Gray, and in Germany Haeckel; these were the most important of Darwin's supporters outside the circle of friends. Haeckel was the most unreserved adherent to Darwinism, and yet, on the matter of priority he had very particular opinions. This was revealed when in 1866 he published his *Allgemeine Entwickelungsgeschichte der Organismen*, the second volume of his *Generelle Morphologie der Organismen*, which had the subtitle *Allgemeine Grundzüge der organischen Formen-Wissenschaften, mechanisch begründet durch die von Charles Darwin reformierte Descendenz-Theorie*. This second volume was dedicated to 'der Begründern der Descendenz-Theorie, den denkenden Naturforschern, Charles Darwin, Wolfgang Goethe, Jean Lamarck'.[78]

This was a very original way to divide the honour between the three leading civilised nations; yet, I think that only chauvinism could make Geothe a co-founder of the general theory of evolution. However, Haeckel made a very important distinction between what he called *Descendenztheorie* and *Selectionstheorie*. He writes:

It is this *selection theory* which quite rightfully may be called *Darwinism*, to honour its singular originator, but it is not correct as recently often happens, to bestow this name to the whole *theory of evolution*, which already by *Lamarck* was introduced into biology as a scientifically formulated theory, and which therefore correspondingly ought to be labelled *Lamarckism*.[79]

Haeckel sent a copy of his book to Darwin, who wrote back: 'I have read several parts, but I am too poor a German scholar and the book is too large for me to read it all . . . I fully expect that your book will be highly successful in Germany, and the manner in which you often refer to me in your text, and your dedication and the title, shall always look at as one of the greatest honours conferred on me during my life.'[80] The editors of Darwin's letters did not think o, for in a footnote they wrote: 'As regards the dedication and title this seems a strong expression', hinting, I suppose, at the shared dedication and the word 'reformierte' in the title.

233

What was Haeckel's message?

It was a curious production, this first book of Haeckel's, and representative not so much of Darwinian as of pre-Darwinian thought. It was a medley of dogmatic materialism, idealistic morphology, and evolution theory . . .

It was scarcely modern even on its first appearance, and many regarded it, not without reason, as a belated offshoot of *Natur-philosophie* . . .

As a book, the *General Morphology* suffers a good deal from the arid, schematic, almost scholastic manner of exposition adopted. Haeckel's Prussian mania for organisation, for absolute distinctions, for iron-bound formalism, is here given full scope. A treatment less adequate to the variety, fluidity and changeableness of living things could hardly be imagined.[81]

Whatever the merits of the book, there are only two points which need concern us here. First, defining teleology as a metaphysical doctrine, Haeckel concluded that Darwin had done away with teleology. Second, Haeckel adopted the biogenetic law, implied in *On the Origin of Species* and propounded in 1864 by Fritz Müller in his book *Für Darwin*. This question has been dealt with in previous chapters.

There are certain similarities between Darwin and Haeckel. Both were relatively conservative in outlook, but they advocated a materialist theory of evolution at the right moment, and they addressed themselves to a public far beyond the range of specialists. And although they gained few supporters among the latter, they gained a reputation which, even in the case of Haeckel, has lasted to the present day. And in both cases their fame rests on borrowed plumes. Darwin is renowned as the father of Lamarck's first theory of evolution, and Haeckel as the father of the biogenetic law first propounded by Fritz Müller.

THE CANVASSERS

Whoever is led to believe that species are mutable will do good service by conscientiously expressing his conviction; for thus only can the load of prejudice by which this subject is overwhelmed be removed.[82]

Charles Darwin

The three persons dealt with in this chapter did much to advertise Darwinism. And yet, both Wallace and Asa Gray realised, like the friends and like many critics, that natural selection cannot possibly accomplish all that was claimed by Darwin. However, they did not, like most objectors, resort to macromutations as an evolutionary agent, rather they both invoked metaphysical forces, thereby tearing down the edifice raised by Darwin. With Haeckel it was the other way round, he accepted Darwin's theory so uncritically that the specialists at least were forced to react.

It is also interesting to note the difference between Gray and Haeckel with respect to teleology. It was Darwin's intention to account for evolution without the interference of any metaphysical agents. And without a Creator or any other intelligence, there cannot be any kind of design behind the living organisms. Haeckel was right, Darwin had done away with teleology. But 'teleology' is an ambiguous concept, it implies 'design', but it also implies 'purpose'. And Darwin's natural selection ensures that living organisms are supplied with useful, or purposeful features. Natural selection *is* a teleological mechanism in this second sense, so Asa Gray was also correct, Darwin had re-introduced teleology.

9

The Critics

We had not dreamt that because the objections to a theory could not be proved to be absolutely insuperable, we were called upon to accept it as true . . .

Tant pis pour les faits, is a taunt which has frequently been thrown out against philosophers whose boldness has somewhat exceeded their discretion; and we cannot help thinking that Mr. Darwin must be prepared to submit to it largely . . .

We venture to assert, without fear of contradiction, that any physical theory of inorganic matter which should rest on no better evidence than the theory we are considering, would be instantly and totally rejected by every one qualified to form judgement upon it.[1]

William Hopkins

Darwin's book was more than a treatise on biology, it was a manifest on the philosophy of life and a challenge to the ruling religion: at least, so it was conceived. And for that reason Darwin's critics were not just natural scientists, even the clergy joined the controversy. In England the borderline between churchmen and scientists was virtually non-existent as long as the Church controlled the universities; in fact, many parsons were outstanding amateur scientists, and the university professors were generally ordained members of the Anglican Church.

So some critics turned against Darwin's teachings for religious reasons, but they were a minority; most of his opponents, even when they had religious hesitations, argued on a completely scientific basis. Among the scientists Darwin's most formidable critics were Richard Owen, Fleeming Jenkin and St George Jackson Mivart. Of these we have already dealt with Owen, the others will be discussed here together with Samuel Butler, the last of Darwin's great foes.

HENRY CHARLES FLEEMING JENKIN (1833–1885)

Fleeming Jenkin was professor of engineering at University College in London when he published his view of Darwin's *On the Origin of Species* in *The North British Review* in 1867. In this he writes:

Some persons seem to have thought his theory dangerous to

236

religion, morality, and what not. Others have tried to laugh it out of court. We can share neither the fears of the former nor the merriment of the latter; and, on the contrary, own to feeling the greatest admiration both for the ingenuity of the doctrine and for the temper in which it was broached, although, from a consideration of the following arguments, our opinion is adverse to its truth.[2]

Jenkin begins by discussing *Variability*: 'Darwin's theory requires that there shall be no limit to the possible differences between descendants and their progenitors, or, at least, that if there be limits, they shall be at so great a distance as to comprehend the utmost differences between any known forms of life. *The variability required, if not infinite, is indefinite*' (my italics).[3]
He further observes that the differences known from domestic animals

. . . are infinitely small as compared with the range required by his theory, but he assumes that by accumulation of successive differences any degree of variation may be produced; *he says little in proof of the possibility of such an accumulation*, seeming rather to take for granted that if Sir John Sebright could with pigeons produce in six years a certain head and beak of say half the bulk possessed by the original stock, then in twelve years this bulk could be reduced to a quarter, in twenty-four to an eighth, and so farther. (My italics)[4]

By citing observations made on various domesticated plants and animals Jenkin concludes that this kind of accumulation is not possible, the breeder may initially be highly successful, but soon he reaches an impassable limit. And he asks:

What argument does Darwin offer showing that the law of variation will be different when the variation occurs slowly, not rapidly? The law may be different, but is there any experimental ground for believing that it *is* different? Darwin says . . . 'The struggle between natural selection, on the one hand, and the tendency to reversion and variability on the other hand, will in the course of time cease, and that the most abnormally developed organs may be made constant, I can see no reason to doubt'. But what reason have we to *believe* this? (The last italics are mine)[5]

The argument advanced here by Jenkin has been used by many other of Darwin's critics, and it has never been refuted.

Jenkin next turns to the *Efficiency of Natural Selection*. He first observes: 'The mere existence of a species is a proof that it is tolerably well adapted to the life it must lead; many of the variations which may occur will be variations for the worse, and natural selection will assuredly stamp these out.'[6] Thus, in the first instance selection will have a function opposite to that envisaged by Darwin. He continues:

. . . two distinct kinds of possible variation must be separately considered: *first*, that kind of common variation which must be conceived as not only possible, but inevitable, in each individual of the species, such as longer and shorter legs, better or worse hearing, etc.; and, *secondly*, that kind of variation which only occurs rarely, and may be called a sport of nature . . . as when a child is born with six fingers on each hand . . . If we could admit the principle of a gradual accumulation of improvements, making the hare of the present generation run faster, hear better, digest better, than his ancestors; his enemies, the weasels, greyhounds, etc., would have improved likewise, so that perhaps the hare would not be really better off; but at any rate the directon of the change would be from a war of pigmies to a war of Titans . . . We freely admit, that if an accumulation of slight improvements be possible, natural selection might improve hares as hares, and weasels as weasels, that is to say, it might produce animals having every useful faculty and every useful organ of their ancestors developed to a higher degree; more than this, it may obliterate some once useful organs when circumstances have so changed that they are no longer useful . . .

But it may be urged, although many hares do not burrow, one may, or at least may hide in a hole, and a little scratching may just turn the balance in his favour in the struggle for life. So it may, and this brings us straight to the consideration of '*sports*', the second kind of variation above alluded to. *A hare which saved its life by burrowing would come under this head*; let us here consider whether a few hares in a century saving themselves by this process could, in some indefinite time, make a burrowing species of hare. It is very difficult to see how this can be accomplished, even when the sport is very eminently favourable indeed; and still more difficult when the advantage gained is very slight, as must generally be the case. The advantage, whatever it may be, is utterly outbalanced by numerical inferiority. A million creatures are born; ten thousand survive to produce offspring. One of the million has twice as good a chance as any other of surviving; but the chances are fifty to one against the gifted individuals being one of the hundred survivors . . . *the chances are against the preservation of any one 'sport' in a numerous tribe . . . Unless* [*the sports*] *breed together, a most improbable event*, their progeny would again approach the average individual. (The last two italic phrases are mine)[7]

This part of Jenkin's article made a very great impression upon Darwin; unfortunately this does not hold for those parts where he was right, but only for this one where he was wrong. Jenkin clearly saw that Darwin's natural selection can concern only already existing useful properties and characteristics, innovations require the occurrence of macromutations, called 'sports' by him. Like Darwin, Jenkin assumed blending inheritance, and this is a handicap for the establishment of mutations as compared with Mendelian particulate inheritance. But that is not the main reason why he finds difficulties for the establishment of variations, great or small. Rather, as we see from the statements emphasised by me, Jenkin, like Darwin, excluded inbreeding and isolation, the expedients which ensure the breeder's success. If he had allowed for these events his objections would have lost their force. Jenkin continues:

Another argument against the efficiency of natural selection is, that animals possess many peculiarities the special advantage of which it is almost impossible to conceive . . . A true believer . . . may take refuge in the word correlation, and say, other parts were useful, which by the law of correlation could not exist without these parts; and although he may not have one single reason to allege in favour of any of these statements, he may safely defy us to prove the negative, that they are not true . . . *The believer who is at liberty to invent any imaginary circumstances, will very generally be able to conceive some series of transmutations answering his wants.*

He can invent trains of ancestors of whose existence there is no evidence; he can marshal hosts of equally imaginary foes; he can call up continents, floods, and peculiar atmospheres, he can dry up oceans, split islands, and parcel out eternity at will; surely with these advantages he must be a dull fellow if he cannot scheme some series of animals and circumstances explaining our

239

assumed difficulty quite naturally.[8]

If Darwin had self-criticism these words ought to have hurt him deeply.

The next point in Jenkin's criticism concerns *Lapse of Time*. Lyell and Darwin needed hundreds of millions of years to account for their theories. Lord Kelvin, with whom Jenkin co-operated, had calculated the age of the Earth and arrived at a value far below that assumed by Darwin. We now know that Kelvin based his estimations on false premises; Darwin was nearer the truth than Kelvin, and therefore the objections in this section may be ignored.

The last section is called *Observed Facts supposed to support Darwin's Views*. Here we may read:

> The general form of his argument is as follows: — All these things may have been, therefore my theory is possible, and since my theory is a possible one, all those hypotheses which it requires are rendered probable. There is little direct evidence that any of these maybe's actually *have been*.[9]

This is a very shrewd exposition of Darwin's approach. Jenkin's conclusion is:

> What can we believe but that Darwin's theory is an ingenious and plausible speculation, to which future physiologists will look back with the kind of admiration we bestow on the *atoms of Lucretius*, or *the crystal spheres of Eudoxus*, containing like these some faint half-truths, marking at once the ignorance of the age and the ability of the philosopher. Surely the time is past when a theory *unsupported by evidence* is received as probable, because in our ignorance we know not why it should be false, though we cannot show it to be true. Yet we have heard grave men gravely urge, that because Darwin's theory was the most plausible known, it should be believed. (My italics)[10]

Many of Darwin's critics had voiced views similar to Jenkin's, but it appears that the latter made a deeper impression on Darwin, possibly because Jenkin substantiated his arguments with mathematical calculations. Darwin wrote to Hooker: 'It is only about two years since last edition of *Origin*, and I am fairly disgusted to find how much I have to modify, and how much I ought to add;

but I have determined not to add much. Fleeming Jenkin has given me much trouble, but *has been of more real use to me than any other essay or review*' (my italics).[11]

A week later he wrote to Wallace:

I have been interrupted in my regular work in preparing a new edition of the 'Origin', which has cost me much labour, and which I hope I have considerably improved in two or three important points. I always thought individual differences more important than single variations [macromutations], but now I have come to the conclusion that they are of paramount importance, and in this I believe I agree with you. Fleeming Jenkin's arguments have convinced me.[12]

This letter upset Wallace who answered:

Will you tell me *where* are Fleeming Jenkin's arguments on the importance of single variations? Because I at present hold most strongly the contrary opinion, that it is the individual differences or *general variability* of species that enables them to become modified and adapted to new conditions.

Variations or 'sports' may be important in modifying an animal in one direction, as in colour for instance, but how can it possibly work in changes requiring coordination of many parts, as in Orchids for example, I cannot conceive.[13]

But this, of course, was a misunderstanding. So Darwin replied:

I must have expressed myself atrociously; I meant to say exactly the reverse of what you have understood. F. Jenkin argued in the 'North British Review' against single variations ever being perpetuated, and has convinced me, though not in quite so broad a manner as here put. I always thought individual differences more important; but I was blind and thought that single variations might be preserved much oftener than I now see is possible or probable. I mentioned this in my former note merely because I believed that you had come to a similar conclusion, and I like much to be in accord with you. I believe *I was mainly deceived by single variations offering such simple illustrations, as when man selects.* (My italics)[14]

Jenkin actually argued that evolutionary innovations, and hence

241

THE CRITICS

trans-specific evolution, require what Darwin called 'single variations'. Subsequently adopting Darwin's assertion that isolation and inbreeding do not occur in Nature, he had to conclude that such macromutations cannot become established, and consequently that evolution is not possible. But Darwin knew that 'when man selects', they may become established, and therefore he had formerly been willing to allow for macromutations, to a limited extent at least, even if he himself had rejected the importance of isolation and inbreeding in Nature. But the breeder's expedient involves isolation and inbreeding, and therefore the logical approach would have been to refute Jenkin's and his own premise. As we have seen, Jenkin's article did not convince Darwin to the extent that he gave up the involvement of 'single variations' advocated by so many people.

Darwin was now in a precarious situation, for Jenkin had shown that individual differences could become established only when present in a large number of individuals. What did he have to say on this subject in the later editions in which he discusses Jenkin's views? He begins by mentioning Jenkin's arguments against the establishment of 'single variations' and goes on:

It should not, however, be overlooked that certain variations, which no one would rank as mere individual differences, frequently recur owing to a similar organisation being similarly acted on, — of which fact numerous instances could be given with our domestic productions. In such cases, if a varying individual did not actually transmit to its offspring its newly-acquired character, it would *undoubtedly* transmit, as long as the existing conditions remained the same, a *still stronger tendency* to vary in the same manner. The conditions might indeed act in so energetic and definite a manner as to lead to the same modification in all the individuals of the species *without the aid of selection*. But we may suppose that the conditions sufficed to affect only a third, or fourth, or tenth part of the individuals . . . Now, in such cases, if the variation were of a beneficial nature, the original form would soon be supplanted by the modified form, through *the survival of the fittest*.

With reference to the effects of intercrossing and of competition, it should be borne in mind that most animals and plants keep to their proper homes, and do not needlessly wander about; we see this even with migratory birds, which almost always return to the same district. Consequently each newly-formed variety would generally be at first local, as seems to be *the common rule*

242

with varieties in a state of nature; so that similarly modified individuals would soon exist in a small body together, and would often *breed together*. If the new variety was successful in its battle for life, it would slowly spread from a central spot, competing with and conquering the unchanged individuals on the margin of an ever-increasing circle . . . It may be objected by those who have not attended to natural history [among whom Fleeming Jenkin], that the long-continued accumulation of individual differences could not give rise to parts or organs which seem to us, and are often called, new. But, as we shall hereafter find, it is difficult to advance any good instance of a really new organ; even so complex and perfect an organ as the eye can be shown to graduate downwards into mere tissue sensitive to diffused light. (My italics)[15]

We see here that Darwin begins by refuting his own and Jenkin's notion on blending inheritance; 'single variations' may reappear after being absent in one or more generations. This is explained, however, as a reaction to the conditions, and this effect may indeed be so strong that natural selection becomes superfluous! Is this mechanism Buffonism or Lamarckism? In passing it may be noticed that even if evolution can manage without natural selection, it still needs the participation of 'the survival of the fittest', which is the synonym of 'natural selection'. And then Darwin goes on to demonstrate that isolation and inbreeding may occur in nature, a circumstance which completely invalidates Jenkin's argument against the establishment of 'single variations'.

But of course, he was aware that Jenkin had rejected the notion that evolutionary innovations can arise through the accumulation of 'individual differences'. This objection Darwin had to meet, and he did by arguing that there are no parts or organs which deserve to be called 'new'. This statement, I suppose, must be valid for the evolution of life from micro-organisms to angiosperms and mammals.

It seems clear that Darwin did not understand much of Jenkin's argument; the question remains whether he *could not* or *would not*.

ST GEORGE JACKSON MIVART (1827–1900)

Mivart was the son of a successful hotel owner in London. At the age of sixteen he converted to Catholicism, much to the distress of his parents. Having thus excluded himself from entering a university, he studied law at Lincoln's Inn; he finished his studies, but never practiced as a barrister; rather, having no need to make a living he began to study biology. During the following years Mivart established very good contacts with Owen, and later he became Huxley's student and friend. These two together helped him to enter a career as a teaching biologist at St Mary's Hospital Medical School.[16]

Mivart was personally acquainted with Darwin, whom he regarded highly, and Wallace was his friend. As far as their theory was concerned he was initially neutral, neither adherent nor opponent. But this situation changed, as related by himself:

> It was in 1868 that difficulties as to the theory of Natural Selection began to take shape in my mind, and they were strongly reinforced by the arguments of . . . the Rev. W.W. Roberts . . . The arguments he again and again urged upon me were the difficulties, or rather the impossibilities, on the Darwinian system, of accounting for the origin of the human intellect, and above all for its moral intuitions — not its moral *sentiments*, but its ethical *judgements* . . .
>
> After many painful days . . . I felt it my duty first of all to go straight to Professor Huxley and tell him all my thoughts, feelings, and intentions in the matter without the slightest reserve, including . . . the theological aspect of the question. *Never before or since have I had a more painful experience than fell to my lot in his room* at the School of Mines on that 15th. of June, 1869. As soon as I had made my meaning clear, *his countenance became transformed as I had never seen it.* Yet he looked more sad and surprised than anything else. He was kind and gentle as he said *regretfully, but most firmly, that nothing so united or severed men as questions such as those I had spoken of.*
>
> Nevertheless no positive breach took place, though the following day . . . the conversation became rather sharply controversial. Yet, family friendly relations continued. (My italics, except for the first two words)[17]

Huxley's reaction is completely incomprehensible. Was he not himself an agnostic, and as such obliged to tolerance? Did he not know of Mivart's religious convictions? Was not the stand taken by Mivart similar to the one professed by Lyell, Darwin's friend and master, and by Wallace, co-founder of the theory of natural selection?

Rather than attempting to answer any questions at this stage let us turn to the work which resulted from Mivart's doubts. In 1871 he published the book *On the Genesis of Species*,[18] in which he pointed out certain insurmountable difficulties in the theory of natural selection, submitting the necessity of assuming that many evolutionary modifications must have occurred by macromutations.

In the introduction Mivart writes:

> The problem then is . . . by what combination of natural laws . . . is an individual embodying . . . new characters produced?
> For the approximation we have of late made towards the solution of this problem, we are mainly indebted to the invaluable labours and active brains of Charles Darwin and Alfred Wallace.
> Nevertheless, important as have been the impulse and direction given by those writers to both our observations and speculations, the solution will not (if the views here advocated are correct) ultimately present that aspect and character with which it has issued from the hands of those writers.[19]

On the background to the problem Mivart makes a statement which is very interesting:

> Remarkable is the rapidity with which an interest in the question of specific origination has spread. But a few years ago it scarcely occupied the minds of any but naturalists. Then the crude theory put forth by Lamarck, and by his English interpreter, the author of the 'Vestiges of Creation', had rather discredited than helped on a belief in organic evolution — a belief, that is, in new kinds being produced from older ones by the ordinary and constant operation of natural laws. Now, however, this notion is widely diffused. Indeed, there are few drawing-rooms where it is not the subject of occasional discussion, and artisans and schoolboys have their views as to the permanence of organic forms.[20]

Mivart is here caught with substantial inaccuracies: Chambers was not a Lamarckian, he rejected specifically Lamarckism and advocated a macromutation theory, coinciding with the one proposed by Mivart himself. And as witnessed by the tremendous success of *Vestiges of the Natural History of Creation* the general public had been very much interested in evolution before Darwin, in contrast, perhaps, to the naturalists.

After a completely fair presentation of the theory of natural selection and a brief discussion of some of the difficulties it encounters he goes on:

> Thus, whether this theory be true or false, all lovers of natural science should acknowledge a deep debt of gratitude to Messrs. Darwin and Wallace, on account of its practical utility. But the utility of a theory by no means implies its truth . . .
>
> With regard to Mr. Darwin (with whose name, on account of the noble self-abnegation of Mr. Wallace, the theory is in general exclusively associated), his friends may heartily congratulate him on the fact that he is one of the few exceptions to the rule respecting the non-appreciation of a prophet in his own country.[21]

As we have seen, they might congratulate themselves also, for the status of Darwin was at least in part of their making. Mivart continues:

> . . . it was inevitable that very many half-educated men and shallow thinkers should accept with eagerness the theory of 'Natural Selection', or rather what they think to be such (for few things are more remarkable than the manner in which it has been misunderstood), on account of a certain characteristic it has in common with other theories which should not be mentioned in the same breath with it, except, as now, with the accompaniment of protest and apology. We refer to its remarkable simplicity and the ready way in which phenomena the most complex appear explicable by a cause for the comprehension of which laborious and persevering efforts are not required, but which may be represented by the simple phrase 'survival of the fittest'. With nothing more than this, can, on the Darwinian theory, all the most intricate facts of distribution and affinity, form, and colour, be accounted for; as well as the most complex instincts and the most admirable adjustments, such as those of the human eye and ear . . . At the same time it must be admitted that a similar 'simplicity' — the apparently easy explanation of complex phenomena — also constitutes the charm of such matters as hydropathy and phrenology, in the eyes of the unlearned or half-educated public . . . It is not, of course, meant to imply that its 'simplicity' tells at all against 'Natural Selection', but only that the actual or supposed possession of that quality is a strong reason for the wide and somewhat hasty acceptance of the theory, whether it be true or not.[22]

We may further read:

It is easy to complain of onesidedness in the views of many who oppose Darwinism in the interest of orthodoxy; but not at all less patent is the intolerance and narrowmindedness of some of those who advocate it, avowedly or covertly, in the interest of heterodoxy. This hastiness of rejection or acceptance, determined by ulterior consequences believed to attach to 'Natural Selection', is unfortunately in part to be accounted for by some expressions and a certain tone to be found in Mr. Darwin's writings. That his expressions, however, are not always to be construed literally is manifest. His frequent use metaphorically of the theistic expressions, 'contrivance', for example, and 'purpose', has elicited . . . criticisms which fail to tell against their opponent, solely because such expressions are, in Mr. Darwin's writings, merely figurative — metaphors, and nothing more.

It may be hoped, then, that *a similar looseness of expression will account for passages of a directly opposite tendency to that of his theistic metaphors.*

Moreover, it must not be forgotten that he frequently uses that absolutely theological term, 'the Creator', and that he has retained in all the editions of his 'Origin of Species' an expression which has been much criticized: he speaks 'of life, with its several powers, having been originally breathed by the Creator into a few forms, or into one'. This is mentioned in justice to Mr. Darwin only, and by no means because it is a position which this book is intended to support. For, from Mr. Darwin's usual mode of speaking, it appears that by such Divine action he means a supernatural intervention, whereas it is *here* contended that throughout the whole process of *physical* evolution — the first manifestation of life included — *supernatural* action is assuredly not to be looked for. (My italics, except for the last ones)[23]

Hence, as far as physical evolution was concerned, Mivart, the Roman Catholic, was ready publicly to go one step further than Darwin.

One can imagine that Darwin was less than happy when reading the quoted statements. But on the whole they are justified, and, in spite of the irony, I personally think that Mivart kept within the bonds of civility. However, as we shall see, Darwin and his friends soon came to consider Mivart's book as sacrilege.

Mivart ends the Introduction by enumerating the difficulties encountered by the theory of natural selection, the subjects of the successive chapters of his book:

> What is to be brought forward may be summed up as follows:—
> That 'Natural Selection' is incompetent to account for the incipient stages of useful structures.
> That it does not harmonize with the co-existence of closely similar structures of diverse origin.
> That there are grounds for thinking that specific differences may be developed suddenly instead of gradually.
> That the opinion that species have definite though very different limits to their variability is still tenable.
> That certain fossil transitional forms are absent, which might have been expected to be present.
> That some facts of geographical distribution intensify other difficulties.
> That the objection drawn from the physiological difference between 'species' and 'races' still exists unrefuted.
> That there are many remarkable phenomena in organic forms upon which 'Natural Selection' throws no light whatever, but the explanations of which, if they could be attained, might throw some light upon specific origination.

And he continues with a criticism which today will be endorsed even by the most ardent Darwinians:

> Besides these objections to the sufficiency of 'Natural Selection', others may be brought against the hypothesis of 'Pangenesis', which, professing as it does to explain great difficulties, seems to do so by presenting others not less great — in fact almost to be explanation of *obscurum per obscurius*.[24]

And so Mivart goes on to show chapter by chapter, example by example, how the difficulties facing Darwin's micromutation theory are resolved by the macromutation theory proposed by him. In the last chapter but one he summarises his views, and I think they deserve to be quoted in full, but before we reach this point we may notice the following statement: 'The view of evolution maintained in this work, though arrived at in complete independence, yet seems to agree in many respects with the views advocated by Professor Owen in the last volume of his Anatomy of Vertebrates, under the term derivation.' And he even adds in a footnote: 'Since the publication of the first edition of this book, its author has become aware that similar views were enunciated more than ten years ago by Professor Theophilus Parsons.'[25]

Here Mivart reveals his ignorance as concerns the history of evolutionary thought; the theory advocated by Parsons, Owen and himself is nothing but the epigenetic macromutation theory. As the readers of this book will know, this theory dates back to Etienne Geoffroy Saint-Hilaire, and it had been upheld by several persons both before and after 1859, among whom Robert Chambers. But Mivart's statement is also remarkable because it shows that some people besides Owen himself realised that he believed in evolution, if not in Darwin's theory.

And now to Mivart's theory:

It is believed: That [the] conception of an internal innate force will ever remain necessary, however much its subordinate processes and actions may become explicable. That by such a force, from time to time, new species are manifested by ordinary generation . . . these new forms not being monstrosities but harmonious self-consistent wholes . . .

That these 'jumps' are considerable in comparison with the minute variations of 'Natural Selection' — are in fact sensible steps, such as discriminate species from species.

That the latent tendency which exists to these sudden evolutions is determined to action by the stimulus of external conditions.

That 'Natural Selection' rigorously destroys monstrosities, and abortive and feeble attempts at the performance of the evolutionary process.

That 'Natural Selection' removes the antecedent species rapidly when the new one evolved is more in harmony with surrounding conditions.

That 'Natural Selection' favours and develops useful variations, though it is impotent to originate them or to erect the physiological barrier which seems to exist between species.

By some conception as this, the *difficulties* here enumerated, *which beset the theory of 'Natural Selection'* pure and simple, *are to be got over.* (My italics)[26]

Some comments: (i) The 'internal innate force' has by some Darwinians been proposed to be a metaphysical agent. This is, of course, nothing but slander; as we have seen above, Mivart expressly excluded 'supernatural action'. In fact, the forces in question are those epigenetic mechanisms involved in the creation of the body in the course of ontogenesis. (ii) There is undue weight laid on the evolution of species; Nature has been responsible for the origin of all categories of animals and plants. (iii) The realisation of the innovations is not affected by the environment, but their survival is. (iv) Mivart neatly outlines the various functions of natural selection, including that of *progressive evolution*.

It was no doubt inevitable that Mivart's faith should affect his evolutionary views. Thus, in the last chapter, called 'Theology and Evolution', he contends that a theory of physical evolution is not at all incompatible with religious belief, but he makes a reservation with respect to the evolution of man, the last step of which, the acquisition of a soul, has been *spiritual* evolution. In this chapter, and also in the Introduction, he mentions a 'post-medieval theologian . . . Suarez, who has a separate section in opposition to those who maintain the distinct creation of various kinds — or substantial forms — of organic life'.[27] It is important to note in this context that the references to Suarez occupy nine lines in a book of 333 pages.

Darwin and his friends were deeply concerned by Mivart's book, particularly because it emphasised the suspicion entertained by public opinion as to the general validity of the theory of natural selection. We shall return to this question; here we must first deal with Darwin's reaction. In fact, he had only one possible road to take — meet the criticism. But Darwin realised that it would be difficult. He wrote to Wallace: 'I feel very doubtful how far I shall succeed in answering Mivart, it is so difficult to answer objections to *doubtful points*, and *make the discussion readable*. I shall make only a selection' (my italics).[28] And so he set out to prepare an additional chapter to the forthcoming edition of *On the Origin of Species*, called 'Miscellaneous Objections to the Theory of Natural Selection', where he discussed objections raised by Mivart and other biologists. We must discuss this rejoinder in rather great detail because it is so revealing of Darwin's style of argumentation.

[Darwin writes:] A distinguished zoologist, Mr. St. George Mivart, has recently collected *all* the objections which have *ever* been advanced by *myself* and others against the theory of natural selection, as propounded by Mr. Wallace and myself, and has illustrated them with admirable art and force. When thus marshalled, they make a formidable array; and as it forms no part of Mr. Mivart's plan to give the various facts and considerations opposed to his conclusions, no slight effort of reason and memory is left to the reader, who may wish to weigh the evidence on both sides. When discussing special cases, Mr. Mivart passes over the effects of the *increased use and disuse* of parts, which I have always maintained to be *highly important* . . . He likewise often assumes that I attribute nothing to *variation, independently of natural selection* . . . My judgment may not be trustworthy, but after reading with care Mr. Mivart's book, and comparing each section with what I have said on the same head, I never before felt *so strongly convinced* of the general truth of the conclusions here arrived at, subject, of course, in so intricate a subject, to much partial error. (My italics).[29]

Let us first record that *all* is false, Mivart considered the most weighty objections, but not all. And then we must conclude that Darwin did not grasp the aim of Mivart's book, which was to refute Darwinism, that is, the theory of natural selection. And under these conditions it is of course irrelevant to mobilise Lamarckism (use and disuse), a theory rightly rejected by Mivart, and macromutations (variation, independently of natural selection), the evolutionary agent advocated by Mivart.

And then Darwin proceeds to discuss details, beginning with the objection 'that natural selection is incompetent to account for the incipient stages of useful structures'. The first example concerns the giraffe.

The giraffe, by its lofty stature, much elongated neck, forelegs, head and tongue, has its whole frame beautifully adapted for browsing on the higher branches of trees . . . So under nature with the nascent giraffe, the individuals which were the highest browsers and were able during dearths to reach even an inch or two above the others, will often have been preserved; for they will have roamed over the whole country in search of food . . . These slight proportional differences, due to the laws of growth and variation, are not of the slightest use or importance to most species. But it will have been otherwise with the nascent giraffe, considering its *probable habits of life*; for those individuals which had *some one part* or several parts of their bodies *rather more elongated* than usual, would generally have survived. These will have intercrossed and *left offspring*, either *inheriting* the same bodily peculiarities, or with a *tendency* to vary again in the same manner; whilst the individuals, *less favoured in the same respects*, will have been *most liable to perish*. (My italics)[30]

It will be seen that the 'nascent giraffes' were already giraffes as far as their habits were concerned, and perhaps even in their structure. Whether the tallest ones would indeed leave offspring is most questionable, for, as has been pointed out repeatedly, among the 'less favoured' giraffes with respect to 'lofty stature' are the females and, of course, the young ones. Darwin's explanation of the evolution of the giraffes raises some further questions. Does it suffice 'during dearth' to have 'a tendency to vary' in the beneficial direction? Does the giraffe evolve only during dearths? Does it evolve in the opposite direction when there is plenty of food?

We may proceed:

To this conclusion Mr. Mivart brings forward two objections. One is that the increased size of the body would obviously require an increased supply of food, and he considers it as 'very problematical whether the disadvantages thence arising would not, in times of scarcity, more than counterbalance the advantages'. But as the giraffe does actually exist in large numbers in S. Africa, and as some of the largest antelopes in the world, taller than an ox, abound there, *why should we doubt that*, as far as size is concerned, intermediate gradations could formerly have existed there, subjected as *now* to severe dearths. Assuredly the being able to reach, at each stage of increased size, to a supply of food, left untouched by the other hoofed quadrupeds of the country, would have been of some advantage to the nascent giraffe. (My italics)[31]

This is not exactly an answer to the objection raised by Mivart. However, the larger body size may or may not entail a relative improvement in food supply during a dearth, but it certainly has other advantages:

Nor must we overlook the fact, that increased bulk would act as a protection against almost all beasts of prey excepting the lion; and against this animal, its tall neck, — *and the taller the better* — would . . . serve as a watch-tower. It is from this cause . . . that no animal is more difficult to stalk than the giraffe. This animal also uses its long neck as means of offence or defence, by violently swinging its head armed with stump-like horns. *The preservation of each species can rarely be determined by any one advantage, but by the union of all, great and small.* (My italics)[32]

[Darwin continues:] Mr. Mivart then asks (and this is his second objection), if natural selection be so potent, and if high browsing be so great an advantage, why has not any other hoofed quadruped acquired a long neck and a lofty structure . . .? With respect to S. Africa, which was formerly inhabited by numerous herds of the giraffe, *the answer is not difficult*, and can best be given by an *illustration*. In every meadow in England in which trees grow, we see the *lower* branches trimmed or planed to an exact level by the browsing of the *horses* or *cattle*; and what advantage would it be, for instance, to sheep, if kept there, to acquire slightly longer necks? In every district some one kind of animal will almost certainly be able to browse higher than the others; and it is almost equally certain that this one kind alone could have its neck elongated for this purpose, through natural selection and the effects of increased use. In S. Africa the competition for browsing on the higher branches of the acacias and other trees must be between giraffe and giraffe, and not with the other ungulate animals. (My italics)[33]

If Darwin had here followed the rules of logic, he would have seen that in England it was the horses or perhaps the cattle, but not the sheep, which should transform into giraffes, at least during 'dearths'. And he also forgot that the 'nascent giraffe' would compete with different animals of equal size, for if it already was taller than its rivals, there would be no reason for it to grow taller.

Darwin continued with a discussion on 'incipient stages of useful structures'; among the examples he used I find his explanation of the origin of the whale-bone whales through micromutations is very entertaining, however here we shall deal only with the following example.

The Pleuronectidae, or Flat-fish, [Darwin writes] are remarkable for their asymmetrical bodies . . . But the eyes offer the most remarkable peculiarity; for they are both placed on the upper side of the head. During early youth, however, they stand opposite to each other, and the whole body is then symmetrical . . . Soon the eye proper to the lower side begins to glide slowly round the head to the upper side . . .

Mr. Mivart has taken up this case, and remarks that *a sudden spontaneous transformation in the position of the eyes is hardly conceivable*, in which I quite agree with him. He then adds: 'If the transit was gradual, then how such transit of one eye a minute fraction of the journey towards the other side of the head could benefit the individual is, indeed, far from clear. It seems, even that such an incipient transformation must rather have been injurious'. (My italics)[34]

Is Mivart now also beginning to contradict himself? No, he wrote: 'If the condition had appeared at once, if in the hypothetically fortunate common ancestor of these fishes an eye had suddenly become thus transferred, then the perpetuation of such a transformation by the action of "Natural Selection" is conceivable enough. Such sudden changes, however, are not those favoured by the Darwinian theory, and indeed the incidental occurrence of such a spontaneous transformation is far from probable. But if this is not so . . .'[35] and then he goes on as quoted above by Darwin.

Mivart contends that the preservation of the flatfishes through natural selection is conceivable if the transformation occurred in one step, an event 'far from probable', but not 'hardly conceivable'. On the other hand, he rejected the possibility of the *origination* of the flatfishes through a long succession of small steps. It seems that Darwin is here misinterpreting Mivart, a point of some interest as we shall presently see.

I shall not deprive my readers of the pleasure of learning how the flatfishes arose or, rather, arise:

But [Mivart] might have found an answer to this objection in the excellent observations published in 1867 by Malm. The Pleuronectidae, whilst very young and still symmetrical . . . cannot long retain a vertical position, owing to the excessive depth of their bodies, the small size of their lateral fins, and to their being destitute of a swimbladder. Hence *soon growing tired, they fall to the bottom to one side.* Whilst thus at rest *they often twist . . . the lower eye upwards, to see above them;* and they do this so vigorously that the eye is pressed hard against the upper part of the orbit. The forehead between the eyes consequently becomes, as could be plainly seen, temporarily contracted in breadth. (My italics)[36]

The discussion of this remarkable 'Lamarckian' macromutation trails on for almost two pages, with Darwin observing on one occasion: 'Our great authority on Fishes, Dr. Günther, concludes his abstract of Malm's paper, by remarking that "the author gives a very simple explanation of the abnormal condition of the Pleuronectoids".'[37] Indeed!

And then a final thrust towards Mivart: 'We thus see that the first stages of the transit of the eye from one side of the head to the other, which Mr. Mivart considers would be *injurious*, may be attributed to the habit, no doubt *beneficial* to the individual and to the species, of endeavouring to *look upwards with both eyes, whilst resting on one side at the bottom*' (my italics).[38]

Overall, Darwin concentrated his rejoinder on the 'incipient stages of useful structures'; he did discuss some of the other objections too, but, as far as I can see, not all of them. Towards the end he writes:

At the present day [1872] almost all naturalists admit evolution under some form. Mr. Mivart believes that species change through 'an internal force or tendency', about which *it is not pretended that anything is known*. That species have a capacity for change will be admitted by all evolutionists [sic!]; but there is no need . . . to invoke any internal force beyond the *tendency to ordinary variability*, which through the aid of . . . natural selection would . . . give rise by graduated steps to natural races or species. (My italics)[39]

But must not internal forces participate whenever any transformation of the body occurs? Furthermore, Mivart's 'internal force or tendency' appears to be indistinguishable from Darwin's 'correlated variation', by which 'I mean . . . that the whole organisation is so tied together during its growth and development, that when slight variations in any one part occur, and *are accumulated through natural selection, other parts become modified*. This is a very important subject, *most imperfectly understood*, and no doubt wholly different classes of facts may be here easily confounded together' (my italics).[40] Thus one may ask whether the 'correlated variation', occurring during 'growth and development', will not occur whether or not natural selection gets a chance to interfere? And finally, Darwin could hardly demand that Mivart should know something that was 'most imperfectly understood' by himself? Darwin rounded off his defence with the following statement:

255

He who believes that some ancient form was transformed suddenly through an internal force or tendency . . . will be almost compelled to assume, in opposition to all analogy, that many individuals varied simultaneously. It cannot be denied that such abrupt and great changes of structure are widely different from those which most species apparently have undergone. He will further be compelled to believe that many structures beautifully adapted to all the other parts of the same creature and to the surrounding conditions, have been suddenly produced; and of such complex and wonderful co-adaptations, he will not be able to assign a shadow of an explanation. He will be forced to admit that these great and sudden transformations have left no trace of their action on the embryo. To admit all this is, as it seems to me, to enter into the realms of miracle, and to leave those of Science.[41]

It must be difficult to find, in any of the major works recorded in the history of biology, another statement which, to a similar degree is beside the point. For he who believes in macromutations will readily assume that only single individuals, or members of the same clutch, vary. Provided the variation is hereditary he is assured that, in conformance with the breeders' experience, it may be preserved through inbreeding. He will presumably admit that such changes are 'widely different' from those which are usually observed in wild and domesticated organisms. But since the changes invoked are supposed to account for the evolution of the living world, they must be of a kind which *all* 'species apparently have undergone'.

Since he has accepted that living creatures have arisen through macromutations, this must of course involve their 'complex and wonderful co-adaptations'. But he will assume that the numerous less successful attempts succumbed through the action of natural selection, either immediately or when, by chance, Nature produced something better. And his explanation is that most of these modifications, certainly all morphological ones, have arisen through changes in the embryonic development, the phase of life during which living bodies are constructed. He will therefore strongly contend that they have indeed left traces in the embryo. Referring to von Baer's studies on comparative embryology he will claim that once we understand the epigenetic mechanisms responsible for the formation of the embryos, say, in the various vertebrate classes, we shall also know the changes that occur when evolution causes a change from one major taxon to another. To admit all this may be to enter the 'realms of miracle', but it does not imply that we leave the realms of science.

How did Darwinism fare at the time of Mivart's attack? A study of the British periodical papers has led to the following conclusion:

It has often been asserted that the first reaction to Darwin's theory was uniformly hostile. That is, however, hardly correct . . .

The attitude towards Natural Selection was one mixed admiration and hesitation: admiration of the ingenuity of the theory, and hesitation as to the extent of its applicability. One did not quite grant to it the power to work such wonders as Darwin claimed for it . . .

There was also a tendency to regard sudden and spectacular mutations between parents and offsprings as furnishing a clue to the mystery of the origin of species . . ,

What happened may be briefly described by saying that the majority of the general public were in the end prepared to *accept the Evolution part of Darwin's doctrine*, at least for the organic world below man, while they rejected Darwin's explanation of it, namely, the theory of Natural Selection . . .

[During 1870–2] the number of adherents to [Natural Selection] seem to have declined. This was probably *chiefly due to the influence* of Mivart's *Genesis of Species*, where the arguments against Natural Selection were put forth ably and effectively. (My italics)[42]

Indeed, the fact that Mivart accepted the salient points in Darwin's theory and yet could demonstrate its shortcomings was a tremendous blow against Darwin. Darwin was very much upset by the book as shown by several letters; for instance one to Wallace:

I have just read (but not with sufficient care) Mivart's book, and I feel *absolutely certain* that he meant to be *fair* (but he was stimulated by theological fervour); yet I do not think he has been quite fair . . . The part which, I think, will *have most influence* is where he gives *the whole series of cases like that of the whalebone*, in which *we cannot explain gradational steps* . . . Mivart is savage or contemptuous against my 'moral sense', and so probably will you be. I am extremely pleased that he agrees with my position, *as far as animal nature is concerned*, of man in the series; or if anything, thinks I have erred in making him too distinct. (My italics, except for the first and the last ones)[43]

This letter requires some comments: (i) As we see, Darwin acknowledges gratefully that Mivart accepts physical evolution without reservation. (ii) When Mivart rejects that the spiritual endowments of man can have been acquired through natural selection, he assumes the standpoint also adopted by Wallace, as Darwin admits in the letter. On this point there is no reason to mention fairness or religious fervour, as such criticism will hit even Wallace. (iii) The expression 'moral sense' does not concern Darwin's own moral sense, but his views on the evolution of this faculty.

At this time Wallace got another letter:

I send by this post a review by Chauncey Wright, as I much want your opinion of it as soon as you can send it. I consider you an incomparably better critic than I am. The article, though not very clearly written, and *poor in parts from want of knowledge, seems to me admirable. Mivart's book is producing a great effect against Natural Selection, and more especially against me.* Therefore if you think the article even somewhat good I will write and get permission to publish it as a shilling pamphlet . . .

I grieve to see the omission of the words by Mivart, detected by Wright. I complained to Mivart that in two cases he quotes only the commencement of sentences by me, and thus modifies my meaning; but I never supposed he would have omitted words. There were other cases of what I consider unfair treatment. *I conclude with sorrow that though he means to be honourable, he is so bigoted that he cannot act fairly.* (My italics)[44]

Let us first cast a glance at the 'omissions', discovered by Chauncey Wright, which so much grieved Darwin. The editor of Darwin's *Life and Letters* (his son Francis, whose comments usually are aimed at improving his father's image) adds a footnote in this context, stating: 'It should be mentioned that the passage from which words are omitted is not given within inverted commas by Mr. Mivart.'

We learn something about the misrepresentations in a letter from Wallace:

I must say . . . I do not see any great reason to complain of the 'words' left out by Mivart, as they do not seem to me materially to affect the meaning. Your expression 'and tends to depart in a slight degree', I think hardly grammatical; a *tendency* to depart cannot be very well said to be in a slight degree, a departure can, but a tendency must be either a *slight tendency* or a *strong tendency*.

In your chapter on Natural Selection the expressions 'extremely slight modifications', 'every variation even the slightest', 'every grade of constitutional difference', occur, and these have led to errors such as Mivart's. I say all this because I feel sure that Mivart would be the last to intentionally misrepresent you, and he has told me that he was sorry the word '*infinitesimal*', as applied to variations used by Natural Selection, got into his book. (The last italics are mine)[45]

This answer shows that Wallace did his best to defend his friend Mivart, and also that Darwin had lost all sense of proportion — particularly as he himself, as we have seen, misquoted Mivart.

But let us return to Chauncey Wright's review. We have seen that Darwin was not greatly impressed by it, and he had several reasons for this attitude. In the review it was stated: 'It would seem, at first sight, that Mr. Darwin has won a victory, not for himself, but for Lamarck. Transmutation, it would seem, has been accepted, but Natural Selection, *its explanation*, is still rejected by many converts to the general theory, both on religious and scientific grounds' (my italics).[46]

Yet, the review was a criticism of the macromutation theory advocated by Mivart and to an important extent an acceptance of Darwin's theory. And that must have been why Darwin decided to publish Wright's review in England. He wrote to Wright:

I have hardly ever in my life read an article which has given me so much satisfaction as the review which you have been so kind as to send me. I agree to *almost* everything which you say. *Your memory must be wonderfully accurate*, for you know my works as well as I do myself, and *your power of grasping other men's thoughts is something quite surprising*; and this, as far as my experience goes, is a very rare quality. As I read on I perceived how you have acquired this power, viz. by thoroughly analyzing each word.

. . . Now I am going to beg a favour. Will you provisionally give me permission to reprint your article as a shilling pamphlet? I ask only provisionally, as I have not yet had time to reflect on the subject. It would cost me, I fancy, with advertisements, some

£20 or £30; but the worst is, as I hear, pamphlets never will sell. And this makes me doubtful. (My italics)[47]

Darwin's vindictiveness was stronger than his thriftiness; the pamphlet was published that year under the name *Darwinism: Being an Examination of Mr. St. George Mivart's 'Genesis of Species'*.

But worse was to come. About this time Darwin's *The Descent of Man, and Selection in Relation to Sex* was published, in which he tried to account for the evolution of man through natural and sexual selection, in opposition to the views of Mivart and Wallace. The former reviewed the book in *The Quarterly Review*. In a letter to Wallace Darwin wrote: 'There is a most cutting review of me in the 'Quarterly'; I have only read a few pages. The skill and style makes me think of Mivart. I shall soon be viewed as the most despicable of men.'[48]

In his review Mivart, although paying tribute to Darwin's factual and theoretical contributions to the natural sciences, juxtaposed quotations to show that Darwin, far from being convinced of the validity of his own theories, had consistently modified and contradicted earlier statements with respect to his conclusions:

While willingly paying a just tribute of esteem to the candour which dictated these several admissions . . . it would be idle to dissemble, and disingenuous not to declare, the amount of distrust with which such repeated over-hasty conclusions and erroneous calculations inspire us. When their Author comes before us anew . . . with opinions and conclusions still more startling . . . we may well pause before we trust ourselves unreservedly to a guidance which thus again and again declares its own reiterated fallibility . . . This is the more necessary, as the Author, starting at first with an avowed hypothesis, constantly asserts it as an undoubted fact, and claims for it, somewhat in the spirit of a theologian, that it should be received as an article of faith. Thus the formidable objection to Mr. Darwin's theory, that the great break, in the organic chain between man and his nearest allies, which cannot be bridged over by any extinct or living species, is answered simply by an appeal 'to a *belief* in the general principle of evolution' . . . or by a confident statement that 'we have *every reason to believe* that breaks in the series are simply the result of many forms having become extinct . . .' So, in like manner, we are assured that 'the early progenitors of man were, *no doubt*, once covered with hair, both sexes having beards; their ears were pointed and capable of movement; their bodies were provided with a tail, having the proper muscles' . . . And finally, we are told, with a dogmatism little worthy of a philosopher, that, *unless we wilfully close our eyes*, we must recognize our parentage . . .

These are hard words; and, even at the risk of being accused of wilful blindness, we shall now proceed, with an unbiased and unprejudiced mind, to examine carefully the arguments upon which Mr. Darwin's theory rests.[49]

Ignoring Darwin's ludicrous details it must be acknowledged that he was wrong and Mivart and Wallace were right with respect to the evolution of our mental powers; that they were *not* acquired through micromutations accumulated through natural selection, they could not be. I believe that this assertion is beyond dispute today, when we know that chimpanzees can learn to use a formal language.

Of course, by invoking a metaphysical agent for this purpose, Darwin's opponents were wrong too. And it is surprising, but understandable at the same time, that they did not arrive at the proper answer which, evidently, must be that macromutations were involved. This solution ought to have been obvious to Mivart, the Macromutationist, were it not for the fact that, according to his religious convictions, man has a soul; and this, presumably, was more than a macromutation could accomplish. Wallace was not loaded with religious restraints, but as a true Darwinist he could not accept macromutations.

We may observe that Mivart's description of Darwin's approach and style is a clean hit and not unfair at all; Darwin was changing, modifying, correcting, and generally 'wriggling' in order to appease every form of criticism, and very often he did not heed the contradictions which thereby ensued.

I suppose that many others had observed how the Darwinian theory was continually changing, but Mivart was the first who ventured to unmask Darwin. He was going to suffer the rest of his life for this audacity. What we have learned so far would not seem to deserve so hard a penalty, but Darwin and his friends claimed that, apart from the purely factual criticism, the book, and in particular the review, contained personal attacks on Darwin.

Was this accusation substantiated?

Mivart's remarks of a personal nature fall into two categories. The first, and less important, is that in which Mivart repeatedly reminds the reader that Darwin was not the sole originator of the theory which had come to carry his name. Mivart was careful, perhaps too careful, to pay tribute to Wallace as the co-discoverer of the hypothesis of natural selection. Such statements Huxley righteously [?] regarded as an 'oblique and entirely unjustifiable attempt to depreciate Mr. Darwin'. Perhaps they were. To Mivart's mind, however, it was justifiable and, in a sense, honorable, to set the record straight. He felt, perhaps too strongly and with insufficient reason, that too much homage and trust was being tendered Darwin in admiration for a mind which some might regard as superhuman because of its ability to give birth to the evolutionary theory. To counter such hero-worship, that could lead only to a degradation of science, which must be based on the authority of fact alone and not that of a person, he felt it necessary to point out that the theories laid down in the *Origin*, a book ranked by some alongside Newton's *Principia*, were a product of the times and could emerge from the minds of at least two independent investigators. Furthermore, Mivart was extremely careful, in his own writings and in his treatment of those of others, regarding the matter of priority. It is not surprising that, with his regard for and friendship toward Wallace, he should seek to pay his friend the honor due to him. When set alongside many other passages in both works, in which lavish praise is paid to Darwin for his many contributions to the natural sciences, these alleged depreciations pale into insignificance; and it takes a mind peculiarly sensitive to and perceptive of the nature of personal criticism and invective to regard them in that light.

The same may be said for the more numerous passages of the second category in which Mivart takes Darwin to task for errors of method, of fact, or of philosophical views, in order to demonstrate the fallibility of the prophet. As works of criticism, neither the *Genesis* nor the review lacks statements which are critical of the author of the doctrines under review. Naturally, these critical remarks are not laudatory; nor were they intended to be. But neither can such references as these from the pen of an avowed critic be constructed as either 'insolent' or as 'unjust and unbecoming', as they were both by Huxley and by others of the Darwinian circle. When they are balanced against statements of admiration toward Darwin, contained in the same works, it is difficult to see how such critical remarks could have been interpreted as personal abuse.[50]

If Mivart's attempts to honour Wallace was a fight against the hero-worship of Darwin, then, as we know, his endeavours were a dismal failure. But under any circumstances, I cannot see that injustice was committed towards Darwin in emphasising that Wallace was one of the founders of the theory of natural selection. As to the second category we must observe that here it is the academic freedom of speech which is at stake. Does it imply a personal attack to criticise publicly the views advanced by a peer? In assuming this stand I think the Darwinian clique acted with 'religious fervour' as guardians of the infallible truth.

However this may be, Mivart had gone too far — the friends decided that he had to be punished. And Huxley voluntarily offered to be the hangman. As a personal friend Mivart's motives should have been obvious to Huxley. Mivart later formulated them as follows: 'My first object [in writing *On the Genesis of Species*] was to show that the Darwinian theory is untenable, and that natural selection is not *the* origin of species. This was and is my conviction purely as a man of science, and I maintain it upon scientific grounds only. My second object was to demonstrate that nothing even in Mr. Darwin's theory, as then put forth, and *a fortiori* in evolution generally, was necessarily antagonistic to Christianity.'[51]

To a latter-day reader Mivart's intentions are quite evident, and also that the first object was by far the most important to him, occupying the bulk of the book. And we should recall that he proposed as an alternative to Darwin's theory, a macromutation theory, coinciding, partly at least, with, and no doubt inspired by, the stand taken by Huxley at several occasions. Certainly, if the views advocated in the present volume are correct then Mivart was in the right. As far as the second object is concerned it seems that Mivart has been vindicated; even the Catholic Church has discovered that beyond the bounds of human knowledge there will always be room for God.

But Huxley set to work, writing a review called 'Mr. Darwin's critics', which appeared in the *Contemporary Review*. To Hooker he wrote from Edinburgh:

I have been reading Mivart's book . . . and the devil has tempted me to follow up his very cocky capsuling of Catholic theology based as he says upon Father Suarez. So I got some of the old Jesuit's folios out of the Library here and have been revelling in scholastic philosophy and catholic theology with the effect of discovering that Master Mivart either gushes without reading or reads without understanding . . . I am sorry . . . as Mivart is clever and not a bad fellow but he allows himself to be insolent to Darwin and I mean to pin him out. Only fancy my vindicating Catholic orthodoxy against the Papishes themselves.[52]

Darwin was also informed, and in his answer we may read:

Your letter has pleased me in many ways to a wonderful degree. I laughed over Mivart's soul till my stomach contracted into a ball, but that is a horrid sensation which you will not know. What a wonderful man you are to grapple with those old metaphysico-divinity books. It quite delights me that you are going to some extent to answer and attack Mivart. *His book, as you say, has produced a great effect* . . . It was this that made me ask Chauncey Wright to publish at my expense his article, which seems to me very clever, though ill-written. He has not knowledge enough to grapple with Mivart in detail . . . I am preparing a new Edit. of the Origin and shall introduce a new chapter in answer to miscellaneous criticisms, and I shall give up greater part to answer *Mivart's cases of difficulty of incipient structures being of no use; and I find it can be done easily*. He never states his case fairly and makes wonderful blunders . . . I shall confine myself to *details* and not enter on any general discussion with Mivart. His Genesis at first *appeared to me very formidable*, on the principle of aggregation; but after maturely considering all that he has said, *I never before in my life felt so convinced* of the *general* truth of the Origin. (My italics, except for the last ones)[53]

Nine days later Darwin had read the proofs of Huxley's attack and wrote back:

It was very good of you to send the proof-sheets, for I was *very* anxious to read your article. I have been delighted with it. How you do smash Mivart's *theology* . . . Mivart under his mild and pleasing and modest manners must have a good stick of self-sufficiency, not to say arrogance. Nothing will *hurt him so much* as this part of your review . . . I am mounting climax on climax; for after all there is nothing, I think, better in your whole review than your argument v. *Wallace* on intellect of savages. I must tell you what Hooker said to me a few years ago — 'When I read Huxley, I feel quite infantile in intellect'. By Jove I have felt the

truth of *this* [?] throughout your review. What a man you are.
There are scores of splendid passages, and vivid flashes of wit.
(My italics, except for the first ones)[54]

Let us note in passing that even Wallace belonged to those of 'Mr.
Darwin's critics' who should be exposed to Huxley's wit — or whip.

Huxley was equally admired by Hooker, who wrote to Darwin:
'I return Huxley's article which I have read with all the admiration
I can express. What a wonderful Essayist he is, and incomparable
critic, and *defender of the faithful*. Well I think you are avenged on
your enemy' (my italics).[55]

As for the review itself it turns out that '. . . nearly half of
Huxley's review, which was directed against Wallace as well as
Mivart, concerns itself with this single aspect of the theological
question [the harmony between Christian dogma and evolution],
while almost the whole of the remainder, where it does not deal with
Wallace, attempts to refute Mivart's distinctions between human and
animal intellect . . . As for his scientific objections to Darwinism,
Mivart could justifiably complain that his critic had, to an important
extent, ignored them'.[56]

And much of the review was based on Mivart's alleged misinterpretation of Suarez, the nine-line incident in his book. Huxley's
rejoinder has been called 'one of the most deadly in the history of
controversy',[57] by a judge anything but impartial, Huxley's son
Leonard. I permit myself to doubt that the general public cared about
what a Jesuit had said or not said some centuries earlier. In my
opinion 'silly' would be a better description than 'deadly'.

Mivart's reaction to Huxley's criticism was stated in a public
reply where we may read:

I felt that, as a subaltern in science, I was being severely
reprimanded by my superior officer; that I might apprehend a
sentence of degradation to the ranks, if not actual expulsion from
the service . . .

Now, recognizing as I do that, in physical science, Professor
Huxley is *indeed* my superior officer, having his just claim to
respect and deference on the part of all men of science, I also feel
that I am under special obligations to him, both many and deep,
for knowledge imparted and for ready assistance kindly rendered.
No wonder then that the expression of vehement disapproval is
painful to me.

It was not however without surprise that I learned that my one unpardonable sin — the one great offence disqualifying me for being 'a loyal solider of science' — was my attempt to show that there is no real antagonism between the Christian revelation and evolution.[58]

Mivart apparently had one great fault — he could not learn from past experience. And therefore he ventured, in a review of some works on anthropology, to criticise an article on matters of eugenics, published by young George Darwin, Charles' son. I shall not enter into details about the justification of this criticism, but only observe that this act had the consequence that Mivart was excommunicated from the scientific Establishment, and for the same reason that he was later excommunicated from the Catholic Church; his assertion of the right of freedom of speech.

Mivart had not 'acted as a gentleman', and both Darwin and Huxley broke off all relations with him, although Mivart went to great lengths in his attempts to mollify them. In fact, Huxley and Hooker and the men around them used their positions of power to ostracise Mivart. Several times, the last time in 1888, they succeeded in preventing his election to the prestigious Athenaeum Club, much desired by Mivart.[59] Irrespective of the errors he may have committed, the treatment of Mivart is a second 'black mark on the characters' of Darwin and his entourage.

I shall end this discussion of Mivart on a note of irony. In 1885 Mivart had written an article on Darwin, and sent it to Huxley, asking for comment. Huxley answered:

My dear Mr. Mivart — I return your proof with many thanks for your courtesy in sending it. I fully appreciate the good feeling shown in what you have written, but as you ask my opinion, I had better say frankly that my experience of Darwin is widely different from yours as expressed in the passages marked with pencil. I have often remarked that I never knew any one of his intellectual rank who showed himself so tolerant to opponents, great and small, as Darwin did. Sensitive he was in the sense of being too ready to be depressed by adverse comment, but I never knew any one less easily hurt by fair criticism, or who less needed to be soothed by those who opposed him with good reason
. . .

I cannot agree with you, again, that the acceptance of Darwin's views was in any way influenced by the strong affection entertained for him by many of his friends. What that affection really did was to lead those of his friends who had seen good reason for his views to take much more trouble in his defence and support, and to strike out much harder at his adversary than they would otherwise have done. This is pardonable if not justifiable — that which you suggest would to my mind be neither. (Italics superfluous)[60]

St George Mivart certainly was not an outsider by birth, but he seems to have had an unfortunate ability to make one of himself. The first time this happened was when he as a young man converted to Catholicism, thereby excluding himself from a normal academic career. Yet, his personal and intellectual qualities helped to surpass this handicap. But when later in life he dared to challenge the Establishments, first that of Darwinism, later that of the Catholic Church, his status as an outsider was irremediably established.

SAMUEL BUTLER (1835–1902)

Samuel Butler, the grandson of Dr Samuel Butler, Darwin's teacher at Shrewsbury, was also involved in a controversy with Darwin, modest compared with that of Mivart, but not without interesting points.

We may begin by hearing the testimony of Darwin, as he presented the case in his autobiography:

In 1879, I had a translation of Dr. Ernst Krause's *Life of Erasmus Darwin* published, and I added a sketch of his character and habits from materials in my possession . . . *Owing to my having accidentally omitted to mention that Dr. Krause had enlarged and corrected his article in German before it was translated, Mr. Samuel Butler abused me with almost insane virulence. How I offended him so bitterly, I have never been able to understand. The subject gave rise to some controversy in the* Athenaeum *newspaper and* Nature. I laid all the documents before some good judges, viz. Huxley, Leslie Stephen, Litchfield [his son-in-law], *etc., and they were all unanimous that the attack was so baseless that it did not deserve any public answer; for I had already expressed privately my regret to Mr. Butler for my accidental omission. Huxley consoled me by quoting some German lines from Goethe, who had been attacked by someone, to the effect 'that every Whale has its Louse'.* (My italics, except for the book title)[61]

The italicised section was deleted by the Darwin family in the published version of Darwin's autobiography; only in 1958 was the first uncensored edition published by his grand-daughter, Nora Barlow. The information thus supplied is not very illuminating, the reader rather gets the impression that Butler must indeed have been insane, if he attacked Darwin 'with almost insane virulence' because 'Dr. Krause had enlarged and corrected his article in German before it was translated'. Fortunately, Nora Barlow undertook to investigate the case closer, finding that 'the whole incident appeared to me in such a new light that I felt it must be retold in all its detail'.[62]

Initially, Butler embraced Darwin's theory with great enthusiasm, but like so many others, he later came to realise that natural selection cannot accomplish all it is supposed to do according to the Darwinian doctrine. And so he began to think and study, and developed his own theory which was in part founded on Lamarckism, in part an invention of his own, involving 'development of structure and instinct by intelligence and memory'. This theory was published in the book *Life and Habit* in 1878.[63] Here we can learn of his main criticism against Darwinism: 'To me it seems that the "Origin of Variation", whatever it is, is the only true "Origin of Species".'[64] Butler correctly points out that Darwin has neglected one very important component in the complex of theories of evolution, the one here called 'the epigenetic theory on mechanism of evolution'.

As concerns Darwin's contribution he writes:

Any one can make people see a thing if he puts it in the right way, but Mr. Darwin made us see evolution, in spite of his having put it, in what seems to not a few, an exceedingly mistaken way. Yet his triumph is complete, for no matter how much any one now moves the foundation, he cannot shake the superstructure, which has become so currently accepted as to be above the need of any support from reason, and to be as difficult to destroy as it was originally difficult of construction. Less than twenty years ago, we never met with, or heard of, any one who accepted evolution . . . Yet, now, who seriously disputes the main principles of evolution.[65]

These, certainly, were not flattering words, and I do not think that the following statement did much to improve the situation, although *prima facie* a tribute to Darwin:

It is not he who first conceives an idea, nor he who sets it on its legs and makes it go on all fours, but he who makes other people accept the main conclusion, whether on right grounds or on wrong ones, who has done the greatest work as regards the promulgation of an opinion. And this is what Mr. Darwin has done for evolution. He has made us think that we know the origin of species, and so of genera, in spite of his utmost efforts to assure us that we know nothing of the causes from which the vast majority of modifications have arisen — that is to say, he has made us think we know the whole road, though he has almost ostentatiously blindfolded us at every step of the journey. But to the end of time, if the question was asked, 'Who taught people to believe in evolution?', there can only be one answer — that it was Mr. Darwin.[66]

But as he delved into the problems he discovered Darwin's lack of originality, the idea of evolution, by then Darwin's priority, and even that of selection having been stated long before Darwin. This led him to write the book *Evolution, Old and New; Or, the Theories of Buffon, Dr. Erasmus Darwin, and Lamarck, as compared with that of Charles Darwin.*[67]

The book was published in March 1879, just as Darwin was preparing the book on Erasmus Darwin. While Krause was editing his essay for the translation, he received from Darwin a copy of Butler's book. The knowledge thus gained induced Krause to make various additions to his article, among which the following one at the end: 'Erasmus Darwin's system was in itself a most significant first step in the path of knowledge which his grandson has opened for us, but to wish to revive it at the present day, as has actually been seriously attempted, shows a weakness of thought and a mental anachronism which no one can envy.'[68] Thus, Darwin had got an ally against Butler. Unfortunately, the readers were not notified about the changes, so when Butler read the book and discovered the piques, he ordered a copy of the original article, found out about the changes and concluded that they were a covert attack on himself.

Now, in the book on Erasmus Darwin, Charles Darwin had written a Preface, containing two footnotes. The first, referring to Krause's article in *Kosmos*, reads: 'Mr. Dallas has undertaken the translation, and his scientific reputation, together with his knowledge of German, is a guarantee for its accuracy.' The second states: 'Since the publication of Dr. Krause's article, Mr. Butler's work, "Evolution, Old and New, 1879", has appeared, and this includes an account of Dr. Darwin's life, compiled from the two books just mentioned, and of his views on evolution.'[69]

Taken together, these two statements seem to exclude that Krause's contribution could contain any reference to Butler's work, and Butler therefore wrote and asked for an explanation. Darwin answered:

> Dr. Krause, soon after the appearance of his article in *Kosmos*, told me that he intended to publish it separately and to alter it considerably, and the altered MS. was sent to Mr. Dallas for translation. *This is so common a practice that it never occurred to me to state that the article had been modified*; but now I much regret that I did not do so . . . I may add that I had obtained Dr. Krause's consent for a translation, and had arranged with Mr. Dallas before your book was announced. (My italics)[70]

The last statement is interesting in so far as Darwin here assures that *Erasmus Darwin* was not planned as an attack on Butler. However, Darwin knew that Krause had seen Butler's book, and if he had read the alterations he would also know that they referred to this work. Under these circumstances it is understandable that his answer was unsatisfactory to Butler, who wrote a letter to the *Athenaeum* which ends thus:

> Mr. Darwin further says that, should there be a reprint of the English life of Dr. Darwin, he will state that the original as it appeared in *Kosmos* was modified by Dr. Krause. He does not, however, either deny or admit that the modifications of the article was made by the light of, and with a view to, my book.
>
> It is doubtless a common practice for writers to take an opportunity of revising their works, but it is not common when a covert condemnation of an opponent has been interpolated into a revised edition, the revision of which has been concealed, to declare with every circumstance of distinctness that the condemnation was written prior to the book which might appear to have called it forth, and thus lead readers to suppose that it must be an unbiased opinion.[71]

Now the matter had become public, and Darwin therefore took the trouble to look through his papers. What he found there led him to compose a letter to the *Athenaeum* in which we may read:

In my private letter to Mr. Butler I said that it was so common a practice for an author to alter an article before its republication, that it never occurred to me to state that this had been done in the present case. Afterwards a dim recollection crossed my mind that I had written something on the subject, and I looked at the first proof . . . and found in it the following passage, here copied verbatim:—

To the Compositor; Be so good as to insert inverted commas to the whole of this extract:—

'*Dr. Krause has taken great pains, and has added largely to his essay* as it appeared in *Kosmos*; and my preliminary notice, having been written before I had seen the addition, unfortunately contains much repetition of what Dr. Krause has said. In fact, the present volume contains two distinct biographies, of which *I have no doubt that by Dr. Krause is much the best*. I have left it almost wholly to him to treat of what Dr. Darwin has done in science, *more especially* in regard to evolution'.

The proof sheets were sent to Dr. Krause, with a letter in which I said that . . . as my Notice was drawn up chiefly from unpublished documents, it appeared to me best that *my account alone should appear in England* . . . Dr. Krause . . . agreed instantly to my suggestion . . . He then expressly asked me to strike out the passage above quoted, which I did; and having done so, it did not occur to me to add, as I ought to have done, that the retained parts of Dr Krause's article had been much modified . . .

[Mr. Butler] is mistaken in supposing that *I was offended by* [his] *book*, for I looked only at the part about the life of Erasmus Darwin; I did not even look at the part about evolution; for I had found in his former work that I could not make his views harmonize with what I knew. I was, indeed, told that this part contained some bitter sarcasms against me; but this determined me all the more not to read it.

As Mr. Butler evidently does not believe my deliberate assertion that the omission of any statement that Dr. Krause had altered his article before sending it for translation, was unintentional or accidental I think I shall be justified in declining to answer any future attack which Mr. Butler may make on me. (My italics)[72]

This letter was rejected by the family, so a second version was prepared:

In regard to the letter from Mr. Butler . . . I wish to state that the omission of any mention of the alterations made by Dr. Krause in his article before it was re-published had no connection whatever with Mr. Butler. I find in the proofs received from Messrs. Clowes the words: '*Dr. Krause had added largely to his essay* as it appeared in *Kosmos.*' These words were afterwards accidentally omitted, and when I wrote privately to Mr. Butler I had forgotten that they had ever been written . . . It is a mere illusion on the part of Mr. Butler to suppose that it could make any difference to *me* whether or not the public knew that Dr. Krause's article had been added to or altered before being translated. The additions were made quite independently of any suggestion or wish on my part. (My italics)[73]

Darwin's efforts on this account are honourable, both he and some of his sons were anxious to clear the air through a public statement, even though I still think that he avoided the real issue, namely, that Krause had used the book given to him by Darwin to launch an attack on Butler. But the letter was subjected to the scrutiny of the family, and Mrs Darwin, the daughter Henrietta Litchfield and her husband opposed its publication. A frantic correspondence was exchanged between Down and London. I shall quote only one letter, from Henrietta to her father:

I foresee one result of your letter that Butler will say you have been guilty of another quibble, — first you say to him that it never occurred to you to state that Krause had altered his article and then that you actually had it in the proof sheets and as you say accidentally omitted to publish it. Now Butler will say which of these two statements are true — and so it gives him scope for a whole set of fresh insults, — and with his clever pen he can make something very disagreeable out of this.[74]

Yes, no doubt. And so it was decided to let the master of polemics, Huxley, settle the matter. And he recommended to ignore Butler, writing:

I am astounded at Butler — who I thought was a *gentleman* though his last book appeared to me to be supremely foolish.
Has Mivart bitten him and given him Darwinophobia?
It is a horrid disease and I would kill any son of a

I found running loose with it without mercy. But don't you worry
with these things. Recollect what old Goethe said about his
Butlers and Mivarts:

'Hat doch der Wallfisch seine Laus
Muss auch die Meine haben?'

(Still, as the whale has his louse, I must also have mine.)[75]

Butler repeated the story in *Unconscious Memory*, published in
1880, and the family was upset again. It seems that after Darwin's
death his son Francis Darwin was anxious to reach an understanding
with Butler, but unfortunately he did not take the initiative needed.
Be this as it may, I think that the treatment of Butler is the third black
mark — a minor one perhaps — on the character of Darwin and,
notably, his advisers.

Butler's most serious criticism of Darwin is found in the book
Luck, or Cunning, As the Main Means of Organic Modification?
published in 1887, thus after the death of Darwin.[76] The book
contains a detailed analysis of the various editions of *On the Origin
of Species*, demonstrating the inconsistencies and contradictions.
Butler states that 'there is hardly an opinion on the subject of descent
with modification which does not find support in some one passage
or another of the "Origin of Species".'[77] He also clearly shows
that in the first edition of his book Darwin claimed priority for
Lamarck's first theory of evolution, by referring to it, more or less
directly, as 'my theory', etc. Butler points out that most of these
'*my*'s' were deleted in later editions, possibly under the impact of
Haeckel's works.

As far as Butler's own theory of evolution is concerned we may
observe that it is metaphysical speculation, worthy of little notice.
However, there are two rather ironical points that deserve attention.

First, since they are not empirically testable, it is always difficult
to distinguish between metaphysical theories, much depending upon
the wording with which they are formed. Nevertheless, if we try to
get at the basic idea behind the words it seems to me that Butler's
theories of 'Life and Habit' and 'Unconscious Memory' are
indistinguishable from Darwin's theory of Pangenesis, both of them
concerned about explaining the inheritance of acquired characters.

Second, it seems that Butler found an adherent to his theory in Francis Darwin, the botanist. This, at least, is the impression one gets from his article 'The Analogies of Plant and Animal Life'. In this he inquires 'whether among plants anything similar to memory or habit, as it exists among animals, may be found'.[78] These concepts are so similar to those adopted by Butler, that one understands that the latter was pleased to quote the young Darwin.

THE DISSENTERS

I have got fairly sick of hostile reviews.[79]

I must be a very bad explainer . . . Several reviews and several letters have shown me too clearly how little I am understood. I suppose 'natural selection' was a bad term.[80]

Charles Darwin

Very few of the reviews of *On the Origin of Species* accepted Darwin's views. We may get an overview of Darwin's critics by considering those compiled by David L. Hull in his book *Darwin and his Critics*,[81] namely, Joseph Dalton Hooker, William Benjamin Carpenter, Heinrich Georg Bronn, Thomas Vernon Wollaston, François Jules Pictet, Adam Sedgwick, Richard Owen, Samuel Haughton, William Hopkins, Henry Fawcett, Frederick Wollaston Hutton, Fleeming Jenkin, St George Jackson Mivart, Chauncey Wright, Karl Ernst von Baer and Louis Agassiz.

Two of these (Sedgwick and Agassiz) reject evolution outright, and three (Hooker, Hutton and Wright) accept Darwin's views with little or no reservation. The remaining eleven point out grave difficulties, and seven of them suggest that these may be overcome on the assumption that macromutations may occur. Several of the reviewers point out that Darwin's theory is Lamarckism disguised — or revised — and Chamber's book was also mentioned a couple of times. And as we have seen, of the three critics discussed above two clearly saw the need for macromutations. The only exception was Butler, and this, I think, is easily explainable by the fact that he was not a biologist.

Darwin complained this his critics did not understand him, but he did not seem to realise that almost everybody, friends, supporters and critics, agreed on one point, his natural selection cannot account for the origin of the variations, only for their possible survival. And the reasons for rejecting Darwin's proposal were many, but first of all that many innovations cannot possibly come into existence through accumulation of many small steps, and even if they can, natural selection cannot accomplish it, because incipient and intermediate stages are not advantageous. As this criticism mounted, Darwin became more and more convinced that he was right, at least he said so, and that everybody else was wrong.

10

The Interregnum

In 1883, when Weismann published his first essay on Heredity, the only English or American naturalist of note who was not subscribing to some form of the Lamarckian principle was Alfred Wallace.[1]

Henry Fairfield Osborn

The general results of this work will form an important support for the doctrine, at present especially represented by Bateson and de Vries, of the great significance of 'discontinuous' variation or 'mutation' for the theory of heredity [evolution?]. For selection in populations acts in my cases only in so far as it chooses *representatives of already existing types*. These types are not successively formed . . . but they are *found* and *isolated*.[2]

Wilhelm Johannsen

Is it possible that the significant deviations which we know as 'individual variations' can form the beginning of a process of selection? Can they decide which is to perish and which to survive? . . . To this question even one who, like myself, has been for many years a convinced adherent of the theory of selection, can only reply: *We must assume so, but we cannot prove it in any case*. It is not upon demonstrative evidence that we rely when we champion the doctrine of selection as a scientific truth; we base our argument on quite other grounds.[3]

August Weismann

We have seen that by 1870 nobody, and this includes Charles Darwin himself, believed that natural selection can accomplish all the wonders originally ascribed to it. With some notable exceptions this situation prevailed for more than half a century. However, from about 1920 an ever growing number of biologists have declared themselves adherents to a modified version of Darwin's theory or, rather, to the postulated synthesis of Darwin's and Mendel's theories.

The fifty years between 1870 and 1920 is here called the *interregnum*. We know that, owing largely to Darwin's contribution, by 1870 most people had accepted that evolution had taken place, and they even admitted that natural selection might have been involved in *the survival of the fittest*, but in agreement with criticism raised for instance by Mivart and Butler, it was repeatedly asserted that Darwin had not accounted for *the origin of the fittest*. Or, in the terminology of the present book: Through his natural selection Darwin had explained at least part of the ecological theory on the

276

mechanism of evolution, but he had made no contribution what-soever to the corresponding epigenetic theory. It was therefore natural that during the interregnum the anti-Darwinian Evolutionists sought for mechanisms capable of explaining the origin of variation, and for this purpose they turned in two directions, some became Neo-Lamarckians and some became Macromutationists.

The Neo-Lamarckians were a most influential faction during the final decades of the last century, the leading figures being American palaeontologists. We have traced the origin of the macromutation theory to Geoffroy Saint-Hilaire in France and von Baer in Germany, but subsequently the movement spread to England, being there championed by people like Chambers, Owen, Huxley and Mivart. In the continuation, particularly in the early years of the present century, the macromutation theory was on the rise, both in England and on the Continent, but less so, it seems, in America. Besides these groupings there was a dwindling flock of Darwinians who made interesting, if somewhat pathetic contributions to the history of evolutionary thought.

We shall became acquainted with these three movements in the following subsections.

THE NEO-LAMARCKIANS

There always was something seductive about Lamarckism: If organisms are adapted to their environment, then it is because they have gradually adapted themselves to the environment. This argu-ment is even simpler than Darwin's, and that may be why many people have endeavoured to revive Lamarck's theory, even in recent times.[4]

The most initiated, though not necessarily the most authentic chronicle of Neo-Lamarckism may be the one given by Alpheus S. Packard, Professor of Zoology and Geology at Brown University, in his biography of Lamarck,[5] on which the following account is based.

We shall permit Packard to state his views:

Neolamarckism . . . has for its foundation a combination of the factors suggested by the Buffon and Geoffroy St. Hilaire school, which insisted on the direct action of the *milieu*, and of Lamarck, who relied both on the direct (plants and lowest animals) and on the indirect action of environment, adding the important factors of need and of change of habits resulting either in the atrophy or in the development of organs by disuse or use, with the addition of the hereditary transmission of characters acquired in the lifetime of the individual . . .

Neolamarckism . . . adds those [factors] of geographical isolation or segregation (Wagner and Gulick), the effects of gravity, the effects of currents of air and of water, of fixed or sedentary as opposed to active modes of life, the results of strains and impacts (Ryder, Cope, and Osborn), the principle of change of function as inducing the formation of new structures (Dohrn), the effects of parasitism, commensalism, and of symbiosis — in short, the biological environment; together with geological extinction, natural and sexual selection, and hybridity.

It is to be observed that the Neolamarckian in relying mainly on these factors does not overlook the value of natural selection as a guiding principle, and which began to act as soon as the world became stocked with the initial forms of life, but he simply seeks to assign this principle to its proper position in the hierarchy of factors.

Natural selection . . . is not a *vera causa*, an initial or impelling cause in the origination of new species and genera . . .

Were the dogma of natural selection to become universally accepted, further progress would cease, and biology would tend to relapse into a stage of atrophy and degeneration. On the other hand, a revival of Lamarckism in its modern form, and a critical and doubting attitude towards natural selection as an efficient cause, will keep alive discussion and investigation.[6]

Some of the statements in the last paragraph we may endorse, but it seems doubtful if embracement of Packard's Neo-Lamarckism really is any conspicuous advance relative to the last pluralist version of Darwin's theory. Rather, in both cases we are dealing with a hotchpotch of assertions which in no way constitute a synthesis. Indeed, the elements are to a remarkable degree the same in the two instances, for it will be noticed that the macromutation theory has made its way into Packard's theory *via* Etienne Geoffroy Saint-Hilaire, whose theory is equated more or less with Buffon's.

Packard quotes about 40 American and European biologists in support of Neo-Lamarckism; in this survey he is not quite fair, for he mobilises all critics of Darwinism as supporters of his theory, among whom T.H. Huxley. There is no need to name all these people, but among them some are still remembered: Edward D.

Cope, Alpheus Hyatt, Henry F. Osborn, Herbert Spencer, George J. Romanes, J.A. Thomson, Hans Driesch, Ernst Haeckel, Wilhelm Roux, Julius von Sachs, Karl Semper, Yves Delage and Alfred Giard. It cannot be doubted that these persons were anti-Darwinians, but I wonder if all of them would have been happy to be classified as Neo-Lamarckians.

THE MACROMUTATIONISTS

Many of Darwin's continental opponents were Macromutationists, although they often did not formulate their views very explicitly. In fact, it seems that most of the people who during, and even after, the interregnum rejected Darwinism were Macromutationists. In the present context we shall discuss only three persons, William Bateson, Hugo de Vries and Wilhelm Johannsen; all three were most influential during the first two decades of the present century.

William Bateson

Studying at Cambridge, Bateson started out as a comparative embryologist and morphologist.[7] However, he soon became fascinated by the problem of evolution and came to realise, as many before him, that the mechanism of variation is the key to the mechanism of evolution. He rejected Darwin's micromutation theory and, ironically enough, also the embryological approach to the mechanism of evolution initiated by von Baer, as resting 'on an error in formal logic'.[8] As a Macromutationist he is exceptional in not being influenced by von Baer; it will be understood that from the present point of view he was thereby committing 'an error in formal logic'.

However this may be, Bateson set out to look for variations and in 1894 he published his material, collected from the literature, in *Materials for the Study of Variation, Treated with Especial Regard to Discontinuity in the Origin of Species*. The book was not a success, possibly because it was heretic, but most probably because it is, in my view, one of the most boring books on evolution ever written.

There were some people, however, who approved of Bateson's general thesis on evolution through macromutations. Thus Francis

279

Galton, Darwin's cousin, stated: 'It was . . . with the utmost pleasure that I read Mr. Bateson's work bearing the happy phrase in its title of "discontinuous variation", and rich with many original remarks and not a few trenchant expressions.'[9] And Huxley, who also received a copy, wrote to Bateson: 'I see you are inclined to advocate the possibility of considerable "saltus" on the part of Dame Nature in her variations. I always took the same view, much to Mr. Darwin's disgust, and we often used to debate it.'[10] Bateson's book initiated his controversy with the Biometricians, the defenders of Darwin's theory at the time; we shall return to this point.

The position of Bateson was radically changed in 1900, when Mendel's theory was rediscovered. As so many others, he felt that the two primary weaknesses of Darwin's theory were: (i) The negligible selective value of small variations, and (ii) the swamping effect of blending inheritance. In his view both of these difficulties were overcome by Mendel's observations and the theory to which they gave rise, which, he asserted, support 'discontinuous evolution', i.e. macromutations.[11]

Hugo de Vries

Hugo de Vries had written extensively on biological inheritance before he rediscovered Mendel's work in 1900. He believed that each hereditary character is represented and determined by a definite material particle located in the germ cell; he called such particles 'pangens'. He had further become convinced that evolutionary changes are associated with alterations, 'mutations', in these pangens. Through his experimental work, especially on *Oenothera lamarckiana*, he had observed that the effects of mutations at times may be quite extensive, and thus he became a Macromutationist. This of course implies that he rejected the power of natural selection to accomplish large changes through the accumulation of slight ones. He published his views in the two-volume work *Die Mutationstheorie*, the first part of which appeared in 1900, the year he became aware of Mendel's paper published 35 yers earlier.

Bateson and de Vries met in 1899 at an international conference in England, and finding common interests in the macromutation theory and in their dislike of the Darwinian Micromutationists, they immediately became friends. But in contrast to Bateson de Vries did not consider Mendelism very important for evolution, a circumstance which impaired their relationship.

The impact of de Vries's *Mutationstheorie* upon biologists was enormous. For many reasons biologists had become disillusioned with Darwin's idea of natural selection, and de Vries presented the first experimental evidence to support another view of the mechanism of evolution. Many biologists accepted de Vries's new theory outright, and the response was generally favourable. There were, to be sure, many old-guard Darwinists who retained their ideas. But the idea of evolution in the first decade[s] of the twentieth century was dominated by the surge of interest in the mutational leaps of de Vries.

The effect of de Vries's mutation theory was heightened by the growing interest in Mendelian heredity, which was demonstrated so many times with discontinuous characters between 1900 and 1910. The connection between Mendel's discontinuous variations and discontinuous evolution, although not emphasised by de Vries himself, was made by many other biologists. *Many of the important adherents of Mendelian heredity during these years were also adherents of discontinuous evolution.* (My italics)[12]

As the Darwinians began to close their ranks in the last years of the second decade, de Vries's *Oenothera* experiments were heavily criticised.

In 1918 H.J. Muller suggested . . . that the *Oenotheras* . . . represent a complicated case of balanced lethals. The proof of Muller's hypothesis had already been demonstrated for *Oenothera Lamarckiana* by Renner in 1917, but his work was not generally known until later. The reliability of mutations in *Oenothera* as a proof of the mutation theory of evolution was severely shaken by 1918 even though the actual genetic mechanisms were not generally known. Because de Vries's major proof had come from the *Oenotheras*, skepticism about his mutation theory increased.[13]

This scepticism was partly misdirected, but de Vries could blame himself. He had made the claim that his various strongly divergent varieties of *Oenothera* represent new species, which were duly named according to the established rules. This notion certainly does not conform to general observation, and makes *Oenothera* a rather unique genus. But this extravagant claim made by de Vries ought not to overshadow the fact that he had observed and experimented with one-step variations which justifiably may be called 'macro-mutations'.

Wilhelm Johannsen

Johannsen gained world fame from his studies on the heredity of 'pure lines' in beans, which were aimed at settling the issue between the macromutation theory advocated by Bateson and de Vries, and Darwin's micromutation theory.

Johannsen also made a contribution to biology by coining the names of 'gene', 'genotype' and 'phenotype'. The relationship between the last two concepts may be stated thus: genotype + environment → phenotype. From this expression it follows that two organisms of the same genotype may well have different pheno-types, if, that is, they live in different environments. Lamarckians will claim that such phenotypic variations are inheritable, but all other biologists expect identity of the offspring with respect to mean and range of variation to be completely independent of the pheno-type in this special case.

Johannsen's pure lines represent the offspring of single beans from a particular crop, each of which is characterised with respect to various size parameters. It is well known that the size of peas and beans depends on their position in the pod, and if the variation in Johannsen's peas depended *only* on this factor, then he should be able to record the expected invariance in the offspring. Johannsen claimed that his results confirmed the prediction, and thus, on his own premises he had falsified Lamarckism.

Had he also falsified Darwinism? In order to do this, it is necessary to operate with inheritable variations, and this evidently requires the occurrence of different genotypes. However, beans can reproduce through self-fertilisation, and under these circumstances the various plants have identical genotypes. If this situation obtains, all variation is due to environmental influences, and selection should therefore be without any effect. So if Johannsen's pure lines were indeed homozygous, then his finding '. . . that selection has had no reliably demonstrable influence'[14] had no bearing on the question he set out to answer, namely whether there are individual differences which are inheritable. The importance of such variations for the process of evolution is of course quite a different matter.

THE NEO-DARWINIANS

In a quotation at the head of this chapter it is stated that in 1883 Wallace was the only English or American naturalist who had not to some extent accepted Lamarck's notion on the inheritance of acquired characters. This assertion is correct only to the extent that the Macromutationists are neglected; Owen and Mivart certainly had no Lamarckian leanings. Darwin had died the year before, but it would have made no difference if he had been alive, for as we have seen, Darwin felt obliged to supplement his own theory with Lamarck's theory on the mechanism of evolution. In fact, Wallace was a rather unfortunate example in the given context; he might have refuted Lamarckism, but he admitted that natural selection alone cannot account for evolution.

The question therefore arises: Were there any naturalists towards the end of the last century who believed that Darwin's natural selection suffices to explain the mechanism of evolution? There were indeed such persons around — for instance August Weismann in Germany, and Walter F.R. Weldon and Karl Pearson in England; in the present context they are treated together under the slightly misleading name 'Neo-Darwinians'. As will appear, these three persons turn out to be quixotic figures in the history of biology.

August Weismann

August Weismann published his book *On Heredity* in 1883, in which he set forth his germ plasm theory. Influenced by von Nägeli and Haeckel he started out from unicellular organisms, observing that the mutual resemblance from one generation to the following one is a consequence of the fact that the individual organisms propagate by division. Hence, every protistan is a segment of a previous one, and therefore there exists in them a '*Continuität des Individuums*'.[15]

In multicellular organisms this continuity exists only in the germ cells; these, and these alone, can ensure the origin of new organisms similar to the old ones. The soma, that is, the body, is just a side branch to the succession of germ cells, the germ line, which constitutes the basis of life. The germ cells thus contain the information, in the form of a germ plasm, which is required for the creation of a new body. This idea was not particularly original; Galton, for instance, had published similar views before.

Weismann further claimed that the germ cells are completely shielded off from the soma, so that no changes in the latter can ever affect the former. Hence, acquired characteristics *cannot* be inherited, and Lamarck's theory is therefore refuted. Even this had been said before by Galton, a fact which went largely unnoticed.

In fact, Weismann became 'more Darwinian than Darwin himself', considering that if 'Lamarckism' and Buffonism had been refuted, all that remained of 'Darwinism' was natural selection. This, of course, was a mistake since Darwin also allowed for macromutations.

Weismann was criticised by Spencer, who wrote an article on 'The Inadequacy of Natural Selection',[16] in which he declared that natural selection cannot account for what Darwin called 'correlated variation', and Wallace, less appropriately, called 'co-adaptation'. These expressions are used to denote the fact that when one component of the body, say, the vertebrae in the neck of the giraffe, undergoes changes, then various other components, muscles, nerves, blood vessels, etc., must change correspondingly. In Spencer's view all these modifications could not possibly proceed harmoniously, if they were the result of the accumulation of slight fortuitous variations.

Wallace, who became involved in the dispute, very sensibly observed

> . . . that the very thing said to be impossible by variation and natural selection has been again and again effected by variation and artificial selection. During the process of formation of such breeds as the greyhound or the bull-dog, of the race-horse and cart-horse, of the fantail pigeon or the otter-sheep [Ancon sheep], many co-ordinate adjustments have been produced; and no difficulty has occurred, whether the change has been effected by a single variation — as in the last case named — or by slow steps, as in all the others.[17]

Wallace is here admitting the existence of macromutations in the one case specifically recorded in the literature, the Ancon sheep. But ought he not then to admit that the evolution of some other mammals, otters, martens, ermines, squirrels, etc., had originated by homologous mutations? And with what right did he assert that *all* the other forms had arisen in small steps, this certainly is not true for the 'bull-dog', and hardly any other domesticated animals either, even if the relevant knowledge may not have been available to Darwin and himself?

To the volume celebrating the 50th anniversary of *On the Origin of Species* Weismann contributed an article called 'The Selection Theory'. After having rejected, if not refuted Lamarckism and the macromutation theory on three pages, he proceeds in the Darwinian fashion to present observational evidence to sustain the theory of natural selection. In this context he poses various questions, among which the first, and his answer to it, are quoted at the head of this chapter.

Another question is the following one:

How does it happen *that the necessary beginnings of a useful variation are always present?* . . .

It is of no use answering to this that the question is wrongly formulated and that it is the converse that is true; that the process of selection takes place in accordance with the variations that present themselves. This proposition is undeniably true, but so is also another, which apparently negatives it; the variation required has in the majority of cases actually presented itself. Selection cannot solve this contradiction; it does not call forth the useful variation, but simply works upon it.[18]

He goes on to discuss 'Coadaptation', beginning by refuting Spencer's solution which involves Lamarck's theory. Yet, he must still have found the objections against his theory weighty, for he sacrifices one of its fundamental principles, the separation between germ cells and soma in order to explain the occurrence of co-adaptation. He writes:

In every being of complex structure thousands of primary constituents must go to make a single id; these I call *determinants*, and I mean by this name very small individual particles, far below the limit of microscopic visibility, vital units which feed, grow, and multiply by division. These determinants control the parts of the developing embryo, — in what manner need not here concern us. The determinants differ among themselves, those of a muscle are differently constituted from those of a nerve-cell or a glandular cell, etc., and every determinant is in its turn made up of minute vital units, which I call *biophors*, or the bearers of life. According to my view, these determinants not only assimilate, like every other living unit, but they *vary* in the course of their growth, as every living unit does; they may vary qualititatively if the elements of which they are composed vary, they may grow and divide more or less rapidly, and their variations give rise to *corresponding* variation of the organ, cell, or cell-group which they determine. That they are undergoing ceaseless fluctuations in regard to size and quality seems to me the inevitable consequence of their unequal nutrition; for although the germ-cell as a whole usually receives sufficient nutriment minute fluctuations in the amount carried to different parts within the germ-plasm cannot fail to occur.

Now, if a determinant, for instance of a sensory cell, receives for a considerable time more abundant nutriment than before, it will grow more rapidly — become bigger, and divide more quickly, and, later, when the id concerned develops into an embryo, this sensory cell will become stronger than in the parents, possibly even twice as strong. This is an instance of a *hereditary individual variation*, arising from the germ.[19]

Weismann's theory reminds of Darwin's Pangenesis theory, except that the soma is not claimed to decide which determinants shall be better nourished than the remaining ones. But in that case only two possibilities prevail, either the plan of nutrition is predetermined in the germ cell, or else it is settled by chance. In the former case both ontogenesis and evolution seem to be predetermined, in the latter the advance is fortuitous. In either case there is little to do for natural selection. Furthermore, it is questionable whether a random doubling of one particular cell type is compatible with harmonious development, and surely this mechanism is not borne out by any empirical observations.

Weismann ends his article in the following way: 'All parts of the organism are tuned to one another, that is, *they are adapted to one another*, and in the same way *the organism as a whole is adapted to the conditions of its life, and it is so at every stage of its evolution*.

But all adaptations *can* be referred to selection, the only point that remains doubtful is whether they all *must* be referred to it.

However that may be, whether the *Lamarckian principle* is a factor that has cooperated with selection in evolution, or whether it is altogether fallacious, the fact remains, that selection is the cause of a great part of the phyletic evolution of organisms on our earth.[20]

The preceding discussion shows that with time Weismann changed his view as regards the continuity of the individual, displacing it from the cell to the 'germ-substance', which he envisaged to be located in the chromosomes. This idea of his is current orthodoxy today, but it is hardly correct; personally I have more confidence in Weismann's first theory — that the germ-plasm is located in the germ cells proper, notably, of course in the egg.[21]

Walter F.R. Weldon and Karl Pearson

Weldon was a biologist who after initial studies in London went to Cambridge in 1878 to study with Francis Balfour. The latter was influenced by von Baer and Haeckel, and wanted to study evolution from the epigenetic angle, that is, through comparative embryology. Weldon did some work on embryology, and continued this work after Balfour's death in 1882.[22]

However, it later turned out that he had a truly Empiricist leaning; he wanted to do quantitative biology, to *measure the pace of evolution* under the influence of natural selection. On one occasion he stated his view on the study of evolution in the following way:

> It cannot be too strongly urged that *the problem of animal evolution is essentially a statistical problem*: that before we can properly estimate the changes at present going on in a race or species, we must know accurately (a) the percentage of animals which exhibit a given amount of abnormality with regard to a particular character; (b) the degree of abnormality of other organs which accompanies a given abnormality of one; (c) the difference between the death rate per cent in animals of different degrees of abnormality with respect to any organ; (d) the abnormality of offspring in terms of the abnormality of parents and *vice versa*. These are all questions of arithmetic; and when we know the numerical answers to these questions for a number of species, we shall know the deviation and the rate of change in these species at the present day — *a knowledge which is the only legitimate basis for speculations as to their past history, and future fate*. (The first and the last italics are mine)[23]

Considering that Weldon was an avowed Micromutationist and that he wanted to study the evolution of wild animals, the programme outlined is extremely ambiguous; particularly in the light of his

287

desire to predict the future course of evolution.

Initially, Weldon did not know enough mathematics to realise his plans, so he welcomed Galton's *Natural Inheritance*, published in 1889, which furnished him with what he needed — a statistical method for analysing correlations. As an Empiricist, his interest was focused on Galton's *method*, not his conclusions. For Galton had committed himself to macromutations in 1869, and he had also submitted a law of regression according to which the mean of the offspring with respect to a characteristic always lies closer to the mean of the total population than to that of the parents. This generalisation, which seems to be ignored today, would if true represent the falsification of Darwin's micromutation theory.

In 1891 Weldon came to University College in London, where he became a colleague of the mathematician Karl Pearson, who also was much influenced by Galton's book. They became friends, and as good Darwinian Micromutationists they set out to save Darwinism from Galtonism, just as Weismann had saved it from Lamarckism. It fell upon Pearson to demonstrate that Galton had got his mathematics all wrong and that, consequently, his law of regression was a flaw. I believe that Pearson was right in his claim, but it should be noted that a falsification of Galton's law of regression does not imply a vindication of the micromutation theory.

This was what Weldon, the zoologist, tried to supply. We have already seen that the information he deemed necessary to demonstrate evolutionary change is impossible to obtain in a natural population. Nevertheless he tried to establish whether selection takes place between birth and the adult stage in crabs found at Plymouth. I shall not enter into details except to mention that he found the chosen parameter, the relative frontal breadth of the carapace, to change with age, and from this he concluded that in the course of life there is a selective elimination which is somehow associated with the shape of the carapace.[24]

Weldon's paper contained a lot of mathematics, but rested on a frail biological basis, and therefore it was heavily attacked. According to Pearson the reason was the following: 'The very notion that the Darwinian theory might after all be capable of statistical demonstration seemed to excite all sorts and conditions of men to hostility . . . The need for further investigation of the law of growth had been frankly admitted by Weldon in the remarks issued at the discussion of the report, but the critics declined to wait till further results were published.'[25] But Pearson himself joined the chorus of complaint, denying 'that Weldon had demonstrated the operation of a selective death rate, pointing out that the report's conclusion rested on assumptions about the crab's mode of growth that were both *unproven* and *improbable*' (my italics).[26]

But the burning issue at the time, and still today, is not selection but mutation; that is, macromutations versus micromutations. As we know, many English biologists at the time were in favour of the first alternative; these included Galton and Bateson who were also in close contact with Weldon and Pearson. The former was hailed by Weldon and Pearson as the founder of biometrics, and by Bateson as a Macromutationist.

Apparently the work published in Galton's and Weldon's early papers made impact, for the Royal Society reacted positively to a proposal suggesting the establishment of a committee on biometrics. With Galton as chairman the 'Committee for Conducting Statistical Inquiries into the Measurable Characteristics of Plants and Animals' was set up in 1894. From the name of this committee the biometricians were entitled to believe it would be a forum for their work, conducted in a Micromutationist spirit. In the following year the dispute began between Bateson and Weldon, which resulted in the break-up of their friendship and ultimately to a change in the membership of Galton's committee, and in its name, which became the 'Evolution Committee of the Royal Society'.[27] This was the first great defeat of the biometricians.

When Mendel's theory was rediscovered in 1900, it was claimed by the Macromutationists to be a vindication of their theory. It is true that the characteristics used by Mendel in his studies on peas were relatively large variations — green or yellow, wrinkled or smooth, etc. But there were good reasons why Mendel's work ought not to upset the biometric defenders of Darwinism: (i) If the variations had been so slight as supposed by the micromutation theory, Mendel could not have observed them in the first place. Mendel's observations might substantiate the existence of relatively large variations, but it surely did not disprove the existence of slight ones. (ii) Anyhow, the variations studied by Mendel were not of the type involving gradual variation, which by necessity forms the biometrician's object of study.

Nevertheless, Weldon and Pearson bet on the wrong horse and rejected Mendelism. This had little consequence for Weldon, who died prematurely in 1906. Pearson lived for another 30 years, long enough to experience the rise of Mendelian population genetics. This theory is claimed to be a micromutation theory of evolution; in R.A. Fisher's view even a synthesis between Darwinism, Mendelism and biometrics. Yet, Pearson's aversion towards Mendelism was so great that he never accepted this attempt at reconciliation.

THE CRUSADERS

Towards the close of the nineteenth century the influence of Darwinism began noticeably to wane.[28]

Erik Nordenskiöld

The final decades of the last and the first decades of the present century were a period of fighting between advocates of theories of evolution intended to be alternatives to Darwinism, and those few who remained faithful to Darwin's theory. As we have seen, the defence of Darwinism was either awkward or treacherous, and certainly the champions were not able to bring forward empirical evidence in favour of their view. But the opponents did not fare much better, so it was a war of believers, a crusade.

But during the first decades of this century one could observe the signs of the Darwinian 'renaissance', and in the 1920s the revolution had seriously begun. But that is the subject of the next chapter.

11

The Neo-Mendelians

When we cast our minds back over the history of biological theories, both in the last quarter of the nineteenth century and in the first quarter of this, it is, I submit, a question worth considering whether a sympathetic contract with mathematical ideas would not have induced such continuity in the grasp of the logical purport of the arguments used at different periods as would have obviated the chaotic misunderstandings which are so marked a feature of this history. Incidentally I believe that the popular reputation of biology will be raised, and some of the *point* of mathematics will be more widely recognized, the more thorough and extensive such intellectual contact can be made.[1]

R.A. Fisher

The present chapter deals with the founders of the currently acclaimed theory of evolution. This theory is usually called *Neo-Darwinism*, but as this term had been applied to Weismann's theory, the names *The Synthetic Theory* or *The Modern Synthesis* are considered more appropriate by many. These names imply that the ruling theory is a synthesis between Darwinism and Mendelism. Before we come to the end of this chapter I hope it shall be apparent that this is a mistake; the current theory has little, if anything, in common with Darwinism except that it is a micromutation theory. But since Lamarckism is also a micromutation theory, it is evident that both names mentioned above are misleading; as already pointed out, the theory ought to be called either *Mendelian Population Genetics* or, better still, *Neo-Mendelism*.[2]

R.A. Fisher, J.B.S. Haldane and Sewall Wright are the founding fathers of Neo-Mendelism; it was their work which inspired those who ensured the triumph of the theory.

RONALD ALYMER FISHER (1890–1962)

R.A. Fisher was a mathematical prodigy. He came to Cambridge in 1909, and very soon began to produce papers which were so sophisticated that accomplished and established mathematicians could not follow his reasoning!

At Cambridge he became acquainted with the work of Karl

291

Pearson, and began to take an interest in evolution. But Fisher accepted Mendelism, and aspired to reconcile this theory with the Darwinian micromutation theory and biometrics; as might be expected, he was opposed in these endeavours as much by the Macromutationists as by the biometricians. Fisher spent many years at the Rothamsted Experimental Station, where he made outstanding contributions to science by developing the theory and practice of statistical evaluation of experimental data. Finally he became Arthur Balfour Professor of Genetics at Cambridge University.[3]

It must be understood that Fisher first and foremost was a mathematician; his whole approach to science was influenced by this fact. An example of his dogmatic belief in the virtues of mathematics is quoted at the head of this chapter. Elsewhere in the same paper he makes the following statement:

A mathematician, if he is of *any* use, is of use as an expert in the process of reasoning, by which we pass from a theory to its logical consequences, or from an observation to the inferences which must be drawn from it. Speaking thirty years ago, it would have been proper to speak of mathematics as providing the technique only of deductive reasoning. Such a limitation would no longer be appropriate at the present time; for, owing primarily to the work of 'Student' [W.S. Gosset], mathematically exact inferences *can* now be drawn from the sample to the population — from the particular to the general — in an important and increasing class of cases. I refer to the Tests of Significance. The importance of this advance, for human thought in general, is, I believe, roughly equivalent to that of the first mathematically exact use of deductive reasoning, by the Greek geometers of the generation of Euclid. It is not my purpose now to enter into the logical revolution effected by 'Student's' work; but it has this immediate bearing on our subject, that, whereas the points in which the physicist requires mathematical aid lie chiefly in the deduction from a theory of its logical consequences, the biologist most frequently needs assistance in the inductive process by which general theoretical conclusions are drawn from bodies of observational data.[4]

Fisher here makes some extraordinary epistemological assertions. First, he claims that the fundamental shortcoming of induction, the impossibility to proceed from the particular to the general, has been overcome by the invention of statistical methods of

292

significance, notably 'Student's' *t*-test. This, I believe, is somewhat of an exaggeration. Statistical evaluations of empirical observations are of great value, notably when there are many observations to survey, and when the differences are slight. But a conclusion based on a few distinct values is as certain and empirically significant as one derived by means of statistics. And what can we say about the 'mathematical exactness' of an inference based on a value of P lying between 0.05 and 0.10? It is true that a 'conclusion' based on many observations is less likely to be falsified than one based on a handful, but we do not know what the future hides; we can never be sure that our next observation will not falsify all those preceding it.

The application of a test of significance implies the testing of at least one hypothesis, the null hypothesis. But such a testing entails nothing more than the establishment of a fact. Facts *per se* represent *knowledge*, but what we strive for is *understanding*, and this we obtain by establishing causal connections between some of the several facts we know. And such connections are conjectures which can be corroborated by logically deducing their empirical consequences, and testing the validity of the latter through observation.

This is the approach which Fisher envisages to hold for physics, but it is generally valid for all empirical sciences; so he is mistaken when he asserts that a difference obtains between physics and biology in this respect. There are more objections that could be raised against Fisher's epistemology, but the present ones may suffice.

Fisher's confidence in the supremacy of mathematics as an infallible guide towards the truth has an interesting consequence; he appears to believe that his mathematical demonstrations constitute empirical evidence. Thus, as far as his theory of evolution is concerned, '. . . he is quite *indifferent* as to the *cause* of mutations, *so long as they are produced somehow*, with the *rather minute frequency* necessary to maintain a stock, or pool, of heritable variability. *Given that heritable variability*, it can be seen, or rather, I should say, it can be *rigorously demonstrated*, that differences in the rates of death and reproduction will produce a *constant modification* of the species, in whatever directions lead to a *more perfect adaptation* to the circumstances in which it exists' (my italics).[5]

It is beyond my comprehension that anybody engaged in the study of evolution can 'be quite indifferent as to the cause of mutations'. It would be easy to explain Fisher's attitude as a consequence of his being a mathematician, but I believe that many biologists have shared this view. The quoted statement will probably be readily endorsed by population geneticists, but it should be pointed out that in spite of Fisher's assurance, the phenomenon he describes has never been observed taking place.

But now it is time to study his particular theory of evolution. Beginning with a paper in 1918, Fisher published a series of articles on the mathematics of Mendelian inheritance, and also some experimental observations, all with reference to the problem of evolution. In 1930 his main views were put forth in the book *The Genetical Theory of Natural Selection*.[6]

Immediately we meet with some noteworthy statements in the Preface.

> Natural Selection is not Evolution. Yet, ever since the two words have been in common use, the theory of Natural Selection has been employed as a convenient abbreviation for the theory of Evolution by means of Natural Selection, put forward by Darwin and Wallace. This has had the unfortunate consequence that the theory of Natural Selection itself has scarcely ever, if ever, received separate consideration . . . The overwhelming importance of evolution to the biological sciences partly explains why the theory of Natural Selection should have been so fully identified with its role as an evolutionary agency, as to have suffered neglect as an independent principle worthy of scientific study.
>
> The other biological theories which have been put forward, either as auxiliaries, or as the sole means of organic evolution, are not quite in the same position. For advocates of Natural Selection have not failed to point out, what was evidently the chief attraction of the theory to Darwin and Wallace, that it proposes to give an account of the means of modification in the organic world *by reference only to 'known', or independently demonstrable causes*. The alternative theories of modification rely, avowedly, on hypothetical properties of living matter which are inferred from the facts of evolution themselves. Yet, although this distinction has often been made clear, its logical cogency could never be fully developed in the absence of a separate investigation of the independently demonstrable modes of causation which are claimed as its basis. The present book, with all the limitations of a first attempt, is at least an attempt to consider the theory of Natural Selection on its own merits. (My italics)[7]

There are two points to notice here: (i) Fisher attempts to distinguish between 'the theory of Evolution by means of Natural

Selection' and 'Natural Selection' proper, proposing to present a separate study of the latter. This claim seems rather astounding; is it really possible to have natural selection without having evolution at the same time? From the book it does not appear to be so, for it deals to a very large part with evolution. (ii) The confidence in the theory of Darwin and Wallace is remarkably high, as revealed by the statement emphasised by me.

The first chapter deals with *The Nature of Inheritance*. Fisher here compares blending and Mendelian inheritance, asserting that a main source of Darwin's difficulties depends on the fact that he believed in the former theory which implies a steady loss of variation, and therefore requires a constant supply of new variation. We have already seen that this is a misunderstanding; if Darwin had allowed for inbreeding, he could have resolved this obstacle readily. In this context Fisher also declares his absolute adherence to the micromutation theory, and his belief that the mutations, observed for instance in *Drosophila*, are representative of the variation, whether deleterious or beneficial, which is involved in evolution.

In the summary Fisher makes an interesting assertion:

The whole group of theories which ascribe to hypothetical physiological mechanisms, controlling the occurrence of mutations, a power of directing the course of evolution, must be set aside, once the blending theory of inheritance is abandoned. The sole surviving theory is that of Natural Selection, and it would appear impossible to avoid the conclusion that *if any evolutionary phenomenon appears to be inexplicable on this theory, it must be accepted at present merely as one of the facts which in the current state of knowledge does seem inexplicable.* (My italics)[8]

Fisher does not exactly state that if empirical facts do not agree with his theory, then the facts must be false. But he is not very far from this point, and he certainly seems to have raised a shield protecting the theory from any attempts at falsification.

The following chapter, called *The Fundamental Theorem of Natural Selection*, is, I believe, the most important in the book. I have mentioned that, as a young man, Fisher managed to write papers unintelligible to his seniors and this appears to be a habit which followed him through life, for later in his career '. . . mathematical statisticians and geneticists were to complain that Fisher's proofs contained intuitive leaps which were not obvious'.[9]

It seems that Fisher was aware of and not too much concerned

295

by this state of affairs, for he writes in the Preface: 'No efforts of mine could avail to make the book easy reading.'[10] Perhaps not, but I am sure he could have done a lot to make it *easier* reading. In this context I am thinking less of the mathematics, with respect to which I am in the same predicament as the vast majority of biologists, and perhaps a substantial number of geneticists, namely, that I cannot follow the argument. No, I refer to the written text, of which the following is an example:

> This definition will appear the more appropriate if, *as is necessary for precision*, the population used to determine its value comprises, not merely the whole of a species in any one generation attaining maturity, but is conceived to contain all the genetic combinations possible, with frequencies appropriate to their actual probabilities of occurrence and survival, whatever these may be, and if the average is based upon the statures attained by all these genotypes in all possible environmental circumstances, with frequencies appropriate to the actual probabilities of encountering these circumstances. The statistical concept of the excess in stature of a given gene substitution will then be *an exact one*, not dependent upon chance as must *any practical estimate* of it, but only upon the genetic nature and environmental circumstances of the species. (My italics)[11]

I vaguely grasp Fisher's meaning. However, in aiming at a precision superior to anything empirically observable, I think we witness another example of Fisher's preference for the ideal world. It is not so easy to use calculus on the green and yellow colours of Mendel's peas, and Fisher was therefore obliged to adopt a biometric approach. Thus, he used actuarial tables dealing with human mortality and fertility as models for survival and reproduction. In this context he introduced a new concept, which '. . . measures the relative rate of increase or decrease of a population when in the steady state appropriate to any such system. In view of the emphasis laid by Malthus upon the "law of geometric increase" m may appropriately be termed the Malthusian parameter of population increase. It evidently supplies in its negative values an equally good measure of population decrease, and so covers cases to which, in respect of mankind, Malthus paid too little attention.'[12]

Malthus lived in a period when, like today, human ingenuity allowed for an increase in food supply, and hence in the number of people. This may be why he was especially concerned about the danger involved in the numerical increase of the human population. But Darwin and Wallace were sufficiently acquainted with biological reality to understand that this situation does not prevail under natural conditions. *Except for some very rare occasions, it holds that* $m = 0$. This is Darwin–Wallace's *Malthusian axiom*, which implies that *Nature generally is sated with the organisms living at any point of time; for every organism born another similar one must die.* For some reason Fisher does not mention this axiom, which surely is the foundation of any theory claiming to be Darwinian.

It should be noted that if m represents the *relative* rate of increase, one might expect that $m = 1$ would represent numerical constancy, with values above and below this value standing for increase and decrease, respectively. It may be inferred from the quotation that to Fisher $m = 0$ symbolises constant census. A remarkable thing about the Malthusian parameter is that besides representing the change in population number, we learn that m also 'measures fitness by the objective fact of representation in future generations'.[13]

We must now turn to what Fisher himself considered his greatest contribution to evolutionary theory, *the fundamental theorem of natural selection.* Mathematically, it has the following form:

$$\Sigma \alpha d p = W d t,$$

where α is the average effect upon m of introducing a certain gene, and p its frequency, W the total genetic variance in fitness and t the time. Formulated in words the theorem says: '*The rate of increase in fitness of any organism at any time is equal to its genetic variance in fitness at that time.*'[14] As Fisher assumes $W > 0$, his creation might also be called the *theorem of progressive evolution*, at least if 'organism' is replaced by 'population' or 'species'. On this point there is thus a distinct difference between Darwin and Fisher.

An immediate concern is the testability of the predictions of the theorem. Fisher apparently did not question the feasibility of this undertaking, for he wrote: '*The rigour of the demonstration* requires that the terms employed should be used *strictly as defined*; the ease of its interpretation may be increased by *appropriate conventions of measurement.* For example, the frequencies p should *strictly be evaluated at any instant by the enumeration, not necessarily of the census population, but of all individuals having reproductive value, weighted according to the reproductive value, of each*' (my italics).[15] From this quotation one gets the impression that Fisher is as ambitious as Weldon was with respect to the Plymouth crabs!

Yet, even if it may be difficult to make exact measurements, we can at least try to derive some of the consequences of Fisher's ideas. First, having two measures of fitness, we may write

$$m \approx \Sigma\alpha\mathrm{d}p = W\,\mathrm{d}t.$$

Before we discuss Fisher's theorem, let us first look at his own comments:

It will be noticed that the fundamental theorem proved above bears some *remarkable* resemblances to the second law of thermodynamics. Both are properties of populations, or aggregates, true irrespective of the nature of the units which compose them; both are statistical laws; each requires the constant increase of a measurable quality, in the one case the entropy of a physical system and in the other the fitness, measured by m, of a biological population. As in the physical world we can conceive of theoretical systems in which dissipative forces are wholly absent, and in which the entropy consequently remains constant, so we can conceive, though we need not expect to find, biological populations in which the genetic variance is absolutely zero, and in which fitness does not increase. Professor Eddington has recently remarked that 'The law that entropy always increases — the second law of thermodynamics — holds, I think, the supreme position among the laws of nature'. It is not a little instructive that so similar a law should hold *the supreme position* among the biological sciences. While it is possible that both may ultimately be absorbed by some more general principle, for the present we should note that the laws as they stand present profound differences — (1) The systems considered in thermodynamics are permanent; species on the contrary are liable to extinction, although *biological improvement must be expected to occur up to the end of their existence*. (2) Fitness, although measured by a uniform method, is qualitatively different for every different organism, whereas entropy, like temperature, is taken to have the same meaning for all physical systems. (3) Fitness may be increased or decreased by changes in the environment, without reacting quantitatively upon that environment. (4) Entropy changes are exceptional in the physical world in being irreversible, while irreversible evolutionary changes form no exception among biological phenomena. Finally, (5) entropy changes lead to a progressive disorganization of the physical

298

world, at least from the human standpoint of the utilization of energy, while evolutionary changes are generally recognized as producing *progressively higher organization in the organic world*. (My italics)[16]

We have seen that according to the Malthusian axiom $m = 0$ is the most usual state in Nature; consequently both fitness and variance in fitness will generally assume the value zero. Fisher does not arrive at this conclusion; rather, he claims that, like entropy, the fitness will always increase. He can conceive populations in which fitness and fitness variance are zero, but, most surprisingly, he does not expect to find any. The situation corresponding to negative values of these parameters is not mentioned at all, or rather, it is asserted that in species on the way to extinction ($m < 0$) biological improvement (i.e. increase in fitness, thus $m > 0$) ought to occur as long as they exist. This seems to imply a contradiction in terms of mathematics, and surely one in biology too; just imagine a population becoming more and more fit the closer it comes to extinction.

It seems to me that Fisher's definitions imply that when the members of two taxa are engaged in competition, the typical outcome is a numerical census increase in one of them, and a corresponding decrease in the other one. As long as the fight goes on, the former taxon — or population — has positive, and the latter negative values of fitness and fitness variation. When the replacement is completed, i.e. when only one taxon survives, the fitness of the victors returns to zero.

This fluctuation in the value of m shows that it does not represent something which is typical of the organisms themselves: rather, it is a function of their environment. Although it is true that the environments must be involved in deciding what is, and what is not fitness, the general opinion will probably assert that fitness is a measure of properties possessed by living organisms. But whereas the majority of Evolutionists presumably will agree with Darwin that the accomplishment of natural selection is adaptive and not progressive evolution, Fisher clearly states that evolution 'produces progressively higher organization in the organic world'.

In a later chapter (see pp. 382–4) I propose to show that the phenomenon of dominance, responsible for progressive evolution, corresponds closely to Fisher's 'fitness', for it shares the property with entropy that it can change only in one direction, having undergone a steady increase in many phylogenetic lineages in the course of evolution.

However, subsequently Fisher claims that even adaptation is associated with a progressive increase of fitness, and in this context Fisher gives the following definition of adaptation:

An organism is regarded as adapted to a particular situation, or to the totality of situations which constitute its environment, only in so far as *we can imagine* an assemblage of *slightly different situations, or environments, to which the animal would on the whole be less well adapted*; and equally only in so far as *we can imagine* an assemblage of *slightly different organic forms, which would be less well adapted to that environment*. This I take to be the meaning which the word is intended to convey, *apart altogether from the question whether the organisms really are adapted to their environment, or whether the structures and instincts to which the term has been applied are rightly so described*. (My italics)[17]

This definition seems to imply that the phenomenon of adaptation is foremost a mental operation, whose concordance with the real world is rather irrelevant. Can this really be true? And furthermore, human imagination being highly variable, Fisher's definition seems to be rather subjective. I think that in order to have sense the expression 'we can imagine' must be replaced by 'there can exist'. Under any circumstances it is obvious that Fisher envisages adaptation to be a *maximum* state.

We shall not try to follow Fisher when he gives a mathematical description of adaptation, but proceed to the *Deterioration of the Environment*. This section begins with a discussion of mutations with large effect, that is, macromutations. With reference to the definition of adaptation given above it follows that such events can only lead to a decrease in adaptation, or fitness. This is indeed the view of Fisher, as expressed in the following statement: 'A considerable number of such mutations [with large effects] have now been observed, and these are, I believe, without exception, either definitely pathological (most often lethal) in their effects, or with high probability to be regarded as deleterious in the wild state.'[18] This assertion, which excludes the involvement of macromutations in biological evolution, I have called *Fisher's axiom*.[19] The most remarkable thing about this axiom is the context in which it occurs, surely it should have been placed in a section called *Deterioration of the Organism*. However, allowing for this event would involve a contradiction of the fundamental theorem of natural selection for, as we have learned, species increase their fitness 'to the end of their existence'.

And therefore we can explain extinction only as *deterioration of the environment*. So Fisher writes:

> As to the physical environment, geological and climatological changes *must* always be slowly in progress, and these, though possibly beneficial to some few organisms, *must* as they continue become harmful to the greater number, for the same reasons as mutations in the organism itself will generally be harmful. For the majority of organisms, therefore, *the physical environment may be regarded as constantly deteriorating*, whether the climate, for example, is becoming warmer or cooler, moister or drier, and this will tend, in the majority of species, constantly to lower the average value of *m*, the Malthusian parameter of the population increase. (My italics)[20]

Here we must take a moment for reflection. We have learnt that any species at any time increases in fitness, and we have seen that this fitness concerns adaptation to the environment. It may well be that like macromutations, terrestrial catastrophes are harmful to living beings, but if the same holds for slowly progressing changes, then surely the fundamental theorem of natural selection loses sense, for the constant increase in fitness must imply that the organisms are able to follow suit with the environmental changes, perhaps even to race ahead of them.

But, of course, the environment also consists of living beings, so Fisher continues: 'Probably more important than the changes in climate will be the evolutionary changes in progress in associated organisms. As each organism increases in fitness, so will its enemies and competitors increase in fitness; and this will have the same effect, perhaps in a much more important degree, in impairing the environment, from the point of view of each organism concerned.'[21]

But here again, if the enemies and competitors increase in fitness relatively more than the organisms on which our attention is focused, then that must imply that the relative fitness of the latter is decreased. Thus, once more the fundamental theorem is falsified. In fact, if we accept Fisher's fundamental theorem and his definition of fitness and adaptation, then extinction is excluded, except as caused by catastrophes. It will be noticed that lethal macromutations may well eliminate individuals, but not species, as they have no chance to become fixed.

On one occasion Fisher surveyed the history of the criticism of Darwin's theory:

The cases of special difficulty, which were advanced in great numbers, and which were discussed by Darwin, and by his supporters and opponents at very considerable length, are all closely similar in the kind of difficulty which they present, although this difficulty may be framed in three distinguishable phases.

(*a*) An organ, such as the wing of a bat . . . may be so specialized for the particular functions to which it is adapted as to bear little resemblance to the prototype, as illustrated by the fore-limb of an insectivore, from which it must be presumed to have arisen. The difficulty *felt* here is that of *imagining* a series of organisms presenting organs of intermediate grades connecting these widely separate extremes.

(*b*) An organ of extreme perfection, such as the eye in the higher vertebrates, may show such perfect and detailed adaptation to its important function that by comparison with the obstacles which the design of such an apparatus would present to human ingenuity, *the mind is staggered by the effort of conceiving it as the product of so undirected a process as trial and error.*

(*c*) Some organs of seemingly trifling importance are yet so clearly adapted to the function they perform [for instance, fly-flapper] that they cannot be regarded as accidental. In these cases it may be asked how can the efficacy of this trifling function have ever been a matter of life and death to the organism, and so have determined its survival in the struggle for existence.

Of these three types of objection the first is opposed to evolutionary theory of all kinds, while the second and third, though I have stated them in the form in which they should be presented to a selectionist, can only be evaded by evolutionists of other schools by postulating a creative power in living matter equivalent to the ingenuity of a benevolent creator. They are all, in somewhat different ways, *difficulties less of the reason than of the imagination. The cogency and the wealth of illustration* with which Darwin was able to deal with these cases was, perhaps, the largest factor in persuading biologists of the truth of his views, and would in itself to a great extent explain the enormous influence which he exerted upon biological opinion. The *difficulty of imagining the intermediate stages* in the evolution of the wing

302

of a bat Darwin met by pointing to the existence in Nature, not of the intermediate stages themselves, which must necessarily be extinct, but of the analogues of a chain of intermediate adaptations, in the flying squirrels and in *Galeopithecus*, in which less specialized means for gaining assistance from the air, in leaping and gliding, indicate a series of stages, each of practical service to its possessor, without the latter enjoying the advantages of true flight. In considering such a series of stages it becomes apparent that it is the theory of evolution of continuous adaptation . . . which makes such transitions possible. What would be incredible in such a case would be a non-adaptive orthogenetic urge leading straight from the fore-limb of an insectivore to the wing of a bat through some thousands of generations of intermediate types encumbered with useless appendages; or, to allude to a rival *absurdity*, the appearance of the bat's wing by a *saltation* among a litter of primitive insectivorous animals. (My italics, except for the Latin name and the last ones)[22]

Time is ripe for a semantic clarification. Whether we are dealing with organs of extreme perfection or trifling importance, they have always been created *inside*, and *by* living organisms. This statement is completely independent of whether the organs are created in a few large, or in many small steps. In either case selection is involved to eliminate mistakes and to ensure the survival of useful features. It is true that the second alternative allows for ascribing a *more directive* role to natural selection, but in either case it is certainly necessary 'posulating a creative power in living matter'. Whether or not this power is 'equivalent to the ingenuity of a benevolent creator' is a metaphysical problem which is beyond the realms of natural science.

It appears that Fisher did not read *On the Origin of Species* with care, for neither cogency nor wealth of illustration are distinctive features of that book. As pointed out repeatedly, Darwin did not mobilise one single fact which convincingly corroborated the micromutation theory. The history of biology would not have been the same, if he had done that. It should also be observed how Fisher turns the argument upside down. Darwin's critics disowned that the wing of a bat could arise 'through some thousands of generations of intermediate types encumbered with useless appendages', a conclusion which follows from the micromutation theory. As it is, Fisher makes it appear that most of Darwin's adversaries must have been lunatics supporting an absurdity. Fisher repeatedly stresses that lack of imagination is the main element in the opposition to Darwin's theory. This assertion seems to imply that he considered himself better endowed with this faculty and it must be regretted that he did not demonstrate his superiority with some practical examples.

It is tempting to continue the analysis of Fisher's study of Darwinism, but we must confine ourselves to two quotations. First we look at how he defends the selectional value of micromutations:

> The case to which the life and death test is most immediately applicable is that of capture by or escape from a predator. If we consider no outcome to such an encounter, other than escape or death, then it is manifest that the amount of difference in alertness, speed or endurance, which may decide the issue, *is smaller than any assignable quantity*. The difference needed to determine life or death is, *in mathematical strictness, infinitesimal*. For, however small the difference which we choose to consider, a finite number of increments of this magnitude will suffice, in any particular case, to determine the difference between easy capture, at the one extreme, and easy escape at the other. And some particular one of these increments, *however small they may have been chosen*, will therefore have sufficed to bridge the gulf between death and safety. (My italics)[23]

We have seen it before, haven't we? This appears to be nothing more than Zenon's paradox of Achilles and the turtle in an evolutionary disguise. It is remarkable to see how Fisher was convinced that his mathematics was directly applicable to real life. Surely, his argument implies *ceteris paribus*, other things being equal. But how often would it happen in Nature that two infinitesimally different organisms are hunted by predators which are likewise infinitesimally different with respect to alertness, speed and endurance, and in an environment where the impediments to flight are exactly alike?

The last comment brings in a ray of hope. Fisher discusses Julian Huxley's work on allometric growth, pointing out

> . . . that relatively simple modifications in the system of growth-gradients (by which the form of organisms, both in their general structure and in that of their parts, is governed in the later stages of development) will bring about harmoniously adapted modification of form, involving numerous structural elements, and which might have appeared to require equally numerous modifications of the germinal material . . . It would, I believe, be an entire

overstatement to deny an extreme degree of genetic complexity in the evolutionary development of some structures such as the eye. *A better understanding, however, of the developmental process, may well show that conspicuous phylogenetic changes in the external form can be brought about more simply than many far less striking adaptations in detail of the organism to its environment, or of its parts to their mutual relations.* (My italics)[24]

Indeed, that is the whole point. If for a moment we forget about genetics and turn to epigenetics — or development — then we shall find that slight changes in the early stages may cause substantial modifications in later development, through *epigenetic amplification*. But the resultant of such events are saltations; thus, unknowingly, we may suppose, Fisher is here advocating the macromutation theory. Clearly, it was not so absurd after all.

Fisher was a great statistician, whose work on the design of scientific experiments is of lasting value. But by placing his authority in support of an obsolete theory of evolution he has been a reactionary force in the history of biology.

JOHN BURDON SANDERSON HALDANE (1892–1964)

J.B.S. Haldane was also a mathematical prodigy, although he did not measure up to Fisher in this respect.[25] But he was a scholar; the subjects of his published books range from enzyme kinetics and genetics to evolution and politics. At Cambridge University he studied mathematics, classics and philosophy, but he got a fine introduction to biology by attending Edwin S. Goodrich's lectures in comparative morphology. Although he never was much of an experimental biologist, his publications show that he was much more familiar with biology than Fisher. He became interested in genetics very early, and in the question about the relevance of Mendelism to Darwin's theory of natural selection. By the time he published the book we are going to discuss here he had become Fullerian Professor of Physiology at the Royal Institution, Dunn Reader in Biochemistry at Cambridge University and Head of the Genetical Department at John Innes Horticultural Institution in Merton.

He introduced the first of a series of papers dealing with *A Mathematical Theory of Natural and Artificial Selection* (1924) with the statement: 'A satisfactory theory of natural selection must be quantitative. In order to establish the view that natural selection is capable of accounting for the known facts of evolution we must show not only that it can cause a species to change, but that it can cause it to change at a rate which will account for present and past transmutations.'[26]

Although it is modest compared to the declaration made by Weldon some 30 years before, this programme seems very ambitious. And we are entitled to ask if it is really true that a theory on evolution must be quantitative to be satisfactory. The circumstance that a scientific theory is quantitative implies that the data can be dealt with mathematically. In such contexts mathematics is used as a tool to facilitate the logical deductions of predictions which can be tested empirically. But it should be recalled that the theories — mostly physical and chemical ones — in which mathematics may be applied, do not allow for the prediction of future events in general, but only of phenomena occurring under narrowly circumscribed conditions, particularly such as they prevail in a laboratory. But evolution cannot be studied in laboratories, the best we can do is to study phenomena which we, with more or less justification, presume are of the kind that have been involved in evolution. I do not believe that either Haldane or any other mathematician has shown that 'natural selection is capable of accounting for the known facts of evolution'.

Be this as it may, in 1932 Haldane published a learned and delightful little book called *The Causes of Evolution*.[27] In this book he summarised his own work on Mendelian population genetics, and compared it with the contributions of Fisher and Sewall Wright. Almost all the mathematics was relegated to a large appendix, and we shall leave it there.

I will not present the evidence considered by Haldane to support the Darwinian micromutation theory, for if he had been successful in this, he would have been acclaimed as a second Darwin. Rather, I intend here to demonstrate that he was aware that in many cases evolution had advanced in large steps, and that he also in other instances had a very good understanding of the biological aspect of evolution.

Yet, we must begin by a critical note. In the Introduction he writes:

Darwinism has been a subject of embittered controversy ever since its conception. The period up till Darwin's death saw a vast mass of criticism. This was mostly an attack on the doctrine of

306

evolution, and was almost entirely devoid of scientific value. The few really pertinent attacks were lost amid a jabber of ecclesiastical bombinations. The criticism was largely dictated by disgust or fear of this doctrine, and it was natural that the majority of scientific men rallied to Darwin's support. By the time of Darwin's death in 1882, Darwinism had become orthodox in biological circles. The next generation saw the beginnings of a more critical attitude among biologists.[28]

This is history as the Darwinians would like it to be, but the readers of the present book will know that it is false. By 1870 almost everybody had accepted evolution, that is, Lamarck's first theory of evolution, while rejecting emphatically Darwin's theory on the mechanism of evolution. This stand was taken even by 'the majority of scientific men'; the only ray of hope for the theory of natural selection was constituted by the biometricians at the close of the century.

It will be recalled that Fisher considered the stature of humans to be the outcome of the co-operation of many genes. Haldane makes the following remark, worthy of a professor in physiology: 'Ultimately it may well be found that of the genes influencing human height some act through the thyroid gland, others through the pituitary, others through the gonads in delaying maturity, others again more directly on the bones, and so on. That is mere speculation.'[29] It is, but it is creative speculation, showing where to look for the terminal, the phenotypic action of the genes. Surely, there is room for several genes in Haldane's mechanism, but there is also scope for all kinds of interactions which reduce the need for the many mutations envisaged by Fisher. And above all, although it is not directly mentioned by Haldane, it allows for macromutations: many single mutations affecting the pituitary are known to have a large effect on the form and the function of the body.

Somewhat later he makes another striking observation: 'Genetics can give us an explanation of why two fairly similar organisms, say a black and white cat, are different. It can give us much less information as to why they are alike.'[30] Evidently, they are alike because they have undergone the same ontogenetic processes, but that is something which lies beyond the realm of genetics.

Haldane also writes: 'But the change from one stable equilibrium to the other may take place as the result of the isolation of a small unrepresentative group of the population . . . This case seems to me very important, because it is probably the basis of progressive evolution of many organs and functions in higher animals, and of the break-up of one species into several.'[31]

Isolation may at times lead to progressive evolution, but this outcome is more likely under the conditions of selection imposed by competition. Yet, Haldane is evidently right when he proposes that isolation may lead to evolutionary divergence. And he realised that in isolation selection is temporarily suspended, thereby allowing for the survival of forms which might otherwise succumb:

> But where natural selection slackens, new forms may arise which would not survive under more rigid competition, and many ultimately hardy combinations will thus have a chance of arising . . . This seems to have happened on several occasions when a successful evolutionary step rendered a new type of organism possible, and the pressure of natural selection was temporarily slackened. Thus the distinction between the principal mammalian orders seems to have arisen during an orgy of variation in the early Eocene which followed the doom of the great reptiles, and the establishment of the mammals as the dominant terrestrial group. Since that date mammalian evolution has been a slower affair, largely a progressive improvement of the types originally laid down in the Eocene.[32]

What perspicacity! Too bad that many later Evolutionists did not read Haldane carefully enough; if they had done, they would know that divergent evolution ('adaptive radiation') is not a consequence of an augmented *selection pressure*, but rather of a reduced one, owing to the fact that ample possibilities for isolation prevail. In the next chapter we read:

> But if we come to the conclusion that natural selection is probably the main cause of change in a population, we certainly need not go back completely to Darwin's point of view. In the first place, we have every reason to believe that new species may arise quite suddenly, sometimes by hybridisation, sometimes perhaps by other means. *Such species do not arise, as Darwin thought, by natural selection. When they have arisen they must justify their existence before the tribunal of natural selection, but that is a very different matter* . . .
>
> Secondly, *natural selection can only act on the variations available, and these are not*, as Darwin thought, *in every direction* . . . [Rather,] mutations only seem to occur along certain

lines, which are very similar in closely related species, but differ in more distant species.[33]

We need not use more quotations to demonstrate that Haldane's views on biological problems were based on extensive knowledge and common sense, even if mathematics had the upper hand as concerns his explanation of biological evolution. I shall now discuss one point where, in my view, he was led astray by this option.

Some people have repudiated Darwin's theory of natural selection for ideological reasons, because it implies death and extinction.[34] However a certain consolation has been found in the currently adopted theory because it replaces differential elimination by differential reproduction. It cannot be denied that there is something appealing in replacing death by sex, but apart from that the idea is, of course, rather naive. For living beings, plants as well as animals, are being eaten every day; this is the basic precondition for life. Most often, I presume, individuals fortuitously fall victim to this course of events, but should it happen that there is a selection such that the survivors represent the ablest and the healthiest among their peers then, surely, it can only be to the future advantage of their species that their inferiors are sacrificed. From this point of view natural selection is not a bad thing at all.

Yet, when we come to our own species a particular asymmetry obtains; as long as we stay alive we do not join the cycle of Nature, we consume other beings, but are not ourselves consumed. Still, even in this case we cannot completely avoid the interference of natural selection, for as all other living organisms, we find in human beings a number of gene mutations which impair the viability or the fertility of their carriers. These deleterious mutations are kept down, if not necessarily eliminated, owing to the fact that the individuals in which they reside die leaving no, or at best a reduced number of successors, compared to the other members of their species. From a very restricted point of view this circumstance may be said to involve a 'genetic load', as first suggested by H.J. Muller in 1950.[35] Since human beings seldom exploit their maximum reproductive capacity, the application of the 'load' concept may seem rather questionable in this particular instance, but in Nature the situation is quite different. The reproductive capacity varies widely from one species to another, but there is no birth control.

Haldane, who never missed a chance to do mathematics, set out '. . . to make quantitative the fairly obvious statement that natural selection cannot occur with great intensity for a number of

Table 1

Genotype	AA	Aa	aa
Frequency	p^2	$2pq$	q^2
Fitness	1	1	$1 - s$
Frequency after selection	p^2	$2pq$	$q^2 - sq^2$
Overall fitness after selection	$p^2 + 2pq + q^2 - sq^2 = 1 - sq^2 < 1$		

characters at once'.[36] The basis of Haldane's reasoning and calculations is a modification of Hardy–Weinberg's equation which allows for selective elimination of one genotype. In Table 1 we may observe the frequencies obtaining for the three combinations of the two alleles A and a, before and after selection. It is seen that the fitness of the genotype aa is lowered by s, the selection coefficient, and as fitness by definition is measured by the reproductive success, the frequency of aa must be proportional to the fitness, thus $q^2 - sq^2$.

The remarkable thing is that the *total* number of the population is reduced by the same number as aa, namely sq^2. This phenomenon is of course reiterated so long as the inferior allele is present in the gene pool, and Haldane calculated that the number of individuals which must thus be eliminated prematurely to substitute one allele by another may be something like 30 times the number in any one generation. This staggering number of deaths was called by Haldane 'the cost of Natural Selection'; currently it is more usual to talk of 'genetic load'. Clearly, the number of generations required to carry the substitution to the end must be much larger — a value of $n = 300$ was suggested. Haldane also discussed the origin of new species, stating: 'If two species differ at 1000 loci, and the mean rate of gene substitution, as has been suggested, is one per 300 generations, it will take at least 300,000 generations to generate an interspecific difference.'[37]

I shall not discuss the concept of 'genetic load' in detail, but it may be pointed out that it has a number of counter-intuitive consequences, which have been debated by various authors. In fact, although the discussion of the genetic load continues in the literature, it seems that the problem was solved many years ago by Bruce Wallace,[38] who pointed out that when the population number is 'normalized' in each generation by dividing with $1 - sq^2$, the genetic load vanishes.

It is indeed true that the elimination of disadvantageous mutations may entail the death of the individuals which carry these genes.

However, if we look at the question from an ecological rather than a population genetical perspective, we know that, allowing for fortuitous oscillations, it holds that for each pair of parents only two individuals can survive. Whenever the number of offspring oversteps this number, the excess must be eliminated. This elimination may be called 'the Malthusian load', ML. If, in a population of N_0 individuals, the mean offspring per generation is N_1, then we have $ML = N_1 - N_0$.

A certain genetic load, GL, is bound to prevail, and we therefore face the possibilities: $GL > ML$, $GL = ML$ or $GL < ML$. In the first case the population — the species or taxon — must become extinct; in the two remaining cases the genetic load cannot be appreciated, quantitatively at least, because it is balanced or outnumbered by the Malthusian load.

The idea of 'genetic load' is so unreasonable that it is no wonder it has been rejected many times. But none of the various counter-arguments seems to have been completely convincing, for the concept reappears again and again in the literature. Thus, less than ten years ago Dobzhansky wrote: 'Substitution of neutral genes entail no genetic deaths and no substitutional load. This is perhaps the strongest argument in favour of the panneutralist position.'[39] If this can be stated by one of the leading figures in population genetics then the 'genetic load' is not a dead issue to be neglected in the present context.

SEWALL WRIGHT (1889–)

Sewall Wright studied biology at the University of Illinois where he became acquainted with William Castle's observations on the inheritance of coat colour in the laboratory rat. Fascinated by this work he became Castle's assistant during the years 1912–15. From 1915 to 1925 he worked at the Animal Husbandry Division of the United States Department of Agriculture, and in 1925 he became Professor at the University of Chicago and later at the University of Wisconsin.[40]

At an early stage Wright became involved in genetical experiments on animals, partly Castle's hooded rats and partly guinea pigs. Under laboratory conditions inbreeding is a natural and common expedient, which, it seems, may be expected to increase the homozygosity. This prediction was contested by Raymond Pearl in 1913, and Wright undertook to prove him wrong by means of mathematical calculations. Since then a great part of Wright's contribution to science came to consist of mathematical equations. However, the feature distinguishing this early work has remained typical of Wright's achievements; it was practical biological problems which urged him to find a mathematical solution, biology always came before mathematics.

This circumstance also meant that he acquired a much broader view on the mechanisms behind evolution than his compeers. There are three points which clearly show his thorough understanding of biological matters: (i) his unremitting insistence on the effect of interaction between the various genes; (ii) his understanding of the significance of epigenetic processes for, above all, morphogenetic events; and (iii) his frank admission that many other agents than mass selection of micromutations are involved in the mechanism of evolution.

Wright's concern with gene interactions led to his formulation of the theory of path coefficients, which allows for the mathematical representation of the correlation between various gene interactions. This method has turned out to be extremely successful in the hands of its founder. In fact, the theory was developed for the application to biometric data concerning rabbits and human beings, and Wright was able to show by means of his method that 'most differences between individuals are those which involve the body as a whole'.[41] This conclusion clearly implies that there must be some superior agents which control the growth of the various parts of the body. It follows that the understanding of the morphological changes associated with evolution requires knowledge of the workings of these superior agents. Wright is here approaching the solution of the problem which concerned Darwin and some of his successors, namely, the reciprocal regulation of the size of the legs and the neck of the giraffe.

Observations on various monsters among his guinea pigs led Wright to assume a still more outright epigenetic position. In a review he stated:

On this view the genes are highly specific chemically, and thus called into play only under very specific conditions; but their morphological effects, if any, rest on quantitative influences of *immediate* or *remote* products on *growth gradients, which are resultants of all that has gone on before in the organism* . . .

More or less similar views have been expressed by other geneticists almost since the rediscovery of Mendelian heredity.

Goldschmidt, of course, has been urging for years that gene action is through control of developmental rates . . . Huxley has discussed the genetic control of growth gradients. I suspect that most of you have felt that I have been uttering platitudes. But the human mind slips back so easily into the ancient groove of sympathetic magic — preformation with its almost inevitable corollary, the inheritance of acquired characters — that *it is perhaps desirable from time to time to reexamine and restate the epigenetic position.*[42]

At several occasions Sewall Wright has attempted to classify the various agents which may contribute to evolutionary change. In a publication from 1977 we may read: 'Evolution includes both the transformation of characters and the splitting of species. These occur simultaneously, indeed, under the mutation theories of de Vries, Goldschmidt and Willis, but are largely distinct under theories generally accepted now.'[43] Wright is here making a distinction between transformation of characteristics and splitting of species which, as an approximation, perhaps corresponds to progressive and divergent evolution. I am not sure that the mentioned Macromutationists would accept the quoted statement, they asserted that the 'splitting of species' requires 'transformation of characters', but not necessarily the other way round.

We still need to be informed about Wright's view upon the origin of taxa above the species level. This we may obtain from the following citation:

Summing up, the characteristic evolutionary process may be described as the *emergence* of a complex of adaptations of general significance, the rapid exploitation of this in diverse ways of life by adaptive radiations at successively lower levels, leading ultimately to gradual *orthogenetic* advance along each line, accompanied in some cases by extensive diversification of genera and species with jointly *nonadaptive* and *minor adaptive* aspects. On *rare occasions* a new, relatively general, adaptive complex may *emerge* at any stage in the proccess, initiating a new cycle. The broad course of evolution has the appearance of being guided by *selective expansion and elimination* among the higher categories. (My italics)[44]

There are some points, but not many, in this statement with which a Macromutationist cannot agree, but what about the Micromutationists? Can a person who, in the spirit of Darwinism, believes that evolution is a matter of fixation and recombination of micromutations, really endorse the above quotation?

I hope I have managed in the preceding pages to express my great admiration for Sewall Wright. He is unquestionably the outstanding figure among the founders of the Neo-Mendelian theory, the reason being that he was the one best acquainted with biology. Experience has repeatedly shown that every time a doctrine acquires supporters enough to build up a power-wielding hierarchy, the demands on discipline increase and the doctrine hardens into orthodoxy. This is what happened with Neo-Mendelism in the 1950s and 1960s, but Sewall Wright was recalcitrant and stuck to his old views. Consequently

> Wright continued to receive lip service in the ritualistic invoca-
> tion 'Fisher, Haldane and Wright' in obligatory historical
> sentences of various works, but his views on levels of evolution
> and interdemic selection were effectively removed from the
> developing (and constricting) synthesis [i.e. the synthetic theory
> of evolution]. The current rediscovery of his work and its general
> vision is one of the greatest signs of health in our profession.
>
> In October 1980, I spoke with Dr. Wright about his perception
> of his role in the synthesis as it developed. He remarked, 'I was
> out of it' and said that he wasn't invited to major meetings (indeed
> — and incredibly — he was not invited to attend the major
> historical conference on the definition, impact and meaning of the
> synthesis — Mayr and Provine 1980). He said that the genetics
> in the modern synthesis was Fisher's, that an alliance with E.B.
> Ford was important in establishing Fisher's role, and that
> references to his own work were generally 'perfunctory'. He
> cited 'emphasis on individual selection' as his primary
> characterization of the modern synthesis and complained that his
> views on interdemic selection had been ignored.[45]

I have made this quotation to demonstrate how fashion rules in biology. Dissenters are frozen out, without regard to their previously established merits. I agree with Stephen Jay Gould in the above quotation that it is a 'sign of health' that we can again discuss and recognise the importance of Sewall Wright's contribution to evolutionary thought.

314

THE MATHEMATICIANS

Having examined the views of evolution of Fisher, Haldane, and Wright, it is illuminating to compare the general view each took of the work of the other two in the early 1930s. Haldane stated that the work of Wright 'resembles the work of Fisher more than that of Haldane' . . . Wright believed that the strong emphasis upon the deterministic effect of mass selection of single genes in the work of Fisher and Haldane distinguished their work sharply from his own, which emphasized the selection of interaction systems of genes. Fisher thought Wright and Haldane failed to appreciate the importance of very small selection pressures acting over long periods of time in evolution of natural populations. He often lumped Wright and Haldane together as critics of his views. Thus the relationship between the three appears to have been symmetrical.[46]

William B. Provine

. . . the mathematical geneticists either claim for selection far more than Darwin did himself, or use the term in a totally different sense.[47]

Lancelot Hogben

[Fisher, Wright and Haldane] have worked out an impressive mathematical theory of genetical variation and evolutionary change. But what, precisely, has been the contribution of this mathematical school to evolutionary theory, if I may be permitted to ask such a provocative question.[48]

Ernst Mayr

Les modèles mathématiques de l'évolution semblaient donc avoir peu de rapport avec la réalité.[49]

Marcel Blanc

Neo-Mendelism was from the outset a mathematical discipline, and this tradition has been preserved. Today it has developed into a highly sophisticated subject[50] which, I believe, is accessible only to a small minority of biologists. But although they must have had some premises in common, the mathematical systems developed by the three founders of population genetics are widely different. The outsider who with great efforts has penetrated the equations of one of the three should not expect to master simultaneously those developed by the others.

But, as pointed out by Provine in the above quotation, they differed still more with respect to the biological interpretations of the data. In the preceding text they have been ranged alphabetically, and fortuitously in such a way that their mathematical affiliation is represented by a descending, and their biological affiliation by an ascending line. Under these circumstances it would be natural if Fisher thought that Haldane and Wright had something in common. In fact, although this is ignored by Provine, they both allowed for the occurrence of unique beneficial macromutations. Likewise,

315

Wright might well think that his English colleagues shared some views. Most remarkable is that even Haldane could group the other two as opponents to his work.

Nevertheless, what unites the three or, at least, what is considered to unite them, is the belief in the micromutation theory, which claims that it is possible to bring about substantial changes in living organisms through the gradual accumulation of mutations with slight effects on the reproductive success of the organisms in question.

The reproductive success is measured by the number of offspring which in general widely exceeds that required by the Malthusian axiom, according to which the number of offspring must equal the number of parents. The recorded differences in numbers of offspring may reasonably be referred to the genetic load, but on top of this there is a further elimination, representing the Malthusian load. If the observed values of progeny are to have any sense, we face the following alternatives: either (i) the effects of all other properties serving to promote the survival of the organisms under natural conditions are proportional to the reproductive capacity, or (ii) the further elimination must be random.

The former of these possibilities is hardly acceptable as a general premise. The latter implies that most of the elimination occurring in nature is fortuitous, and thus non-selective. This circumstance seems to preclude that natural selection exerts its putative function, the adaptation of the organisms to their environment. In this context it cannot be emphasised too much that if natural selection is allowed for, then there is no reason whatsoever to presume that the number of reproductively active adults is proportional to the original number of progeny. Experience rather seems to indicate that the chances of survival often is inversely related to the number of offspring. This state of affairs cannot be accounted for within the framework of Mendelian population genetics.

However this may be, we may still investigate some of the implications of the population genetic theory, using an example proposed by Dobzhansky: '. . . the carriers of genotypes AA and Aa contribute on the average 100 gametes to the gene pool of the next generation, whereas the aa carriers contribute only 90 gametes.'[51] The three genotypes clearly represent three individuals, so that when the ecological demands have been met with, only three offspring will remain of the 290 produced. Since only whole individuals can survive, we can record a difference between the three genotypes only by multiplying all numbers by ten. We then have a progeny of 2,900 of

Table 2: Poisson distribution showing the probability for various numbers of progeny

Number of progeny	0	1	2	3	4	5	...
Probability	0.135	0.271	0.271	0.180	0.090	0.036	

which 29 will survive, ten *AA*, ten *Aa* and nine *aa*.

So the score is the following: 30 individuals should theoretically yield a progeny of 3,000, but owing to natural selection this number is reduced such that only 2,900 reach sexual maturity. Before these organisms are allowed to reproduce, another 2,871 have to be eliminated by chance, and yet in such a way that the original ratio is preserved. A large measure of luck is necessary if this expectation is to be fulfilled. Under any circumstances the calculation shows that in this example, taken from a secular text in population genetics, the Malthusian load is ecologically much more important than the genetic load supposed to represent Darwin's natural selection.

In the literature we may encounter values for the selection coefficient s as low as 0.001, and if we allow for sufficiently large exponents in the equations, we may be sure that a substantial effect is obtained. However, in the present context we may attempt to answer the question: how small values of s is it realistic to operate with?

According to Darwin–Wallace's Malthusian axiom the mean offspring for each pair of parents is two, which may be expected to follow a Poisson distribution as shown in Table 2. Referring to the three genotypes discussed above, it is evident that the *lowest* value of s is obtained if *aa* has one offspring less than *AA* and *Aa*. In this case the only reasonable alternatives are 1, 1 and 0 or 2, 2 and 1 or 3, 3 and 2. In the first case $s = 1$, and since the probabilities for getting either one or two progeny are equal, the second case gives $s = 0.5$. In the third case the genotypes *AA* and *Aa* are superior corresponding to $s = 0.33$, thus $1 - s = 0.67$. Yet, because it is 1.5 times more likely to get two than to get three offspring, their superiority is not paid off as a higher reproductive success. When the selection coefficient is thus weighted we have $s = 0$. Apparently $s \geqslant 0.5$ is the most realistic expectation.

It is as common today as it was in Darwin's time that people object vigorously to the notion of 'macromutations', presumably because it is thought to be some mysterious or miraculous kind of event. On the basis of the preceding discussion we may define the concept quantitatively, and at the same time deprive it of any metaphysical implication. Thus, we may assert that a macromutation is a hereditary variation which significantly augments or reduces the reproductive survival of the carrier of the mutation in question. For a macromutation to avail it must hold that $|s| \geqslant 0.5$.

Neo-Mendelism is based on the assumption that micromutations (that is, relatively frequent but phenotypically insignificant mutations) are of evolutionary significance. This is a necessity because only micromutations are frequent enough to be studied in population genetic experiments and equations. Macromutations, some of which are supposed to have occurred only at intervals of millions of years, are obviously not fit for direct study. This may not hold for all macromutations.

However this may be, we have given above a relatively specific definition of a macromutation, and we are therefore entitled to frame the question: are the observations made on mutations outside the laboratory micromutations or macromutations? It is difficult to test this problem, but it seems that two instances frequently encountered in the literature offer this possibility, industrial melanism and sickle-cell anaemia, both of which refer to the effect of single genes. In the former case 'Haldane found that the fertility of the [melanic] dominants must be 50% greater than that of the recessives', which he called a 'not very intense degree of natural selection'.[52] The latter statement seems odd in view of the fact that such a high value of s must entail a tremendous genetic load.

In the second case the selection against the sickle-cell gene in homozygous individuals is above 0.9. The reason that it is not eliminated is that in malaria-infested regions the carriers of the heterozygous genotype have a greater chance of survival than those possessing a normal homozygous genome.[53]

In this context we must refer to a specialist on the topic of selection in Nature, as opposed to selection in culture, Edmund B. Ford: '. . . Fisher suggested that selection for advantageous qualities in nature might rise to as much as 1 per cent. As a result of the approach by means of ecological genetics, it is now known that values of 20 to 60 per cent and well over are common and usual — a fact of wide evolutionary significance.'[54]

This quotation demonstrates the extent to which Fisher's mathematics was divorced from reality, and it even seems to imply a corroboration of the view advanced above. Thus, on the basis of the given definition macromutations are the driving force of evolution, for they alone have effects large enough to affect substantially the chances of survival. The examples discussed may serve to show that macromutations need not be something wonderful in any sense; in fact, macromutations more radical than those discussed here are well known to the breeders of plants and animals, for it is mainly on these their work is based.

I cannot help mention in this context that industrial melanism, this show-piece of Neo-Mendelism, has turned out to be much more complicated than was formerly assumed. Recent computer studies of a migration-selection model have shown that *strong non-visual selection* and *weak frequency-dependent predation* are needed to explain the actually observed distribution.[55] It is difficult to see what remains of the initial concepts under these conditions.

Neo-Mendelism is an intellectually sophisticated topic. Biologically, its importance increases as less reliance is put on mass selection, and more on inbreeding, for that is the way breeders and Nature alike proceed to ensure the survival of rare mutations. So with respect to biological importance population genetics follows an ascending line from Fisher over Haldane to Sewall Wright.

12

The Rise and the Fall

You will think me very conceited when I say I feel quite easy about the ultimate success of my views, (with much error, as yet unseen by me, to be no doubt eliminated); & I feel this confidence because I find so many young and middle-aged truly good workers, in different branches, either partially or wholly accepting my views, because they find they can thus group & understand many scattered facts.[1]

Charles Darwin

The modern synthetic theory as a generally accepted way of approaching problems of evolution was born in 1937 with the publication of Dobzhansky's *Genetics and the Origin of Species*.[2]

G. Ledyard Stebbins

. . . and the world is our laboratory, evolution itself our guinea-pig.[3]

Julian S. Huxley

Almost every biologist active today has been taught that Darwin's theory of natural selection as modified by Mendelian genetics — in other words, the modern synthesis or Neo-Mendelism — has been demonstrated to account successfully for the mechanisms responsible for the evolution of life on this planet. So the triumph was as complete as it could possibly be, but it was not immediate. Rather, as I have already suggested, the founders were probably too mathematical to make any impact on the biological community and the general public. It was left to persons with less lofty aspirations to bring home the victory.

We shall here analyse the views set forth by some of these advocates with reference to the cardinal point, namely, the empirical evidence they were able to mobilise in favour of the micromutation theory, the theory which had been rejected by so many biologists for such a long time. Anticipating the outcome of this analysis I shall claim that they did not manage to make this theory more credible; indeed some of the facts presented were rather adverse to the theory. And as the search for corroboration went on, it turned out that the events of the real world, now, as a century ago, obstinately refuse to bear out the micromutation theory. It would be an exaggeration to claim that this misfortune has brought down the theory, but at least it is correct to state that a steadily increasing number of people are growing uneasy about its validity. In the second section to follow we shall discuss various kinds of evidence which has been found to be contrary to the predictions of the micromutation theory. In the last section we shall discuss some of the adverse effects of the acceptance of 'the modern synthesis' on biological thought.

THE TRIUMPHATORS

Quite a few people came out in support of the new theory of evolution, so many that a selection must be made in the present context. Those dealt with in the following section: Theodosius Dobzhansky, Julian Huxley, Ernst Mayr and George Gaylord Simpson, have been chosen with the intention of representing the widest possible range of biological disciplines.

Theodosius Dobzhansky

Naturally enough, the speciality to react most readily was genetics, as personified by Theodosius Dobzhansky, who wrote the book *Genetics and the Origin of Species* (1937),[4] primarily an exposition of the extremely important advances which had been made in the field of genetics during the early decades of our century. The presentation is comprehensive; if a large part of the text was to do with *Drosophila*, the reason is simply that at the time, and even today, a very substantial part of genetic science is related to this genus of fruit flies. When read today, the most remarkable difference between Dobzhansky's and current texts concerns the macromolecular level of organisation; this is where the great advances have been made since then. Another conspicuous fact is that there is very little mathematics in the book, a fact which may indicate that the experimentalists were not yet ready to test the elaborate predictions implied by the mathematical achievements of the founders of Mendelian population genetics.

When we pass from genetics to purportedly evolutionary issues it is first reported that variation does in fact occur in natural populations. One point disclosed by these observations is 'that the available data, meagre as they are, tend to show that the effective population sizes may prove to be small, at least in some species. In any case, to suppose that the breeding population equals the total number of

321

individuals in a species is erroneous'.[5] Although it is not pointed out, this finding tends to show that some of the calculations made by Fisher and Haldane are quite unrealistic. Dobzhansky also demonstrates that the phenomenon of selection, as revealed by changes in gene frequencies, occurs in Nature, but above all in the laboratory.

A chapter called *Polyploidy* discusses the phenomenon of polyploidy, common in plants and often the result of hybridisation. Since polyploidy implies sterility *vis-à-vis* the ancestral species, it follows that a sexually isolated taxon has arisen. Dobzhansky admits that this phenomenon allows for the sudden origin of new species, but he rejects that species in general arise through such sudden events. Rather, under normal conditions taxonic divergence usually is preceded by isolation, a circumstance which may ensure the ecological survival of new forms which happen to arise through hybridisation. As hybrids they are protected from inbreeding with the ancestral forms, so their chances of survival are therefore quite high. This may be one reason for the large number of hybrids found in the vegetable kingdom. This is the essential message of the book so far as evolution is concerned. However, even if the arguments are supported by various empirical observations, it cannot be claimed that Dobzhansky succeeded to throw much light on the problem of evolution.

In the first chapter Dobzhansky writes: '. . . genetics as a discipline is not synonymous with the evolution theory, nor is the evolution theory synonymous with any subdivision of genetics. Nevertheless, it remains true that genetics has so profound a bearing on the problem of the mechanisms of evolution that any evolution theory which disregards the established genetic principles is faulty at its source.'[6] May be so, but the same claim could be made with respect to many biological disciplines, and in particular to those which are concerned with the mechanisms responsible for the onto-genetic creation of living organisms, for instance developmental, cellular and molecular biology. Yet, in spite of Dobzhansky's warning, many people believe the study of evolution to be a subdivision of genetics.

Further on Dobzhansky writes:

> The genetics of the transmission, and the genetics of the realiza-tion of hereditary materials are concerned with individuals as units . . .
> Since evolution is a change in the genetic composition of

populations, the mechanisms of evolution constitute problems of population genetics . . . Experience seems to show, however, that there is no way toward an understanding of the mechanisms of macro-evolutionary changes, which require time on a geological scale, other than through a full comprehension of the micro-evolutionary processes observable within the span of a human lifetime and often controlled by man's will. For this reason we are compelled at the present level of knowledge reluctantly to put a sign of equality between the mechanisms of macro- and micro-evolution, and, proceeding on this assumption, to push our investigations as far ahead as this working hypothesis will permit.[7]

Dobzhansky is making a mistake in logic here. Evolution leads to changes in the genetic composition of populations, and it also leads to the origination of populations consisting of new kinds of individuals. However, the information residing in the genome does not explicitly specify the nature of the organism in question, rather, it is utilised in the epigenetic processes responsible for the ontogenetic creation of living organisms. And the latter concern individuals rather than populations, and therefore it follows that a theory accounting for the origin of new forms of life cannot be a theory dealing only with populations.

Even a relatively superficial acquaintance with epigenetics suffices to disclose that there are fundamental, and easily distinguishable differences between 'macroevolution' and 'microevolution'. Dobzhansky did not realise this, and therefore he felt obliged, if only reluctantly, to accept the micromutation theory as the only theory of evolution. There is one point in Dobzhansky's confession to which it is necessary to object, namely, the expression 'at the present level of knowledge'. All that is required to comprehend the difference between the two kinds of evolution is familiarity with von Baer's work. This is furthermore the clue to the falsification of the micromutation theory.

However this may be, Dobzhansky's book was a great success. It is hardly an exaggeration to assert that it has inspired more genetic research than any other single work.

Julian Huxley

In 1942 Julian Huxley published the book *Evolution: The Modern*

323

Synthesis,[8] which outlines the view of a general biologist. Huxley presents the synthesis of Darwinism and Mendelism without using a single mathematical equation. That he, in the footsteps of his grandfather, felt himself an advocate of Darwin is touchingly demonstrated by the fact that he writes 'Darwinian', but 'mendelian', when he uses these words as adjectives. Otherwise the book follows Darwin's 'true Baconian principles'; thus, the reference list contains about twelve hundred items from all relevant disciplines of biology. I believe that Huxley thereby substantially increased the evidence of favour of Evolutionism, that is, Lamarck's first theory of evolution. However, he did not present any facts supporting Darwin's micromutation theory.

On one point Huxley is, if not original then at least brave: as we have seen in a previous chapter (p. 50) he insists on the Lamarckian distinction between two kinds of evolution, which he calls progress and specialisation, respectively. The reason for Huxley's braveness in this context is that, ignoring vector mathematics, one cannot go forwards and sidewards at the same time, and analogously, the same force cannot drive evolution in two different directions. And although it is glaringly true that evolution has been both progressive and divergent, it may be logically correct to deny this fact when there is only one mechanism to propel the process. This was the situation facing Darwin, and when he had to decide whether natural selection should be made responsible for progressive or divergent (adaptive) evolution, he chose the latter. The same stand had been adopted by many of Darwin's followers, but Huxley knew too much about biology to accept this view. However, he might be braver than many other Darwinians, but perhaps less acute, for he did not resolve the dilemma, but rather put his trust in the omnipotence of natural selection: 'We have now dealt with the fact of evolutionary progress, and with the philosophical and biological difficulties inherent in the concept. What of its mechanism? It should be clear that if natural selection can account for adaptation and for long-range trends of specialization, it can account for progress too.'[9]

It should be observed that even if Huxley's book is an apology for 'the modern synthesis', it is not an unreserved acceptance of the mathematical approach. On several points he qualifies his stand, for instance, he objects to 'the one-to-one or billiard-ball view of genetics',[10] that is, the 'one gene — one character' hypothesis. From his own studies on embryogenesis and ontogenesis, notably the phenomenon of allometric growth, Huxley was well aware of the fact that living organisms are created through epigenetic processes, in which many factors interact. In the list of advocates presented here Huxley is the closest to an embryologist who ever defended 'the synthetic theory'. The readers of the present book will understand why.

Ernst Mayr

In the same year as Huxley, Ernst Mayr published his *Systematics and the Origin of Species*,[11] in which the taxonomist and bio-geographer has his say. The book is an outright advocacy of the micromutation theory: '. . . it is now agreed that the great majority of mutations produce small or even invisible changes'.[12] The evolutionary importance of macromutations, as advocated by Gold-schmidt and Schindewolf, is flatly rejected.

To Mayr, the taxonomist, the species assumes a central position, since every organism, past, present and future, by convention must belong to a species. As an adherent to Darwinism, Mayr accepts only one kind of evolution, divergence, which thus is nothing but a transformation of one species into another: '. . . the species is a passing stage in the stream of evolution'.[13] Mayr thus adopts the traditional view that the Linnaean taxa of higher rank are simply conventional groups of species, and hence it follows as a natural conclusion that '. . . there is only a difference of degree, not one of kind, between the two classes of phenomena [viz. macroevolution and microevolution, or the origin of supraspecific taxa and of species]'.[14]

The classical species concepts were all based on the assumption of the immutability of the species, and with the acceptance of evolution they evidently lose their validity. Consequently Mayr, the Evolutionist, felt obliged to introduce a new definition, outlining the 'biological species concept': 'Species are groups of actually or potentially interbreeding natural populations, which are reproductively isolated from other such groups.'[15] Like all other species concepts this one is not universally applicable, a point acknowledged by Mayr, but it focuses on the dynamic aspect of the origin of new species, rather than on the various phenotypic features which distinguish their members.

Before dealing with Mayr's views in detail we may first observe that he at the outset declares his adherence to Mendelian population genetics:

Single individuals are, at least in sexually reproducing species, rarely the immediate ancestors of completely new species. Speciation is, in general, not such a cataclysmic process. It is now becoming more certain with every new investigation that species descend from groups of individuals which become separated from the other members of the species, through physical or biological barriers, and diverge through this period of isolation. The concept of the isolated population as incipient species is of the greatest importance for the problem of speciation.[16]

In order to handle the problem of evolutionary divergence Mayr introduces two concepts: 'Two forms or species are *sympatric*, if they occur together, that is if their areas of distribution overlap or coincide. Two forms (or species) are *allopatric*, if they do not occur together, that is if they exclude each other geographically.'[17] (Since the plants and animals with which the evolutionist is concerned inhabit the Earth, it is of course admissible to use the word 'geographically' in this context, not the least because isolation often occurs on islands and mountains, or in lakes. But isolation may also happen for instance in caves, and therefore it seems that the word 'spatially' would be more generally applicable.) The two concepts are evidently quite trivial if they concern widely different species; it is only when the species or forms are closely related that they become important in an evolutionary context.

Departing from these definitions it is possible to distinguish between allopatric and sympatric speciation. The former event is outlined in the following way: '*A new species develops if a population which has become geographically isolated from its parental species acquires during this period of isolation characters which promote or guarantee reproductive isolation when the external barriers break down.*'[18]

Like Darwin, Mayr thus accepts that reproductive isolation cannot be established through natural selection, and he therefore suggests that spatial isolation is the first step in the process of divergent evolution. Spatial isolation is a completely fortuitous phenomenon; at times, for instance as a consequence of plate tectonics, large populations may become isolated at a single occasion, but often, probably most often, a new species may be founded 'by a single pair or by a single fertilized female'.[19] This assertion contradicts the claim quoted above, namely that single individuals rarely are the ancestors of new species. On the other hand, it seems to imply a corroboration of the macromutation theory, according to which new taxa originate through inbreeding. In small populations the chances are greatly enhanced that new characters become established. Such features may be advantageous under the prevailing conditions of life, but they need not be so. The new characters may be phenotypic or they may promote sexual isolation; these two kinds of phenomena are random and completely independent. Thus, the isolated population may evolve phenotypically to the extent that only the preserved sexual compatibility discloses its affinity with the parental species, or contrariwise, it may be indistinguishable from the latter phenotypically, but sexually isolated. The normal situation presumably lies between these extremes.

If sexual isolation is acquired, it must be a consequence of fortuitous events in which it seems impossible to impute the participation of natural selection. However, if contact with the parent species is established before isolation is complete, if the tendency to heterogeneous mating is inheritable, and if the hybrids have reduced viability, then natural selection may ensure the completion of speciation by establishing an ethological isolation mechanism.

Sympatric speciation involves divergence without any preceding spatial isolation. Mayr writes: 'It is now being realized that species originate in general through the evolution of entire populations. If one believes in speciation through individuals, one is by necessity an adherent of sympatric speciation, the two concepts being very closely connected.'[20] This quotation and the following discussion clearly show that, as might be expected on the given premises, Mayr is quite averse to sympatric speciation.

Allopatric speciation is the work of physical agents external to the organisms themselves. On the contrary, if sympatric speciation is to ensue, then a change must occur in the organisms proper which led to reproductive isolation. This may be obtained in various ways: (i) *Ecological isolation* obtains if the organism can invade a new niche, for instance a new habitat or a new kind of food. (ii) *Ethological isolation* may occur if changes occur in the courtship patterns associated with mating. (iii) *Mechanical isolation* prevails if successful copulation is prevented because of the incompatibility of the sexual organs. (iv) *Genetic isolation* obtains when the offspring is non-viable or sterile.

If one of these various mechanisms was to concern all the members of a population then clearly no isolation would be possible. Rather, as indicated by Mayr, sympatric isolation presupposes that one, or some few individuals acquire the property that allows for isolation. This implies that sympatric speciation is instantaneous, and ensured through inbreeding. Since a mutation, which in one step results in reproductive isolation, rather deserves to be called a 'macromutation', it is no wonder that Mayr is opposed to sympatric speciation, claiming that it is rare in the animal, if not in the vegetal kingdom. We shall return to this question in a later section.

Just as in the case of allopatric speciation, it is seen that sympatric speciation involves that a few individuals become isolated, and under these circumstances natural selection hardly has any role to play in divergent evolution. It is understandable, therefore, that there are few references to natural selection in the index. In fact, Mayr even goes so far as to claim: 'That strong competition [i.e. natural selection] is a retarding factor in evolution has never been seriously questioned.'[21] One really wonders whether this assertion would be endorsed by all those Evolutionists who invoke 'selection pressure' whenever they have to account for any state of affairs prevailing in the animal or vegetal kingdom.

Mayr also deals with the question of adaptation:

Each population is more or less adapted . . . to the particular environment in which it lives. Neighboring environments are similar, and we might therefore expect that neighboring populations would be similar in their external and internal characters. This has been found to be true in areas in which there are no striking environmental changes. In such areas, as for example in neighboring continental districts or on chains of islands, each local climate intergrades with the neighboring ones to form one continuous gradient. It has also been found, as we would expect from these premises, that such morphological characters as tend to be correlated with climate factors — as, for example, size, proportions, and pigmentation — show a similar and parallel gradient . . . The existence of [such] clines . . . is a necessity, if we believe in the adaptive power of natural selection by the environment.[22]

That clines would exist in large continuous areas is natural, for here geographical dispersal may be expected to occur in an orderly and gradual fashion. This may even happen in chains of islands, but there chances are greater that random events may be involved. And in fact, this seems to be the case: 'Of particular interest are the cases in which a small and well-isolated population deviates considerably in size from the rest of the species. This happens particularly on islands or on mountains. It was formerly believed that insular forms were invariably smaller than mainland forms, but this is by no means true. The only generalization we can make is that island forms are often different in size from the other populations of the species.'[23] This observation ought to shake 'the belief in the adaptive power of natural selection'; rather, the empirical facts suggest that not only is the process of spatial isolation random, but so is what happens to become isolated. Thus, although it cannot be questioned that the size of animals is often correlated with the environment in which they live, this is by no means always the case.

Mayr has always had a critical attitude towards Mendelian population genetics, and it is hardly a coincidence that among the founding fathers Wright is quoted most often, and Haldane not at all. This shows that Mayr opted for an outsider variety of population genetics, in which isolation plays a very important role.

As a good empiricist Mayr wanted to substantiate his conviction by means of factual data. Indeed, his book contains a fascinating collection of observations on the natural history of animals in general, and of birds in particular, and many of these are original. But his interests stretch beyond taxonomy and biogeography; thus he also emphasises the importance of the epigenetic aspect of evolution. He writes: 'The organism seems to change as a harmonious entity, and not by random mutation of parts.'[24] It is surprising, however, to find this apt statement being succeeded by the following claim: 'An even-greater puzzle is the question as to why in certain groups entire "blocks of characters" are retained without change, characters that are family, order, or class characters.'[25] These characters are parts of the respective body plans, which are causally engaged in the various epigenetic processes through which the organisms arise. Their suppression would imply the annihilation of the type of organisms in question.

Mayr wrote a very readable book, but he did not succeed in presenting any evidence in support of the view that species arise through the toilsome accumulation of micromutations of trifling value for survival. Although he rejected the macromutation theory, it appears that most of his facts fit better with this than with its rival.

George Gaylord Simpson

The next to rally to the patronage of the new theory was the

329

palaeontologist George Gaylord Simpson, in the book *Tempo and Mode in Evolution* from 1944.[26] As appears from the title Simpson took up the question about the rates at which various organisms have evolved. The answer to this question cannot be derived from the population genetical equations, nor from genetical experiments, so in principle any outcome will be compatible with the theory. However, if it is true that the changes in the environment control evolution by forcing adaptation upon the organisms, then the most plausible supposition would be that contemporaneous organisms evolve at approximately equal rates, since they appear to share, more or less, the same environment.

With reference to the fossil record Simpson found that the observable rates of evolution differ widely; some do not change at all during hundreds of million years, others, the 'bradytelic' forms, evolve very slowly, while the 'tachytelic' forms evolve fast. The taxa evolving at about standard rates were called 'horotelic'. This result did not upset anybody, for it is easy enough to challenge the presumption that organisms living side by side have a common environment. If this premise is rejected, then it is no longer difficult to understand that the brachiopod *Lingula* has remained unchanged for 400 million years, whereas human beings have originated from ape-like forms in the course of a few million years.

One question which must haunt the palaeontologists who have converted to the micromutation theory is the size of evolutionary steps. We have already seen that Darwin himself admitted the lack of agreement between expectation and observation in the fossil record, and accounted for this with reference to its incompleteness. As Simpson was writing almost a century later than Darwin, one might expect that the situation had been remedied in the intervening period.

Simpson discusses the problem in a chapter called *Micro-Evolution, Macro-Evolution, and Mega-Evolution*. Here we may read: 'Micro-evolution involves mainly changes within potentially continuous populations, and there is little doubt that its materials are those revealed by genetic experimentation. Macro-evolution involves the rise and divergence of discontinuous groups, and it is still debatable whether it differs in kind or only in degree from micro-evolution. *If the two proved to be basically different, the innumerable studies on micro-evolution would become relatively unimportant and would have minor value in the study of evolution as a whole*'[27] (my italics). There is nothing to disagree with here, except to point out that even differences in degree, if they are large enough, may serve to invalidate the micromutation theory.

The subject is complicated, however, by Simpson's introduction of three terms, and it is necessary to state their implications. Thus, as we have seen, 'micro-evolution' is the phenomenon studied in the genetic laboratory. The other two concepts are defined as follows: 'If the term "macro-evolution" is applied to the rise of taxonomic groups that are at or near the minimum level of genetic discontinuity (species and genera), the large-scale evolution studied by the paleontologist might be called "mega-evolution" . . . As will be shown, the paleontologist has more reason to believe in a qualitative distinction between macro-evolution and mega-evolution than in one between micro-evolution and macro-evolution.'[28]

Further on we read:

> Nevertheless, when the materials are available and have been carefully studied, the development of *discontinuity* between species and genera, and sometimes between still higher categories, so regularly follows one sort of pattern that it is only reasonable to infer that this is normal and that *the sequences missing* from the record would tend to follow much the same pattern. The development of the *discontinuity* between *Merychippus* and *Hypohippus* . . . is one of the most complete examples. There can hardly be a question in such a case that the differentiation of the two lines involved *no qualitatively distinct process* peculiar to macroevolution. *They diverged gradually, almost imperceptibly at first, by the segregation and further modification of genetic factors analogous to those already involved in the store of variability present in their common ancestry.* (My italics, except for the Latin names)[29]

I am afraid that we here catch Simpson in fallacious reasoning. In a discussion of whether or not discontinuities exist, it is not warranted to presume that observable discontinuities represent missing sequences. And discontinuity between the two early horses need not be qualitatively distinct, it might be quantitative. Morphologically the main difference between the okapi and the giraffe may be explained as a quantitative mutation concerning the control of the skeletal growth. It should be noted that the last phrase, dealing with the *discontinuity* between *Merychippus* and *Hypohippus*, contains statements which must be classed as mere assertions. Simpson continues:

This and innumerable other examples show beyond reasonable doubt that the horizontal discontinuity between species, genera, and at least the next higher categories can arise by a process that is continuous vertically and that new types on these taxonomic levels often arise gradually at rates and in ways that are comparable to some sorts of subspecific differentiation and have greater results only because they have had longer duration. Two *serious* questions remain: whether this really is the usual or universal pattern on these levels, and whether it also occurs or is normal for still higher taxonomic categories. The *facts* are that many species and genera, *indeed the majority, do appear suddenly in the record*, differing sharply and in many ways from any earlier group, and that this *appearance of discontinuity* becomes *more common the higher the level, until it is virtually universal as regards orders and all higher steps in the taxonomic hierarchy.*

The face of the record thus does *really* suggest normal discontinuity at *all* levels, most particularly at high levels, and some paleontologists (e.g., Spath and Schindewolf) insist on taking the record at this face value. Others, (e.g., Matthew and Osborn) discount this evidence completely and maintain that the breaks neither prove nor suggest that there is any normal mode of evolution other than that seen in continuously evolving and abundantly recorded groups. (My italics)[30]

Evidently one century of arduous work had not brought forth the slightest evidence in favour of the micromutation theory. No wonder that palaeontologists who take their trade seriously, and believe that they unearth *reliable* facts, generally consider that the empirical evidence falsifies the micromutation theory. In this context one might really want to know more about the 'normal mode of evolution . . . seen in continuously evolving and abundantly recorded groups'.

Prima facie, the palaeontological evidence thus rather seems to favour the macromutation theory, so the case cannot be settled without further *Explanations of Systematic Discontinuities of Record*. Thus we read on:

In the early days of evolutionary paleontology it was assumed that the major gaps would be filled in by further discoveries, and even, *falsely*, that some discoveries had already filled them. As it became more and more evident that the great gaps remained, despite wonderful progress in finding the members of lesser transitional groups and progressive lines, it was no longer satisfactory to impute this absence of objective data entirely to chance . . .

The paleontological evidence for the saltation theory of mega-evolution is *solely* the systematic nature of the breaks in the record. The evidence *against* this theory is largely *indirect*, but it is *cumulative* and in sum is *conclusive* . . . In other words, if intermediate types never existed, obviously they would never be found; but they are sometimes found. *The gaps are not completely filled* by such *isolated* discoveries, so *it is always possible to maintain that saltation did occur earlier or later*; but the facts certainly suggest that the sampling of the transition periods has been inadequate, and they lend no real support to the saltation theory. It has previously been pointed out how *very unlikely, if not impossible*, it is that such major saltations have occurred, according to present understanding of the *genetic* mechanism. The most nearly concrete suggestion of a mechanism adequate for saltation is that of Goldschmidt . . . and he quite fails to adduce factual evidence that his postulated mechanism ever has produced or ever really could produce such an effect.

As I see it, then, all the evidence *except that of the breaks in the record*, is opposed to this theory, which thus merits further serious consideration, in the light of present knowledge, only if no alternative hypothesis is equally or more probable as an explanation of the breaks and is fully consistent with the other data. (My italics)[31]

And then Simpson begins to present alternative explanations of the gaps, beginning with the imperfection of the fossil record. Next he outlines a theory of 'punctuated equilibria', as Darwin had done before, and Eldredge and Gould after him.[32]

It thus appears that Simpson finds himself in exactly the same situation as Darwin: the fossil record does not support the micromutation theory. And like his predecessor he does not accept falsification of the theory he has adopted, and therefore he follows the Darwinian example and explains away the empirical evidence by means of *ad hoc* hypotheses. Thus, as far as palaeontology is concerned, no progress has been made since Darwin. I readily admit that fossil evidence does not, and cannot prove the validity of the macromutation theory. But it is certainly not true that the cumulative evidence is against it; rather, in spite of no doubt arduous attempts to collect evidence in favour of the micromutation theory the gaps remain which ominously corroborate the rival theory.

THE LOST CAUSE

The arguments raised by the early critics of Darwin's micromutation theory were so telling that, as we have seen, the theory was generally, if not unanimously, rejected for half a century. However, to a public brought up in the supremacy of Empiricism, this refutation has a serious shortcoming, it is based largely on logical reasoning, not on facts. To be sure, the prevailing empirical data were rather embarrassing to the micromutation theory, but as we have seen, neither Darwin nor his followers accepted them as falsifying evidence.

So the relation between the two theories remained a matter of preference or belief, an unstable equilibrium which for a long time favoured the macromutation theory. However, when the popularisers of Neo-Mendelism enthusiastically announced that the newly founded theory was indeed supported by facts representing several biological disciplines, the scales were tipped and all the previous objections were soon forgotten.

At this stage it is necessary to make a clarification. The validity of Neo-Mendelism as a theory of population genetics has never been challenged; as such, it is indeed one of the finest achievements in biology. However, it does not follow that it is also a theory of evolution, reaffirming and extending Darwin's micromutation theory. If this were true, then the population geneticists might rightly claim that biologists of all other brands must adjust the interpretations of their observations to fit the Neo-Mendelian theory. In fact, this has happened to a considerable extent: for several decades most biologists saw fit to explain almost every biological phenomenon as an 'adaptation' established through the action of a 'selection pressure'. However, to some biologists this claim seemed incongruous; there was always an almost silent opposition in which, it appears, dissatisfaction was slowly building up. As time went on, the opponents did not any longer have to rely merely on logical arguments, for falsifying evidence began to accumulate.

This is what we shall discuss in the following subsections.

The breeders' testimony

In his 'Essay of 1844' Darwin asserted that '. . . sports [i.e. carriers of macromutations] are known in some cases to have been parents of some of our domestic races'.[33] We have already seen that in

THE RISE AND THE FALL

1859 the micromutation theory was so close to his heart that he felt bound to belittle the importance of macromutations, *even in the context of domestic breeding*.

This was a completely unnecessary concession, made against his better judgement, and it has been refuted at various occasions by people acquainted with the practice of breeding plants and animals. In the present subsection I shall quote only one such instance. Referring to the statement by August Weismann quoted on p. 276, Raymond Pearl wrote in 1917:

> Even since 1909 a good deal of water has flowed under all our bridges, and particularly under the evolutionary ones. Among other changes in viewpoint there is evident a marked disinclination in science nowadays to regard as 'scientific truth' anything which is not based upon demonstrating evidence. But it is also a fact, perhaps at first thought to be regarded as curious, in view of the opinion of Weismann . . . that there are here with us to-day those who assert, with great zeal and pertinacity, that in selection is to be found the chief cause of evolutionary change. These things being so, it has seemed that possibly it might be profitable to spend a little time upon the selection problem, trying to determine whether the case is any better now than Weismann conceived it to be seven years ago, *from the viewpoint of tangible objective evidence*. It is to be hoped that it is, for among working geneticists just now *any theory which has to depend for its sole support upon its 'interpretative value' is sure to receive scant attention*. (My italics)[34]

After discussing a number of inconclusive observations made on natural phenomena, Pearl turns to his own speciality: *The Experience of the Practical Breeders*. Pearl begins thus:

> At the outstart it may be recalled that it was on the supposed results of artificial selection, as set forth in the experience of practical breeders, that Darwin chiefly relied for objective evidence in favour of natural selection.
>
> In general this evidence has been accepted very uncritically by followers of Darwin. This is not strange in view of the fact that there have been, and are now, relatively few trained biologists who know anything at first hand about the practical breeding of animals.
>
> This fact has led to some entirely unwarranted inclusions in the

technical literature of biology. Statements in the agricultural press which were intended by their breeder-authors merely as harmless generalities . . . have been accorded, by the laboratory evolutionist, the dignity and authority of detailed reports of actual breeding operations, and cited as valuable evidence on the problem of evolution.

This confusion has played particular havoc in discussions of the selection problem because of the general and usually quite irresponsible use of the term 'selection' by practical breeders. In the literature of live stock breeding the word 'selection' has been, and is being used to-day, to designate, upon occasion, every known kind of breeding operation. To illustrate: a fancier who bred a new variety of poultry started with a mongrel male bird which happened to possess just the combination of characters which he wanted in his new breed, as the result of a previous series of indiscriminate crossings. This male was crossed with a female of a well established breed which possessed some of the desired characters. The daughters from this mating were back-crossed to their sire, the original male bird, and so in turn were his granddaughters. The granddaughter's progeny constituted the new breed, full blown and breeding tolerably true. This was an entirely legitimate, and indeed usual, way of making a new breed. But the point lies in the fact that the breeder who did all this always refers publicly to the series of matings which has just been described as 'this process of *selection*'.[35]

But the breeder was right, of course; he was indeed selecting, in the sense of 'choosing', 'picking out', 'isolating', etc. And his *selection* was for the purpose of *inbreeding*. Since Darwin rejected that inbreeding takes place in Nature, it follows that 'selection' must mean different things to the breeder and to the Darwinian, a circumstance which partly leads to confusion and partly undermines the value of the breeders' observations for the support of Darwin's theory. There can be no doubt that this lax terminology, on the parts of the breeders *and* the geneticists has been of great harm to evolutionary discourse.

Pearl continues:

So fixed in the minds of most biologists not acquainted with agricultural matters at first hand is the idea that the vast majority of improved varieties of plants and animals owe their origin, or their improvement, or both, to cumulative selection of slight differences, that it appears desirable to review briefly a few of the actual facts . . . the 'experience of practical breeders' shows that the principle of the gradual accumulation by continued selection of minute somatic variations has had no essential part in the origin or amelioration of certainly a great many of the best varieties of agricultural plants which we have to-day. The essential factors which have been involved in the production of our best fruits, grains, vegetables, flowers, etc., have been (1) the improved conditions of domestication, (2) *mutations, leading at once to new and better forms*, (3) hybridization, which by new combinations of characters . . . has led to amelioration, and (4) the purification of previously mixed races of varieties by selective sorting. It is to the overwhelming importance of one or a combination of these factors that the 'experience of breeders' points and not to Darwinian selection. (My italics)[36]

According to Pearl the situation is less clear-cut as concerns animals, but I am sure that many of the domestic races of poultry, pigeons, dogs and horses owe their origin to macromutations rather than micromutations. However, the other of Pearl's factors listed above may also be influential in this instance.

More than half a century has passed since Pearl wrote his article; nevertheless, I am convinced that his views have preserved their validity to the present day.

The classical and the balance theory

We shall now discuss two theories which have been applied to the interpretation of the results obtained in population genetical experiments. The first of these, the *classical theory*, advocated notably by H.J. Muller, asserts that the genomes of plants and animals are largely homozygous with respect to various 'wild type' genes, which represent a state of maximum adaptation. Since the majority of mutations are disadvantageous, natural selection is mainly concerned with the elimination of such mutations as they happen to arise; it thus must strive to establish a state of minimum variability. This theory has a serious shortcoming, it does not account for the genetic variation required for the process of adaptation which is supposed to occur under changing environmental conditions.

Actually, the classical theory is hardly compatible with the notion that natural selection is the driving force in evolution, and in fact, it turned out that it does not conform with empirical observations. It was found that in many organisms, and notably in various species of *Drosophila*, there is an enormous amount of variation hidden in the form of recessive mutations. This discovery implies the existence of a large amount of material on which natural selection can work, the logical provision for the notion that living organisms through a 'selection pressure' become 'adapted' to their environment.

One problem arose from these observations, namely, the unexpected occurrence of a large proportion of heterozygotes. This phenomenon has been interpreted in three different ways: (i) There is only one niche in which the organisms prevail, and the heterozygotes are better adapted to it than any of the homozygotes. Under these circumstances, Dobzhansky suggested, natural selection must be balancing, striving towards an equilibrium where all three genotypes are represented.[37] (ii) There are two niches, one for each of the homozygotes; the heterozygotes arise from fortuitous crossings.[38] (iii) There are three niches, one for each of the genotypes.[39] This clearly shows the rich explanatory power of the *balance theory*, although a certain apprehension is felt in view of the illimitable number of niches which must exist, if three are required for each pair of alleles. I am rather inclined to agree with Marcel Blanc: 'It is seen that in most of these models the question about "the survival of the fittest" is inverted: each individual carrier of particular genetic characters is "fittest" in the milieu which fits to it.'[40]

After the discovery that a great genetic variation obtains under normal conditions, and the consequent acceptance of Dobzhansky's balance theory:

. . . evolutionary biologists . . . held the following opinions virtually unanimously.

(a) There is always sufficient genetic diversity present in any natural population to respond to any selection pressure. Therefore actual mutation rates always are in excess of the evolutionary needs of the species.

(b) There is no relationship between the mutation rate and the rate of evolutionary change.

(c) Because mutations tend to recur at reasonably high rates, any clearly adaptive mutation is certain to already have been fixed. Therefore, natural populations are at, or very near, either the best of all possible genetic constitutions, or an adaptive peak of genotype frequencies . . .

(d) Since all possible adaptive mutations are fixed, and since neutral mutations are unknown, virtually all new mutations are deleterious, unless the environment has changed very recently. Even a recent change in the environment does not make new mutations necessary, because of (a).

(e) Evolution is directed entirely by natural selection, acting on genetic variability that is produced by recombination, from 'raw materials' produced by recurrent mutation a long time ago.

(f) Mutation is random with respect to function.[41]

In the original work on population genetics the experimentalists had to content themselves to working with random mutations exhibiting visible phenotypic effects. The latter are widely separated from the location where the mutations are supposed to take place, namely, the genotype. This situation has changed radically in recent years as new molecular biological methods have become available, permitting the demonstration of enzyme alleles through electrophoresis, the linear amino acid composition in proteins, etc.[42] Through these means it is possible to study directly the effects of the various mutations.

The electrophoretic studies have shown that for a number of enzymes it is quite normal to find several alleles, representing differences with respect to at least one, and sometimes several amino acids. This implies the complete falsification of the classical theory, leaving only the balance theory to account for the observations. Thus, if the enzyme alleles vary from one locality to another, the variation must be considered an adaptation; if they are similar, there are two alternative interpretations, either there is no environmental variation or else the prevailing alleles represent the superior heterozygote. Evidently, there are so many possibilities to account for empirical data that it may be impossible to falsify the balance theory. From an empirical point of view it is thus not a very good theory, and it is therefore interesting to note that its most serious challenge, involving probably its refutation, came from a theoretical quarter.

The neutral theory

Like the Phoenix, the classical theory rose from the ashes in the form of a *neutral theory*. One of the founders of this theory, Motoo

339

Kimura, a theoretical population geneticist, was started on this new line of thought by some logically disturbing facts, revealed by studies on the amino acid sequences in various proteins: (i) the rate of amino acid substitution is nearly the same in many diverse lineages; (ii) the substitutions seem to be random rather than exhibiting a particular pattern; (iii) the overall rate of change at the level of DNA is much higher than could reasonably be anticipated; and (iv) the wealth of genetic variation observable by electrophoresis has no distinguishable phenotypic effects and no *obvious* correlation with environmental factors.[43] These facts are puzzling to the Neo-Mendelians, as well as to Evolutionists in general. To the former, the great genetic variability is troublesome because it implies an enormous genetic load, so great indeed that it is inconceivable that the organisms survive at all. The latter are aware that evolutionary divergence is a matter of changing phenotypes, notably at the morphological level, whereas little evolutionary change has occurred at the lower levels of organisation. The observations rather indicate the opposite relation.

Kimura suggested an ingenious solution to these difficulties: the observed amino acid substitutions are neutral, or at least quasi-neutral; that is, as long as a protein preserves its function, it matters little if an amino acid at a particular site is exchanged for another one. In this context it should be mentioned that certain sites are known to be 'invariant', that is, they do not allow for any exchange whatever, presumably because such substitutions seriously impair the function of the protein in question. If a random mutation happens at such a site, it will be eliminated immediately by selection. However, this situation concerns only a relatively small part of the total number of sites, and does not affect the main tenets of the neutral theory.

By this stratagem Kimura overcame the objections against the balance theory as concerns the genetic load, for if a mutation is neutral it is not subject to natural selection, and therefore it cannot carry any load. Thus it may appear that Kimura has salvaged the balance theory, but this is not the case, for if the mutations are neutral, they cannot contribute either to adaptation or to hetero-zygotic superiority. Instead Kimura's theory has been suggested to substantiate the classical theory. This may be right in so far as the counterarguments concerning the genetic load are invalidated, but it is difficult to see in which other way the neutral theory brings forth any support of the classical theory.

From the preceding discussion it appears that there is no need to obliterate the genetic load, for it does not exist. But the validity of the neutral theory is completely independent of the notion of 'genetic load'. This is evidenced by the fact that the other champions of the neutral theory, Thomas Hughes Jukes and Jack Lester King, do not mention it in their development of the theory, which is based on observations concerning amino acid substitutions associated with mutations in various proteins.[44]

From the population genetical point of view the neutral theory creates a serious problem, since natural selection does not allow for the fixation of neutral mutations. Yet, as shown by Sewall Wright, they may yet survive by chance, through genetic drift, if the populations in which they occur are very small. From the traditional Neo-Mendelian point of view this is a rather demanding requirement, since it is customary to operate with populations comprising relatively large numbers of individuals.

The neutral theory only concerns evolution at the molecular level, but as far as it goes it has indeed very astounding consequences. These were stated by King in the following way:

(a) *most specific allelic states* achievable by even the simplest and most common form of mutation — single nucleotide substitution — *are highly unlikely to be present within a species at any point of time*;

(b) there is a *simple and direct relationship between the mutation rate and the rate of evolutionary change* on the molecular level;

(c) *specific mutations do not recur at reasonable high rates*; a species may have to wait millions of years before a specific adaptive mutation occurs and begins to increase toward fixation;

(d) *an evolutionary significant proportion of new mutations are either neutral or very slightly advantageous*;

(e) an increased mutation rate may be beneficial to a population or a species;

(f) mutation is not random with respect to function on the molecular level. (My italics)[45]

I have emphasised some parts of these statements, but I could as well have stressed every word, for clearly the message conveyed is extremely startling from the traditional point of view.

The conclusions listed by King are based on results obtained by various approaches, which all concur in yielding a value of around 2×10^{-9} substitutions per year in each line of descent. On the currently accepted presumption that a substantial part of the DNA in the genome is genetically inactive, the frequency of potentially significant mutations will be still smaller. It is evident that this outcome is difficult to reconcile with many current notions. Thus: 'This rate [of substitution] is so low that it is almost nonsensical to consider recurrent mutations to specific alleles to be evolutionarily significant . . . It is quite false to suppose that the requisite genetic variability is present to meet every evolutionary need, *if one conceives of evolutionary needs in terms of specific molecular changes.*'[46]

It appears that the advocates of the neutral theory are here facing a manifest dilemma, namely, that their observations on the molecular level of organisation seem to disagree with those obtained at the higher levels of organisation. This disagreement is implied by the two sets of statements by King quoted above, and it is therefore of interest to see how he stands up to this challenge: 'The remarkable thing about this consensus of opinion on the role of mutation in evolution is that it is generally true on the level at which it was formulated, namely, morphological and physiological evolution; at the same time, every statement is untrue at the level of molecular change in evolution.'[47]

This dilemma was also discussed by Kimura:

Darwinian selection acts mainly on phenotypes shaped by the activity of many genes. Environmental conditions surely play a decisive role in determining what phenotypes are selected for; Darwinian, or positive selection cares little how those phenotypes are determined by genotypes. *The laws governing molecular evolution are clearly different from those governing phenotypic evolution.* Even if Darwin's principle of natural selection prevails in determining evolution at the phenotypic level, down at the level of the internal structure of the genetic material a great deal of evolutionary change is propelled by random drift. *Although this random process is slow and insignificant in the time frame of man's ephemeral existence, over geological time it makes for change on an enormous scale.* (My italics)[48]

Many present-day biologists are Reductionists; that is, they hold that ultimately all biological phenomena can be accounted for in terms of physics and chemistry. The fabulous advances made in molecular biology during the past few decades have of course served to strengthen this belief. In the last two quotations we have seen the foremost representatives of the neutral theory to claim that there is a clear dissociation between evolution at the molecular and the organismic level; a hard blow, it seems to me, to Reductionism in general and to molecular genetics in particular. If I have not misunderstood the last emphasised clause, it appears that Kimura tries to mitigate the effect of the conclusion by claiming that, given sufficient time, an essentially random molecular process may have been responsible for evolution as we know it.

The defenders of the traditional view have come out against the Neutralists, because they cannot accept that once we came to know the nature of the genome and the mutations it undergoes, this knowledge turned out to be of little service for our understanding of the mechanism of evolution. Wanting the observable mutations to represent those changes which lead to adaptation, they have attacked the neutralist theory without in any case being able to falsify it or to corroborate their own view convincingly.[49]

In a way this adverse attitude is quite astonishing, for if the Neutralists had been more bold, they could have claimed their data to show that the observable molecular events have little to do with evolution. To be sure, it cannot be excluded that an accumulation or recombination of neutral mutations *per se* may accomplish a miracle, for instance a protein with new catalytic properties, or a combination of enzymes allowing for the occurrence of a new set of reactions. Indeed, such happenings must have occurred at several occasions, but they do not correspond to the stepwise accumulation through natural selection of slightly advantageous mutations envisaged by the Micromutationists.

In point of fact, evolutionary innovation is not really a matter of molecules. This view was stated by Peter B. Medawar: '. . . in a certain important sense all chemical evolution in living organisms stopped millions of years before even our faintest and most distant records of life began. So far as I know, no new *kind* of chemical compound has come into being over a period of evolution that began long before animals became differentiated from plants . . . I have no views on the processes of evolution that brought new kinds of chemical compounds into existence, but I should not be surprised to find them very different from the forms of evolution that have been in progress since.'[50] Clearly, this citation is an eloquent argument in favour of the logical consequence of the neutral theory derived above. This assertion has subsequently been substantiated by Britten and Davidson who showed that 93 per cent of the enzymes present in eukaryotes are also present in prokaryotes.[51]

Since so little change has taken place on the chemical level in the course of evolution, it seems reasonable to assume that it matters little whether the electrical charge of a protein is slightly changed by amino acid substitution. So there may be much truth in the following statement made by another of the advocates of the neutral theory, Tomoko Ohta: 'Once the structure and function of a molecule are determined in the course of evolution, natural selection acts mainly to maintain them, because all later evolutionary changes proceed under selective constraints. Natural selection then becomes mostly 'negative' and positive Darwinian selection is only a minor part of both total selection and the total number of mutant-substitutions.'[52]

Richard C. Lewontin has attempted to give an objective evaluation of the relative merits of the two theories:

> On the one hand, there are strong reasons for rejecting a balance theory because it predicts tremendous inbreeding depressions that are not observed, because the rates of evolution of different molecules strongly suggest that the least functional evolve fastest, because heterozygosity does not seem to be sensitive to ecological stringency, and because selection has proved extremely difficult to find in operation. On the other hand, the theory that standing variation and most substitutions of amino acids have been neutral also strains our credulity to the limit, because it requires us to believe that population sizes for all species are effectively the same, because it requires adaptive mutation to be several orders of magnitude less frequent than neutral changes, because there is too much variation from locus to locus in the amount of divergence between populations, because of striking similarities in allelic frequency distributions in closely related species, and because the majority of polymorphic substitutions do alter the functional properties of enzymes.[53]

In a review of Lewontin's book, King describes how the author has come to the conclusion that the controversy between the neo-classical (= neutral) and the balance model '. . . will never be resolved . . . because the different viewpoints are less a matter of the observable facts of nature than a matter of the philosophical, sociological and political conditioning of its adherents: not a matter of what we observe, but of what we believe, which is, of course, what we want to believe.'[54] Apparently, present-day Evolutionists are here facing an issue which seems to belong to the realms of metaphysics.

Personally, I feel that the schism is based on a mistake, stemming from failing knowledge about the creative aspect of evolution. Molecules are the tools and the materials of epigenesis, and the information concerning their formation is stored in the genome. So there can be no question about the extreme importance of the genome and the genetical mechanisms through which this information is transferred from generation to generation. And yet, the changes of *architectural* style through the ages, at least up to recent times, show that the output may vary even if the tools and the materials remain unchanged. This, I believe, is the key to the understanding of phylogenetic evolution, namely, that it is primarily an exercise in changing styles.

It has been suggested by Francis Crick that the genetic code is a 'frozen accident',[55] and the same notion has been suggested by Susumu Ohno to hold even with regard to the location of the various genes on the chromosomes.[56] The viewpoint outlined here suggests that phylogenetic evolution in general may consist of 'frozen accidents'. Thus, the archetypes or body plans which represent the several superior taxa arose through unique events several hundred millions of years ago, and they have endured because they happened to be exposed to environments where their bearers could live in isolation. Their continued survival and divergence did not depend upon any particular adaptation to the environment. Rather, besides catastrophes the only phenomenon which could threaten their continued existence was the fortuitous origination of new dominant forms which could invade their particular niche.

If the ideas outlined here are correct, then the connection between molecular and phylogenetic evolution must be, if not non-existent, then at least very tenuous. This, I believe, is the resolution of the dissent mentioned above. It should not be insupportable to the Neutralists, but those geneticists who believe that the testimony of molecular evolution has a significant bearing on phylogenetic evolution, will hardly welcome it with enthusiasm. It may therefore be relevant to stress that in recent years much evidence has been observed indicating '. . . that enzyme-coding loci are relatively insensitive markers of speciation and macro-evolutionary events in general'.[57] To those who do not appreciate my conclusion, I shall quote the following words by Lewontin: 'To concentrate only on genetic change, without attempting to relate it to the kinds of physiological, morphogenetic, and behavioral evolution that are manifest in the fossil record and in the diversity of extant organisms and communities, is to forget entirely what it is we are trying to explain

345

in the first place.'[58]

There is still another paradox in the antagonism between the classical–neutral and the balance theories. We have seen that the neutral theory allows for a considerable variation at the molecular level which, being neutral, is without evolutionary significance, a circumstance which implies that beneficial variations must be extremely rare events. The consequence of this view is stated by Lewontin in the following way:

> If populations are almost entirely homozygous [or heterozygous with respect to neutral mutations], then speciation must await the occurrence of new mutations that may be advantageous in a new environment in which an isolated population is found . . . The classical hypothesis comes close to reintroducing the paradox about speciation that Darwin thought he had solved. Darwin had resolved the problem of passing from one type or mode to another, which is what appears to occur in species formation, by fastening attention on the variation within species and by postulating that this intragroup variation was converted into variation between groups by isolation and natural selection . . . But if organisms are really very homozygous and therefore genetically identical within species, where is that variation on which Darwin supposed natural selection to operate?[59]

This is indeed a very relevant question. For if the neutralist theory is correct, then it seems that the various changes recorded by the breeders are more important for our understanding of evolution than those observed by the molecular biologists. In fact, it appears that the classical–neutral theory may be interpreted to constitute a strong support of the macromutation theory.

Morphological and chemical evolution

The neutral theory seems to imply a serious, if indirect challenge to the current molecular biological notion that major characters, among which the various morphological features used for classification, arise through the accumulation of chemical modifications which may be referred to mutations in the genomic DNA. This hypothesis, which predicts a relatively direct correlation between chemical and morphological evolution, has been further studied in a series of investigations by Allan C. Wilson and his colleagues. First it was shown that the serum albumins in frogs belonging to the same genus in many cases exhibit differences larger than those found in mammals placed in distinct families and sub-orders.[60] Next the relative rates of protein evolution and chromosomal evolution were compared in frogs and mammals. It was found that whereas the rate of protein evolution is approximately the same in frogs and mammals, the chromosomal evolution is 20 times faster in the latter. The rapid rate of gene rearrangement in mammals parallels the rates of their morphological evolution and their loss of potential for interspecific hybridisation. It was therefore concluded that gene rearrangements may be more important than point mutations for taxonomic divergence.[61]

In order to account for the very high rate of chromosomal evolution in mammals it was suggested that social behaviour may be an important factor. It is a typical feature of many mammals that they live in small groups, a circumstance which favours inbreeding. This in turn promotes the fixation of new gene arrangements, and consequently taxonic divergence.[62]

A corresponding study on birds showed that similar to mammals the birds have undergone rapid anatomical evolution, the rate being highest in songbirds and in primates. To explain the contrasts in rates of anatomical evolution it was suggested that behaviour is the major driving force for evolution at the organismal level. Reasoning that behavioural flexibility may be correlated with mental capacity, it was demonstrated that there is a correlation between relative brain size and anatomical evolution in birds and land vertebrates. When interpreted from my point of view, the correlation is based on the fact that an increase in mental capacity facilitates the invention of new niches in which individuals of a particular species may become isolated.[63]

The most startling results obtained by Wilson and his collaborators concern their comparison between the chimpanzee and man. Using a number of different methods it was found that on the macromolecular level the similarity between the two taxa exceeds 99 per cent. The genetic distance based on these findings corresponds to that observed between sibling species of *Drosophila* or of mammals. It thus appears extremely difficult to account for the substantial differences between chimpanzees and human beings with reference to chemical features. On the other hand, some chromosomal rearrangements (inversions, translocations and one chromosomal fusion) have occurred since the two taxa separated. It seems likely that the striking differences obtaining between the two sister taxa may be related to these genomic changes.[64]

Once more we thus find that the empirical facts do not support the predictions of the micromutation theory, whereas they conform neatly with the macromutation theory.

Sympatric speciation

It is a logical consequence of the micromutation theory that whenever neighbouring environments differ slightly with respect to their ecological qualities, different populations of the same species may undergo divergent evolution as they become adapted to a particular milieu. In spite of Moritz Wagner's insistence upon isolation as a necessary antecedent for taxonic divergence, Darwin did not quite give up the idea that organisms may diverge in the midst — more or less — of their companions. Owing primarily, I believe, to the work of Sewall Wright and Ernst Mayr, this view has long been abandoned; today nobody questions that reproductive isolation of some kind is a prerequisite for divergent evolution.

In an earlier section it was observed that reproductive isolation is the outcome of fortuitous events which may involve either factors in the environment or in the organisms themselves. The former instance may lead to allopatric, the latter to sympatric speciation. It is likely that Mayr is correct in his insistence that the most common cause of divergent evolution follows from allopatric isolation, but it appears that the biological events which may lead to sympatric speciation are more common than has hitherto been assumed. It often happens that very closely affiliated taxa, including sibling species, occupy separate but adjacent and sometimes overlapping territories. Under these conditions it is close at hand to presume that the isolation of the taxa is accomplished by one of the biological mechanisms outlined above (p. 327).

Among these mechanisms the most common may be genetic isolation, which involves that the offspring is non-viable or infertile. In general this infertility may be referred to karyotypic incompatibilities, stemming from some kind of chromosomal rearrangement. Michael White has observed that

> . . . it appears as if such rearrangements, of many different types, have played the primary role in the majority of speciation events. It by no means follows, however, that their significance in speciation is always of the same type. In fact, each chromo-

somal rearrangement — whether fusion or dissociation, trans-location, inversion, gain or loss of heterochromatin — must be regarded as a *unique event* whose consequences will be almost impossible to predict in the present state of our knowledge. *It is thus extremely difficult to incorporate chromosomal rearrange-ments into mathematical models of speciation and phyletic evolu-tion, which may be one reason why they have been relatively neglected by many evolutionary geneticists.* (My italics)[65]

The last phrase is correct with the amendment that the importance of karyotypic mutations has long been recognised for speciation in plants; in this case the evidence was too perspicuous to be ignored.

White has further observed:

When one compares the attitudes of biologists to problems of speciation, say, fifteen years ago and today, two important changes can be observed . . .

The first is an increasing awareness of the prevalence and importance of chromosomal rearrangements in speciation . . . The second aspect in which thinking has changed very greatly in recent years is in regard to closely related taxa with contiguous, i.e. parapatric, ranges. In 1967 Blair . . . could still take the view that such distribution patterns were rare and exceptional; it is doubtful if any informed biologist would uphold that idea today. This is due in part to the realization that many groups of organisms identified as species 10 or 20 years ago are in fact complexes of several sibling species . . . that conform to the biological concept of the species . . . When we look at the taxonomic units that make up these complexes, we find that parapatric distributions, instead of being rare, are in fact extremely common.[66]

Under these circumstances it seems to follow that sibling species, whatever their spatial relationships, prevail in their particular niche not because they are adapted to it, but because they happen to be isolated there.

In my view the data compiled by White, and the conclusions he draws, are a most powerful support of the macromutation theory, and thus also of the basic ideas advocated by Goldschmidt. I am therefore somewhat surprised to find that the latter are referred to as 'discredited and out-of-date models of speciation'.[67]

The other isolation mechanisms prevent mating taking place, and they therefore seem to prevent or lessen the loss in progeny resulting from unsuccessful hybridisation. On these premises natural selection has a chance to work, and that may be the reason why the pre-mating isolation mechanisms have been so popular among the Neo-Mendelians. I think that this standpoint has been rather myopic; without asserting that it is impossible, I think that in many situations it cannot work in the gradual fashion implied by the micromutation theory, but rather in the either/or macromutation model. For instance, a temporal shift amounting to twelve hours might very likely lead to a successful isolation, where a change of some minutes one way or the other would be of no avail. Likewise, adopting a new pheromone might easily lead to reproductive isolation, but our knowledge of pheromone chemistry does not seem to allow for transitions incorporating innumerable steps.

FALSIFICATION, EXTINCTION AND THE EVOLUTION OF INDIVIDUALS

. . . population genetics theory is built on the concept of gene frequencies and the actual studies of evolution are conducted at the phenotypic level, and there is no direct way of unambiguously connecting the two . . .

For many years, attempts have been made in vain to estimate the number of gene substitutions that actually occurred in the course of evolution, transforming one species into another, one genus into another, and so forth. But now, by the methods that can measure gene differences in molecular terms, this has become feasible.[68]

M. Kimura and T. Ohta

All that is explicit in the theory is that they will leave more offspring.

There, you do come to what is, in effect, a vacuous statement: Natural selection is that some things leave more offspring than others; and you ask, which leave more offspring than others; and it is those that leave more offspring; and there is nothing more to it than that.

The whole real guts of evolution — which is, how do you come to have horses and tigers and things — is outside the mathematical theory. So when people say that a thing is vacuous, I think they may be thinking of this part of it, this type of statement. The sheer mathematical statement is largely vacuous.[69]

C.H. Waddington

The synthetic theory possesses a remarkable elasticity: when under attack it expands to exclude almost anything, but once the pressure is relaxed it contracts.[70]

Peter T. Saunders and Mae-Wan Ho

Yet, we think we see objectively and therefore interpret each new datum as an independent confirmation of our theory. Although our theory may be wrong, we cannot confute it.[71]

Niles Eldredge and Stephen Jay Gould

350

I hope that the preceding discussion has shown that *nobody has ever been able to present empirical data which corroborate the Darwinian micromutation theory*. Lest I am misunderstood I hasten to make two amendments: (i) I do not assert that no case of selection has been observed in Nature, only that in the cases recorded the effects of the selected variations were not almost imperceptible, as implied by the micromutation theory; and (ii) barring some quantitative changes, neither in Nature nor under experimental conditions have any substantial effects ever been obtained through the systematic accumulation of micromutations.

I have already flatly asserted that the prevailing state of affairs is due to the fact that the micromutation theory is false. However, before this conclusion is accepted, there are two other possibilities which must be considered: (i) the theory may be correct, but suffer from the terrible shortcoming that it cannot be tested empirically; or (ii) it may be a mere tautology.

Superficially, the two alternatives may perhaps seem less detrimental than my first assertion, but this is not really the case. An untestable theory, like belief in God, may indeed be true, but it may just as well be false. However, since no objective choice can be made between these alternatives, the issue is a metaphysical one, entirely beyond the realm of empirical science. I presume that few population geneticists would choose this option. The only person who has had the courage to proclaim the metaphysical essence of the selection theory is, I believe, Karl Popper.[72]

A tautology, like $2 + 2 = 4$, is universally valid, and therefore it does not make any falsifiable predictions. On several occasions it has been claimed that the Darwinian theory is a tautology. This assessment has been made on the basis of a logical analysis of Herbert Spencer's maxim: the survival of the fittest. At the time of Darwin it was still possible to equate 'the fittest' with 'the one with sharpest eyes or longest claws', but in the modern version of the theory 'the fittest' is 'the most reproductive one', and since survival is ensured through reproduction, survival and fitness become equivalent. Hence, it has been argued, Spencer's dictum may be rendered: the survival of the survivor.

Although I am far from sure that it is unassailable, I shall not contest the logic of this argument. However, I seriously disapprove of the shallowness implied by the belief that it is possible to test the validity of a scientific theory through a logical analysis of a catchword meant to popularise it. Who would think of testing Einstein's theory on the basis of the statement: everything is relative?

351

It is something of a consolation that most of the people engaged in this venture have been philosophers and not biologists.

After this step-wise elimination, only one possibility remains: the Darwinian theory of natural selection, whether or not coupled with Mendelism, is false. I have already shown that the arguments advanced by the early champions were not very compelling, and that there are now considerable numbers of empirical facts which do not fit with the theory. Hence, to all intents and purposes the theory has been falsified, so why has it not been abandoned?

I think the answer to this question is that current Evolutionists follow Darwin's example — they refuse to accept falsifying evidence. We have already seen how Darwin supplemented natural selection with three other mechanisms to account for evolution, and furthermore invented several *ad hoc* hypotheses to circumvent the deplorable fact that the testimony of Nature does not accord with his theory. This expedient might work reasonably well with only one person involved, but reflecting on the case of Darwin *versus* Wallace, we realise that already with two persons the situation becomes complicated. And today the modern synthesis — neo-Darwinism — is not a theory, but a range of opinions which, each in its own way, tries to overcome the difficulties presented by the world of facts.

It is not possible to present a comprehensive survey of this state of affairs, but some examples will be given here. However, in order to make my case I must in a few sentences outline the logical consequences of the theory — those to which it must conform if it is to be a scientific theory at all. The Darwinian micromutation theories assert that whenever changes occur in the environment of any particular organism, it must undergo some modification to adjust to the change. The variation necessary for this adjustment is *always* present in some members of the species, and through natural selection it may thus be ensured that the proper modifications are established. On these premises it is warranted to assert that living organisms are 'adapted' to their environment, and that this phenomenon is achieved through a 'selection pressure'.

Since the variations are of slight effect, it may take many generations to realise a particular modification, so organisms can become adapted only to slow environmental changes. Quick alterations must be experienced as 'catastrophes', and should lead to extinction, at least if 'adaptation' is a requirement for survival.

It remains an unsatisfactory state of affairs that the fossil record stubbornly fails to deliver one single bit of evidence in support of the 'phyletic gradualism', which is supposed to be a prediction of the micromutation theory. Darwin maintained the incompleteness of the geological observations to be the main reason for this state of affairs, succeeding at the same time in making the micromutation theory unfalsifiable. However, he also advanced the idea that the environment, and with it the living organisms, may remain constant for long periods of time, to change more or less abruptly in more or less confined areas. Under these circumstances the gaps in the fossil record no longer falsify the micromutation theory but the palaeontological data do not necessarily corroborate it either, because such gaps are also predicted by the macromutation theory.

This Darwinian hypothesis has been reasserted many times, in recent years by two American palaeontologists, Niles Eldredge and Stephen Jay Gould, who have gained reputation for a theory they call 'punctuated equilibria'. This theory is claimed to be a 'macroevolution' theory, but it is definitely not a macromutation theory, as appears from the following quotation: 'Beliefs in "saltative" evolution, buttressed by de Vries' "mutation theory", collapsed when population geneticists of the 1930's welded modern genetics and Darwinism into our 'synthetic theory'' of evolution. The synthetic theory is completely Darwinian in its identification of natural selection as the efficient cause of evolution.'[73] Since the authors clearly reject the macromutation theory, all they achieve is to revive Darwin's *ad hoc* attempt to avoid a glaring falsification of the micromutation theory. The fundamental differences between the Gradualist and the Punctualist micromutation theories, and the macromutation theory are shown diagrammatically in Figure 5.

Most of the taxa which have lived on our planet have become extinct. On the premises of the theory of natural selection extinction represents a failure of the empirical world to behave as predicted by the theory. This fact may be allowed for if the environmental changes have been faster than the rate at which natural selection can work. Considering that, as we have just seen, the micromutation theory requires rather long periods of constancy to conform with the fossil record, it does not seem plausible that most living organisms have become extinct because the environment did not remain constant. The alternative interpretation of the factual situation has been given by Mayr: 'Natural selection comes up with the right answer so often that one is sometimes tempted to forget its failures. Yet the history of the earth is a history of extinction, and every extinction is in part a defeat for natural selection, or at least it has been so interpreted. Natural selection does *not* always produce the

Figure 5: Schematic illustration of three theories on the mechanism of evolution

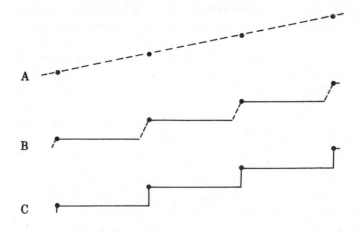

The closed circles represent taxa, and the stippled lines *periods* of transition. (a) Darwinism or phyletic Gradualism postulates that evolutionary change results from the steady accumulation of micromutations in response to an ever changing environment. (b) The theory of punctuated equilibria claims that for extended periods environments and organisms remain constant, but when, at times, the environments do change, there is a rapid and corresponding change in the organisms, accomplished by means of accumulated micromutations. (c) The macromutation theory claims that organisms representing new taxa may originate in one step. The environment does not, or only to an insignificant extent, affect the *creation* of new kinds of organisms, but it is of course very important for their *survival*.

needed improvements.'[74]

Since Mayr elsewhere in the same context states that 'more than 99 per cent of all phyletic lines that existed in the past are now extinct',[75] the expression '*not* always' is something of an understatement, to me it would seem more appropriate to write 'hardly ever'. In other words, the phenomenon of extinction is a terrible load for the micromutation theory. I believe this is demonstrated by the fact that in many of the standard texts on evolution extinction is either not mentioned at all or only very cursorily. In those cases where a more detailed discussion is entered upon, it appears that four different mechanisms are proposed.

The first one was suggested by Simpson:

In other words, the phylum approached or reached an optimum

without passing it, and the optimum then shifted to a previous position, or to one outside the given line, faster than the population could follow, an aspect of what Darlington . . . calls 'lag', failure of the genotype to produce mutation as rapidly as selection requires. Indeed, this is probably the most general cause of extinction, and when the optimum shifts to an earlier point, the character may appear to have, but will not really have, progressed beyond the optimum.[76]

This statement contains several clauses which, I believe, will forever be exempt from empirical testing; in other words, Simpson indulges in metaphysics. But apart from that he introduces an idea which is, or at least ought to be alien to a Darwinian theory, if not to Darwin; lack of necessary mutations. This clearly amounts to a falsification of the modern synthesis, and is a completely unnecessary assumption, for as mentioned above, it suffices to presume that the environment changes too fast for selection to follow suit, even if the necessary mutations prevail.

The second explanation, among the advocates of which we find J. Huxley, is based on the notion of orthogenesis:

There can be little doubt that the apparent orthogenesis which pushes groups ever further along their line of evolution until . . . they are balanced precariously upon the edge of extinction . . . is due, especially in its later stages, to the hypertely induced by intraspecific competition.[77]

The notion of orthogenesis has for various reasons been rejected by most supporters of the selection theory. In the present case it seems obvious that if natural selection is as powerful as it is claimed to be, then it surely should be able to prevent some organisms to evolve towards extinction. Even this explanation therefore seems to constitute a falsification of the micromutation theory.

The third interpretation asserts that extinction results from fortuitous elimination in small populations. This alternative has been suggested, among others, by Lewontin:

Phyletic evolution (adaptation), speciation, and extinction are the three processes of evolution. Fisher demonstrated that Mendelism allows us to understand the first. Only in the synthetic work of Wright do we get hints (and only hints) of the way in which both speciation and extinction can flow mechanically from the processes of modulation and variation. This is the role of chance in evolution.[78]

Evidently it is once more confirmed that extinction is not really an inherent component of Neo-Mendelism; it ought not to occur, and if, nevertheless, it does it is sheer bad luck. But if chance has to account for 99 per cent of all observations, then very little remains for the theory to explain.

The last hypothesis submits that both in the past and in the present the occurrence of new forms of life in a given environment causes extinction of those prevailing there at the time. Thus, with reference to palaeontological data Grant has written: 'Episodes of mass extinction are followed by the formation and development of new groups.'[79] And Mayr contends: 'The introduction of an alien species was in many cases the apparent cause of extinction [of bird species on isolated islands].'[80]

If fitness and adaptation are associated, then the territory occupied by any species should never be exposed to the risk of invasion by any other organism, for no other form can be better adapted to a particular environment than those actually inhabiting it. But this dilemma is solved in a very simple way if it is admitted that there are two kinds of evolution, divergent (adaptive) and progressive, respectively. For in that case the appearance of new dominant forms will automatically lead to the extinction of ancestral inferior forms through selection, if not natural selection. So many of the actually observed instances of extinction, in the past and in the present, find a very simple explanation on this assumption. Yet, this mechanism is based on the macromutation theory. Thus, once more it appears that this theory is well substantiated by empirical facts.

The Neo-Mendelian theory has many bizarre consequences. For one thing, since it is based on sexual reproduction it does not concern asexual organisms. The fact that the latter are known to have undergone evolution shows that the recombination of genes which issues from sexual reproduction may further evolution, in particular by accelerating the rate, but it is not an indispensable prerequisite. Besides, as a micromutation theory it entails a further complication: usually groups of individuals, populations and sometimes entire species are supposed to be involved in evolution, and the process must by necessity advance in so small steps that a taxonomically important step, say, the origination of a new species, must span over innumerable generations. Hence, it clearly does not make sense to talk of evolving individuals; only populations evolve.

It is commonly assumed that organisms are individuals, and that collections of organisms, like populations or species, are classes of individuals. This state of affairs has been questioned from a Neo-Mendelian point of view, first by Ghiselin, who summarised his views as follows:

> Traditionally, species (like other taxa) have been treated as classes (universals). In fact, they may be considered individuals (particular things). The logical term 'individual' has been confused with a biological synonym for 'organism'. If species are individuals, then: 1) their names are proper, 2) there cannot be instances of them, 3) they do not have defining properties (intensions), 4) their constituent organisms are parts, not members . . . Species are to evolutionary theory as firms are to economic theory.[81]

At first sight this analogy is not obvious, firms are organised, generally in hierarchies where the various levels are specialised for particular functions; nothing similar holds in Nature for whole species, even if it may be found in smaller populations. Under these circumstances it is difficult to see the justification for leaving the common view, and a closer scrutiny of Ghiselin's paper reveals assertions rather than arguments. An approach to the latter is found in the following definition: 'Species, then, are *the most extensive units in the natural economy such that reproductive competition occurs among their parts.*'[82] This suggests that the idea which inspired Ghiselin's reformist zeal is that sexually reproducing species form a common gene pool of which each individual is a member. And since, in the Neo-Mendelian interpretation, evolution occurs through changes in the composition of the gene pool, the latter is constantly changing. Now it is typical of classes, at least in the inorganic world (e.g. elements and planets) that they do not change, a circumstance which allows for establishing the defining characters of a class. If species evolve, then Ghiselin faces two alternatives: (i) classes of living beings differ from classes of inorganic entities or (ii) species are not classes. These two alternatives are not clearly stated; yet, although it is admitted to imply certain disadvantages, Ghiselin has adopted the second one.

This standpoint has been better argued by Hull:

> If species are to be units of evolution, they need not be composed of similar organisms; instead they must be made up of organisms

related by descent . . . In addition to spatiotemporal continuity, species must also possess a certain degree of unity to function as units of evolution. Gene exchange is one means by which such unity can be promoted. The mechanisms by which asexual species maintain a similar unity are problematic; higher taxa pose an even more serious problem. However, if species are chunks of the genealogical nexus, they cannot be viewed as classes. Instead they possess all the characteristics of individuals — that is, if organisms are taken to be paradigm individuals. The major difference between organisms and species as individuals is that organisms possess a largely fixed genetic makeup which constrains their development, whereas species do not.[83]

Since 'the genealogical nexus' is the temporal extension of the gene pool, the meaning is clear — species change in the course of time, just like individuals. Classes should not change, and therefore species are individuals rather than classes: '. . . if species are classes, it is difficult to see how they can evolve — but they do!'[84]

It must be stressed that this whole argument stands or falls with the micromutation theory. In fact, in my view Ghiselin and Hull surrender common sense in order to adapt certain concepts to this theory. It seems, however, that many of the arguments which are advanced are mere affirmations, which may fit in a particular case without therefore being generally valid. For instance:

But no matter how hard they tried, taxonomists could rarely find sets of traits which divided living organisms into neat little packets. Some divisions were fairly sharp; others exhibited even gradation . . .

The lists of traits which taxonomists include in their diagnoses and descriptions do not perform the functions of definitions but are, at most, definite descriptions. They help biologists decide whether or not the specimen before them belongs to a particular species.[85]

It is true that taxonomists observe gradations in many cases, but mostly, or perhaps exclusively within what they call species. This may cause some concern, but not more than that. And surely, the taxonomist is happy if his descriptions can help him to perform his work, which is to determine the species, or more generally the terminal taxon to which a specimen belongs.

Subsequently Hull asserts: 'Evolution is a selection process, and selection processes require continuity.'[86] But against this it may be countered, with the blessings of many Evolutionists: Evolution is an isolation process, and isolation processes require discontinuity. We have seen that divergent evolution requires the isolation of one or a few individuals. The very model on which the iconoclasts build their case is false. Evolution does not occur within a genealogical nexus, but through escape from the latter. Ghiselin and Hull are right: classes cannot evolve, only individuals. But what evolves are individual organisms, and as they do, the class (taxon) to which they belong remains unchanged, at the same time as it gives rise to two new subordinate taxa. This is the quintessence of evolution, and as we have seen, it is corroborated by empirical observations.

Once this point is accepted the other difficulties facing Ghiselin and Hull are resolved at the same time. Rare mutations occur in asexual organisms as well as in sexual ones, and the former do not even have to face the problem that the innovations must be established through inbreeding. On the other hand it must be admitted that they cannot combine valuable characters through recombination. So although asexual organisms may be somewhat handicapped *vis-à-vis* those which reproduce sexually, the disadvantage appears to be slighter than generally claimed by the population geneticists. If this was not the case, I suppose we might expect asexual organisms to have become eliminated through natural selection.

As far as the superior taxa are concerned they can evolve creatively only in the sense that among the taxa they include new terminal ones may arise. They also may 'evolve' if they, or some included taxa, undergo extinction. Finally, in some taxa features may be lost which otherwise distinguish a higher taxon in which they are included. In that case the absence is a taxonomic character in the respective inferior taxa.

The cases discussed here vindicate the claim by Eldredge and Gould quoted above. The micromutation theory has led to an epistemological *cul-de-sac*; the logical consequences of the theory requires that common sense views are abandoned. When shall we come to see that the best solution to our current predicament would be to abandon the micromutation theory?

13

A Survey of the Theories on the Mechanisms of Evolution

The other alternative put by Professor Kölliker — the passage of fecundated ova in the course of their development into higher forms — would, if it occurred, be merely an extreme case of variation in the Darwinian sense [sic!], greater in degree than, but perfectly similar in kind to, that which occurred when the well-known Ancon Ram was developed from an ordinary Ewe's ovum.[1]

T.H. Huxley

[i] Evolution most probably goes on by definite single mutations, which cause structural alterations, which may, but by no means necessarily must, have some functional advantage attached. If such an advantage appears in the mutation, natural selection will likely allow it to survive. There is no necessary reason why the immediate ancestor should die out.

[ii] Evolution goes in what one may call the downward direction from family to variety, not in the upward, required by natural selection . . .

[iii] Varieties are the last stages in the mutation, and are not, as a rule, incipient species.

[iv] Chromosome alterations are probably largely responsible for the mutations that go on . . .

[v] [Natural selection] comes in principally as an agent to fit into their places in the local economy of the place where they are trying to [live], the forms there furnished to it, whether newly evolved, or only newly arrived, killing out those in any way unsuitable . . .

[vi] The mutations supposed in differentiation would at one step cross the 'sterility line' between species, which has always been a great stumbling block to natural selection; and thus at once isolate the new form, preventing its loss by crossing.[2]

J.C. Willis

Das Wesen der Stammesentwicklung besteht nicht in der Rassen—und Artbildung, nicht in Differenzierungen und Anpassungen, sondern entscheidend für das Fortschreiten der Entwicklung und die Aufrechterhaltung des Lebens ist die Herausgestaltung von Bauplänen höherer Ordnung, neuer Typen, die immer wieder die entstandenen einseitigen Anpassungen zurückschrauben.[3]

Otto H. Schindewolf

Our geometrical analogies weigh heavily against Darwin's conception of endless small continuous variations; they help to show that discontinuous variations are a natural thing, that 'mutations' — or sudden changes, greater or less — are bound to have taken place, and new 'types' to have arisen, now and then.[4]

D'Arcy W. Thompson

C'est ne pas être anti-évolutioniste que de n'être pas satisfait par les explications de l'evolution qui nous sont actuellement proposées. L'immense renommée de l'illustre CHARLES DARWIN ne peut être atteinte lorsque l'on conteste à la sélection naturelle, cependant d'une importance considérable dans la lutte pour l'existence, la substitution des espèces et leur répartition, de n'être pas un facteur créateur dans les transformations évolutives des êtres vivants.

Ce n'est pas ignorer ni méconnaître la signification de la génétique mendélienne ni la génétique moléculaire qui sont parmi les plus belles conquêtes de la pensée humaine, ce n'est pas les mettre en doute lorsque l'on ne tient pas les gènes pour les seuls facteurs déterminants des différenciations histogénétiques et morphogénétiques, lorsque l'on prétend que l'évolution est plus épigénétiques que génétique dans l'apparition des formes et des structures qui en resultent.

Ce n'est point verser dans le vitalisme, avoué ou honteux, ni reveiller les fantômes du spiritualisme téléologique, du finalisme métaphysique, que de reconnaître aux êtres vivants, parce qu'ils sont vivants, la faculté autocréatrice de leurs propres organisations nécessairement et suffisamment finalisées en leurs ajustements pour être fonctionelles et viables.

Ce n'est point d'un esprit rétrograde que de voir dans la phylogénèse, les manifestations les plus tangibles de l'évolution, puisque c'est l'étude comparative des 'series', des 'lignées' végétales et animales qui seul fait apparaître ce qu'il y a de plus concret, de plus certain dans l'évolution.[5]

Paul Brien

It may sound like a commonplace to state that only those individuals survive and propagate themselves that can find some place in nature where they can exist and leave descendants; and yet this statement may contain all that it is nececssary to assume, in order to account for the fact that organisms are, on the whole, adapted.

The causes of the change of whatever kind should be our immediate quest. The destruction of the unfit, because they can find no place where they can exist, does not explain the origin of the fit . . .

. . . I am not unappreciative of the great value of that part of Darwin's idea which claims that the *condition* of the organic world, as we find it, cannot be accounted for entirely without applying the principle of selection in one form or another. This idea will remain, I think, a most important contribution to the theory of evolution . . .

Animals and plants are not changed in this or that part in order to become better adjusted to a given environment, as the Darwinian theory postulates. Species exist that are in some respects very poorly adapted to the environment in which they must live. If competition were as severe as the selection theory assumes, this imperfection would not exist.[6]

T.H. Morgan

It has already been pointed out that evolution comprises two aspects, the creation of living organisms and their survival. Since Darwin ascribed both phenomena not only to the same agent, his natural selection, but lumped them together into one process, the criticism of Darwinism has always been associated with a certain measure of ambiguity. The reason for this is that most people realised that natural selection may indeed have an evolutionary role, being concerned with the survival of plants and animals. However, many did not accept the role of natural selection as a creative evolutionary agent, working through the accumulation of small individual variations. In short, the critics contended that the creation of evolutionary innovations was the accomplishment of 'internal forces', that is, forces active within the confines of the organism. This expression has (undeservedly) been violently criticised by the Darwinians, suggesting that it has metaphysical implications, but that is evidently wrong; even the Darwinian individual variations must be dependent upon 'internal forces'.

By disowning the creative power of natural selection, the opponents more or less frankly opted for the macromutation theory, which, as we have seen, was in vogue for half-a-century, ending in the 1930s. The last major works on the macromutation theory to be published were Richard B. Goldschmidt's *The Material Basis of Evolution* (1940), John C. Willis's *The Course of Evolution by Differentiation or Divergent Mutation rather than by Selection* (1940) and Otto H. Schindewolf's *Grundfragen der Paläontologie* (1950). In the Francophone realm, where earlier in the century the opposition had been adamant, valiant, but largely ignored, protests against Neo-Mendelism were raised even after the latter date,[7] but all was in vain. The Macromutationists were either attacked, ridiculed or neglected. An attempt to evaluate objectively the merits of the two theories was made by Marjory Grene, who compared Simpson's and Schindewolf's approaches to evolution in a very stimulating essay.[8]

Although I cannot endorse every point of view advanced by the authors mentioned, I would say that they gave a fair representation of the major aspects of the macromutation theory. The main shortcoming is that none of them explicitly emphasised the Lamarckian distinction between divergent and progressive evolution. However, most of the Macromutationists have made it clear that the direction of evolution implied by Darwin's theory, that is, from the species to the kingdom, is mistaken; logical reasoning suffices to show that evolution must proceed from the superior to the inferior taxa.

Among the publications referred to here, Goldschmidt's book was the one that attracted most attention (and most spite), probably because Goldschmidt was the one among the Macromutationists who had the highest standing in the biological community. We shall concentrate on this work in the present context. The book was published just as Neo-Mendelism was gaining momentum. The reaction was violent. He described it himself as follows: 'The Neo-Darwinians reacted savagely. This time I was not only crazy but almost a criminal.'[9]

The crime committed by Goldschmidt was the following claim: '*Subspecies are actually, therefore, neither incipient species nor models for the origin of species. They are more or less diversified blind alleys within the species. The decisive step in evolution, the first step toward macroevolution, the step from one species to another, requires another evolutionary method than that of sheer accumulation of micromutations.*[10] And the solution proposed by Goldschmidt is the occurrence of 'systemic mutations', that is, mutations concerning either one or more chromosomes or the genome as a whole. The outcome of such radical changes may at some occasions be imperceptible, sometimes they may give rise to monsters, but Goldschmidt thought that once in a while it may be a 'hopeful monster', destined to inaugurate a new phylogenetic lineage.

Goldschmidt frankly admitted that the idea of 'hopeful monsters' was not his own and mentions

> . . . a little-known and in many respects rather amateurish book by Bonavia (1895) in which a whole chapter is devoted to the subject . . . Bonavia pointed out that monstrosities might actually have played a large role in evolution by providing specific adaptations in a single step. He even anticipated the idea of preadaptation when he declared that such monsters might have been able to occupy new habitats and there continue a special evolution. He also insisted strongly upon the possibility of single large steps in evolution for which the monsters provide the proper material, and he mentioned a number of writers on evolution who had realized this. He even had a vague idea of the embryological basis of large sudden deviations, when he wrote that 'a little more atomic disturbance here, a little less there, during the embryonic stage may produce a new *compound*, which then may be called a species, a genus, or even an order, as the case may be'.[11]

Goldschmidt substantiated his notion about 'systemic mutations' with several references. So even at that time there was a certain measure of empirical support for his theory. Nevertheless, mutations of this kind are so rare that the acceptance of their evolutionary importance would imply a falsification of population genetics, which operates with observable rates of mutation. So perhaps it was only natural that Goldschmidt's view was rejected 'by the consensus of geneticists'.[12]

The evidence discussed in the preceding chapter shows beyond doubt that the Macromutationists are right to the extent that important evolutionary changes have been associated with, or caused by macromutations. So no evolutionary theory is complete which ignores the macromutations. However, the existence of micromutations is equally well, or even better established; hence, it is not justified to oppose separately the micromutation and the macromutation theories, for only a theory which embodies both kinds of mutations can account for all aspects of evolution. This theory may be called *the comprehensive theory on the mechanism of evolution*, and it is a component of the epigenetic theory, which we shall discuss in the following section. However, as emphasised repeatedly, evolution is not merely a matter of creation of new forms through epigenetic processes, it is also a question of survival, and this topic is dealt with in the ecological theory.

THE EPIGENETIC THEORY

It has been claimed that among the mutations which happen in living organisms only the macromutations are of more than marginal consequence for evolution. This point will be dealt with in the first subsection. Subsequently we shall discuss various aspects of the phenomenon of epigenesis.

The spectrum of mutations

In the present section I am only discussing mutations, although I am aware that the Neo-Mendelians consider many evolutionary innovations to arise through the concurrence between mutation and recombination. My option does not imply that I underrate the importance of recombination; this phenomenon is probably of as great importance for a macromutation as for the micromutation theory. However, it may be neglected here where the main object is to compare the evolutionary importance of micromutations and macromutations.

Mutations vary with respect to the size of their effect on the phenotype and also as regards their value; some are advantageous, some are disadvantageous. I shall make the following three assumptions: (i) mutations constitute a continuum with respect to the extent of their effect; (ii) their frequency is inversely related to the their effect; and (iii) disadvantageous mutations are more common than advantageous ones. On these premises the distribution of mutations may be represented, for example, as in Figure 6, in which I have

Figure 6: A schematic representation of the correlation between the effect and the frequency of mutations stipulated by the macromutation theory

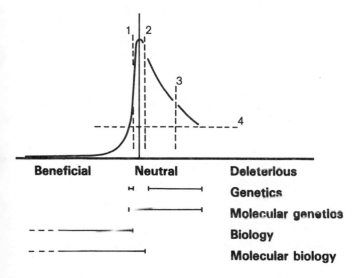

submitted that greatly beneficial mutations are possible, but highly improbable events. From this figure we may outline the range of mutations that can be observed by researchers in various biological disciplines. Thus, geneticists can work only with mutations which occur at relatively high frequencies, as indicated by line 4. The frequency implied by the latter must be quite high in evolutionary terms. Since probability is involved, it is evidently impossible to establish a sharp boundary; geneticists may happen upon very rare mutations, but they cannot expect them to recur.

The range of neutral or quasi-neutral mutations is indicated by the vertical lines 1 and 2, at some distance from the line of neutrality. If we accept the *neutral theory*, many of the mutations observed by the molecular biologists belong to this category, as indicated in the figure. According to the *classical theory* the prevalence of any character testifies to its usefulness, for it is only by being useful that it may become fixed through natural selection. But Darwin himself got ensnared by the consequences of this argument, for there are indeed features for which it is very difficult to envisage any use. One possibility to save the theory, which has often been employed, by Darwin as well as others, is the assumption that the character in question is useless itself, its origination being associated with the epigenetic formation of some useful feature. Whenever this hypothesis is true, ordinary geneticists may indeed observe neutral characters, contrary to what is shown in Figure 6.

At a certain point deleterious mutations become lethal, as indicated by line 3. It is not necessary to compare the extent of the effect of lethal mutations, but the curve has been continued till the intersection with line 4, because lethal mutations are observed in genetical laboratories. The molecular geneticist may thus in theory observe all mutations lying between the curve and line 4, and the geneticist the same, except for most of the neutral and quasi-neutral mutations.

All other biologists do not work with mutating genes, but study the effects of mutations in living and extinct organisms. Their working range is in principle cut off to the right by the line of viability. However, the mutations lying between the lines 2 and 3 are likely to affect the survival adversely, so the effects of these mutations should rarely be observable in Nature. Under these circumstances the mutations to the left of line 1 are observable to the ordinary biologist, molecular biologists may further study the mutations lying between the lines 1 and 2. It is unlikely that the beneficial macromutations lying to the left below line 4 really form a continuous curve, a stippled curve would probably correspond better to the actual state of matters.

The interpretation of Figure 6 given here corresponds very closely to the claims made by most Micromutationists about the nature of mutations, based on observational experience, namely, (i) that neutral mutations do not exist, (ii) that beneficial mutations are rare and of a slight effect and (iii) that deleterious mutations are much more frequent and often extensive in their effects.

We have seen above that Goldschmidt wanted to account for evolutionary innovations by means of a special kind of mutation, called 'systemic mutations'. This idea has often been criticised, and here I think his opponents are right. If we class mutations into three groups: gene mutations, chromosome mutations and genome mutations, then this enumeration probably represents a sequence of decreasing frequency, and perhaps also of increasing effect. But there are exceptions to this rule, some genome and chromosome mutations have imperceptible consequences, and some gene mutations may have very considerable effects, whether deleterious or beneficial. It therefore seems possible to infer that *there is no absolute correlation between the genotypic nature of a mutation and its effect on the phenotype.*

For more than a century now biologists have been engaged in a discussion for or against micromutations and macromutations, respectively. I shall here survey the most important arguments which have been advanced in this context, beginning with the micromutations.

The objections may be epitomised by the statement: Individual variation cannot accomplish what it is attributed with. More specifically the criticism may be subsumed under the four following points. (i) Intraspecific variation does not allow for evolution beyond the species limit. For instance, no amount of variation within one, or even all species of the taxon Crocodilia would allow for the origin of the taxon Aves, the birds. For in the latter we find a number of innovations of which there are no trace in any crocodile, and if there was, then it would not be a crocodile. (ii) Quite generally it holds that the micromutation theory fails to explain the origination of innovations, for it cannot account for the preservation and amplification of the initial stages, before the novel structure or organ has begun to exert its function. (iii) In some cases the micromutational transformation from one form to another may be dismissed because the intermediate stages cannot be useful to the extent implied by the theory. Examples are the transformation of the front limbs of an insectivore into the wings of a bat, or of the teeth into whalebone in whales. A similar situation, although residing at a different level of organisation, is represented by the avian feather. Clearly, a transitional stage between the latter and the reptilian scale is hardly imaginable, and even if it was, it would not have the fantastic properties which makes the feather so useful to the birds. (iv) It has been claimed repeatedly that the transfer from one species to another one, involving the loss of interfertility, cannot be accomplished through the accumulation of micromutations.

Some of the examples mentioned above, and many others from the early anti-Darwinian literature, have been assembled by Michael Denton, in a work which thus significantly contributes to the falsification of the micromutation theory. However, the author feels compelled to refute the macromutation theory as well, with the result that evolution becomes 'a theory in crisis'.[13]

Turning now to the objections against macromutations, we may first notice that it has been contended that macromutations, and particularly beneficial ones, must be so rare as to be without any practical importance for evolution. To this we may observe that the infrequency of beneficial macromutations is not a weighty argument

367

against their evolutionary importance, since the extent of their effect may more than outweigh their rarity. However, macromutations are much more common than the Micromutationists are willing to admit; the breeding of plants and animals is to a considerable extent based on their occurrence. The forms which have been thus produced show that the characters preserved by the breeders often are much more extensive than those otherwise distinguishing separate species. The several races of dogs bear out this point.

What, in fact, do we know about the size and the frequency of the mutations which have propelled evolution? George Ledyard Stebbins has discussed the major advances associated with metazoan evolution, such as 'the origin of multicellular from unicellular organisms, of the digestive tube, coelom, and central nervous system of animals, of vertebrate limbs, lungs, elaborate sense organs, warm blood, the placenta, and elaborate social behaviour', arriving at the conclusion that about '100 major advances . . . have occurred throughout the evolutionary history of the eucaryotes' — thus, one every ten million years. As to minor advances in grade, most of which 'would be recognized only by taxonomists and comparative morphologists',[14] one would have arisen every 2,000 years. Evidently the chances of observing even a 'minor advance in grade' are minimal, and this holds whether macromutations or micromutations are involved. Thus, if we allow, say, 400 micromutations for the establishment of such a change, it would mean that a survey of all living eukaryotes would permit the discovery, if perceptible, of an evolutionary successful micromutation every five years.

Second, the Macromutationists often stress the identity between the breeders' stratagem and that of Nature as far as the preservation of new varieties is concerned: inbreeding. Against this is countered that the two kinds of event cannot be compared since the breeders do not produce new species, but only new races or subspecies. This argument is often supported with reference to the fact that fertility has been preserved between the various races of dogs. However, Darwin himself pointed out (i) that natural selection cannot account for the step-wise origin of reproductive isolation, this process must therefore be an all-or-nothing phenomenon, that is, a macromutation, and (ii) that certain dogs living in South America cannot be crossed with other dogs. It seems that this process is going on continuously, new races having since then become reproductively isolated: in fact, if the fertility criterion were taken seriously, we should accept that today *Canis vulgaris* is not a species, but a species group.

Third, it has been asserted again and again that since macromutations are so rare, it is unlikely that two similar individuals of opposite sex arise at the same time and place, and without this occurrence the innovation cannot survive. To this we may first observe that breeders repeatedly have found that a variation arising in one individual may survive through inbreeding. On the other hand, a macromutation may, for one reason or another, exclude interbreeding with members of the original stock. Yet, in this case the innovation may be preserved if it happens to occur in the germ line, giving rise to sisters and brothers representing the new phenotype.

Fourth, it may be claimed that macromutations give life to monsters: even Goldschmidt admitted this, but insisted that they were 'hopeful monsters'. I have already dismissed this argument: in my view the various races of dogs are no more monstrous than many wild animals.

Fifth, it has been argued that domesticated plants and animals, being the results of macromutations, are generally degenerate forms which could not prevail in 'the struggle for existence' supposedly distinguishing life in Nature. However, we know that many domesticated plants and animals survive splendidly in the feral state. It may be contended that most often they live in the outskirts of human habitations and hence in a state of isolation that saves them from competition. But this overlooks two facts, (i) that some wild organisms also have become specialised to life in villages and cities, and (ii) that, as we shall see later, most organisms survive in isolation.

It thus appears that all the objections against the macromutation theory may easily be met, and this is in itself perhaps the most compelling evidence in its favour.

Considering the various examples used for illustration it should not be too difficult to envisage the nature of macromutations. Nevertheless, an advocate of this theory is repeatedly confronted with the question: What exactly is a macromutation? I can come up with nothing new as far as this point is concerned, but by specifying some particular macromutations I hope that some readers may be convinced about the reality and the necessity of macromutations.

(i) I have above, a little provocatively perhaps, defined a macromutation by $|s| \geq 0.5$. Yet, I am ready to accept that any mutation which increases the reproductivity by 50 per cent is macromutation, irrespective of its effect on the phenotype.

(ii) One important group of macromutations comprises polypeptides with new properties. The proteins may be structural, regulatory or catalytic, and in the latter case they may be involved in the production of structural, metabolic or regulatory substances. The origin of such new polypeptides may often be referred to gene duplications. However, if more than one step is required for the transformation of the gene, then clearly the agent involved is chance, not natural selection, for the latter cannot do anything before the new protein has entered into action. Once this has occurred, natural selection may possibly serve to improve the function, and in particular prevent its loss.

(iii) We have seen that reproductive isolation cannot be accomplished by the accumulation of micromutations by means of natural selection. It was asserted above that biological events which lead to reproductive isolation and sympatric speciation clearly deserve the epithet 'macromutations'.

(iv) If we disregard the taxa which undergo metamorphosis, it holds that newborn or newly hatched individuals generally manifest their species affiliation. From this it follows that the features which distinguish the various taxa to which the individual belongs must be elaborated epigenetically during the earlier stages of ontogenesis. In fact, ever since the publication of von Baer's important monograph in 1828,[15] it has been known that the various properties are laid down in a sequence which corresponds to the succession of taxa into which they are included. In other words, if we want to account for the change from one major taxon to another, then we must look for epigenetic happenings during the earliest stages of development.

In order to substantiate this assertion I shall discuss two features which have been of decisive importance for the evolution of the taxon Craniata. In Figure 7 are shown the fate maps for a polychaete and a urodele blastula. It may be noticed that the distribution of the various cell types exhibit great similarities; this holds in particular for the presumptive nerve cells which are seen to occupy almost the same position in the two blastulae. In spite of this the nerve system in the annelid worm consists of ventrally located chains of ganglia, whereas in the newt, as in all craniates, the central nervous system resides at the dorsal side. The change in location in the former case is due to the fact the animal cells migrate on the surface of blastula, thus ending up at the ventral side. The differences obtaining between the two embryos cannot be explained on the assumption that the urodele cells are less motile than their annelid counterparts, for Holtfreter has shown that if a sheet of animals cells is excised from

Figure 7: Fate maps of the blastula in Polychaeta and Urodela

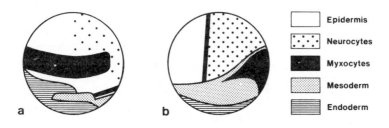

a, *Podarke*; b, *Triton*. The term 'myxocytes' stands for cells, which either swell through extensive uptake of water (goblet cells, notochordal cells), or else are imbedded in a swollen, hyaline matrix secreted by themselves (mesenchyme cells). From SLP, after D. I. Anderson[10] and W Vogt.[17]

a blastula and placed on an aggregate of vegetal cells, then the animal cells will spread on the latter and cover it more or less completely.[18] The different fates of the presumptive nerve cells in the two cases may be accounted for by another discovery made by Holtfreter, namely, that the cells in the urodele embryo are kept together by an extracellular 'surface coat', which prevents the cells of the blastula from migrating on top of each other.[19] I presume that the presence of a surface coat is an all-or-nothing phenomenon, and hence that the mutation which gave rise to this structure in the first instance was a macromutation. However this may be, the presence or absence of a surface coat may explain one of the most fundamental differences between vertebrates and invertebrates.

In Figure 8 is shown a drawing of a urodele neurula. In the middle of the neural plate is seen a dark line, the median neural groove. The dark pigmentation in the groove results from a condensation of the pigmented surface, accomplished by cells in the neural plate which become anchored to the notochord. The groove demonstrates that only the posterior part of the neural plate is attached to the notochord, and consequently it is only this part which becomes elongated when subsequently the notochord is stretched. The anterior part of the neural plate is reserved for the formation of the brain, and we may therefore conclude that the attachment

371

Figure 8: Neurula from the newt *Ambystoma punctatum*

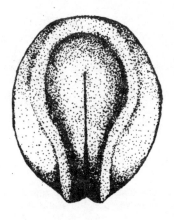

From R. Rugh,[20] after N. Leavitt.

between neural plate and notochord is a precondition for the distinguishing feature of the craniates, namely, the subdivision of the central nervous system into a brain and a neural tube. This conclusion is corroborated by the situation prevailing in *Amphioxus*, where no such attachment occurs. In this animal the notochord stretches to the snout, and no distinct brain is present. We do not know specifically what ensures the observed attachment in the craniates, but once more we are evidently dealing with an all-or-nothing phenomenon, and the mutation responsible for its origination must be a macromutation.

Epigenesis and information

The genome comprises a set of discrete lumps of information, the genes. In the structural genes this information concerns the one-dimensional amino acid sequence in various polypeptides, whereas the information required to regulate the function of the structural genes is assumed to reside in special regulatory genes. The question about regulatory genes is still largely *terra incognita*, although some headway has been made in three instances, *Drosophila*, a nematode worm *Caenorhapditis elegans* and maize, *Zea mays*.[21] The sum total of this genomic information is by many molecular biologists supposed to constitute a blueprint specifying the construction of the body bearing the genome. Phylogenetic evolution is envisaged to be the outcome of the accumulation of changes in the information located in the structural and regulatory genes.

In the early days of the triumph of molecular biology this hypothesis was generally acclaimed, but I think that, considering its consequences, it is now accepted only with some reservation. Thus, the notion that the genome contains a blueprint must imply that *all* the information required for the realisation of normal ontogenesis resides there. This assertion is easily refuted if we consider the fertilised egg, the initial stage in the existence of all bisexual organisms. In this the genome clearly contains the information required to elaborate all the substances needed for making a cell, and yet I believe that nobody would expect a cell nucleus, placed in an otherwise appropriate medium, to surround itself by cytoplasm and cell membrane, thus forming a cell. Rather, the living cell embodies a certain structural information — 'to be a cell' — that is beyond the reach of the genome, and which is transferred from generation to generation through cell division.

Similarly, the centriole is known to contain the information specifying how to 'divide a cell'. It appears that centrioles may arise spontaneously in some cases, but this cannot be the general state of affairs, for most eggs do not begin to divide unless supplied with a centriole by the fertilising sperm. Some of the information required to make a mitochondrion is found in the mitochondrial DNA, and some in the nuclear DNA. But even in this case it seems that the mitochondrion itself embodies the structural information required to make a new mitochondrion.

It follows from these considerations that the genome does not contain all the information required to account for ontogenesis: rather, it is the whole embryo, the *epigenotype*, which incorporates this information. For this reason alone the molecular biologists' claim may be rejected.

In fact, the only *explicit* information which may be stored in the structural genes is that specifying the linear amino acid composition of proteins. However, when the polypeptide has been assembled by the ribosomes it most often spontaneously folds to assume a three-dimensional conformation, determined partly by the amino acid sequence and partly by some little known physico-chemical principles. The information specifying this folding concerns a higher level of organisation than that represented by a one-dimensional polypeptide, and therefore it cannot be encoded in the genome. The three-dimensional structure is thus not explicitly, but only *implicitly* determined by the genome. And the same holds for the function assumed by the protein, whether catalytic or structural.[22]

It is of particular interest to note that although the information concerning the composition of the various nucleic acids and proteins involved in protein synthesis is found in the genome, their co-operation in the actual execution of this process, which takes place at a much higher level of organisation than that represented by the genome, is not and could not be specified there. The same phenomenon may be observed also with respect to some of the information residing outside the nucleus. Thus, the egg cell plus the centriole together hold the information required for cell divisions. Yet, whenever this information is exploited in the metazoan embryo, the result is a multicellular organism, which represents a level of organisation above that of the fertilised egg, and still further above that of the centriole.

Returning to the mentioned analogy we may observe that a blueprint is a necessary, but not a sufficient part of most constructions; nothing will be built in the absence of materials, tools and energy. Traditionally, manpower would also be required, but nowadays this component may be dispensable. Present knowledge implies that the supply of energy is no great problem. If the information in the structural genes may be compared to a blueprint, then it would be one specifying the elaboration of the materials and the tools. But that implies that there is no blueprint containing information about the organism to be. There is thus an abyss between the realm represented by the information present in the genome and that of the presumptive adult organism, an abyss which must be bridged by a link of some kind. And this link must be supplied by the extra-nuclear part of the fertilised egg which together with the nucleus forms the epigenotype. The latter constitutes 'a generative algorithm . . . a sort of carefully spelled out and fool-proof recipe for producing a living organism'.[23] The process in question may appropriately be called *autocreation*[24] or *autogenesis*.

Epigenetic mechanisms

Epigenesis may be said to consist of a transformation of the epigenetic substrate by means of the epigenetic mechanisms. The epigenetic substrate is of course the developing organism itself, being represented initially by the fertilised egg. The epigenetic mechanisms may be listed under three headings: *cell division, cell differentiation* and *morphogenetic processes*. The order in which they are ranged corresponds to the sequence in which they appear, and also to the causal dependence: cell division is a prerequisite for cell differentiation, and cell differentiation for morphogenesis.

Since the egg usually is a very large cell, one of the earliest epigenetic tasks is to subdivide the egg into a large number of cells of 'normal' size. This process goes on during the early phases of ontogenesis, subsequently each dividing cell doubles its volume before it undergoes mitosis.

It is an uncontested dogma that — disregarding mutations — the genome is faithfully replicated each time a cell divides. Yet, most multicellular organisms contain several kinds of cells, each of which is distinguished by its utilisation of a particular repertoire of the genes contained in the genome. If the latter is the same in all cells, then the differential transcription, which by inference must be associated with cell differentiation, cannot be directed by the genome; in fact, many observations indicate that this control is exerted by cytoplasmic or extracellular factors. Cell differentiation thus presupposes the existence of cells differing with respect to their content of or exposure to such factors. These cells must arise through *unequal cell divisions*, and the process of cell division is therefore an epigenetic prerequisite for cell differentiation. Hence we may specify that during ontogenesis some strategic cell divisions must be unequal with respect to factors influencing the transcription of DNA. The preconditions responsible for such unequal divisions during early development are represented by the so-called *polarities*, prevailing in the form of variations of cortical or cytoplasmic properties along some vector across the fertilised egg. It is obvious that the number of such polarities must be quite modest, one or two is the most usual number, and therefore other mechanisms have to be involved to account for even the relatively few patterns of differentiation found during early, and still more during late development.

Morphogenesis is the outcome of co-operation between the various cell types which arise as a consequence of cell differentiation, and various extracellular substances — notably collagens, proteoglycans and glycoproteins — produced and secreted by differentiated cells. Very few cell types are present in the early embryo, when the most decisive morphogenetic events occur, compared to that found in later developmental stages. The fact that the number of morphogenetic agents is so slight weighs heavily against the micromutation theory, and its case is not improved when it is realised that most of the cell types and differentiation products are found in many of the animal phyla. *The advent of a new morphogenetic agent, cellular or extracellular, as the case may be, must have been an extremely rare evolutionary event.* The really extensive utilisation of the genomic information begins only during larval development, where the cytodifferentiation takes place that is the precondition for the function of the various organs.

The preceding discussion of the epigenetic mechanisms and their importance shows that evolution only to a limited extent has involved innovations on the macromolecular level, the one for which the genome is primarily responsible; *evolution is not a question of making new materials, but rather of using old materials for new purposes.*[25] If we confine ourselves to the evolution of form, then we may observe that evolution, notably of the superior taxa, has consisted in the origination of new morphogenetic mechanisms, capable of creating new kinds of body plan. The subsequent taxonic divergence has most often involved either slight modifications of the body plan during morphogenesis, or further changes accomplished through differential growth.

Epigenetic phases

The present section might as easily have been called 'Ontogenetic phases', for ontogenesis and epigenesis are parallel phenomena. In fact, ontogenesis may be said to comprise the observable and describable events taking place during individual development, whereas epigenesis represents the mechanisms responsible for their occurrence. As an approximation one might say that the study of ontogenesis coincides with comparative embryology, and the study of epigenesis may be represented by developmental biology or epigenetics.

An understanding of the epigenetic mechanisms is facilitated by the fact that, following an idea originally submitted by Haeckel and extended by Sewertzoff, it is possible to subdivide ontogenetic development into a number of separate phases.[26] Here we must first observe the complication imposed by metamorphosis. Especially in invertebrates this phenomenon is so extensive that it is most expedient to discriminate between two completely distinct processes of morphogenesis.

Disregarding this particular problem, it is possible to distinguish two main ontogenetic stages, one *progressive* and one *regressive*. The first phase usually lasts from fertilisation to sexual maturation, the second from then on to death. The progressive stage may be subdivided into four phases, *pregastrulation* (blastulation), *form creation, larval* and *postlarval* development. In many cases the last two phases may better be characterised as the phases of *differential* and *allometric* growth, respectively. These various names imply that at the end of the phase of form creation a larva has been formed which possesses all the essential features of the body plan of the adult form, although the latter may be reached only through processes involving differential and allometric growth. (The expression 'form creation' is, of course, identical with 'morphogenesis'. The reason why a particular name has been proposed for the second phase is that morphogenesis of some kind takes place during all epigenetic phases.)

The phase of pregastrulation is concerned with a subdivision of the mass of the fertilised egg through successive cell divisions. In a certain way it may be claimed that this process involves form creation, thus in many instances a transformation of the egg, a solid sphere, into a blastula, a hollow sphere. Especially in view of the phenomenon of recapitulation, the subject of the following section, it seems more consistent to consider this phase simply as preparatory to that of form creation. The latter may be said to begin with the onset of gastrulation, a process which in general happens to be a consequence of the fact that cell differentiation has begun. This phase ends when the larval stage has been reached, that is, when the embryo has acquired all or almost all features which distinguish *the body plan* or *archetype* of the adult form.

Typically for this stage of ontogenesis is that in principle all important structures prevail, even if many of them are not yet functional. Under these circumstances the subsequent epigenetic events may be confined to a process of differential growth during which the various parts of the body, in the vertebrates notably the endoskeleton, are adjusted so as to correspond to the morphology of the more inferior taxa to which the organism belongs. At birth or hatching the specific affiliation is generally evident, but a process of allometric growth is required before the morphological differences between infants and adults are levelled out.

Epigenesis and recapitulation

In a previous chapter (see pp. 72–3), we discussed von Baer's four 'laws' of embryogenesis. The wording of these generalisations is obsolete today, and they also contain some contradictions, but in modern terminology the quintessence of the laws may be stated in the following *von Baer's rule*:

> *Features distinguishing the taxa to which a metazoan animal belongs appear in the developing organism in a succession corresponding to the subordination of the several taxa.*

It has already been pointed out that according to this rule we may expect that an embryo passes through stages corresponding to all the taxa to which it belongs, beginning with the most superior one. If von Baer's rule is correct, then it must hold that each pair of twin taxa follow a common path until they separate. This inference may be stated in the form of *von Baer's theorem*:

> *During their ontogenesis the members of twin taxa follow the same course up to the stage where they diverge into separate taxa.*

If it is true that the phylogenetic classification outlines the course of evolution, then it follows that there is a precise recapitulation of phylogenesis in the course of ontogenesis; this recapitulation I have proposed to call *von Baerian recapitulation*.[27] This phenomenon implies that von Baer's rule may be tested with reference to the hierarchy of phylogenetic classification.

I believe that von Baer's theorem is the *most parsimonious generalisation ever stated in biology*. For if it was not true, it might be inferred that in order to reach the stage corresponding to the common origin of two twin taxa Nature would in some cases, maybe in general, have had to devise two different epigenetic pathways. According to von Baer's theorem the course of epigenesis for a pair of twin taxa is identical until they actually separate; in this way the demands on the inventiveness of Nature are radically diminished.

THE ECOLOGICAL THEORY

Once created, the problem facing living organisms is their survival.

(In this context 'survival' is used as the antonym to 'extinction' rather than to 'death'.) It is true that survival depends upon what goes on inside the living organisms in so far as no organism can survive if, say, it carries a lethal gene. But if such instances are disregarded, then it holds that survival is primarily a matter of interaction between organism and environment, that is, an ecological problem, dealing with happenings at levels of organisation above that of the organism.

Ecology embraces phenomena concerning the relations between members of the same species, between members of different species, and between living organisms and their inanimate environment. Under these circumstances it might be envisaged that the ecological theory of evolution is as elaborate as the one dealing with the epigenetic aspects. I propose to show that it is possible to formulate the problems in such a way that the theory is greatly simplified.

We are going to deal here primarily with the influence of the organic elements of the environment, but it is true, of course, that even the inorganic elements may markedly affect survival. Thus, if one of the parameters of the environment, for instance temperature or humidity, is changed beyond the range of tolerance for a given organism, then it must perish. According to the micromutation theory this happens only if the change is catastrophic; if it occurs at a slow rate the organism will have time enough to adjust itself gradually to the new conditions. The macromutation theory does not exclude that such adjustments may take place, but only by chance and not as a predictable event.

There are two circumstances that may ensure the survival of a particular taxon, *isolation* and *dominance*, giving rise to divergent and progressive evolution, respectively. The effects of these phenomena are dealt with below, followed by a discussion of the phenomenon of adaptation.

Divergent evolution

We shall take the *Axiom of Competitive Exclusion* as the point of departure for the discussion of the correlation between isolation and survival. This axiom, which has a long history,[28] asserts that *the members of two taxa cannot share the same niche.* As always when we deal with biological matters, it is unavoidable that exceptions occur whenever a generalisation is formulated too summarily.[29]

Among the apparent exceptions to this axiom it has been observed that if the organisms are very similar, perhaps members of sibling species, then they apparently can share the same niche; perhaps it would be more correct to assert that it is difficult or impossible to stake out the limits of the niches occupied by each of the taxa.

However, when two taxa, which may be widely separated in the phylogenetic hierarchy, fortuitously come to share the same niche, then one of the taxa will succumb, while the other, the *dominant* one, will prevail. From this it follows that, contrary to all appearances, taxa living side by side are nevertheless isolated from each other. Of particular interest in the present context is the inference that every taxon is isolated from its twin. This in turn implies that, in agreement with current notions, divergent evolution must be preceded by an event of isolation.

How does a taxon become isolated? The answer to this question depends upon the theory adopted to account for the mechanism of evolution. The micromutation theory does not allow for more than slight differences between members of the same species, and hence it follows that *an organism cannot become isolated as a consequence of its own faculties, for wherever it can go, its neighbour can go too.* Clearly, *on this premise divergent evolution can occur only as a consequence of extrinsic random events.* It seems to be a rather discouraging conclusion that what amounts perhaps to the most important aspect of evolution depends entirely on chance events, but it is an unavoidable corollary of the micromutation theory.

If we accept the macromutation theory we may get a more sophisticated view on the phenomenon of isolation, but it must be admitted that even in this case random events play an important role. In order to analyse the problem adequately it is necessary to introduce some specific concepts. Thus, isolation may serve to ensure the origin of new taxa, the phenomenon which usually is called 'speciation'. Since this expression is apt to lead to false notions about the course of evolution,[30] I shall here call it 'taxonic divergence'. The other effect of isolation is to assure the survival of the members of some taxon by preventing the access of potential competitors to their particular niche. This instance may be called 'taxonic survival'. Isolation may arise as the result of circumstances *extrinsic* to the organisms themselves; to this case I shall apply the expression 'random isolation'. However, organisms may also survive because they possess properties themselves which protect them against invasion of their niche. Isolation due to such *intrinsic* properties I shall call 'non-random isolation'. (The adjectives 'random' and 'non-random' are not completely unambiguous, but I have been unable to find any better expressions.)

With these two sets of concepts we have to consider altogether four different alternatives. Beginning with taxonic divergence we may observe that the precondition for this phenomenon is reproductive isolation. This may occur if members of a species fortuitously are sequestered on an island, a mountain, in a lake, etc. As we have seen, if this event leads to the origin of a new taxon, it is called 'allopatric speciation'. Non-random taxonic divergence may occur if members of a species become reproductively isolated from those of the parent species, a relatively common phenomenon which usually arises as a consequence of chromosome rearrangements (pp. 348–50). If the isolated individuals survive, we are dealing with 'sympatric (or parapatric) speciation'. As we have seen Darwin came to the conclusion that this kind of taxonic divergence cannot be established through the accumulation of micromutations.

In both cases discussed it is evident that the isolation can concern only one or a few individuals; in fact, the idea that a whole taxon becomes reproductively isolated seems to imply a contradiction. We may thus conclude that taxonic divergence is a phenomenon involving isolation and inbreeding, and it is therefore completely analogous to the expedient employed by breeders of plants and animals.

Taxonic survival may also depend upon random and non-random circumstances. In the former instance it may often happen that whole taxa become isolated, as a consequence, for instance, of comprehensive geological events. As an example of this kind we may mention the marsupials in Australia. These animals have not survived in great numbers because they are especially adapted to the Australian ambience, but because the continent was separated from South America before the advent of the eutherians. Similar cases in more modest scale abound in biogeographical texts.

Non-random taxonic survival may be said to follow from 'ecological isolation'. The quotation marks indicate that I use the expression in a wider sense than Mayr (p. 327). This phenomenon often concerns specialisations of various kinds, involving for instance the colonisation of a particular element, water, land or air, the faculty to support extreme conditions of, say, temperature and humidity, or the adoption of a particular kind of food. The surviving assortment of odd creatures which have chosen ants as their staple food illustrates strikingly that specialisation may be a cul-de-sac from an evolutionary point of view, but it promotes survival.

Various protective devices may also ensure isolation, leading, for instance, to the prevention of attacks by predators. Protection of the embryo by solid shells or by the maternal body, as realised for instance by the sharks, represents ecological isolation in my interpretation. And the same holds, of course, in those cases where the adult body is protected by armours of various kinds, as found in sea urchins, snails, tortoises and hedgehogs. Even mimicry may belong to this category. On the given premises ecological isolation must be based initially on macromutations.

Several kinds of evidence, but notably palaeontological data, have shown that when a form arises, which can colonise a major division of the biosphere, then it will spread there, occupying smaller compartments in the new environment by forms supposed to be specifically adapted to their particular environment. This phenomenon, called 'adaptive radiation', is thus associated with extensive taxonic divergence.

The divergent evolution associated with adaptive radiation is often exceptionally fast, in geological terms at least. To explain this fact the Darwinians generally invoke a strong 'selection pressure'. This is an *ad hoc* expedient for which there is no support whatsoever. The present theory takes the opposite stand: in the new environment there are innumerable opportunities for ecological isolation, and these are exploited for taxonic divergence whenever possible. Darwin's finches show that the differences associated with this kind of divergence may be quite trivial. The present theory thus claims that divergent evolution follows from isolation, and isolation means suspension — temporarily at least — of selection. *Hence it is not selection pressure, but lack of it which favours taxonic divergence*. As we shall presently see, the most likely outcome of selection pressure is extinction.

Progressive evolution

Progressive evolution occurs whenever two taxa attempt to inhabit the same niche; under these conditions the axiom of competitive exclusion predicts that one taxon must perish, and the other one survive. The latter is the dominant taxon. The continuous repetition of this phenomenon must lead to the survival of ever more dominant taxa. Thus, progressive evolution is the consequence of the axiom of competitive exclusion and the 'struggle for life' implied by Darwin's natural selection.

Various kinds of evidence show that the competition which leads to progressive evolution is interspecific or intertaxonic; the taxa fighting for supremacy may often be widely separated taxonomically, but of course they must nevertheless be so similar that they can inhabit the same niche. Neither from a Darwinian nor from a Neo-Mendelian point of view does this kind of natural selection ensue in evolutionary innovation, so it is not quite the same as Darwin's natural selection.

According to the axiom of competitive exclusion twin taxa must always be isolated from each other. When we consider twin taxa near the base of the phylogenetic hierarchy, that is, at the species level, their isolation is often spatial, being the outcome of survival through random isolation.

With some important exceptions, the superior taxa are represented in most regions of the planet, which means that their isolation must be non-random. Under these circumstances it may be presumed that one of a pair of superior twin taxa is the dominant taxon, from which the other one survives in isolation. When we have established the phylogenetic classification of the major taxa in one of these superior taxa, for instance Craniata, then we shall find that it is possible to determine the relative dominance of each pair of twin taxa by the fact that one of them generally is distinguished either by comprising a smaller number of subordinate taxa, or by its members having a lower organisation than those of the other, or both. In either case the latter taxon is the dominant one.

If the rule is introduced that the dominant taxon is always placed to the right, then we will have a classification where the taxon dominating all others is found in the upper right-hand corner (Figure 1, page 10). The step-wise ascending line bordering the lower edge of the dendrogram represents a dominant phylogenetic lineage, outlining the course of progressive evolution in the particular taxon. The nature of the isolation of the various taxa is discussed in the legend to Figure 1.

We have seen that the phylogenetic classification corroborates the epigenetic theory on the mechanism of evolution, based on the notion of von Baerian recapitulation. The arrangement of the phylogenetic hierarchy proposed here suggests that even the ecological theory is borne out, for it appears that in all cases the taxa are isolated from their twins, randomly or non-randomly, as the case may be. I believe that this is somewhat of a breakthrough for Hennig's phylogenetic classification.

The preceding discussion shows that although there is some truth in Spencer's axiom 'The survival of the fittest', it is not general enough to epitomise evolution. Rather, it should be replaced by the following triplet:

The survival of the dominant (in the struggle for life).

The survival of the cunning (enough to avoid the struggle for life).

The survival of the lucky (enough to avoid the struggle for life).

Adaptation

The basic idea in the Darwinian and Neo-Mendelian theories is that evolution ensures the adaptation of living organisms to their environment. Hence the concept of 'adaptation' has played an enormous role in evolutionary discourse, several books and innumerable articles have been devoted to this problem. However, upon closer, if not necessarily very profound reflection this concept turns out to be ambiguous. I believe this was first pointed out by David Hume: 'It is vain to insist upon the uses of parts of animals and vegetables and their curious adjustment to each other. I would fain to know how an animal could subsist, unless its parts were so adjusted.'[31]

If we follow this train of thought we shall find that it makes no sense to state that an organism is not adapted to its environment. However on these premises the survival of the mentioned theories as non-metaphysical theories clearly depends upon the feasibility of obtaining qualitative, or at least relative measures of adaptation. Since natural selection supposedly increases both adaptation and fitness, it follows that even if these two qualities may not be identical, they ought to vary in the same direction.

As it turns out, population geneticists readily discuss the adaptation of living organisms, but they are only willing to measure their fitness, and this parameter is estimated from relative reproductive success. This is hardly what most people understand by 'adaptation', but even an approximate and biased measure may be better than no measure at all. However, Lewontin has declared: '*To the present moment no one has succeeded in measuring with any accuracy the net fitnesses of genotypes for any locus in any species in any environment in nature.*'[32]

And the situation does not seem to be much better in the laboratory. At least, after discussing the outcome of some *Drosophila* experiments, Lewontin concluded:

> If one simply cannot measure the state variables or the parameters with which the theory is constructed, or if their measurement is so laden with error that no discrimination between alternative hypotheses is possible, the theory becomes a vacuous exercise in formal logic that has no points of contact with the contingent world. The theory explains nothing because it explains everything. It is my contention that a good deal of the structure of evolutionary genetics comes perilously close to being of this sort.[33]

However, if it is impossible to estimate fitness with anything like satisfactory accuracy, and if fitness and adaptation are correlated properties, then the assertion that living organisms are adapted to their environment will either be an affirmation of the fact that they exist, or else a metaphysical proposition.

THE VINDICATION

> . . . it is not only possible, but highly probable, that an internal power or tendency is an important if not the main agent in producing the manifestation of new species on the scene of realized existence . . . the view here advocated, while it is supported by the facts on which Darwinism rests, is not open to the objections and difficulties which oppose themselves to the reception of 'Natural Selection' as the exclusive or even as the main agent in the successive and orderly evolution of organic forms in the *genesis of species*.[34]
>
> St George Mivart

> I am confident that in twenty years my book, which is now ignored, will be given a honorable place in the history of evolutionary thought.[35]
>
> Richard B. Goldschmidt

> In my own, strongly biased opinion, the problem of reconciling evident discontinuity in macroevolution with Darwinism is largely solved by the observation that small changes early in embryology [embryogenesis?] accumulate through growth to yield profound differences among adults.[36]
>
> Stephen Jay Gould

There are a lot of empirical facts which seem to contradict the selectionist micromutation theories; among these may be mentioned evolutionary innovations of every possible kind, the phenomenon of adaptation, the lack of support by the fossil record, etc. If biological science progressed the way envisaged by the philosophers of science then, surely, the falsification of the micromutation theory would have been accepted long ago.

The weakness of the presently accepted Neo-Mendelism does not lie on the ecological side, for it operates with isolation and selection, both of which are important components of the ecological theory of evolution. The only shortcoming on this point is that most population geneticists seem to reject the phenomena of dominance and progressive evolution.

The great inadequacy of the micromutation theory is related to the fact that it neglects completely the epigenetic aspects of evolution. Darwin did not quite understand that whether individual variations are slight or large, they must have a cause or an explanation. He simply premised the necessary variation, and the same has been done by the population geneticists who connect the genotype and the phenotype by means of a 'black box'. This tendency has of course been amplified by the fashions which rule current biological research. On the one hand we have the socially conscious and responsible studies, which concentrate on ecology, the interplay between living organisms and their environment. On the other is the research inspired by the Reductionist 'philosophy' which so strongly affects many biologists, according to which macromolecules and, to a lesser extent, cells are the exclusive clues to the understanding of life.

The organisms proper, the ones in which the creation of living forms takes place, are situated between these two vogues, neglected more or less completely by the majority of biologists.

The epigenetic theory on the mechanism of evolution is based on the work of von Baer, combined with a thorough knowledge of the present stand of embryology. I am sure that the name of von Baer appears in very few modern textbooks on developmental biology. But further than that, it is even difficult to find an embryo in the text and the figures, the subject is primarily molecules and cells. The embryology dealt with is often completely descriptive, occupying only a small part of the total volume.

In the present text the several aspects of epigenesis have been discussed very superficially, but I hope it has been made clear that instead of ignoring it, the macromutation theory concentrates on this part of the mechanism of biological creation. We know that many mutations, responsible for extensive modifications of adult form or function, may be referred to slight modifications in the early embryo. But the large ultimate effect does not depend upon an *accumulation* of many such slight variations, but on an *epigenetic amplification* of the initial effect. Once this is understood it becomes impossible to claim that a resolution of the antagonism between the micromutation and the macromutation theory is possible. They are both valid, but they differ substantially in importance for the understanding of biological evolution. And it should not be forgotten that, as already pointed out by Mivart, *all the difficulties facing the micromutation theory are abolished with the acceptance of the macromutation theory.*

One point which follows from the preceding discussion is the great importance of phylogenetic classification. As we have seen, the testing of both the epigenetic and the ecological theory may be carried out with reference to the established classifications. It is felicitous that the practice of phylogenetic classification has progressed so much in recent years that an appropriate background now exists for testing the theories on the mechanisms of evolution.

A final comment.

During the years I have campaigned for the case of the macro mutation theory I have met several people who believe that the macromutation–micromutation issue is solely a matter of the extent of the effect of single mutations. Very often they even seem willing to accept the existence of macromutations, once they are assured that the effects of the latter *may* be quite slight at the initial stage, say, at the molecular level. This is a mistake, for the macromutation theory is not Darwinism with magnified mutations. What is at stake is a shift of paradigm, which will make much of the discussion on evolution during the last half century completely obsolete.

14

Social Evolution

. . . the Darwinian orthodoxy provided a rallying point for all factions and parties that desired a better world along the lines of their own infallible prophecies. It did not matter how much they fought among themselves on other counts. Fighting was the order of the day.[1]

Jacques Barzun

In the spectrum of opinion that went under the name of Social Darwinism, almost every variety of belief was included. In Germany it was represented chiefly by democrats and socialists; in England by conservatives. It was appealed to by nationalists as an argument for a strong state, and by the proponents of laissez-faire as an argument for a weak state. It was condemned by some as an aristocratic doctrine designed to glorify power and greatness, and by others, like Nietzsche, as a middleclass doctrine appealing to the mediocre and submissive. Some socialists saw in it the scientific validation of their doctrine; others the negation of their moral and spiritual hopes. Militarists found in it a sanction of war and conquest, while pacifists saw the power of physical force transmuted into the power of intellectual and moral persuasion. Mill's doctrine was taken to be a sophisticated form of natural selection, in which the war of arms and might yielded to the war of words and ideas. Some complained because it exalted men to supermen or gods; others because it degraded them to the status of animals. Political theorists read it as an assertion of the need for inequality in the social order corresponding to the inequality in nature, or alternatively as an egalitarian tract in which men as well as animals were in an undifferentiated state of equality.[2]

Gertrude Himmelfarb

If animals arise through a process of evolution, and if man is an animal, then man is also a product of evolution. This is a simple logical conclusion, but one which was of grave concern to many of Darwin's contemporaries. The main reason for this reaction was the following inference: since man has a soul, then animals must also have a soul, or else the origin of man from the apes must have been associated with a miracle, say, the creation of self-reproducing souls. Although those who believe in the human soul generally also believe in miracles, it appears that the acceptance of this particular miracle was too much to ask for.

But it was soon realised that there is room for God as well as for the soul beyond the outermost limits of scientific knowledge; consequently no particular risk was associated with acknowledging man as an outcome of biological evolution. And from this followed a new

388

and exciting question: Are human behaviour, and thus human societies, subject to the laws of evolution?

Many people have taken an interest in this problem. In the present context we shall discuss the views of Darwin and Spencer on this question, and nineteenth-century Social Darwinism. The chapter is concluded by a discussion of the prospect of the future evolution of man.

DARWIN

We have seen that Darwin was fully aware of the risks of discussing man in his book. In the first edition of *On the Origin of Species* he limited himself to the statement: 'In the distant future I see open fields for far more important researches. Psychology will be based on a new foundation, that of the necessary acquirement of each mental power and capacity by gradation. Light will be thrown on the origin of man and his history.'[3]

However, as the opposition to Evolutionism abated, Darwin grew bolder and in 1871 he published *The Descent of Man and Selection in Relation to Sex*,[4] in which the origin of man is discussed without inhibitions. A large part of this book concerns sexual selection, in man and animals alike, and Darwin even admits '. . . that in the earlier editions of my "Origin of Species" I perhaps attributed too much to the action of natural selection or the survival of the fittest'.[5] Nevertheless, this evolutionary agent is involved even in the development of man:

Naturally selection follows from the struggle for existence; and this from a rapid rate of increase. It is impossible not to regret bitterly, but whether wisely is another question, the rate at which man tends to increase; for this leads in barbarous tribes to infanticide and many other evils, and in civilized nations to abject poverty, celibacy, and to the late marriages of the prudent. But as man suffers from the same physical evils as the lower animals, he has no right to expect an immunity from the evils consequent on the struggle for existence. Had he not been subjected during primeval times to natural selection, assuredly he would never have attained to his present rank.[6]

What is most remarkable in this quotation is that the only one of various consequences of natural selection which may possibly lead

389

to differential elimination is 'abject poverty'. 'Celibacy' and 'late marriage of the prudent' rather seem to be attempts to gain 'immunity from the evils consequent on the struggle for existence'.

Anyhow, this question seemed to be of little concern in Darwin's own time: 'With highly civilized nations continued progress depends in a subordinate degree on natural selection; for such nations do not supplant and exterminate one another as do savage tribes.'[7] Darwin made one reservation, however: 'At some future period, not very distant as measured by centuries, the civilized races of man will almost certainly exterminate, and replace, the savage races throughout the world.'[8]

As a prophet — or futurologist — Darwin clearly was not very successful; as we readily observe 'savage races' in various parts of the world are at the moment doing their best to exterminate themselves with arms usually supplied by 'highly civilized nations'. As a matter of fact, once more in contradiction of Darwin's prediction, on top of this 'assistance' the developed countries actually make contributions, if mostly modest, to relieve the plight in which some of the underdeveloped countries find themselves.

Darwin discusses two further points of importance for human evolution. The first of these is co-operative behaviour: 'Finally the social instincts, which no doubt were acquired by man as by the lower animals for the good of the community, will from the first have given to him some wish to aid his fellows, some feeling of sympathy, and have compelled him to regard their approbation and disapprobation'[9] and 'A tribe including many members who, from possessing in a high degree the spirit of patriotism, fidelity, obedience, courage and sympathy, were always ready to aid one another, and to sacrifice themselves for the common good, would be victorious over most other tribes; and this would be natural selection'.[10] Darwin's wording suggests that social instincts were acquired independently by man, but this is hardly correct; rather, to the extent that the kind of co-operative behaviour discussed by Darwin is found in mammals, especially in primates, there is reason to presume that we are dealing with an inheritance from the past.

The second point concerns technical inventions:

Now, if some one man in a tribe, more sagacious than the others, invented a new snare or weapon, or other means of attack or defence, *the plainest self-interest*, without the assistance of much reasoning power, would prompt the other members to imitate him; and all would thus profit. The habitual practice of each new art must likewise in some slight degree strengthen the intellect. If the new invention were an important one, the tribe would increase in number, spread, and supplant other tribes. In a *tribe thus rendered more numerous* there would always be a rather greater chance of the birth of other superior and inventive members. If such men left children to inherit their mental superiority, the chance of the birth of still more ingenious members would be somewhat better, and in *a very small tribe* decidedly better. (My italics)[11]

In organic evolution up to the advent of *Homo sapiens* success or failure have depended upon faculties possessed by the individual organism. However, when man discovered that it is possible to increase the chances of survival by means of implements of various kinds, the situation was suddenly changed. For now it is not the fittest, say, the physically strongest individual, which survives, but the best armed. And since the survivor may have contributed next to nothing to his state of being armed, the struggle for existence no longer ensues in 'natural selection', but in 'selection by proxy'.

It has been asserted above that the struggle for existence which leads to progressive evolution usually concerns organisms rather widely separated phylogenetically, for the reason that only in that case are the differences large enough to decide the outcome of 'the struggle for existence'. With the invention of weapons the differences between members of the same species were amplified to the extent that one tribe might be dominant *vis-à-vis* another one. And as our history has clearly shown, very few tribe leaders have been able to resist the temptation to give practical demonstrations of 'progressive evolution'. Yet, the outcome of such exercises was often mitigated by the behaviour of the victors: they killed the men and raped the women, and the genes of the conquered race thus survived in the progeny of the winners.

There can be no doubt that Darwin was correct that intertribal fighting has been of significant bearing for the early evolution of man. This phenomenon ensued in the progressive development of the taxon, a progression which at least initially was based exclusively on biological features; but Darwin recognised that later on technical inventions may have played an important role in establishing the dominance required for 'progressive' evolution. It should be recalled, however, that survival may follow not only from dominance, but also through isolation. I am sure that isolation has been a major factor in the evolution of man, and one whose consequence may still be felt today.

The situation envisaged by Darwin changed completely when civilisation, notably in the form of agriculture, permitted the formation of large communities organised in hierarchies. For the master classes, the clergy and the military, needed working power to satisfy their personal and social needs; above all, they needed some to fill the lowest ranks of the hierarchies. This work was usually supplied by slaves, most often captured prisoners of war. Thus, if the members of a defeated tribe or race could mentally and physically endure slavery, their chances of survival were very good indeed, otherwise not. I believe that human history, not the least the one of the United States, vindicates this inference.

SPENCER

We have already seen that Spencer put forward a 'General Law of Evolution', valid for all events in our universe. Much of his teaching was gospel on the progress of humankind, ending with a 'Utopian Equilibrium', distinguished by physical, mental and social perfection. Initially Spencer did not doubt that the survival of the fittest, or rather the elimination of unfittest, would ensure the approach towards this distant goal. And he was logically consistent in insisting on the necessity of eliminating handicapped of all shades: 'If they are sufficiently complete to live, they *do* live, and it is well they should live. If they are not sufficiently complete to live, they die, and it is best they should die'; and therefore he 'deplored not only poor laws, but also state-supported education, sanitary supervision other than the suppression of nuisances, regulation of housing conditions, and even state protection of the ignorant from medical quacks'.[12] Such views were not popular in a liberal society, but when 'accused of brutality in his application of biological concepts to social principles, Spencer was compelled to insist over and over again that he was not opposed to voluntary private charity to the unfit, since it had an elevating effect on the character of the donors and hastened the development of altruism'.[13]

There is no reason to deal further with Spencer's philosophical system, which was highly metaphysical, even if, as we have seen, Spencer at times had a marvellous understanding of biological problems. The importance of Spencer lies in the fact that, for some decades, his message about 'the survival of the fittest' was adopted by many people, notably in the United States, because it fitted so well with the liberal economic system which prevailed at the time.

SOCIAL DARWINISM

'The survival of the fittest' is indeed a very delusive maxim, particularly if 'survival' is taken in a metaphorical sense. In fact, in that case it may become a truism, allowing for a multitude of interpretations, and that is the way it was used by the Social Darwinians.

In the very distant past of human history the victors in contests on life and death usually reaped the reward in the form of a progeny well beyond average. With the rise of civilisation, distinguished above all by the creation of power hierarchies of various kinds, new forms of struggle or competition have been introduced. In some instances the life is still at stake, but most often the fight is ritualised and the goal is to win, to reach the top. Whoever succeeds in that may with full justification claim to be 'the fittest'.

Joseph Stalin and Adolph Hitler were the fittest in their particular strife, and so were John D. Rockefeller and Aristoteles Onassis. As far as the former are concerned, we know that their competitors, and many others besides lost their lives; in the latter case the wager was mostly a matter of survival as independent entrepreneurs.

But also sportsmen and sportswomen, entertainers of various sorts, politicians and other members of hierarchies, private as well as official ones, fight to get to the pinnacle, and thereby demonstrate their fitness. However, with civilisation the nature of the prizes has changed; where it used to be progeny, it is now money, power or honour, or any combination of these. It is a peculiar phenomenon that, at least if one may believe the gossip columns, these fruits are often accompanied with lavish opportunities for procreation. That women are so frequently allured by successful men is probably explainable on a sociological basis, but according to the current teachings of sociobiology, this phenomenon may have a deeper biological significance. Sociobiologists may even be prepared to account for the circumstance that the situation is at most only partly reciprocal as far as successful women are concerned.[14]

Before birth control was practised, the biological and the social aspects of triumph were inseparable, the victors gained their biological reward together with the other prizes. However, for a long time now, and particularly in the present century, this coupling no longer exists, and so it happens that we can see social lions waste money, wield power and reap honour, while leaving little or no

393

offspring. This fact shows that the ritualised struggles of civilised man have nothing to do with the biological theory forwarded by Darwin, genetic survival is no longer of primary concern. Even individual survival is of secondary importance compared to success; in fact, in the past and to some extent even today, the chances of individual survival may be greater at some distance from the top of a hierarchy, if not necessarily at the lower and lowest levels.

Obviously, except in the completely trivial sense of 'the winners are the best' or 'the best reach the top', the application of Darwinism to social phenomena is a great mistake. It might therefore be a waste of time to discuss the delusion of some of those who, in the last part of the preceding and the early part of the present century, thought that their case was vindicated by the teachings of Darwin and Spencer, if it were not to show that biologically the situation is exactly the opposite of what these people believed.

As might be expected, military men and nationalists of every shade considered that war is a model example of Darwin's 'struggle for existence'. It is told, for instance, that the Franco–Prussian war in 1870 was the first in which both sides adopted this view.[15] If this is true, it may be surmised that the French, after having lost the war, did not ascribe their 'unfitness' to a biological, and hence presumably incurable cause, for in that case it would have been pointless to think of revenge.

However this may be, a war is, in the last analysis, a combat between two military hierarchies and, disregarding numerical differences, the victory unquestionably goes to the one best equipped and best commanded. This is of course a measure of supremacy which even may be a national characteristic, but it is not in any way a sign of biological superiority. In fact, to a very great extent the outcome depends upon those charged to do the dirty work, that is, the private soldiers, and therefore they are subject to a quality control before they are enlisted. And so it happens that both sides, winners and losers alike, send their best young men out to be killed while leaving to the waste, biologically speaking, the task of ensuring the genetic survival. Surely, it is difficult to imagine an undertaking more un-Darwinian than war.

In the last century most industrial workers spent their lives under appalling conditions, in striking contrast to the leisure of the upper classes, and in particular that of their employers, the 'capitalists'. It might have been difficult for thoughtful people to justify this state of affairs, but again Darwin came to the rescue, for evidently the professional achievements of the industrialists were an indication of their fitness, and the prevailing situation thus the consequence of an inexorable natural law.

Apparently none of those who used Darwinism to vindicate their wealth thought of questioning whether this natural law permitted equating 'survival' with 'material abundance'. In fact, the true survival occurred elsewhere. Before the industrial revolution the populations remained relatively constant for centuries, adjusted to the prevailing productivity. Improved agricultural methods, in conjunction with advances in hygiene and medicine, allowed for substantial increases in population numbers. However, this excess of people could not gain their livelihood in the villages, and they therefore moved to the towns to work in the factories founded by the 'capitalists'. Through their initiative the latter created *wealth* to themselves, but in return they gave *life* and *genetic survival* to their employees. If, as they seem to have believed, they were themselves the fittest, then the industrialists worked for the survival of the 'unfittest', a most un-Darwinian endeavour. In fact, if we accept that altruism is a quality rarely found in human beings, one may see the hoarding of wealth by the 'capitalists' as a kind of compensation.

Many people, then and now, hold another view on these matters, regarding the 'capitalists' as exploiters of their workers. As we know, Marx is the foremost representative of this standpoint. It is a curious fact that in his view 'the struggle for existence' meant 'class struggle', and 'the survival of the fittest' meant 'the subjugation of the capitalists and the wielding of power by the proletariat'. If 'subjugation' here means 'elimination' it cannot be denied that there is a certain measure of 'natural selection' in Marx's theory, even if perhaps the criterion of fitness may be disputed.

Dreams are one thing, reality another. Where adherents of Marx have risen to power, the situation is fundamentally different from that envisaged by him. Rather, where this has occurred, people are ruled by a small elite which seldom can claim to have ever belonged to the proletariat. Furthermore, both during the fight for power and afterwards, millions of people have lost their lives, lives that might otherwise have been spared. And even if members of the elite have been among the victims, it cannot be questioned that the vast majority belonged to the people. Is not, in fact, the socialist society more truly Darwinian than the capitalist one?

Another example of misunderstanding on the part of the Social Darwinians concerns the 'imperialists', as represented by the large European nations and the United States. The colonisation of foreign countries, inhabited by people at the time considered to belong to 'inferior races', was usually declared to be one aspect of 'the white man's burden', involving the spreading of the blessings of civilisation to all parts of the planet. In many cases this 'noble' pursuit did imply sacrifices of human lives, but on the whole the result was similar to what had previously occurred in the industrialised countries: increased survival among the indigenous people. This is clearly an un-Darwinian outcome, the consequences of which are beginning to be felt now, and which will go on aggravating in the coming decades. Perhaps it will some day lead to a true Darwinian struggle for survival; should this occur the victors presumably will not be the biologically fittest, but the technically most advanced people.

There was a movement in the last century which deserves mention in the present context, namely, radicalism, founded by people in England who wanted to improve the conditions of mankind through legislative reforms. The sincere humanitarian zeal of the radicals cannot be doubted. They — the fittest presumably — aimed at raising the underprivileged — the unfit — to their own level. Obviously, nothing could be more un-Darwinian than these efforts, but so were those of the industrialists, and they were successful.

But the endeavours of the radicals could be successful only if the prevailing differences were caused by the environment, for only the milieu can be affected by reforms. So the radical egalitarian ideology led to the refutation of the notion that social and cultural differences between human beings can be explained to any significant extent on the basis of inheritable properties. This stand is clearly at odds with Darwinism, which deals with inheritable characters. Consequently there has been a general tendency among radicals, both biologists and laymen, to reject selection as an important evolutionary agent. Curiously enough, Neo-Mendelism may seem to support the endeavours of the radicals. For according to this theory fitness is measured solely through differential reproduction, and it cannot be doubted that the efforts of the radicals, like those of the industrialists and the colonialists, favoured the reproduction of the socially underprivileged strata.

For understandable reasons the socialists — like the radicals — have tended to play down inheritance, and stressed instead environmental influence. The belief in this doctrine found its extremist representative in Lysenko. It is touching to see that, among those who cheered the downfall of the Soviet–Russian fake, we find many Western radicals who have preserved their belief in the effect of the environment as far as political reform is concerned.

396

I showed above that the elite was wrong in thinking that Darwinism somehow applies to social status and achievement. Rather, it turns out that one part of the elite, the one responsible for the production of material and spiritual goods — not the bureaucratic one — has done a lot during the history of human civilisation which runs counter to the notion implied by 'the survival of the fittest'.

The spectacular numerical increase of humanity which has taken place during the last 10,000 years shows that innumerous individuals which would otherwise have succumbed without leaving progeny have 'survived' for many generations. Who are the 'fittest' under these conditions, those who would have survived under any circumstances, or those additional ones, by far the greatest part of the present human population, who owe their existence to a civilisation, whose existence is due, we may presume, to the contributions of a relatively small number of persons?

How do we explain human development during civilisation on the background of Darwinism? The answer is simple: not at all. For the basic tenet in Darwinism is the Malthusian axiom that the resources of Nature are limited, and hence also the number of individuals of any species, including man. But there are situations in Nature where this situation does not hold, temporarily at least, and then Darwinian selection through selective elimination does not occur — except to a slight extent owing to lethal genes, etc. — rather, every individual survives and reproduces. The success in life is thus measured by reproductive success, implying that the sexual organ becomes the most important weapon in the struggle for survival. But this situation can never be of long duration, sooner or later nature will impose her restrictions.

The preceding discussion tends to show that with respect to social evolution Darwinism gave rise to as much confusion as it did with respect to biological evolution. On this point, however, Darwin may plead 'not guilty', he did discuss human evolution, but he clearly realised that his natural selection cannot act under the conditions of human civilisation. The true sinners are Spencer with his promise of the coming millennium, and those many people of various professions who adopted the gospel, mostly because they believed therein to find a vindication of their privileges.

THE PROSPECT OF HUMAN EVOLUTION

> . . . evolution can end only in the establishment of the greatest perfection and the most completely happiness.[16]
>
> Herbert Spencer

The naive belief in the evolution of mankind towards the millennium which was sponsored partly by the general acceptance of the notion of evolution, but particularly by the writings of Spencer, soon came to an end; even Spencer himself gradually acquired a rather gloomy view of the destiny of man.[17]

Although one may still meet today with people who have kept alive the optimistic view on human evolution, I believe that few biologists will endorse this view. Rather, man has acquired so much power that the evolution of all living species, including *Homo sapiens*, is almost completely under human control. As far as domesticated organisms are concerned, evolution is still going on, and this process is undoubtedly progressive, at least from a human point of view. Among the smaller organisms, like bacteria and insects, divergent, and perhaps even progressive evolution may still occur in Nature, but as far as the larger organisms are concerned, extinction caused by human activities is today a common phenomenon.

What about our own species? We have seen that progressive evolution depends on the origination of unique organisms which, owing to their dominance, can replace ancestral forms. Human societies, whether democratic or totalitarian, are ruled by power hierarchies, against which individuals are powerless. A new 'dominant' form residing outside the hierarchies would have no chance to establish itself. However, the dominance might comprise the faculty to rise to the top in the ruling hierarchy. This would not necessarily entail biological superiority, but in any case, if the ensuing power was exploited according to the laws of Nature, that is, to ensure a prodigious offspring, there is a theoretical possibility that the new form might subsist. However, we have already seen that in human societies the people at the top are seldom exceptionally fertile. Furthermore, even if they were, they would have little chance to succeed in a democracy; sooner or later the people would probably protest against the preferential reproduction of the dominant form.

Divergent evolution depends upon isolation, and as we know, in the past human populations have been isolated from each other, randomly we suppose, to the extent that many different varieties of our species have evolved. But today this trend has been turned; nowhere on our planet can any population persist in complete isolation. Rather, the mixing of the races has begun, and will probably go on at an accelerated rate in the centuries to come. In fact, in a not too distant future it may be expected that the average person will exhibit features representing several of the present races. So even on this point the evolution of man has been reversed.

Except as concerns very serious inheritable diseases, natural selection has been abolished in the taxon *Homo sapiens*. Rather, the advance of medicine has made possible the survival and procreation of people with a variety of hereditary illnesses. As a consequence the predominant direction of human evolution has for centuries been regressive, and there seems to be no way to change this course as long as civilisation prevails.

The situation described here refers to the industrialised countries. In the underdeveloped countries the mortality is still so high that a certain selection must occur. Whether this elimination is such that the biologically valuable individuals are spared is highly doubtful, because it occurs in hierarchically organised societies where individual properties are of secondary importance. Thus, evolution has come to an end because it led to the creation of an organism which gained the power to suspend evolution, his own and that of most of the living world.

I cannot end this resumé without mentioning that in recent years 'Social Darwinism' has been resurrected in the form of sociobiology. This topic is based on the 'Neo-Darwinian' theory, and its basic tenet is that if natural selection has been directing the course of evolution, then it follows that it must also have affected the behaviour of living beings, whenever it makes sense to talk of behaviour. It follows that particularly the higher animals will behave socially, notably in sexual contexts, in such a way as to ensure an optimalisation of their fitness, as evaluated on the basis of their progeny.

Proposing that this state of affairs holds also for human beings, this theory has been violently criticised by present-day radicals, who still, in spite of the innumerable failures testified by history, believe that mankind may be improved by legislative reforms. This reaction, which might be predicted, may not carry much weight, but that does not mean that the criticism of sociobiology is unjustified. As I see it, there are few hard and fast facts which can be mobilised in favour of the theory, and many of the more theoretical calculations into which the sociobiologists have engaged themselves are rather unrealistic. However, in my opinion any believer in evolution through differential survival must accept that all aspects of life, also behaviour, may be subject to trial. Hence, I do not believe that sociobiology is as wrong as claimed by some of its critics.[18]

15

The Myth

. . . while the adept, who can supply the missing links in the evidence from his own knowledge, discovers fresh proof of the singular thoroughness with which all difficulties have been considered and all unjustifiable suppositions avoided, at every perusal of Mr. Darwin's pregnant paragraphs, the novice in biology is apt to complain of the frequency of what he fancies is gratuitous assumption . . .

We should leave a very wrong impression on the reader's mind if we permitted him to suppose that the value of [*On the Origin of Species*] depends wholly on the ultimate justification of the theoretical views which it contains. On the contrary, if they were disproved to-morrow, the book would still be the best of its kind — the most compendious statement of well-sifted facts bearing on the doctrine of species that has ever appeared , . .

Nor is it essential that one should take up any particular position in regard to the mode of variation, whether, for example, it takes place *per saltum* or gradually; whether it is definite in character or indefinite . . .

That Darwin held strong opinions on some or all of these points may be quite true; but, so far as the theory is concerned, they must be regarded as *obiter dicta* [said in passing].[1]

T.H. Huxley

At the same time, it must be steadily remembered that there are many naturalists at the present day, especially among those of the lower order of intelligence, who, while accepting evolutionism in a general way, and therefore always describing themselves as Darwinians, do not believe and often cannot even understand the distinctive Darwinian addition to the evolutionary doctrine — namely, the principle of natural selection. Such hazy and indistinct thinkers as these are still really at the prior stage of Lamarckian evolutionism. It is probable that in the future, while a formal acceptance of Darwinism becomes general, the special theory of natural selection will be thoroughly understood and assimilated only by the more abstract and philosophical minds.[2]

Grant Allen

R.A. Fisher's . . . work gave natural selection so firm a mathematical basis that within a few years a 'synthetic theory' had emerged. Natural selection, Darwin's fundamental contribution, is now as well established as any hypothesis in all the natural sciences. Nonetheless, much biological history was written — and it is remarkable that some continues to be written — from the older point of view. The false premises upon which many writers have based their interpretations affect virtually everything they say. Many such errors have been perpetuated by those who have not gone back to the original works. To find out even the most straightforward facts, therefore, it is dangerous to trust secondary sources.[3]

Michael T. Ghiselin

Even a foreign reader, whose knowledge of the English Language is inadequate, cannot fail to be impressed and stimulated by Darwin's stylistic mastery. His way of writing is exceedingly clear, and he represents the points of importance in a direct manner, without the heavy pseudo-scientific turgidity or over-intelligent

401

stylistic extravagances which may otherwise burden the reader.[4]

Arne Münzing

. . . although the 'Origin' has been close on [one hundred and twenty-five] years before the world, the strangest misconceptions of the essential nature of the theory therein advocated are still put forth by serious writers.[5]

T.H. Huxley (updated)

We have seen that Darwin had not filled many pages in his first notebook before he saw himself as 'the Lyell of Biology', and although it may not have been his original idea, he was acquainted with the fact that some people considered him 'the Newton of Biology'. We have above analysed Darwin's *On the Origin of Species* and the various contributions which have been proposed to be modifications of Darwin's original theory, and we have been able to observe that all these propositions have one serious flaw in common: they are micromutation theories.

It was realised, and argued by many of Darwin's contemporaries, that the micromutation theory does not work, and yet, even today Darwin is claimed, often in panegyrical terms, as the founder of the notion of evolution in general and of the theory of natural selection in particular, and the inspirer of all work on evolution during the last century. This is evidently a myth, but what lies at the basis of this myth: ignorance, incompetence, prejudice, dishonesty or, perhaps worst of all, opportunism?

As little as those who have attempted to do so before me, can I give an exhaustive answer to this question. All I can do in the context of this volume is to discuss some of the mistakes and the misrepresentations that have led to the present state of affairs.

THE MISTAKES

From his notebooks and his correspondence, and less distinctly in his publications, it appears that Darwin's primary goal was to oppose Creationism. According to this creed, current at the time, the living world is the work of God who frequently, perhaps incessantly supervises and interferes with this creation of his.

The antithesis of Creationism is Evolutionism, that is, a theory which asserts that life had arisen on this planet as the result of a series of natural processes, without the involvement of any metaphysical agents. Thus, Creationism is opposed by a theory asserting that evolution has taken place, or in my terminology, the theory on the reality of evolution or Lamarck's first theory on evolution. Darwin did not have to concern himself with the conception and statement of this theory, since it had been advanced by Lamarck almost 40 years before he began to consider the problem, and half-a-century before he published *On the Origin of Species*.

Consequently, on these premises Darwin might have formulated the aims of his contribution in the following way: (i) to collect empirical evidence supporting Lamarck's theory on the reality of evolution and (ii) to advance and corroborate a theory on the mechanism of evolution more plausible than what had been proposed by Lamarck. For reasons which are impossible to explain rationally, Darwin did not accept this distinction; to him the theory on the reality of evolution was a matter of course and only theories on the mechanism of evolution were of any substance. As a consequence he considered that the evidence which he compiled in support of evolution was at the same time a corroboration of his theory of natural selection.[6] Darwin's neglect of his great predecessor is even more flagrant than appears from the preceding discussion, for it has been observed that in his notebooks he mentions 'my theory' many times before he had read Malthus and thus come upon the theory of natural selection. May we not presume that the theory in question is Lamarck's theory, and that even at this early stage Darwin considered this his own invention?

However this may be, Darwin's conceptual confusion was pointed out to him by several persons, supporters as well as critics; as shown above, Lyell was among the former. We have seen that in his private correspondence he might accept the distinction made above, but we may also find examples demonstrating his confusion on the issue. Thus: 'When I say "me", I only mean *change of species by descent*. That seems to me the turning point. Personally, of course, I care much about Natural Selection; but that seems to me utterly unimportant, compared with the question of Creation *or* Modification.'[7]

Among biologists the reputation of Darwin's theory has waxed and waned, but it appears that the general public has remained faithful to Darwin's original claim as the founder of *the* theory of evolution. So when he was resurrected in the biological community through the efforts of the Neo-Mendelians, it was quite normal that the present situation should prevail, namely, that Darwin is generally acclaimed as the founder of Evolutionism. It happens even nowadays that people, who have taken the trouble to read Lamarck, discover that the current opinion is at fault, and publish their discovery. Some examples were quoted above; more could be listed, but so far this has been without effect; it is still the orthodoxy among lay and learned that there is one and only one theory of evolution, and that this theory is a modification of the one submitted by Darwin. It is interesting to contemplate the current situation in the history of biology, if people had not been duped by Darwin's want of conceptual acuity.

The mistake discussed here is unquestionably the most serious of the mistakes made by Darwin and his followers. But there were others, first of all the concept of selection. As we have seen, Darwin was inspired by the work performed by breeders. Yet: 'In moving from artificial to natural, Darwin retains the anthropomorphic conception of *selection*, with all its voluntarist overtones.'[8] Darwin's critics seized upon this ambiguity, and he admitted himself that the expression is infelicitous, and that he ought to have employed instead 'Natural Preservation'.[9] But this would not have helped much for, as I have pointed out, if the breeders use the expression 'selection', they mean 'selection through inbreeding'. It requires little imagination to see that the state of biology would have been widely different if Darwin had contended that evolutionary change results from 'Natural Inbreeding' rather than 'Natural Selec-tion'. I dare not claim that this would have prevented the rise of Neo-Mendelism, but it would surely have prevented the amalgamation of this discipline in Darwin's theory.

The third mistake was to invoke differential survival as a creative force. It was often admitted by Darwin that the working of natural selection presumes the existence of relevant variation. In contrast to many of his successors Darwin actually attempted to penetrate the mystery behind the origin of variation, but owing to his lack of understanding of embryology and morphology, especially the work of von Baer, he could not see that the main evolutionary changes have involved epigenetic changes in the course of embryonic development. If he had grasped this point, and had adopted inbreeding as an essential evolutionary agent, he would have become a Macromutationist, like many of his contemporaries. As it is, he became a Micromutationist, with the consequence that the micro-mutation theory, falsified at the outset, came to survive in biology for a whole century.

Darwin was completely right in insisting that survival is an important factor in evolution, and also in the assertion that survival under certain circumstances may be ensured through 'the struggle for existence'. But this expedient can only ensure progressive evolution, through the survival of dominant forms. Divergent evolution is the result of isolation, involving the avoidance of competition. Darwin touched upon this idea, and it may be met with occasionally in the literature on evolution. However, the great majority of Evolutionists, including Darwin, failed to see that natural selection is not the only means through which survival may be ensured.

For almost two centuries Empiricism has been the ruling orthodoxy in biology. Darwin's approach was to survey the literature for facts supporting his views, and he has often been lauded for his endeavours in this respect. But as we have seen, he never found any data corroborating his own theory, and therefore his main concern became '. . . to explain *away* the *lack* of evidence while repeatedly stressing the greater plausibility of his theory over that of *special creation*'[10] (the last italics are mine). This may be Empiricism, but it is not good science.

Even today most biologists are unaware of the lesson taught by Popper, namely, that facts are interesting only to the extent they may be used in attempts to falsify a theory. And before this can be done, a large amount of work must be done at the desk or in an armchair rather than in the field or the laboratory. This indeed was Darwin's attitude; he did most of his work in his armchair, but his endeavours mostly consisted in searching the literature for corroborating, not *falsifying* evidence.

There are two other mistakes which prevail in evolutionary research today, and for these at least Darwin has no responsibility. The first is the belief which may be traced back to Fisher, namely, that biology becomes better science if it can be formulated in terms of mathematics. It is true that mathematics is an invaluable aid in deductive reasoning, but it is also true that the mathematical derivations are no more correct than the axioms on which they are founded. If a lot of excellent experimental work has been made in genetics on the basis of theoretical population genetics, I still believe that this work has made only a very modest contribution to our understanding of the mechanisms responsible for biological evolution.

The last mistake concerns another philosophical doctrine, Reductionism. The French positivists showed that the sciences may be arranged in an ascending hierarchy: physics, chemistry, biology, ecology (sociology); and Saint Simon envisaged that all the higher sciences may be reduced to, that is, shown to be ruled by one fundamental physical law, namely, Newton's law of gravitation.

Translated in modern terms the notion of reduction would imply that all sciences can be explained on the basis of quantum mechanics. No biologist believes in this, but nevertheless it is frequently asserted that biological phenomena should be explainable in terms of physics and chemistry. For a long time a less extreme form of Reductionism has prevailed in biology in the form of the common, if not ubiquitous belief that the problems of evolution could all be solved in terms of genetics and molecular genetics. In recent years a growing awareness of the invalidity of this tenet has been manifested; evolution is the concern of all disciplines of biology.[11]

THE MISREPRESENTATIONS

History is written by the victors, and it is therefore natural that texts on evolution abound with adulatory references to Darwin and his achievements. In order to keep the discussion of this topic within reasonable limits I shall confine myself almost exclusively to one work, *The Triumph of Darwinian Method* by Michael T. Ghiselin.[12] The reason for my choice is that this book represents a climax as far as misrepresentations are concerned.

Before turning to this work I shall make a brief reference to a paper by Gould and Lewontin where they confess a partial conversion to the macromutation theory. Here we may read:

Since Darwin has attained sainthood (if not divinity) among evolutionary biologists, and since all sides invoke God's allegiance, Darwin has often been depicted as a radical selectionist at heart who invoked other mechanisms only in retreat, and only as a result of his age's own lamented ignorance about the mechanism of heredity. This view is false. Although Darwin regarded selection as the most important of evolutionary mechanisms (as we do), no argument from opponents angered him more than the common attempt to caricature and trivialize his theory by stating that it relied exclusively upon natural selection. In the last edition of the *Origin*, he wrote . . .:

'As my conclusions have lately been much misrepresented, and it has been stated that I attribute the modification of species exclusively to natural selection, I may be permitted to remark that in the first edition of this work, and subsequently, I placed in a most conspicuous position — namely at the close of the Introduction — the following words: "I am convinced that natural

406

selection has been the main, but not the exclusive means of modification.'' This has been of no avail. Great is the power of steady misrepresentation.'[13]

If this apology is carefully scrutinised it turns out to be nothing but a misrepresentation. We have seen that in this same last edition of his book Darwin listed the mechanisms which he considered to be responsible for the evolution of life. The list comprises four items: (i) Accumulation of micromutations through natural selection, (ii) use and disuse, (iii) environmental influence and (iv) macromutations. Darwin's fame, then as well as now, supposedly rests on his theory of natural selection. On this background the pluralism implied by the list, which happens to include all the mechanisms known to Darwin, is rather puzzling. In fact, we have seen that Darwin extended the list in order to explain those phenomena which cannot be accounted for by natural selection. In some cases this shortcoming may have been discovered by Darwin himself, but the list was above all an attempt to placate his opponents. To me it is completely incomprehensible that modern biologists consider Darwin's 'pluralism' anything like a merit, for the points (ii) and (iii) represent theories abandoned long ago, and (iv) is the macromutation theory, which Darwin had rejected repeatedly in the preceding text by asserting: *Nature non facit saltum*.

One might write a whole dissertation on Ghiselin's book, so once more I am obliged to introduce a restriction, in this case by dealing mainly with the Conclusion which begins in the following way:

Nothing hinders the work of genius more than man's incapacity to appreciate original ideas. The fact that Darwin's accomplishment has been controversial merely reflects the degree to which it has been misunderstood. Was Darwin just a naturalist and a good observer, or was he a theoretician of the first rank? Was he unphilosophical, or did he possess sufficient wisdom not to embrace the metaphysical follies of his detractors? Is *The Origin of Species*, in the words of a present-day historian, 'the accumulated observations in a naturalist's commonplace-book', or is it one of the most sophisticated intellectual edifices that the human mind has ever devised? Did Darwin heap fact upon fact, or was it fact upon theory? Do his interests suggest narrowness of understanding, or has the scope of his synthesis proved too much for his critics? The answers are to be found in his works.

To learn of the facts, one reads the latest journals. *To understand biology, one reads Darwin.*

Yet one still may ask just why it was that Darwin attained such remarkable success. For the mere fact of his having produced a series of classic works leaves out the personal element of why it was he, rather than someone else, who wrote them. Intellect alone does not explain why he synthesized upon such vast scale. Zeal or labour are far too common, and his accomplishment was too far beyond the ordinary, to provide a satisfactory answer. The notion that he stole his ideas from his predecessors fails completely with many of his *more* original ideas. Yet Darwin's success may readily be explained by a very simple hypothesis which seems not to have occurred to his critics: *he thought. He reasoned systematically, imaginatively, and rigorously, and he criticized his own ideas.* We have seen, in examining his theories one by one, that he applied much the same manner of reasoning to most varied problems. His models were rich in implications, and he knew full well how to exploit a promising lead. *Through his grasp of the logic of his argument, he saw what facts to seek for critical testing of his hypotheses* . . . His way of thinking — in effect, his heuristic — provides that explanation which alone can withstand rational criticism. (My italics)[14]

Clearly, whoever cannot accept Darwin's theories whole-heartedly and unreservedly, and that includes people like Lyell, Hooker, Huxley, Wallace and hundreds of other Evolutionists who claimed adherence to Darwinism, have in common one grave short-coming: they cannot think, at least not in the Darwin–Ghiselin mode! Ghiselin's attitude towards Darwin is completely uncritical, his worship is such that one feels inclined to ask if Darwin has not in fact attained divinity in the eyes of Ghiselin?

Reading on we find the following remarks:

In observing that Darwin's major innovations had roots in his earlier work, one might ask if this should detract from our esteem of him . . .

This generation of new ideas from old ones was a synthetic and innovative process, not to be confused with mere compiling. However true it may be that the spadework of fact-gathering is indispensable in the erection of theoretical edifices, it is rightly the architect whom we most admire. Just as boards and stones are not buildings, raw data are by no means properly called knowledge. We have an understanding only when the data are arranged in a system, and not every kind of order will do. To berate Darwin for borrowing elements in his theories, or to dismiss him as a compiler, is to misconstrue the role of theory in science. It is to confound scholarship with pedantry.

Darwin's theories were certainly original. But his work is not valued simply because of its novelty as such. He had a peculiar gift for developing ideas of the kind that scientists can use. *The Origin of Species* is less to be valued for the answers it gives than for the questions it asks . . . The evolutionary writings of Lamarck have proved barren from the time of their publication; Darwin's have continued to serve as the foundation for new research. This was Darwin's fundamental contribution to scientific thought, and it will endure regardless of whether his particular hypotheses are ultimately confirmed.[15]

This citation really represents a paradigm of misrepresentation, stemming from the fact that the author is unable to distinguish between the theory on the reality of evolution, one of Lamarck's contributions, and Darwin's theory of natural selection. For surely, Lamarck's writings were no less barren than that they converted Darwin and made him a compiler of empirical evidence corroborating Lamarck's theory. It may be that later Evolutionists have set out to confirm even Darwin's theory, but if that is the case, they have not been particularly successful. They may have found evidence of selective forces in Nature, but surely not working the way envisaged by Darwin. So the compliments paid to Darwin by Ghiselin would be better paid to Lamarck, Darwin's inspiration.

Ghiselin also discusses Darwin's intellectual status:

Darwin himself admitted, in characteristically modest terms, to his great originality. But he did not believe that he possessed intelligence to a remarkable degree. Certainly his intellectual powers, although marked by personal weaknesses and strengths, were far above average. He did experience difficulty with algebra and foreign languages, and he showed no astonishing facility for verbal reasoning. Nonetheless, he does remark upon his delight in Euclid. His talent for geometry is manifest in his geology, taxonomy, embryology, and morphology. Thus it is evident that he did possess uncommon ability in certain kinds of reasoning. By the conventional indices, his intelligence quotient would probably indicate intellectual superiority, but not genius. Yet such standards can have little meaning in judging a unique individual with such unusual talents. Whatever may have been Darwin's intellectual resources, he used them with almost superhuman effectiveness. The fact of his accomplishment may be explained in at least two ways. Perhaps he was gifted with enormous power of intellect, and if so, he was indeed a remarkable man. Alternatively, he somehow accomplished all his feats of reasoning in spite of his limitations; if this latter possibility be accepted, we have reason to esteem him all the more. And there may be a residuum of truth in this second point of view. Perhaps we should attribute his accomplishment less to intelligence than to wisdom. As we have seen, Darwin was remarkable for his capacity to apply a characteristic manner of thought. His reasoning was at once imaginative and critical. While willing to entertain any hypothesis, he subjected each one to the most demanding tests.[16]

Ghiselin here raises the point about the qualifications of a genius. These are undoubtedly many, and among these are, in my opinion, the following two: (i) a genius has a creative imagination, he must be a theory maker, and (ii) he has a high level of intelligence, not necessarily as measured by IQ tests, but certainly demonstrated by a great facility for mathematical and verbal reasoning. We have seen that Darwin was redundantly endowed with the first faculty, but many judges, including Ghiselin and Darwin himself, have testified to the fact that Darwin was wanting with respect to the second one. And that is the reason he found himself involved in confusions and contradictions, when he had to present and to defend his views. This is borne out by the analysis of *On the Origin of Species* given above, which also shows that the evaluation of Darwin's approach in the last clauses quoted above is a grotesque misrepresentation.

Further on Ghiselin writes: 'Bacon wrote that it is "the first distemper of learning, when men study words and not matter". The substance of an argument is propositions, not names. What *matters is ideas*, not the language in which they are expressed'[17] (my italics). This surely is a fundamental misunderstanding, for Bacon wanted people to deal with facts rather than ideas; however, by an elegant, if deceptive pun Ghiselin transforms matters into ideas, and consequently ideas must also be converted into something else, and so they become names or even language. This rendering of Empiricism is hardly shared by anybody else, certainly it does not conform with the one professed by Darwin.

410

On the next page we may read: 'Many have argued that since they, personally, disagree with Darwin's conclusions, we should heap contempt upon the scientist or his thinking.'[18] Anybody who has publicly stated his opinion on any topic must be prepared to be exposed to criticism, not of his person, but of his views. It is possible that some people mix their criticism with contempt, but that is a rather unusual state of affairs. More often does it happen that sensitive souls take any criticism to imply a measure of contempt, and I am afraid that Darwin belongs to this category.

And now the last citation:

The quality of his satisfaction is especially apparent when, in recounting an early geological triumph, he says: 'All this shows how ambitious I was; but I think that I can say with truth that in after years, though I cared in the highest degree for the approbation of such men as Lyell and Hooker, who were my friends, I did not care much about the general public'. Darwin possessed an aristocrat's system of values. What counted was not reputation, but his personal sense of honor. It evidently mattered little to him that ignorant or foolish persons misinterpreted his writings. The satisfaction lay more with expressing the truth than with communicating it. If only the best minds understood him, so much the better.[19]

The quoted statement shows that neither Darwin nor Ghiselin has grasped the source of Darwin's triumph. If he had won the approbation of Lyell, Hooker and some other persons in the English Establishment of science, and been neglected by the general public, Darwin would have been unknown today. The point is that his theory was rejected by almost all who had the power to judge, *but his name was associated by the general public with the notion of evolution, and therefore it is still with us today.*

THE ANTIMYTH

It was this long preparation on both sides, the climax coming just when the Church had been defeated in the English universities, that gave the excitement to the ultimate clash and the ultimate victory. And it was this excitement which gave rise to the illusions of what we may call the Darwinian myth. The belief that Darwinism was simply the work of Darwin and that its success was simply a scientific success, to be judged by intellectual criteria alone. The belief that it is concerned merely with the historical fact of evolution, that the process of

411

evolution, the future of evolution, did not concern Darwin and, since it is so very, very slow, it need not seriously concern us. The belief that the man who liberated mankind succeeded also in liberating himself — which unfortunately he did not. All these are parts of the Darwinian myth. If we understand them, Darwin's work becomes a base for discovery. If we do not understand them it becomes . . . a block to discovery.[20]

C.D. Darlington

But when one tries to relate the accounts of historians of science to the problem of Darwin's place in intellectual history one finds a gap between the generality of his influence and the particularity of his theory.[21]

Robert M. Young

Darwin was not a thinker and he did not originate the ideas he used. He vacillated, added, retracted, and confused his own traces. As soon as he crossed the dividing line between the realm of events and the realm of reality he became 'metaphysical' in the bad sense . . .
Darwin ended by disowning Darwinism, thinking he had poorly set forth his ideas. Marx said that for his part he was no Marxist.[22]

Jacques Barzun

No educated person, not even the most ignorant, could suppose that I mean to arrogate to myself the origination of the doctrine that species had not been independently created. The only novelty in my work is the attempt to explain *how* species became modified.[23]

Charles Darwin

I do not believe that success proves anything.[24]

Karl R. Popper

As appears from the statement by Darlington quoted above, the Darwinian myth comprises several aspects. We cannot here follow the outline presented in the citation, but we may consider the following points.

In his publications Darwin conveys the impression that the general theory of evolution, the theory on the reality of evolution, originated with him; his 'Historical Sketch' did very little to amend this perception. As concerns this point Darlington writes:

It seems incredible that the apostle of evolution should have been so deficient in historical sense; so much so that, although deeply interested in his own priority, he never realized that his own ideas were second hand. He thought he had worked them out himself, even when he had only sorted them out. Moreover his ideas were less clearly sorted out and less clearly expressed and, worst of all, less strictly and less openly held and maintained than the ideas of those who first thought of them.[25]

412

It is possible that Darwin's assertions may have convinced the general public, but the contemporaneous biologists in general, and his supporters in particular should have known better — and yet many of them joined the chorus praising Darwin's genius.

Sometimes a more modest claim is made. Admitting that Darwin did not himself originate the idea that evolution had taken place, it is asserted that through his painstaking compilation of supporting evidence he converted the world to the belief in Evolutionism. There is certainly a measure of truth in this claim, but the merit of this achievement should be measured on the basis of the view stated by Ghiselin, the admirer of Darwin, which was quoted above: 'However true it may be that the spadework of fact-gathering is indispensable in the creation of theoretical edifices, it is rightly the architect whom we most admire.'

So we are facing a very peculiar situation: if people celebrate Darwin as the founder of the general theory of evolution — and this is a notion which has survived almost uninterruptedly to this day — then they are committing a serious mistake. If, on the other hand, Darwin's main achievement is the successful advocacy of a theory advanced by somebody else, then it would seem reasonable that when Darwin is lauded, this somebody else (that is, Lamarck) should at least be mentioned in the context.

I think it is one of the great puzzles in the history of biology that Darwin succeeded where everybody else had failed. I shall begin by mentioning a reason which cannot be invoked, namely that, in my opinion, Darwin wrote a book which charmed the readers through its content and style, for On the Origin of Species is a boring book. When I first came to this conclusion, I thought that the cast of the book reflected the style of its day, and to a certain extent this is indeed the case. However, as I subsequently read Lamarck, Geoffroy Saint-Hilaire, von Baer, Chambers, Owen, Huxley, Mivart and even Haeckel, I came to understand that when allowances are made for the time, Darwin is outstanding as an author, but not in a commendatory sense. I appreciate finding my view supported by the judgement of Huxley, Darwin's contemporary friend: 'Exposition was not Darwin's forte — and his English is sometimes wonderful.'[26] Needless to say, this outspoken criticism was confided in a private letter.

Among the explanations which have been proposed to account for Darwin's success is that he came out at the right time and the right place. The former notion was current when Darwin was still alive, and he commented upon it as follows:

It has sometimes been said that the success of the 'Origin' proved 'that the subject was in the air', or 'that men's minds were prepared for it'. I do not think this is strictly true, for I occasionally sounded not a few naturalists, and never happened to come across a single one who seemed to doubt the permanence of species.[27]

We may be sure that all those interviewed by Darwin were acquainted with Lamarck's theory, and yet none of them was willing to accept it. I believe that one main reason for this situation is that Lamarck, the hermit, was completely out of time with the intellectual movements of the day. In the early nineteenth century the intelligentsia reacted against the Rationalism of the Enlightenment by converting to pantheistic Romanticism. It is easy to understand that in this milieu Lamarck's theory failed to find response in both the general public and the intellectual Establishment. When Darwin published his book half-a-century later, the replacement of Romanticism by Naturalism was on the way, and people were prepared to accept a Naturalistic explanation of the origin of life.

The negative outcome of Darwin's enquiries may have an alternative explanation. It has been proposed by Thomas S. Kuhn[28] that scientific revolutions — shifts of paradigm — are always accomplished by outsiders. The most likely explanation of this fact is that the insiders — the members of the scientific Establishment — have founded their reputations on the ruling dogmas and consequently are reluctant to acquiesce in their overthrow. This interpretation has previously been suggested by Darlington, in the statement quoted at the head of this section, and in the following one: 'Likewise we can see that by taking all the credit and all the blame for "my theory" Darwin simplified the tasks of both friends and foes. For his foes had a false excuse for concentrating their attack on one dangerous innovator and his friends had a false excuse for not having acknowledged earlier what had long been perfectly obvious to laymen like Chambers or Spencer.'[29]

Darwin also came out in the right place. There can be no doubt that in spite of the French revolution the intellectual Establishment in general, and the clerical one in particular, were much less conservative in England than in France. It took a long time before evolution became accepted in France.

But Darwin also profited from his epistemological confusion or delusion. We have seen that Lamarck frankly stated that speculation, that is, theory construction, forms a very important aspect of the

414

chores of the scientist. With Empiricism on the rise in France at the time, under the guidance of Cuvier, this was a very daring stand to take. Darwin was as much a theory maker as Lamarck, but publicly he portrayed himself as an Empiricist, thus disarming many potential critics, even though, as we have seen, quite a few of them unmasked him.

I have asserted above that as scientists both Lamarck and Darwin were outsiders, and that part of their accomplishments may be referred to this state of affairs. But apart from this there is a great difference between the two; Lamarck was a poor man and a social outcast, whereas Darwin was a wealthy man who, in spite of his voluntary isolation in the countryside, could keep in contact with the leading scientific circles in England. This is a circumstance which must have contributed significantly to Darwin's recognition.

The suggestions made here do not pretend to explain the establishment of the Darwinian myth. But to the extent it contains a grain of truth, I would like to compare the history of evolutionary thought with a pitcher, partly filled with water, into which pebbles are thrown, one by one. It so happens that one single pebble will cause the water to spill over, and this pebble may thus be declared *the cause* of this event. Yet, it should not be forgotten that its effect sprang from all the other pebbles that went before.

The statement by Young quoted above was unquestionably correct when it was published in 1971, and it still is. But we know that it was not always so, some few adherents to Darwin's theory may have lingered on between 1870 and 1940, but according to the unanimous testimony of the historians of biology Darwinism was dead.[30] The general attitude towards this theory was succinctly, but belatedly stated by J. Gray: 'No amount of argument, or clever epigram, can disguise the inherent improbability of orthodox [Darwinian] theory; but most biologists feel it is better to think in terms of improbable events than not to think at all; there will always be a few who feel in their bones a sneaking sympathy with Samuel Butler's scepticism.'[31]

I think it is quite unusual that abandoned scientific theories are revived, and it is therefore of some interest to see if we can find some acceptable explanation of this phenomenon. Personally I believe that one reason may be found in the fact that the revival took place in England. Even if science is international, it may be presumed that Fisher and Haldane would have been more inclined to rehabilitate Darwin than biologists of other nationalities. But to this we may add Fisher's early contact with the Darwinian biometricians, and his personal acquaintance with Major Leonard Darwin, Charles' son, whose assistance is acknowledged in Fisher's book. I frankly admit that the reasons proposed here do not weigh very heavily, but I insist that emotional or personal reasons may have been involved. If this was not the case, Fisher ought to have stated that his was a new micromutation theory in which Darwin's differential survival had been replaced by differential reproduction.

Jacques Barzun, quoted at the head of this section, was the first to point out the similarities between Darwin and Karl Marx. He has been followed by others, for instance A.R. Manser: 'Perhaps Darwin should be called ''Biology's Karl Marx'' rather than its ''Newton''. In both cases there is a basic picture which seems to render a complex mass of facts comprehensible without giving either the power of control or of prediction.'[32] This may be right, but the most distressing similarity lies in the fact that although both Darwin and Marx advanced falsifiable theories that have been falsified long ago, there are still lots of people who declare themselves adherents to Darwinism and Marxism. And since falsified theories belong to the realm of metaphysics, we may infer that what were once 'empirical theories' have become religions.

In the case of Darwinism the consequences of this metamorphosis prevail mostly on the intellectual level; no persons are harmed, but the advancement of the biological sciences has been seriously hampered. With Marxism the opposite relation holds, the economic sciences have advanced far beyond the stage set by Marx, but myriads of people live under a yoke, whose existence is justified in the name of 'Marxism'. In fact, I would like to challenge Manser's assertion with respect to the predictions allowed for by the two theories. Experience has shown that whenever Marxism is exposed to empirical tests, the outcome is exactly the opposite of the theoretical predictions. Thus, it is not that slaves are made to free men, but the opposite which occurs, and the economic exploitation, as measured by the privileges of the ruling class, is increased rather than reduced.

In this respect there are indeed certain similarities between the two theories, for even in Darwin's case is the real world exactly the opposite of that stated by his theory. Thus, the major evolutionary changes are macromutations, not micromutations, Darwin's adaptive evolution is accomplished by isolation, rather than by selection, and the process for which the latter answers, progressive evolution, was rejected by Darwin.

And thus it comes about that for Marx as for Darwin the myth became an antimyth.

16

Conclusion

. . . there is not a single belief that it is not a bounden duty with them to hold with a light hand and to part with cheerfully, the moment it is really proved to be contrary to any fact, great or small.[1]

T.H. Huxley

A long-enduring and regrettable effect of the success of the *Origin* was the addiction of biologists to unverifiable speculations. 'Explanations' of the origin of structures, instincts, and mental aptitudes of all kinds, in terms of Darwinian principles, marked with the Darwinian plausibility but hopelessly unverifiable poured out from every research centre.[2]

W.R. Thompson

How is it, we may now ask ourselves, that so much obscurity overhangs the development of the greatest of modern ideas. After a hundred years we are almost as uncertain of the authorship or editorship of Darwin's writings as we are of those attributed to Homer or Hippocrates. This is due on the one hand to the fact that people who investigate the history of science are historians who are not entirely clear about the meaning of its ideas. Changes in the key words of technical speech break their formal continuity. They also often believe what the discoverer writes about his own discoveries, which, as we see, is not a wise thing to do.

On the other hand among scientists there is a natural feeling that one of the greatest of our figures should not be dissected, at least by one of us. The myth should be respected.[3]

C.D. Darlington

But if it is important for later generations not to deny the fact of revolution because they cannot concede its truth or justice, it is no less important not to concede the truth or justice merely because they cannot deny the fact of revolution.[4]

Gertrude Himmelfarb

It seems clear as an obvious historical fact that zoology and botany have constantly neglected to sharpen their higher thinking in the implicit assumption that, in regard to thinking at this level, Darwin said in 1859 the very last word.[5]

Leon Croizat

To propose that intellectual progress in biology is possible for anyone who is prepared to shake the scales from their eyes may seem like dangerous mystical adventurism to the members of the neo-Darwinian establishment, but in the larger realm of the human intellect it should go without saying.[6]

Robert G.B. Reid

417

For more than a century the biological community has accepted that *the* theory on evolution is a theory on the mechanism of evolution. During most of the last half century it has been conceded that this theory is the one first submitted by Darwin and Wallace in 1858, the theory of natural selection, which passes under the name of 'Darwinism'.

Both of these suppositions have been refuted repeatedly. In the present book I have shown that simple reasoning suffices to bring out that no fewer than four theories of evolution are necessary to account for the various aspects of the phenomenon of evolution. However, during the century following the publication of *On the Origin of Species* it has been pointed out many times that at least two theories of evolution are necessary, one stating the reality of evolution and one dealing with the mechanism of evolution. And those who have made this distinction have not failed to observe that the first theory properly ought to be called 'Lamarckism'. As I have demonstrated here, Darwin's micromutation theory implies incongruities so conspicuous that the great majority of biologists rejected it right away. It was disowned even by the general public, but in this case the name of Darwin remained associated with Lamarck's theory.

However, today the officially accepted evolutionary paradigm, the synthetic theory or Neo-Mendelism is claimed to be a modification of Darwinism. How did this resurrection come about? Some aspects of this question have been answered above; I shall here give a brief recapitulation and discuss some more general issues.

(i) First of all, it is not really true that Neo-Mendelism is a revision of Darwin's theory. The former explains evolutionary change as the outcome of differential reproduction plus random survival, whereas the latter involves random reproduction coupled with differential survival. This difference is so fundamental that I find it beyond comprehension that it was not acknowledged a long time ago by the specialists. The discrepancy was pointed out by a complete outsider, Norman Macbeth, as late as 1971.[7]

(ii) Several of the authors quoted at the head of this section suggest that the state of biological thought is less than satisfactory, and the observation made in the preceding paragraph supports this proposition. I have already indicated the most likely explanation of this state of affairs, namely, that modern biologists to an overwhelming extent are Reductionist Empiricists, who believe that problems are solved by making observations, preferably experimental ones obtained by modern laboratory equipment. As a consequence they have lost the sense of history: work published 50 or 100 years ago is considered so obsolete that it is not even necessary to know it, let alone teach it.

But what we aim at is understanding, and that we do not obtain through observations, but through theories which attempt to establish causal relations between our observations. This fact was recognised by Lamarck and Geoffroy Saint-Hilaire, and to a certain degree it was accepted by the nineteenth-century biologists. But with the rise of experimental biology in our century and especially, of course, following the breakthrough of molecular biology after the Second World War, this lesson was forgotten completely. It is quite usual to read in the discussion of an experimental paper that the solution of some problem requires the acquisition of further experimental results. I think it has never occurred that authors assert as their conviction that the only way to crack their problem is to sit down and read and think.

Popper has for many years fought a lonely battle against Empiricism — or Positivism. In recent years he has gained some adherence among biologists, but typically mostly among those, palaeontologists and morphologists, who cannot easily apply the experimental approach. The circumstance that many present-day biologists believe that all problems must be solved by experiments, when coupled with the lack of knowledge of the history of biology, has had some bad and sad consequences: (1) since 'speculation' is banned, the experiments are often quite unimaginative — at best descriptive, rather than explanatory; (2) it often happens that experiments published long ago are repeated and published as original observations; and (3) very seldom is it realised that the answers to many of the problems facing us today may be found in the literature, either because the original authors were unable to draw the consequences of their own observations, or else because the proper interpretations depend upon more recently acquired knowledge.

(iii) In the statement quoted above, Darlington claims that the historians of science in general are incompetent, owing to the circumstance that they are not familiar with technical aspects of the topic with which they deal. There is a certain truth in this statement, but it is not the whole truth. Before I explain myself, I propose to extend the charge to include even the philosophers of science.

It is true that today, as in 1959 when Darlington's book was published, the large majority of historians and philosophers of science excel in the glorification of Darwin as the founder of *the* theory of evolution, a theory which is believed to have prevailed to the present day. By adopting this stand they are joining forces with the opinion acclaimed by the professional biologists. And what else can they do? If the biologists cannot themselves find out that the ruling orthodoxy is false, how can we expect outsiders to do the job for them?

Some readers may perhaps think that I am now contradicting myself, since I have earlier in this book proclaimed that we may expect the essential innovations in science to be the accomplishments of outsiders. But this is not the case, for we must distinguish between two kinds of outsiders, the professional and the social ones. From a biologist's point of view, historians and philosophers of science are outsiders by training, but they commonly belong to the same social hierarchy. And among the unwritten laws of scientific hierarchies one is that you must respect the scholarship and authority of all your colleagues. Anyone who violates this law is certain to suffer ostracism, as Lamarck was to learn.

And therefore Darlington's criticism may be unjustified; if today historians and philosophers salute Darwin and his work, then it is because the biologists do so. I think I can vindicate this postulate by referring to the fact that when, during the first third of our century, biologists in general did not believe in Darwinism, the historians and the philosophers did not either.[8]

(iv) If we return to the statement of Darlington, it seems to follow from the last clause that the biologists themselves are aware of the fact that the significance of Darwinism is a myth, but that for reasons of piety they do not divulge the truth. This interpretation, which may not represent Darlington's personal view, is wide of the mark. In fact, the Empiricistic and non-historical approach distinguishing current biology has the consequence that students may get the impression that what they are taught are facts, not ideas. And since facts cannot be disputed, the critical faculty is not adequately developed; very few people dispute what they learn at school. This, I believe, is the main reason why the 'Neo-Darwinian' myth has survived for more than half-a-century.

(v) Must we criticise Darwin? Is it not rather despicable to slate the reputation of a man who indisputably deserves a place in the annals of biology? I fear that such objections may be raised against my book, and therefore I want to emphasise that it is not in any way meant as a criticism of Darwin, the person. All the available testimonies agree in showing Darwin as a person with extraordinarily fine qualities, a loyal son, a caring husband and a loving father, a considerate employer and, not the least, the friend of his friends. This picture is troubled by a few instances where he was less

than generous towards rivals and critics, but by and large Charles
Darwin, the person, as known by posterity is an unusually sympathetic human being.

However, the present work is primarily concerned with *Darwinism*, not with *Darwin*. If the criticism of the former entails a certain
measure of censure of the latter, then it is because he and many of
his friends and followers systematically have degraded the contribution of those persons who simultaneously or before Darwin contributed to the development of evolutionary thought. Today, thanks
to the deception of these men, Lamarck is largely considered a
lunatic, Geoffroy Saint-Hilaire an unbridled speculator, Chambers
next to unknown, Owen a mischievous struggler, Spencer an inexhaustible scribbler and Mivart a religious fanatic. Von Baer, who
after all supplied an important clue to the correct solution of the
mechanism of evolution, and even publicly, if belatedly professed
his belief in evolution, is hardly ever mentioned in discourses on
evolution, and if he is, he is claimed to have been an anti-
Evolutionist.

One purpose of the present work is to show that this is a falsification of history; the accomplishments of the mentioned persons to
biology measure up to, and in some instances even surpass that of
Darwin. Some of them did little more than point out Darwin's
mistakes, but in doing so they at least demonstrated that they
mastered biology better than Darwin. And if so many people,
including, as we have seen, most of his friends and supporters, could
see the shortcomings of his theory, we are entitled to conclude that
as a biologist and thinker Darwin was not a genius. He was not 'the
Newton of Biology', not even its Copernicus. In fact, I would rather
be willing to bestow the latter epithet on Lamarck.

As Darwin was told himself, his success did not depend upon
what he said, but that he happened to say it at the right time. All the
ridicule which may follow from challenging the ruling orthodoxy
had been reaped by the vanguard Evolutionists; when Darwin at long
last came out the world was ready to accept the message that life had
originated through evolution.

This attempt to correct a historical falsification is one of the
objectives of my writing this book, but it is not the most important
one. Rather, for half-a-century biology has been caught in a cul-de-
sac represented by the micromutation theory. As I have shown, it
matters little whether this theory is called *Lamarckism, Darwinism,
Neo-Darwinism, Mendelian population genetics, the modern
synthesis*, or *Neo-Mendelism*, for empirically these theories are

indistinguishable. Micromutations do occur, but the theory that these alone can account for evolutionary change is either falsified, or else it is an unfalsifiable, hence metaphysical theory.

I suppose that nobody will deny that it is a great misfortune if an entire branch of science becomes addicted to a false theory. But this is what has happened in biology: for a long time now people discuss evolutionary problems in a peculiar 'Darwinian' vocabulary — 'adaptation', 'selection pressure', 'natural selection', etc. — thereby believing that they contribute to the *explanation* of natural events. They do not, and the sooner this is discovered, the sooner we shall be able to make real progress in our understanding of evolution.

I believe that one day the Darwinian myth will be ranked the greatest deceit in the history of science. When this happens many people will pose the question: How did this ever happen? The present text surveys some of the answers which have been given, but there is no reason to believe that we have yet reached the final one. There will be a lot of work to do for coming generations of historians of biology.

When, more than ten years ago, I began a detailed study of the literature on Evolution, the last two great Macromutationists, Goldschmidt and Schindewolf, had left the scene. For a number of years I felt rather isolated, so it is with great satisfaction that during the last few years I have been able to record a growing opposition to the ruling micromutation theory, both among experimentally and theoretically minded biologists. In fact, the present situation has features typical of a period of paradigm shift, namely, that so many theories float around that one sometimes gets the impression that the phrase holds: One man, one theory.

This is not a stable situation, and we may expect that sooner or later the majority of biologists will agree upon adopting one among the present cornucopia of theories. Darwin recommended the theory of evolution because it answers so many questions left unintelligible by the theory of Creationism. I propose that we adopt the two theories on the mechanism of evolution advocated in this book because they resolve *all* the difficulties facing the micromutation theory in its several disguises.

If in this book harsh words are spoken about some of the greatest among the intellectual leaders of mankind, my motive is not, I hope, the wish to belittle them. It springs rather from my conviction that, if our civilization is to survive, we must break the habit of deference to great men.

Karl R. Popper: *The Open Society and its Enemies*

. . . it made its way through the succession of stages that Whewell had described as the fate of all great discoveries — the first in which people said, 'It is absurd', the second, 'It is contrary to the Bible', and the third, 'We always knew it was so'.

Gertrud Himmelfarb: *Darwin and the Darwinian Revolution*

Comme nous allons rire de nos vieilles idées! Comme nous allons mous moquer de nous-mêmes.

Constant Prévost in *Life Letters and Journals*
of Sir Charles Lyell, Bart

Notes

ABBREVIATIONS

ADB   *The autobiography of Charles Darwin 1809–1882* (ed. N. Barlow). Collins, London (1958).

BDMW   J. Barzun: *Darwin, Marx, Wagner critique of a heritage* (second revised edn.). Doubleday, New York (1958).

DDP   C.D. Darlington: *Darwin's place in history*. Basil Blackwell, Oxford (1959).

DNTS   Darwin's notebooks on transmutation of species (ed. G. de Beer). *Bulletin of the British Museum (Natural History) Historical Series* 2, 23–183 (1960).

DOS (1)   C. Darwin: *On the origin of species A fascimile of the first edition with an introduction by Ernst Mayr*. Harvard University Press, Cambridge, Mass. (1966).

DOS (6)   C. Darwin: *The origin of the species by means of natural selection or the preservation of favoured races in the struggle for life* (sixth edn., with additions and corrections to 1872). John Murray, London (1885).

DOSV   *The origin of species by Charles Darwin A variorum text* (ed. M. Peckham). University of Pennsylvania Press, Philadelphia (1959).

DWNS   Charles Darwin and A.R. Wallace: *Evolution by natural selection* (with a foreword by G. de Beer). University Press, Cambridge (1958).

FGNS   R.A. Fisher: *The genetical theory of natural selection* (second revised edn.). Dover Publications, New York (1958).

GS-HHN   I. Geoffroy Saint-Hilaire: *Histoire naturelle générale des règnes organiques*, trois tomes. Victor Masson, Paris (1854–60).

HDE   T.H. Huxley: *Darwiniana Essays*. Macmillan, London (1893).

HDR   G. Himmelfarb: *Darwin and the Darwinian revolution*. Chatto and Windus, London (1959).

HGM   E. Haeckel: *Generelle Morphologie der Organismen. Allgemeine Grundzüge der organischen Formen-Wissenschaft mechanisch begründet durch die von Charles Darwin reformierte Descendenz-Theorie. Zweiter Band. Allgemeine Entwickelungsgeschichte der Organismen Kritische Grundzüge der mechanischen Wissenschaft von den entstehenden Formen der Organismen, begründet durch die Descendenz-Theorie.* Georg Reimer, Berlin (1866).

HNS   E. Haeckel: *Natürliche Schöpfungsgeschichte Gemeinverständliche wissenschaftliche Vorträge über die Entwickelungslehre im Allgemeinen und diejenige von Darwin, Goethe und Lamarck im Besonderen, über die Anwendung derselben auf den Ursprung des Menschen und damit zusammenhängende Grundfragen der Naturwissenschaft.* Georg Reimer, Berlin (1868).

KEBR   K.E. von Baer: *Reden gehalten in wissenschaftlichen Versammlungen und kleinere Aufsätze vermischten Inhalts,* zwei Bände. H. Schmitzdorff, Sankt Petersburg (1864–76).

LDO   J.B. Lamarck: Discours d'ouverture (An viii, An x, An xi et 1806). *Bulletin Scientifique de la France et de la Belgique* 40, 5–157 (1907).

LHN   J.B.P.A. de Lamarck: *Histoire naturelle des animaux sans vertèbres, présentant les caractères généraux et particuliers de ces animaux, leur distribution, leurs classes, leurs familles, leurs genres, et la citation des principales espèces qui s'y rapportent; précédée d'une introduction offrant la détermination des caractères essentiels de l'animal, sa distinction du végétal et des autres corps naturels; enfin, l'exposition des principes fondamentaux de la zoologie* (deuxième edn., eds. G.P. Deshayes and H. Milne Edwards), tome premier. J.B. Ballière, Paris (1835).

LIM   *Inédits de Lamarck d'après les manuscripts conservés à la bibliothèque centrale du Museum National d'Histoire Naturelle à Paris* (eds M. Vachon, G. Rousseau et Y. Laissus). Masson, Paris (1972).

LLD   *The life and letters of Charles Darwin, including an autobiographical chapter* (ed. F. Darwin), three volumes. John Murray, London (1888).

LLHo   L. Huxley: *Life and letters of Sir Joseph Dalton Hooker, OM, GCSI.* Based on materials collected and arranged by Lady Hooker, two volumes. John Murray, London (1918).

LLHu   L. Huxley: *Life and letters of Thomas Henry Huxley,* three volumes. Macmillan, London (1903).

LLL   *Life, letters and journals of Sir Charles Lyell, Bart.* (ed. [K.M.] Lyell), two volumes. John Murray, London (1881).

LPZ   J.-B.-P.-A. Lamarck: *Philosophie zoologique,* two volumes in one. Reprinted by H.R. Engelmann (J. Cramer) and Wheldon & Wesley, Weinheim and Codicote (1960).

LZP   J.B. Lamarck: *Zoological philosophy An exposition with regard to the natural history of animals The diversity of their organisation and their faculties which they derive from it; the physical causes which maintain life within them and give rise to their various movements; lastly, those which produce feeling and intelligence in some among them* (translated, with an introduction by H. Elliot). Macmillan, London (1914).

MARW   J. Marchant: *Alfred Russel Wallace: letters and reminiscences,* two volumes. Harper, New York (1916).

MLD   *More letters of Charles Darwin A record of his work in a series of hitherto unpublished letters* (eds F. Darwin and A.C. Seward), two volumes. John Murray, London (1903).

NHB   E. Nordenskiöld: *The history of biology A survey.* Tudor Publishing, New York (1946).

PLFE   A.S. Packard: *Lamarck the founder of evolution His life and work*. Longmans, Green, New York (1901).

PTP   W.B. Provine: *The origins of theoretical population genetics*. University Press, Chicago (1971).

SLE   S. Løvtrup: *Epigenetics — a treatise on theoretical biology*. John Wiley, London (1974).

SLP   S. Løvtrup: *The phylogeny of* VERTEBRATA. John Wiley, London (1977).

WD   A.R. Wallace: *Darwinism An exposition of the theory of natural selection with some of its applications*. Macmillan, London (1890).

WML   A.R. Wallace: *My life A record of events and opinions*, two volumes. Chapman and Hall, London (1905).

INTRODUCTION

1. HDE, p. 286.
2. LLD, Vol. 2, p. 179.
3. WML, Vol. 1, p. 372.
4. E. Haeckel: *The history of creation* (third edn., translation revised by E.R. Lankaster). Kegan Paul, Trench, London (1883), p. 106. (HNS, p. 72.)
5. J.R. Oppenheimer: 'Problems, concepts and their history', pp. 1–24 in *Analysis of development* (eds. B.H. Willier, P.A. Weiss and V. Hamburger). V.B. Saunders, Philadelphia (1955). W. Garstang: 'The theory of recapitulation', *Zoological Journal of the Linnean Society* 35, 81–101 (1922).
6. R.B. Goldschmidt: *The material basis of evolution*. Yale University Press, New Haven (1940).
7. SLE.

1. THE FOUR THEORIES OF EVOLUTION

1. E. Krause: *Erasmus Darwin with a preliminary notice by Charles Darwin*. John Murray, London (1879), pp. 139–40.
2. LPZ, pp. 31–2.
3. C.H. Waddington: *The evolution of an evolutionist*. University Press, Edinburgh (1975), p. 168.
4. W. Hennig: *Phylogenetic systematics*. University of Illinois Press, Urbana (1960).
5. SLP. C. Patterson: 'Significance of fossils in determining evolutionary relationships', *Annual Review of Ecology and Systematics* 12, 195–223 (1981).
6. W. Hennig, *Phylogenetic systematics*.
7. SLP.
8. S. Løvtrup: 'The evolutionary species: fact or fiction?', *Systematic Zoology* 28, 386–92 (1979). S. Løvtrup: 'On species and other taxa',

Cladistics (in press).

9. SLP.

10. B.G. Gardiner: 'Tetrapod classification', *Zoological Journal of the Linnean Society* 74, 207–32 (1982).

11. S. Løvtrup: 'On the classification of the taxon Tetrapoda', *Systematic Zoology* 34, 463–70 (1985).

12. SLE.

2. THE PIONEERS

1. M. Barthélemy-Madaule: *Lamarck ou le mythe du précurseur*. Seuil, Paris (1979), p. 12.

2. Ibid.

3. BDMW, p. 74.

4. A. Weinstein: 'How unknown was Mendel's paper?', *Journal of the History of Biology* 10, 341–64 (1977).

5. DDP.

6. H.F. Osborn: *From the Greeks to Darwin The development of the evolution idea through twenty-four centuries* (second edn.) Charles Scribner, New York (1929).

7. S. Butler: *Evolution, old and new; Or, the theories of Buffon, Dr. Erasmus Darwin, and Lamarck, as compared with that of Charles Darwin* (third revised edn.). A.C. Fifield, London (1911).

8. Ibid., pp. 90–1.

9. Ibid., p. 123.

10. GS-HHN.

11. DOS (6), p. xiii.

12. GS-HHN, vol. 2, pp. 390–1.

13. T.S. Kuhn: *The structure of scientific revolutions*. University of Chicago Press, Chicago (1962).

14. D. King-Hele: *Doctor of revolution The life and genius of Erasmus Darwin*. Faber and Faber, London (1977).

15. Ibid., p. 241.

16. Ibid., p. 243.

17. Ibid., pp. 245–6.

18. Ibid., p. 290.

19. LLD, vol. 1, p. 38.

20. D. King-Hele, *Doctor of revolution*, p. 313.

21. MLD, vol. 1, p. 125.

22. Ibid., p. 124.

23. DNTS, p. 41.

24. D. King-Hele, *Doctor of revolution*, p. 310.

25. Ibid., p. 313.

26. E. Krause: *Erasmus Darwin with a preliminary notice by Charles Darwin*. John Murray, London (1879).

27. Ibid., p. 88.

28. Ibid., pp. 131–3.

29. Ibid., p. 211.

30. D. King-Hele, *Doctor of revolution*, p. 323.

31. L. Eiseley: *Darwin's century Evolution and the men who discovered it*. Doubleday, New York (1961).

32. P.J. Vorzimmer: 'The Darwin reading notebooks (1838–1860)', *Journal of the History of Biology* 10, 107–53 (1977).

33. DDP, p. 22.

34. P.G. Mudford: 'William Lawrence and *The natural history of man*', *Journal of the History of Ideas* 29, 430–6 (1958).

35. DDP, p. 22.

36. This book has not, unfortunately, been available to me.

37. K.D. Wells: 'The historical context of natural selection: The case of Patrick Matthew', *Journal of the History of Biology* 6, 225–58 (1973).

38. DDP; L. Eiseley, *Darwin's century*; C. Limoges: *La sélection naturelle Etude sur la première constitution d'un concept (1837–1859)*. Presses Universitaires de France, Paris (1970); K.D. Wells, 'The historical context of natural selection'.

39. DDP, pp. 90–1.

40. Ibid., p. 91.

41. C. Limoges, *La sélection naturelle*; K.D. Wells, 'The historical context of natural selection'.

42. DOS (6), p. xvi.

43. LLD, vol. 2, p. 302.

44. L. Eiseley: 'Charles Darwin, Edward Blyth, and the theory of natural selection', *Proceedings of the American Philosophical Society* 103, 94–158 (1959). According to C. Limoges, *La sélection naturelle*, a similar assertion has been made by C.D. Darlington in the American edition of *Darwin's place in history*. This work has not been available to me.

45. My view accords with those of C. Limoges and K.D. Wells.

46. K.D. Wells, 'The historical context of natural selection', p. 256.

47. L. Eiseley, 'Charles Darwin' (1959).

48. DWNS, p. 27.

49. L. Eiseley, 'Charles Darwin' (1959).

50. Ibid., p. 108.

51. Ibid., pp. 117–18.

52. Ibid., p. 118.

53. Ibid., p. 118.

54. Ibid., p. 147.

55. B.G. Beddall: ' "Notes for Mr. Darwin": Letters to Charles Darwin from Edward Blyth at Calcutta: A study in the progress of discovery', *Journal of the History of Biology* 6, 69–95 (1973).

56. DNTS, p. 106.

57. J.S. Schwartz: 'Charles Darwin's debt to Malthus and Edward Blyth'. *Journal of the History of Biology* 7, 301–18 (1974).

58. DNTS, p. 36.

59. DOS (6), pp. 49–50.

60. P.B. Medawar: *The art of the soluble*. Methuen, London (1967), p. 44.

61. Ibid., p. 49.

62. H. Spencer: *The principles of biology* (revised and enlarged edn.) vol. 1. Williams and Norgate, London (1898).

63. Ibid., pp. 452–3.

64. Ibid., p. 453.
65. Ibid., p. 332.
66. H. Spencer: *An autobiography*. vol. 1. Williams and Norgate, London (1904), p. 389.
67. DOS (6), p. xix.
68. LLD, vol. 2, p. 141.
69. Ibid., vol. 3, pp. 55–6.
70. Ibid., p. 120.
71. R.M. Young: 'Darwin's metaphor: Does Nature select?', *The Monist* 55, 442–503, (1971), p. 459.
72. E. Gilson: *D'Aristote à Darwin et retour*. J. Vrin, Paris, (1971), p. 118.
73. DOS (6), p. xiii.
74. DDP, p. 33.
75. W. Irvine: *Apes, angels, and Victorians A joint biography of Darwin and Huxley*. Weidenfeld and Nicolson, London (1955), p. 223.
76. S. Butler: *Luck, or cunning, As the main means of organic modification: An attempt to throw additional light upon Darwin's theory of natural selection* (second revised edn.). A.C. Fifield, London (1920).

3. JEAN-BAPTISTE DE LAMARCK (1744–1829)

1. LHN, p. 19.
2. C.H. Waddington: 'Evolutionary adaptation', pp. 381–402 in *Evolution after Darwin*, vol. 1. *The evolution of life its origin, history and future* (ed. S. Tax). Chicago University Press, Chicago (1960), p. 383.
3. LIM, p. 291.
4. PLFE.
5. F.A. Stafleu: 'Lamarck: The birth of biology', *Taxon* 20, 397–442 (1971), p. 401.
6. G. Cuvier: 'Eloge de M. de Lamarck', *Mémoires de l'Academie Royale des Sciences de l'Institute de France* 13, i–xxxi (1835), p. xiii.
7. PLFE, p. 76.
8. A. Giard: LDO, p. 12.
9. LZP, p. 40 (LPZ, tome premier, pp. 45–7).
10. LZP, p. 41 (LPZ, tome premier, p. 48).
11. LZP, p. 244 (LPZ, tome second, p. 80).
12. S.W. Fox: 'Proteinoid experiments and evolutionary theory'. pp. 15–60 in *Beyond Darwinism An introduction to the new evolutionary paradigm* (eds. M.-W. Ho and P.T. Saunders). Academic Press, London (1984).
13. LZP, p. 245. (LPZ, tome second, p. 83).
14. LZP, p. 56 (LPZ, tome premier, p. 81).
15. LZP, pp. 58–9 (LPZ, tome premier, pp. 84–7).
16. M. Ruse: *The Darwinian revolution*. University Press, Chicago (1979). See also C.C. Gillespie: 'Lamarck and Darwin in the history of science', *American Naturalist* 46, 388–409 (1958); and J.S. Wilkie: 'Buffon, Lamarck and Darwin: The originality of Darwin's theory of

evolution', pp. 262–307 in *Darwin's biological work Some aspects reconsidered* (ed. P.R. Bell). University Press, Cambridge (1959).

17. A.O. Lovejoy: *The great chain of being*. Harper and Row, New York (1958).

18. LHN, pp. 110–11.

19. See C.C. Gillespie: 'Lamarck and Darwin' and M. Ruse, *The Darwinian revolution*.

20. LDO, p. 32.

21. LZP, p. 46 (LPZ, tome premier, p. 60).

22. Ibid., p. 37.

23. R.W. Burkhardt: *The spirit of system Lamarck and evolutionary biology*. Harvard University Press, Cambridge, Mass. (1977), p. 55.

24. LDO, p. 51.

25. LHN, p. 134.

26. J. Huxley: *Evolution The modern synthesis*. Allen and Unwin, London (1942), pp. 559, 562.

27. DOS (6), p. 121.

28. LHN, p. 152.

29. Ibid., p. 155.

30. Ibid.

31. Ibid., p. 158.

32. Ibid.

33. LDO, p. 81.

34. LZP, p. 59 (LPZ, tome premier, p. 87).

35. LHN, p. 166.

36. C. Zirkle: 'The early history of the idea of the inheritance of acquired characters and of pangenesis', *Transactions of the American Philosophical Society*, NS 35, 91–151 (1946).

37. DDP.

38. LZP, p. 107 (LPZ, tome premier, p. 187).

39. LZP, p. 69 (LPZ, tome premier, p. 108).

40. LZP, p. 122 (LPZ, tome premier, pp. 218–19).

41. H.G. Cannon: 'What Lamarck really said', *Proceedings of the Linnean Society of London* 168, 70–87 (1957).

42. HGM, p. 391.

43. P.-P. Grassé: 'Lamarck, Wallace et Darwin', *Revue d'Histoire des Sciences* 13, 73–9 (1960), p. 73.

44. DNTS, p. 28.

45. G. Nelson: 'Inédits de Lamarck. D'après les manuscripts conservés à la Bibliothèque Central du Muséum National d'Histoire Naturelle à Paris', *Systematic Zoology* 24, 271–4 (1975), p. 272.

46. BDMW, p. 82.

47. ADB.

48. DNTS, pp. 41–2.

49. Ibid., p. 93.

50. Ibid., p. 104.

51. Ibid., p. 138.

52. DOS (6), pp. xiii–xiv.

53. D. King-Hele: *Doctor of revolution The life and genius of Erasmus Darwin*. Faber and Faber, London (1977), p. 245.

54. DNTS, p. 43.
55. Ibid., p. 130.
56. Ibid., p. 180.
57. DOS (6), p. 429.
58. LLD, vol. 2, p. 23.
59. Ibid., p. 29.
60. Ibid., p. 207.
61. Ibid., p. 208.
62. DOS (1), p. 480.
63. LLD, vol. 2, p. 215.
64. LLL, vol. 2, pp. 365–6.
65. LLD, vol. 3, p. 16.
66. Ibid., p. 27.
67. M. Barthélemy-Madaule: *Lamarck ou le mythe du précurseur*. Seuil, Paris (1979). J. Rostand: 'Les précurseurs français de Charles Darwin', *Revue d'Histoire des Sciences* 13, 45–58 (1960). A. Vandel: 'Lamarck et Darwin', *Revue d'Histoire des Sciences* 13, 59–72 (1960). P.-P. Grassé, 'Lamarck, Wallace et Darwin'.
68. J.H.F. Kohlbrugge: 'J.B. de Lamarck und der Einfluss seiner Descendenztheorie von 1809–1859, *Zeitschrift für Morphologie und Anthropologie* 18, 191–206 (1914).

4. THE MACROMUTATIONISTS

1. GS-HHN, vol. 1, p. 325.
2. LIM, p. 137.
3. *Collins dictionary of the English language*. Collins, London (1979), p. 1540.
4. GS-HHN.
5. K.R. Popper: *The logic of scientific discovery*. Hutchinson, London (1959).
6. *Encyclopaedia Britannica* 20 (1964), p. 61.
7. GS-HHN, vol. 1, p. 305.
8. Ibid., p. 305.
9. Ibid., pp. 317–18.
10. Ibid., p. 323.
11. K.R. Popper: *The logic of scientific discovery*.
12. E.S. Russell: *Form and function A contribution to the history of animal morphology*. John Murray, London (1916), pp. 98–100.
13. J.H.F. Kohlbrugge: 'Das biogenetische Grundgesetz. Eine historische Studie', *Zoologischer Anzeiger* 38, 447–53 (1911).
14. E.S. Russell, *Form and function*, p. 93.
15. Ibid., p. 252. Quoted from F. Müller: *Für Darwin*. Wilhelm Engelmann, Leipzig (1864), p. 75.
16. I. Geoffroy Saint-Hilaire: *Vie, travaux et doctrine scientifique d'Etienne Geoffroy Saint-Hilaire*. P. Bertrand, Paris (1847). T. Cahn: *La vie et l'oeuvre d'Etienne Geoffroy Saint-Hilaire*. Presses Universitaires de France, Paris (1962).

17. E. Geoffroy Saint-Hilaire: 'La degré d'influence du monde ambient pour modifier les formes animales; question interessant l'origine des espèces téléosauriennes et successivement celles des animaux de l'époque actuelle', *Mémoires de l'Academie Royale des Sciences de l'Institut de France* 12, 63–92 (1833), p. 64.

18. Ibid., p. 81.

19. Ibid., p. 80.

20. Ibid., p. 74.

21. NHB.

22. DOS (6), p. xiv.

23. K.E. von Baer: *Ueber Entwickelungsgeschichte der Thiere. Beobachtung und Reflexion*, erster Theil. Gebrüder Bornträger, Königsberg (1828), p. 224.

24. S. Løvtrup: 'On von Baerian and Haeckelian recapitulation', *Systematic Zoology* 27, 348–52 (1978).

25. W. Garstang: 'The theory of recapitulation: A critical restatement of the biogenetic law', *Zoological Journal of the Linnean Society* 35, 81–101 (1922), p. 98.

26. KEBR, vol. 1, pp. 37–8.

27. Ibid., p. 52.

28. Ibid., p. 53.

29. Ibid., p. 56.

30. Ibid., p. 60.

31. LLD, vol. 2, p. 329.

32. Ibid., p. 330.

33. KEBR, vol. 2, p. 422.

34. Ibid., p. 423.

35. Ibid., p. 425.

36. Ibid., pp. 425–6.

37. Ibid., p. 426.

38. Ibid., p. 429.

39. Ibid., pp. 435–6.

40. Ibid., p. 436.

41. A.O. Lovejoy: 'Recent criticism of the Darwinian theory of recapitulation: Its grounds and its initiator', pp. 438–58 in *Forerunners of Darwin: 1745–1859* (eds B. Glass, O. Temkin and W.L. Straus). Johns Hopkins Press, Baltimore (1959), p. 455.

42. Ibid., pp. 443–4.

43. S. Løvtrup, 'On von Baerian and Haeckelian recapitulation'.

44. R. Owen: *The life of Richard Owen* (second edn.), two volumes. John Murray, London (1895).

45. DNTS, p. 61.

46. Ibid., p. 62.

47. DOS (6), p. xvii.

48. Ibid., pp. xvii–xviii.

49. R. Owen, *The life of Richard Owen*, vol. 1, pp. 309–10.

50. D. Ospovat: 'The influence of Karl Ernst von Baer's embryology, 1828–1859: A reappraisal in the light of Richard Owen's and William B. Carpenter's "Palaeontological application of 'von Baer's laws'"', *Journal of the History of Biology* 9, 1–28 (1976).

51. R. Owen, *The life of Richard Owen*, vol. 2, p. 299.

52. Ibid., vol. 1, pp. 249–50.

53. E.S. Russell: *Form and function A contribution to the history of animal morphology*. John Murray, London (1916). D. Ospovat, 'The influence of Karl Ernst von Baer's embryology'.

54. R. Owen, *The life of Richard Owen*, vol. 2, pp. 90–1.

55. [R. Owen]: 'Darwin on the origin of species', *The Edinburgh Review* 3, 487–532 (1860), p. 496.

56. Ibid., p. 500.

57. Ibid., p. 504.

58. Ibid., pp. 517–19.

59. LLD, vol. 2, p. 336.

60. MLD, vol. 1, p. 162.

61. Ibid., p. 393.

62. [R. Owen], 'Darwin on the origin of species', p. 530.

63. Ibid., p. 488.

64. Ibid., pp. 515–16.

65. MLD, vol. 1, p. 146.

66. DOS, p xviii.

67. R.M. MacLeod: 'Evolutionism and Richard Owen, 1830–1868: An episode in Darwin's century', *ISIS* 56, 259–80, (1965), p. 277.

68. Ibid.

69. DOS (1), p. 310.

70. A. Desmond: *Archetypes and ancestors Palaeontology in Victorian London 1850–1875*. Blond and Briggs, London (1982).

71. S. Butler: *Evolution, old and new; Or, the theories of Buffon, Dr. Erasmus Darwin, and Lamarck, as compared with that of Charles Darwin* (third revised edn.). A.C. Fifield, London (1911), p. 77.

72. [R. Chambers]: *Vestiges of the natural history of creation* (fourth edn.), John Churchill, London (1845).

73. Ibid., p. 231.

74. Ibid., p. 263.

75. DNTS, p. 44.

76. LLD, vol. 2, pp. 188–9.

77. DOS (1), pp. 3–4.

78. DOS (6), pp. xvi–xvii.

79. Ibid., p. 107.

80. MLD, vol. 1, p. 49.

81. M. Millhauser: *Just before Darwin Robert Chambers and Vestiges*. Wesleyan University Press, Middletown, Conn. (1959).

82. R. Chambers: *Vestiges of the natural history of creation (facsimile of the first edition with an introduction by Gavin de Beer)*. University Press, Leicester (1959), pp. 230–1.

83. Ibid., p. 231.

84. [R. Chambers]: *Vestiges of the natural history of creation*, pp. 202–3.

85. Ibid., pp. 216–18.

86. Ibid., p. 208.

87. Ibid., p. 235.

88. A.W. Benn, quoted by A.O. Lovejoy in *Forerunners of Darwin:*

1745–1859. (eds. B. Glass, O. Temkin and W.L. Straus). Johns Hopkins Press, Baltimore (1959), p. 414.

89. G. de Beer: 'Darwin and embryology', pp. 153–72 in *A century of Darwin* (ed. S.A. Barnett). Heinemann, London (1958), p. 153.

5. CHARLES DARWIN (1809–82)

1. DOS (1), pp. 166, 314.
2. W. Irwine: *Apes, angels, and Victorians A joint biography of Darwin and Huxley*. Weidenfeld and Nicolson, London (1955), p. 44.
3. HDR, p. 100.
4. P.B. Medawar: 'Darwin's illness', pp. 61–7 in *The art of the soluble*. Methuen, London (1967).
5. DOSV.
6. The biographical notes have been extracted from the autobiography in LLD and from A. Keith: *Darwin revalued*. Watts, London (1955).
7. DOS (6), p. 8.
8. Ibid., p. 9.
9. Ibid., p. 9.
10. Ibid., p. 10.
11. Ibid., p. 11.
12. Ibid., p. 19.
13. Ibid., p. 22.
14. Ibid., p. 23.
15. Ibid., p. 22.
16. Ibid., p. 33.
17. Ibid., p. 33.
18. Ibid., pp. 34–5.
19. Ibid., p. 35.
20. Ibid., p. 43.
21. Ibid., p. 50.
22. Ibid., p. 50.
23. Ibid., p. 50.
24. Ibid., p. 59.
25. Ibid., pp. 60–1.
26. Ibid., pp. 62–3.
27. Ibid., p. 64.
28. Ibid., pp. 64–5.
29. Ibid., pp. 68–9. See also W.L. McAtee: 'Survival of the ordinary', *Quarterly Review of Biology* 12, 47–64 (1937).
30. DOS (6), pp. 70–1.
31. Ibid., pp. 81–2.
32. Ibid., p. 82.
33. S. Løvtrup: 'The evolutionary species: fact or fiction?', *Systematic Zoology* 28, 386–92 (1979). S. Løvtrup: 'On species and other taxa', *Cladistics* (in press).
34. DOS (6), p. 97.
35. Ibid., pp. 97–8.

36. Ibid., pp. 98–9.
37. Ibid., p. 99.
38. Ibid., p. 99.
39. Ibid., p. 106.
40. Ibid., p. 109.
41. Ibid., pp. 109–10.
42. Ibid., p. 114.
43. Ibid., pp. 117–18.
44. Ibid., p. 133.
45. Ibid., pp. 133–4.
46. Ibid., p. 134.
47. Ibid., pp. 136–7.
48. LLD, vol. 2, p. 273.
49. DOS (6), pp. 143–6.
50. Ibid., pp. 146–7.
51. Ibid., p. 156.
52. Ibid., pp 156 7.
53. Ibid., pp. 159–60.
54. Ibid., p. 163.
55. Ibid., p. 212.
56. Ibid., p. 212.
57. Ibid., pp. 212–13.
58. Ibid., p. 213.
59. Ibid., pp. 213–14.
60. Ibid., p. 214.
61. Ibid., p. 235.
62. Ibid., p. 241.
63. Ibid., p. 236.
64. Ibid., p. 256.
65. Ibid., p. 257.
66. Ibid., pp. 247–8.
67. MARW, vol. 1, p. 195.
68. Ibid., p. 205.
69. DOS (6), pp. 312–13.
70. LLD, vol. 2, p. 350.
71. DOS (6), p. 133.
72. Ibid., p. 282.
73. Ibid., p. 282.
74. Ibid., p. 295.
75. Ibid., p. 296.
76. Ibid., pp. 307–8.
77. Ibid., p. 320.
78. Ibid., pp. 330–1.
79. L. Croizat: *Space, time, form: The biological synthesis.* Caracas (1962). L. Croizat, G.J. Nelson and D.E. Rosen: 'Centers of origin and related concepts', *Systematic Zoology* 23, 265–87 (1974). G. Nelson and N. Platnick: *Systematics and biogeography Cladistics and vicariance.* Columbia University Press, New York (1981).
80. LLD, vol. 2, p. 243.
81. DOS (6), pp. 363–5.

82. Ibid., p. 365.
83. Ibid., p. 373.
84. Ibid., p. 368.
85. Ibid., pp. 382–3.
86. Ibid., p. 383.
87. Ibid., p. 310.
88. DOS (1), p. 238.
89. DOS (6), pp. 387–8.
90. Ibid., p. 97.
91. Ibid., p. 308.
92. DWNS, pp. 77–8.
93. Ibid., p. 224.
94. Ibid., p. 233.
95. DOS (6), pp. 390–1.
96. A.O. Lovejoy: 'Recent criticism of the Darwinian theory of recapitulation: Its grounds and its initiator', pp. 438–58 in *Forerunners of Darwin: 1745–1859* (eds B. Glass, O. Temkin and W.L. Straus). Johns Hopkins Press, Baltimore (1959), p. 455.
97. J. Oppenheimer: 'An embryological enigma in the *Origin of Species*', pp. 292–322 in *Forerunners of Darwin: 1745–1859* (eds B. Glass, O. Temkin and W.L. Straus). Johns Hopkins Press, Baltimore (1959), pp. 321–2.
98. LLD, vol. 1, pp. 103–4.
99. DOS (1), p. 480.
100. DOS (6), pp. 421–2.
101. BDMW, p. 78.
102. DOS (6), pp. 413–14.
103. Ibid., p. 424.
104. DOS (1), pp. 481–2.
105. Ibid., p. 428.
106. D.L. Hull: *Darwin and his critics The reception of Darwin's theory by the scientific community*. Harvard University Press, Cambridge, Mass. (1973), pp. 16–17.
107. HDE, p. 25.
108. P.J. Vorzimmer: *Charles Darwin: The years of controversy The origin of species and its critics 1859–1882*. Temple University Press, Philadelphia (1970), p. xv.
109. DOS (6), pp. 203–4.
110. ADB, p. 140.

6. THE TWO EVOLUTIONISTS

1. LPZ, p. xxxix.
2. LLD, vol. 1, p. 83.
3. R.W. Burkhardt: *The spirit of system Lamarck and evolutionary biology*. Harvard University Press, Cambridge, Mass. (1977), p. 39.
4. K.R. Popper: *Unended quest An intellectual autobiography*. Fontana/Collins, Glasgow (1976).

5. K.R. Popper: *The logic of scientific discovery*. Hutchinson, London (1959), pp. 279–80.

6. K.R. Popper: *Conjectures and refutations The growth of scientific knowledge*. Routledge and Kegan Paul, London (1972).

7. LHN, p. 15.

8. MLD, vol. 1, p. 195.

9. LLD, vol. 1, p. 149.

10. Ibid., vol. 2, p. 109.

11. PLFE, p. 110.

12. A. Keith: *Darwin revalued*. Watts, London (1955), p. 153.

7. THE FRIENDS

1. ADB, pp. 100, 105, 106.

2. A. Keith: *Darwin revalued*. Watts, London (1955), p. 128.

3. LLL.

4. Ibid., vol. 2, p. 316.

5. Ibid., vol 1, p. 168.

6. Ibid., vol. 2, p. 212.

7. Ibid., p. 166.

8. Ibid., pp. 166–7.

9. Ibid., pp. 164–5.

10. Ibid., p. 174.

11. Ibid., vol. 1, p. 46.

12. LLD, vol. 2, p. 206.

13. Ibid., p. 208.

14. Ibid., p. 209.

15. DOSV, pp. 620–1.

16. C. Lyell: *The geological evidences of the antiquity of man with remarks on the theories on the origin of species by variation*. John Murray, London (1863), pp. 393–5.

17. Ibid., p. 395.

18. Ibid., pp. 405–6.

19. Ibid., pp. 407–8.

20. Ibid., p. 410.

21. Ibid., p. 411.

22. Ibid., p. 421.

23. Ibid., p. 469.

24. LLD, vol. 3, p. 8.

25. LLL, vol. 2, p. 363.

26. Ibid., p. 331.

27. Ibid., pp. 361–2.

28. LLD, vol. 3, p. 14.

29. C. Lyell: *Principles of geology or The modern changes of the earth and its inhabitants considered as illustrative of geology* (tenth and entirely revised edn.), vol. 2. John Murray, London (1868), p. 492.

30. A.R. Wallace: 'Sir Charles Lyell on *Geological climates and the origin of species*', *Quarterley Review* 126, 359–94 (1869), p. 381.

31. LLL, vol. 2, pp. 431–2.
32. Ibid., pp. 435–7.
33. LLHo.
34. MLD, vol. 1, p. 39.
35. LLD, vol. 2, pp. 26–7.
36. Ibid., p. 23.
37. LLHo, vol. 1, p. 520.
38. Ibid., p. 510.
39. Ibid., p. 511.
40. Ibid., vol. 2, pp. 37–8.
41. Ibid., pp. 212–13.
42. Ibid., p. 214.
43. Ibid., pp. 304–5.
44. Ibid., pp. 516–17.
45. LLD, vol. 2, p. 323.
46. LLHu.
47. LLD, vol. 2, p. 189.
48. HDE, p. 13.
49. LLHu, vol. 2, p. 317.
50. LLD, vol. 2, p. 185.
51. Ibid., pp. 192–3.
52. Ibid., pp. 195–6.
53. Ibid., pp. 172–3.
54. Ibid., pp. 230–1.
55. HDE, pp. 35–9.
56. Ibid., pp. 73–4.
57. LLD, vol. 2, p. 300.
58. Ibid., pp. 354–5.
59. HDE, pp. 187–226.
60. Ibid., p. 229.
61. LLHu, vol. 2, p. 229.
62. MLD, vol. 1, p. 386.
63. LLD, vol. 2, p.179.
64. Ibid., p. 198.
65. Ibid., pp. 175–6.
66. MARW, vol. 1, p. 76.
67. LLD, vol. 2, pp. 242–3.
68. HDR, p. 198.
69. Ibid., p. 176.
70. P.J. Vorzimmer: *Charles Darwin: The years of controversy The origin of species and its critics 1859–1882*. Temple University Press, Philadelphia (1970), p. 211.
71. R.M. Young: 'Darwin's metaphor: Does Nature select?', *The Monist* 55, 442–503 (1971), p. 496.
72. DDP, p. 64.

8. THE SUPPORTERS

1. WML, vol. 2, p. 22.
2. LLD, vol. 2, p. 272.
3. HGM, p. 341.
4. MARW.
5. H.L. McKinney: *Wallace and natural selection*. Yale University Press, New Haven (1972), p. 9.
6. Ibid., p. 11.
7. A.C. Brackman: *A delicate arrangement The strange case of Charles Darwin and Alfred Russel Wallace*. Times Books, New York (1980), pp. 312–13.
8. J.L. Brooks: *Just before the origin: Alfred Russel Wallace's theory of evolution*. Columbia University Press, New York (1984), p. 255.
9. H.L. McKinney: *Wallace and natural selection*, p. 34.
10. Ibid., p. 29.
11. Ibid., p. 53.
12. Ibid., p. 98.
13. J.L. Brooks: *Just before the origin*, p. 244.
14. H.L. McKinney: *Wallace and natural selection*, p. 117.
15. LLD, vol. 2, p. 95.
16. Ibid., pp. 108–9.
17. DWNS, pp. 274–5.
18. A.C. Brackman, *A delicate arrangement*, p. 299.
19. LLD, vol. 1, p. 84.
20. DWNS, pp. 33–4.
21. G. de Beer: *Charles Darwin Evolution by natural selection*. Thomas Nelson, London (1963), p. 140.
22. A.C. Brackman, *A delicate arrangement*. J.L. Brooks, *Just before the origin*. H.L. McKinney, *Wallace and natural selection*.
23. LLD, vol. 2, p. 123.
24. G. de Beer (ed.) 'Darwin's journal', *Bulletin of the British Museum (Natural History) Historical Series* 2, 1–21, (1959), p. 14.
25. J.L. Brooks, *Just before the origin*, p. 230.
26. Ibid., p. 232ff.
27. LLD, vol. 2, pp. 124–5.
28. DWNS, p. 34.
29. A.C. Brackman, *A delicate arrangement*, pp. 326–37.
30. 'On the tendency of species to form varieties; and on the perpetuation of varieties and species by natural means of selection', *Journal of Linnean Society* 3, 45–62 (1858).
31. Ibid., p. 274.
32. J.L. Brooks, *Just before the origin*, p. 236.
33. *Charles Darwin's natural selection being the second part of his big species book written from 1856 to 1858* (ed. R.C. Stauffer). University Press, Cambridge (1975), p. 228.
34. LLD, vol. 2, pp. 116–17.
35. H.L. McKinney, *Wallace and natural selection*, p. 140.
36. J.L. Brooks, *Just before the origin*, p. 255.
37. Ibid., p. 233.

38. Ibid., p. 264.
39. A.C. Brackman, *A delicate arrangement*, p. 348.
40. LLD, vol. 2, p. 117.
41. Ibid., pp. 119-20.
42. DWNS, p. 218.
43. B.G. Beddall: 'Wallace, Darwin, and the theory of natural selection A study in the development of ideas and attitudes', *Journal of the History of Biology* 1, 261-323 (1968), p. 301.
44. H.L. McKinney, *Wallace and natural selection*, p. 143.
45. LLD, vol. 2, p. 128.
46. Ibid., p. 129.
47. MARW, vol. 1, p. 71.
48. LLD, vol. 2, p. 145.
49. MLD, vol. 1, p. 119.
50. MARW, vol. 2, p. 39.
51. LLD, vol. 2, p. 309.
52. DOS (1), pp. 1-2.
53. Ibid., p. 355.
54. LLD, vol. 2, p. 264.
55. MARW, vol. 1, p. 76.
56. C.F.A. Pantin: 'Alfred Russel Wallace, F.R.S., and his essays of 1858 and 1855', *Notes and Records of the Royal Society of London*, 14, 67-84 (1954), p. 72.
57. MLD, vol. 1, pp. 267-70.
58. Ibid., pp. 270-1.
59. DOS (6), p. 63.
60. WD, p. 375.
61. Ibid., p. 474.
62. Ibid., pp. 474-6.
63. LLD, vol. 3, pp. 115-16.
64. LLL, vol. 2, pp. 442-3.
65. S. Butler: *Luck, or cunning, as the main means of organic modification An attempt to throw additional light upon Darwin's theory of natural selection* (second revised edn.). A.C. Fifield, London (1920), p. 244.
66. C.F.A. Pantin: 'Alfred Russel Wallace', p. 83.
67. LLD, vol. 2, pp. 121-4.
68. Ibid., p. 135.
69. Ibid., p. 217.
70. Ibid., pp. 271-2.
71. Ibid., p. 273.
72. Ibid., p. 338.
73. Ibid., p. 345.
74. A. Gray: *Darwiniana Essays and reviews pertaining to Darwinism*. D. Appleton, New York (1877), p. 145.
75. Ibid., p. 146.
76. R.M. Young: 'Darwin's metaphor: Does Nature select?', *The Monist* 55, 442-503 (1971), p. 483.
77. ADB, p. 87.
78. HGM.
79. Ibid., p. 166.

80. MLD, vol. 1, pp. 277–8.
81. E.S. Russell: *Form and function A contribution to the history of animal morphology*. John Murray, London (1916), pp. 247–8, 257.
82. DOS (6), p. 423.

9. THE CRITICS

1. D.L. Hull: *Darwin and his critics The reception of Darwin's theory of evolution by the scientific community*. Harvard University Press, Cambridge, Mass. (1973), pp. 264–5.
2. Ibid., p. 305.
3. Ibid., p. 305.
4. Ibid., p. 306.
5. Ibid., p. 309.
6. Ibid., p. 312.
7. Ibid., pp. 312–15.
8. Ibid., pp. 318–19.
9 Ibid., p. 339.
10. Ibid., pp. 343–4.
11. MLD, vol. 2, p. 379.
12. LLD, vol. 3, p. 108.
13. MARW, vol. 1, p. 234.
14. LLD, vol. 3, pp. 108–9.
15. DOSV, pp. 179–80.
16. J.W. Gruber: *A conscience in conflict The life of St. George Jackson Mivart*. Columbia University Press, New York (1960).
17. Ibid., pp. 36–7.
18. St G. Mivart: *On the genesis of species* (second edn.). Macmillan, London (1871).
19. Ibid., pp. 2–3.
20. Ibid., p. 4.
21. Ibid., p. 11.
22. Ibid., pp. 12–13.
23. Ibid., pp. 16–17.
24. Ibid., pp. 24–5.
25. Ibid., p. 273.
26. Ibid., p. 275.
27. Ibid., p. 21.
28. LLD, vol. 3, p. 146.
29. DOS (6), pp. 176–7.
30. Ibid., pp. 177–8.
31. Ibid., p. 178.
32. Ibid., p. 178.
33. Ibid., pp. 178–9.
34. Ibid., p. 186.
35. St G. Mivart: *On the genesis of species*, p. 42.
36. DOS (6), pp. 186–7.
37. Ibid., p. 187.

38. Ibid., pp. 187–8.
39. Ibid., p. 201.
40. Ibid., p. 114.
41. Ibid., p. 204.
42. A. Ellegård: 'Darwin and the general reader The reception of Darwin's theory of evolution in the British periodical press 1859–1872', *Acta Universitatis Gothoburgensis* 64 (7), 1–394 (1958), pp. 29–33.
43. LLD, vol. 3, pp. 135–6.
44. Ibid., pp. 144–5.
45. J.W. Gruber: *A conscience in conflict*, pp. 84–5.
46. D.L. Hull, *Darwin and his critics*, p. 386.
47. LLD, vol. 3, p. 145.
48. Ibid., p. 146.
49. J.W. Gruber: *A conscience in conflict*, pp. 81–2.
50. Ibid., pp. 95–6.
51. Ibid., p. 52.
52. Ibid., p. 87.
53. Ibid., pp. 87–8.
54. Ibid., p. 89.
55. Ibid., p. 90.
56. Ibid., p. 94.
57. LLHo, vol. 2, p. 128.
58. J.W. Gruber: *A conscience in conflict*, p. 97.
59. Ibid., pp. 112–14.
60. LLHu, vol. 2, p. 423.
61. ADB, pp. 134–5.
62. Ibid., p. 167.
63. S. Butler: *Life and habit* (third edn.). Jonathan Cape, London (1935).
64. Ibid., p. 263.
65. Ibid., pp. 275–6.
66. Ibid., pp. 276–7.
67. S. Butler: *Evolution, old and new; Or, the theories of Buffon, Dr. Erasmus Darwin, and Lamarck, as compared with that of Charles Darwin* (third revised edn.) A.C. Fifield, London (1911).
68. E. Krause: *Erasmus Darwin With a preliminary notice by Charles Darwin*. John Murray, London (1879), p. 216.
69. Ibid., pp. ii, iv.
70. ADB, p. 179.
71. Ibid., p. 182.
72. Ibid., pp. 182–4.
73. Ibid., p. 185.
74. Ibid., p. 207.
75. Ibid., p. 211.
76. S. Butler: *Luck, or cunning, as the main means of organic modification? An attempt to throw additional light upon Darwin's theory of natural selection* (second revised edn.) A.C. Fifield, London (1920).
77. Ibid., p. 157.
78. F. Darwin: 'The analogies of plant and animal life', *Nature* 17, pp. 388–91, 411–14 (1878).

79. LLD, vol. 2, p. 354.
80. Ibid., p. 318.
81. D.L. Hull: *Darwin and his critics*.

10. THE INTERREGNUM

1. H.F. Osborn: 'Are acquired variations inherited?', *The American Naturalist* 25, 191–216 (1891), p. 196.
2. PTP, pp. 94–5.
3. A. Weismann: 'The selection theory', pp. 18–84 in *Darwin and modern science Essays in commemoration of the centenary of the birth of Charles Darwin and of the fiftieth anniversary of the publication of The Origin of Species* (ed. A.C. Seward). University Press, Cambridge (1909), p. 25.
4. M.-W. Ho, C. Tucker, D. Keeley and P.T. Saunders: 'Epigenetics and evolution — theory and experiment', pp. 59–75 in *Evolution and environment* (eds. V.J.A. Novák and J. Mlikovský, vol. 1. Department of Evolutionary Biology, Czechoslovak Academy of Science, Praha (1982) R. Matsuda: 'The evolutionary process in talitrid amphipods and salamanders in changing environments with a discussion of "genetic assimilation" and some other evolutionary concepts', *Canadian Journal of Zoology* 60, 733–49 (1982). F.M. Scudo: 'The role of phenocopy in evolution', *Atti Associazione Genetica Italiana* 21, 196–201 (1976). C.H. Waddington: *The evolution of an evolutionist*. University Press, Edinburgh (1975).
5. PLFE.
6. Ibid., pp. 396–9.
7. PTP.
8. Ibid., p. 40.
9. Ibid., p. 44.
10. LLHu, vol. 2, p. 394.
11. PTP, p. 57.
12. Ibid., pp. 68–9.
13. Ibid., p. 122. See further G.L. Stebbins: 'Patterns of speciation', pp. 194–232 in T. Dobzhansky, F.J. Ayala, G.L. Stebbins, J.W. Valentine: *Evolution*. W.H. Freeman, San Francisco (1977).
14. PTP, p. 94.
15. NHB, p. 564.
16. M. Ridley: 'Coadaptation and the inadequacy of natural selection', *British Journal for the History of Science* 15, 45–68 (1982), p. 61.
17. WD, p. 418.
18. A. Weismann, 'The selection theory', p. 27.
19. Ibid., pp. 36–7.
20. Ibid., p. 65.
21. SLE. S. Løvtrup: 'The epigenetic utilization of the genomic message', pp. 145–61 in *Evolution today* (eds G.G. Scudder and J.L. Reveal). Carnegie-Mellon University, Pittsburgh (1981).
22. The following account of the British biometricians is extracted from PTP.

23. PTP, p. 31.
24. B.J. Norton: 'The biometric defense of Darwinism', *Journal of the History of Biology* 6, 283–316 (1973).
25. Ibid., p. 303.
26. Ibid., p. 304.
27. PTP, p. 51.
28. NHB, p. 562.

11. THE NEO-MENDELIANS

1. R.A. Fisher: 'The bearing of genetics on theories of evolution', *Science Progress* 27, 273–87 (1932), p. 287.
2. C.H. Waddington: *The evolution of an evolutionist*. University Press, Edinburgh (1975), p. 168.
3. PTP.
4. R.A. Fisher: 'The bearing of genetics on theories of evolution' (1932), p. 275.
5. R.A. Fisher: 'Adaptations and mutations', *The School Science Review* 15, 294–301, (1934), p. 296.
6. FGNS.
7. Ibid., p. vii.
8. Ibid., p. 21.
9. PTP, p. 140.
10. FGNS, p. x.
11. Ibid., pp. 30–1.
12. Ibid., p. 26.
13. Ibid., p. 37.
14. Ibid., p. 37.
15. Ibid., p. 38.
16. Ibid., pp. 39–40.
17. Ibid., p. 41.
18. Ibid., p. 44.
19. SLP.
20. FGNS, p. 45.
21. Ibid., p. 45.
22. R.A. Fisher: 'Retrospect of the criticisms of the theory of natural selection', pp. 84–98 in *Evolution as a process* (eds J. Huxley, A.C. Hardy and E.B. Ford) (second edn.). George Allen and Unwin, London (1958), pp. 89–90.
23. Ibid., pp. 94–5.
24. Ibid., p. 98.
25. PTP.
26. Ibid., p. 170.
27. J.B.S. Haldane: *The causes of evolution*. Longmans, Green, London (1932).
28. Ibid., pp. 2–3.
29. Ibid., p. 45.
30. Ibid., p. 61.

31. Ibid., p. 102.

32. Ibid., pp. 104-5.

33. Ibid., pp. 138-9.

34. See for instance G.G. Simpson: *The meaning of evolution*. New American Library, New York (1951), pp. 144ff.

35. H.J. Muller: 'Our load of mutations', *American Journal of Human Genetics* 2, 111-76 (1950).

36. J.B.S. Haldane: 'The cost of natural selection', *Journal of Genetics* 55, 511-24 (1957), p. 511.

37. Ibid., pp. 521-2.

38. B. Wallace: *Genetic load Its biological and conceptual aspects*. Prentice Hall, New Jersey (1970), p. 102.

39. T. Dobzhansky: 'Populations, races, subspecies', pp. 128-64 in T. Dobzhansky, F.J. Ayala, G.L. Stebbins and J.W. Valentine: *Evolution*. W.H. Freeman, San Francisco (1977), p. 164.

40. PTP.

41. Ibid., p. 158.

42. S. Wright: 'Genetics of abnormal growth in the Guinea pig', *Cold Spring Harbor Symposia on Quantitative Biology* 2, 137-47 (1934), pp. 142-3.

43. S. Wright: 'Modes of evolutionary change', pp. 679-98 in *Proceedings of the International Conference on Quantitative Genetics* (eds. E. Pollak, O. Kempthorne and T.B. Bailey). Iowa State University Press, Ames (1977), p. 679.

44. S. Wright: 'Evolution, organic', *Encyclopaedia Britannica* 8, 917-29 (1964), p. 923.

45. S.J. Gould: 'But not Wright enough: Reply to Orzack', *Paleobiology* 7, 131-9 (1981), p. 132.

46. PTP, pp. 175-6.

47. L. Hogben: 'Problems of the origin of species', pp. 267-86 in *The new systematics* (ed. J. Huxley). University Press, Oxford (1940), p. 275.

48. E. Mayr: *Evolution and the diversity of life*. Belknap Press, Cambridge, Mass. (1976), p. 310.

49. M. Blanc: 'Les théories de l'evolution aujourd'hui', *La Recherche* 129, 26-40 (1982), p. 31.

50. J.F. Crow and M. Kimura: *An introduction to population genetics theory*. Harper and Row, New York (1970).

51. T. Dobzhansky: *Genetics of the evolutionary process*. Columbia University Press, New York (1970), pp. 101-2.

52. PTP, p. 170.

53. T. Dobzhansky: 'Populations, races, subspecies', p. 111.

54. E.B. Ford: 'Some recollections pertaining to the evolutionary synthesis', pp. 334-42 in *The evolutionary synthesis perspectives on the unification of biology* (eds. E. Mayr and W.B. Provine). Harvard University Press, Cambridge, Mass. (1980), pp. 341-2.

55. G.S. Mani: 'A theoretical study of morph ratio clines with special reference to melanism in moths', *Proceedings of the Royal Society of London* B 210, 299-316 (1980).

12. THE RISE AND THE FALL

1. G. de Beer: 'Some unpublished letters of Charles Darwin', *Notes and Records of the Royal Society of London* 14, 12–66 (1959), p. 35.
2. G.L. Stebbins: 'The nature of evolution', pp. 1–19 in T. Dobzhansky, F.J. Ayala, G.L. Stebbins and J.W. Valentine: *Evolution*. W.H. Freeman, San Francisco (1975), p. 17.
3. J.S. Huxley: 'Introduction towards the new systematics', pp. 1–46 in *The new systematics* (ed. J.S. Huxley). University Press, Oxford (1940), p. 2.
4. T. Dobzhansky: *Genetics and the origin of species*. Columbia University Press, New York (1937).
5. Ibid., p. 145.
6. Ibid., p. 8.
7. Ibid., pp. 11–12.
8. J. Huxley: *Evolution The modern synthesis*. Allen and Unwin, London (1942).
9. Ibid., p. 568.
10. Ibid., p. 19.
11. E. Mayr: *Systematics and the origin of species from the viewpoint of a zoologist*. Dover Publications, New York (1964).
12. Ibid., p. 67.
13. Ibid., p. 113.
14. Ibid., p. 291.
15. Ibid., p. 120.
16. Ibid., p. 33.
17. Ibid., pp. 148–9.
18. Ibid., p. 155.
19. Ibid., p. 237.
20. Ibid., p. 190.
21. Ibid., p. 271.
22. Ibid., pp. 94–5.
23. Ibid., p. 38.
24. Ibid., p. 295.
25. Ibid., p. 296.
26. G.G. Simpson: *Tempo and mode in evolution*. Columbia University Press, New York (1944).
27. Ibid., p. 97.
28. Ibid., p. 98.
29. Ibid., pp. 98–9.
30. Ibid., p. 99.
31. Ibid., pp. 115–16.
32. N. Eldredge and S.J. Gould: 'Punctuated equilibria An alternative to phyletic gradualism', pp. 82–115 in *Models in paleobiology* (ed. T.J.M. Schopf). Freeman, Cooper, San Francisco (1972). See further S. Løvtrup: 'Macroevolution and punctuated equilibria', *Systematic Zoology* 30, 498–500 (1981).
33. DWNS, p. 93.
34. R. Pearl: 'The selection problem', *The American Naturalist* 51, 65–91 (1917), p. 66.

35. Ibid., pp. 75–6.

36. Ibid., pp. 77 and 80–1.

37. T. Dobzhansky: 'A review of some fundamental concepts and problems of population genetics', *Cold Spring Harbor Symposia on Quantitative Biology* 20, 1–15 (1955).

38. H. Levene: 'Genetic equilibrium when more than one ecological niche is available', *The American Naturalist* 87, 331–3 (1953).

39. C.C. Li: 'The stability of an equilibrium and the average fitness of a population', *The American Naturalist* 89, 281–95 (1955).

40. M. Blanc: 'Les théories de l'évolution aujourd'hui', *La Recherche* 129, 26–40 (1982), p. 32.

41. J.L. King: 'The role of mutation in evolution', pp. 69–100 in *Proceedings of the Sixth Berkeley Symposium on Mathematical Statistics and Probability*, vol. 5 (eds. L.M. LeCam, J. Neuman and E.L. Scott), University of California Press, Berkeley (1972), pp. 70–1.

42. R.C. Lewontin and J.L. Hubby: 'A molecular approach to the study of genic heterozygosity in natural populations. II. Amount of variation and degree of heterozygosity in natural populations of *Drosophila pseudoobscura*', *Genetics* 54, 595 609 (1966). F.J. Ayala: 'Phylogenies and macromolecules', pp. 262–313 in T. Dobzhansky, F.J. Ayala, G.L. Stebbins and J.W. Valentine: *Evolution*. W.H. Freeman, San Francisco (1977).

43. M. Kimura: 'The neutral theory of molecular evolution', *Scientific American* 241, 94–104 (1979). M. Kimura: *The neutral theory of molecular evolution*. University Press, Cambridge (1983).

44. J.L. King and T.H. Jukes: 'Non-Darwinian evolution', *Science* 164, 788–98 (1969).

45. J.L. King: 'The role of mutation in evolution', p. 71.

46. Ibid., p. 77.

47. Ibid., p. 71.

48. M. Kimura: 'The neutral theory of molecular evolution', p. 104.

49. G.L. Stebbins and R.C. Lewontin: 'Comparative evolution at levels of molecules, organisms and populations', pp. 23–42 in *Proceedings of the Sixth Berkeley Symposium on Mathematical Statistics and Probability*, vol. 5 (eds. L.M. LeCam, J. Neuman and E.L. Scott), University of California Press, Berkeley (1972). F.J. Ayala: 'Darwinian *versus* non-Darwinian evolution in natural populations of *Drosophila*', *Proceedings of the Sixth Berkeley Symposium*, pp. 211–36. W.F. Bodmer and L.L. Cavalli-Sforza: 'Variation in fitness and molecular evolution', *Proceedings of the Sixth Berkeley Symposium*, pp. 255–275.

50. P.B. Medawar: *The art of the soluble*. Methuen, London (1967), p. 48.

51. R.J. Britten and E.H. Davidson: 'Repetitive and non-repetitive DNA sequences and a speculation on the origins of evolutionary novelty', *Quarterly Review of Biology* 46, 111–38 (1971).

52. T. Ohta: 'Mutational pressure as the main cause of molecular evolution and polymorphism', *Nature* 252, 351–4 (1974).

53. R.C. Lewontin: *The genetic basis of evolutionary change*. Columbia University Press, New York (1974), p. 267.

54. J.L. King: 'Review', *Annals of Human Genetics* 38, 507–10 (1975),

p. 508.

55. F.H.C. Crick: 'The origin of the genetic code', *Journal of Molecular Biology* 38, 367–79 (1968).

56. S. Ohno: 'Ancient linkage groups and frozen accidents', *Nature* 224, 259–62 (1973).

57. A.R. Templeton: 'Modes of speciation and inferences based on genetic distances', *Evolution* 34, 719–29 (1980), p. 719. This paper may be consulted for further references.

58. R.C. Lewontin: *The genetic basis of evolutionary change*, p. 20.

59. Ibid., pp. 27–8.

60. D.G. Wallace, L.R. Maxson and A.C. Wilson: 'Albumin in frogs: A test of the evolutionary clock hypothesis', *Proceedings of the National Academy of Science USA* 68, 3127–9 (1971).

61. A.C. Wilson, V.M. Sarich and L.R. Maxson: 'The importance of gene arrangements in evolution: Evidence from studies on rates of chromosomal protein and anatomical evolution', *Proceedings of the National Academy of Science USA* 71, 3028–30 (1974).

62. A.C. Wilson, G.L. Bush, S.M. Case and M.-C. King: 'Social structuring of mammalian populations and rate of chromosomal evolution', *Proceedings of the National Academy of Science USA* 72, 5061–5 (1975). G.L. Bush: 'Modes of animal speciation', *Annual Review of Ecology and Systematics* 6, 339–64 (1975).

63. J.S. Wyles, J.G. Kunkel and A.C. Wilson: 'Birds, behavior, and anatomical evolution', *Proceedings of the National Academy of Science USA* 80, 4394–7 (1983).

64. M.-C. King and A.C. Wilson: 'Evolution at two levels in humans and chimpanzees', *Science* 188, 107–16 (1975).

65. M.J.D. White: *Modes of speciation*. W.H. Freeman, San Francisco (1978), p. 336.

66. Ibid., pp. 341–2.

67. Ibid., p. 323.

68. M. Kimura and T. Ohta: 'Population genetics, molecular biometry, and evolution', pp. 43–68 in *Proceedings of the Sixth Berkeley Symposium on Mathematical Statistics and Probability*, vol. 5 (eds L.M. LeCam, J. Neuman and E.L. Scott). University of California Press, Berkeley (1972), pp. 43–4.

69. C.H. Waddington: in *Mathematical challenges to the Neo-Darwinian interpretation of evolution* (eds P.S. Moorhead and M.M. Kaplan). Wistar Institute Press, Philadelphia (1961), p. 14.

70. P.T. Saunders and M.-W. Ho: 'Is Neo-Darwinism falsifiable? — and does it matter', *Nature and System* 4, 179–96 (1982).

71. N. Eldredge and S.J. Gould: 'Punctuated equilibria: An alternative to phyletic gradualism', pp. 82–115 in *Models in paleontology* (ed. T.J.M. Schopf). Freeman, Cooper, San Francisco, (1972), p. 86.

72. K. Popper: *Unended quest An intellectual autobiography*. Fontana/Collins, Glasgow (1976).

73. N. Eldredge and S.J. Gould: 'Punctuated equilibria', p. 87. S.J. Gould and N. Eldredge: 'Punctuated equilibria: the tempo and mode of evolution reconsidered', *Paleobiology* 3, 115–51 (1977).

74. E. Mayr: *Evolution and the diversity of life Selected essays*. Belknap

Press, Cambridge, Mass. (1976), p. 110.
75. Ibid., p. 49.
76. G.G. Simpson: *Tempo and mode in evolution*. Columbia University Press, New York (1944), p. 176.
77. J. Huxley: *Evolution*, pp. 484–5.
78. R.C. Lewontin: 'Theoretical population genetics in the evolutionary synthesis', pp. 58–68 in *The evolutionary synthesis Perspectives on the unification of biology* (eds E. Mayr and W.B. Provine). Harvard University Press, Cambridge, Mass. (1980), p. 61.
79. V. Grant: *Organismic evolution*. W.H. Freeman, San Francisco (1977), p. 326.
80. E. Mayr: *Evolution and the diversity of life*, p. 665.
81. M.T. Ghiselin: 'A radical solution to the species problem', *Systematic Zoology* 23, 536–44 (1974), p. 536.
82. Ibid., p. 538.
83. D.L. Hull: 'Are species really individuals?', *Systematic Zoology* 25, 174–91 (1976), p. 174.
84. Ibid., p. 175.
85. Ibid., p. 180.
86. Ibid., p. 181.

13. A SURVEY OF THE THEORIES ON THE MECHANISMS OF EVOLUTION

1. HDE, p. 97.
2. C.J. Willis: *The course of evolution by differentiation or divergent mutation rather than by selection*. University Press, Cambridge (1940), pp. 191–2.
3. O.H. Schindewolf: *Grundfragen der Paläontologie*. Schweizerbart, Stuttgart (1950), p. 405.
4. D'A.W. Thompson: *On growth and form*. University Press, Cambridge (1917), pp. 1094–5.
5. P. Brien: 'L'évolution épigénétique Référence à J.B. de Lamarck', *L'année Biologique* 6, 465–82 (1967), pp. 465–6.
6. T.H. Morgan: *Evolution and adaptation*. Macmillan, New York (1903), pp. 155, 462–4.
7. R.B. Goldschmidt: *The material basis of evolution*. Yale University Press, New Haven (1940). C.J. Willis: *The course of evolution*. O.H. Schindewolf: *Grundfragen der Paläontologie*. P. Brien: 'L'évolution épigénétique'. A. Vandel: *La genèse du vivant*. Masson, Paris (1968).
8. M. Grene: 'Two evolutionary theories', *British Journal of the Philosophy of Science* 9, 110–27, 185–93 (1958).
9. R.B. Goldschmidt: *In and out of the ivory tower*. University of Washington Press, Seattle (1960), p. 324.
10. R.B. Goldschmidt: *The material basis*, p. 183.
11. Ibid., pp. 391–7.
12. G.G. Simpson: *The major features of evolution*. Columbia University Press, New York (1953), p. 85.

13. M. Denton: *Evolution: A theory in crisis*. Adler & Adler, Bethesda (1985).

14. G.L. Stebbins: 'Adaptive shifts and evolutionary novelty: A compositionist approach', pp. 285–306 in *Studies in the philosophy of biology Reduction and related problems* (eds. F.J. Ayala and T. Dobzhansky). Macmillan, London (1974), p. 301.

15. K.E. von Baer: *Ueber Entwickelungsgeschichte der Thiere: Beobachtung und Reflexion*. Gebrüder Bornträger, Königsberg (1828).

16. D.T. Anderson: *Embryology and phylogeny in annelids and arthropods*. Pergamon Press, Oxford (1973).

17. W. Vogt: 'Gestaltungsanalyse am Amphibienkeim mit örtlicher Vitalfärbung. II. Teil. Gastrulation und Mesodermbildung bei Urodelen und Anuren', *Wilhem Roux' Archiv für Entwicklungsmechanik* 120, 384–706 (1929).

18. J. Holtfreter: 'A study of the mechanics of gastrulation. Part II', *Journal of Experimental Zoology* 95, 171–212 (1944).

19. J. Holtfreter: 'Properties and function of the surface coat in the amphibian embryo', *Journal of Experimental Zoology* 93, 251–323 (1943).

20. R. Rugh: *Experimental embryology A manual of techniques and procedures* (rev. edn.). Burgess, Minneapolis (1948).

21. W.J. Gehring: 'The molecular basis of development', *Scientific American* 253, 136–46 (1985). A.S. Wilkins: *Genetic analysis of development*. John Wiley, Chichester (1986). E.F. Keller: *A feeling for the organism The life and work of Barbara McKlintock*. W.H. Freeman, New York (1983).

22. G.S. Stent: *Paradoxes of progress*. W.H. Freeman, San Francisco (1978).

23. M. Eden: 'Inadequacies of the neo-Darwinian evolution as a scientific theory', pp. 5–19 in *Mathematical challenges to the Neo-Darwinian interpretation of evolution* (eds P.S. Moorhead and M.M. Kaplan). Wistar Institute Press, Philadelphia (1967), p. 11.

24. P. Brien: 'L'évolution épigénétique'.

25. L.F.A. Pantin: 'Organic design', *Advancement of Science* 8, 138–50 (1951). P.B. Medawar: *The art of the soluble*. Methuen, London (1967). R.J. Britten and E.H. Davidson: 'Repetitive and non-repetitive DNA sequences and a speculation on the origin of evolutionary novelty', *Quarterly Review of Biology* 46, 111–38 (1971). E. Zuckerkandl: 'Programs of gene action and progressive evolution', pp. 387–447 in *Molecular anthropology Genes and proteins in the evolutionary ascent of the primates* (eds. M. Goodman, R.E. Tashian and J.H. Tashian). Plenum, New York (1976). SLP.

26. HGM. A.N. Sewertzoff: *Morphologische Gesetzmässigkeiten der Evolution*. Gustaf Fischer, Jena (1931).

27. S. Løvtrup: 'On von Baerian and Haeckelian recapitulation', *Systematic Zoology* 27, 348–52 (1978).

28. G. Hardin: 'The competitive exclusion principle', *Science* 131, 1292–7 (1960).

29. G.E. Hutchinson: *The ecological theatre and the evolutionary play*. Yale University Press, New Haven (1965).

30. S. Løvtrup: 'The evolutionary species: fact or fiction?', *Systematic*

Zoology 28, 386–92.
31. A. Woodfield: 'Darwin, teleology and taxonomy', *Philosophy* 48, 35–49 (1973), p. 39.
32. R.C. Lewontin: *The genetic basis of evolutionary change.* Columbia University Press, London (1974), p. 236.
33. Ibid., pp. 11–12.
34. St G. Mivart: *On the genesis of species* (second edn.). Macmillan, London (1871), p. 278.
35. R.B. Goldschmidt: *In and out of the ivory tower.* University of Washington Press, Seattle (1960), p. 324.
36. S.J. Gould: 'The return of hopeful monsters', *Natural History* 86, 22–30 (1977), p. 30.

14. SOCIAL EVOLUTION

1. BDMW, p. 100.
2. HDR, pp. 355–6.
3. DOS (1), p. 448.
4. C. Darwin: *The descent of man and selection in relation to sex.* (second edn.). John Murray, London (1906).
5. Ibid., p. 91.
6. Ibid., p. 219.
7. Ibid., p. 220.
8. Ibid., pp. 241–2.
9. Ibid., pp. 190–1.
10. Ibid., p. 203.
11. Ibid., p. 198.
12. R. Hofstadter: *Social Darwinism in American thought* (revised edn.). Beacon Press, Boston (1955), p. 41.
13. Ibid., p. 41.
14. E.O. Wilson: *Sociobiology: The new synthesis.* Harvard University Press, Cambridge, Mass. (1975).
15. BDMW.
16. R. Hofstadter: *Social Darwinism in American thought*, p. 37.
17. P.B. Medawar: *The art of the soluble.* Methuen, London (1967).
18. P. Kitcher: *Vaulting ambition Sociobiology and the quest for human nature.* MIT Press, Cambridge, Mass. (1985).

15. THE MYTH

1. HDE, pp. 25, 78, 291.
2. G. Allen: *Charles Darwin.* Longmans, Green, London (1888), p. 199.
3. M.T. Ghiselin: *The triumph of the Darwinian method.* University of California Press, Berkeley (1969), p. 8.
4. A. Münzing: 'Darwin's views on variation under domestication in the light of present-day knowledge', *Proceedings of the American Philosophical Society* 103, 190–220 (1959), p. 191.

5. HDE, p. 287.

6. R.M. Young: 'Darwin's metaphor: Does Nature select?', *The Monist* 55, 442–503 (1971), p. 448.

7. LLD, vol. 2, p. 371.

8. R.M. Young: 'Darwin's metaphor', p. 455.

9. MLD, vol. 1, p. 161.

10. R.M. Young: 'Darwin's metaphor', p. 468.

11. *Beyond reductionism* (eds. A. Koestler and J.R. Smythies). Beacon Press, Boston (1969). M. Polanyi: 'Life's irreducible structure', pp. 225–39 in M. Polanyi: *Knowing and being*. Routledge and Kegan Paul, London (1969). *Studies in the philosophy of biology Reduction and related problems* (eds. F.J. Ayala and T. Dobzhansky). University of California Press, Berkeley (1974). S. Løvtrup: 'Reduction and emergence', *Rivista di Biologia*, 76, 437–51 (1983).

12. M.T. Ghiselin: *The triumph of the Darwinian method*.

13. S.J. Gould and R.C. Lewontin: 'The spandrels of San Marco and the Panglossian paradigm: A critique of the adaptationist programme', *Proceedings of the Royal Society of London*, B 205, 581–98 (1979), p. 589.

14. M.T. Ghiselin: *The triumph of the Darwinian method*, pp. 232–3.

15. Ibid., p. 234–5.

16. Ibid., pp. 236–7.

17. Ibid., p. 240.

18. Ibid., p. 241.

19. Ibid., p. 242.

20. DDP, pp. 65–6.

21. R.M. Young: 'Darwin's metaphor', p. 443.

22. BDMW, pp. 82, 326.

23. DNTS, p. 26.

24. K.R. Popper: *The open society and its enemies*, volume two. *The high tide of prophecy: Hegel, Marx and the aftermath* (fifth edn.). Routledge & Kegan Paul, London (1966), p. 32.

25. DDP, pp. 61–2.

26. LLHu, vol. 3, p. 60.

27. LLD, vol. 1, p. 87.

28. T.S. Kuhn: *The structure of scientific revolutions*. University of Chicago Press, Chicago (1962).

29. DDP, p. 64.

30. R. Rádl: *Geschichte der biologischen Theorien*. Zweiter Band. Wilhelm Engelmann, Leipzig (1909). C. Singer: *A short history of science to 1900* (revised edn.). Clarendon Press, Oxford (1959). NHB.

31. J. Gray: 'The case for natural selection', *Nature* 173, 227 (1954).

32. A.R. Manser: 'The concept of evolution', *Philosophy* 40, 18–34, (1965), p. 30.

16. CONCLUSION

1. HDE, p. 469.

2. W.R. Thompson, in C. Darwin: *The origin of species*. Dent, London

(1958), p. xxi.

3. DDP, p. 57.
4. HDR, p. 374.
5. L. Croizat: *Space, time, form: The biological synthesis*. Caracas (1962), p. viii.
6. R.G.B. Reid: *Evolutionary theory: The unfinished synthesis*. Croom Helm, London/Cornell University Press, Ithaca, New York (1985), pp. 360–1.
7. N. Macbeth: *Darwin retried An appeal to reason*. Gambit, Boston (1971).
8. R. Rádl: *Geschichte der biologischen Theorien*, zweiter Band. Wilhelm Engelmann, Leipzig (1909). C. Singer: *A short history of science to 1900* (revised edn.). Clarendon Press, Oxford (1959). NHB.

Index

455

161, 284, 347, 381
man, evolution of 60, 84, 141,
165, 178–9, 181, 184, 210,
226–7, 244, 250, 257–8,
260, 264, 347, 388–92,
398–400
Mani, G.S. 445
Manser, A.R. 416, 452
Marchant, J. 425
Marx, K. 395, 416
materialism 42, 229, 234
mathematics 240, 287–8, 291–4,
296, 299–300, 304–6, 309,
311–12, 315, 318, 320–2,
324, 404, 409
Matsuda, R. 443
Matthew, P. 15, 24–7, 38,
89–90
Maxson, L.R. 448
Mayr, E. 314–15, 321, 325 9,
348, 353–4, 356, 381, 424,
445–6, 448–9
mechanism of evolution, theories
on see ecological theory;
epigenetic theory;
macromutation theory;
micromutation theory; Neo-
Mendelism
Meckel, J.F. 63, 67, 198
Meckel-Serres' law 67–8, 72–3,
77, 79, 85, 96, 154–7
Medawar, P.B. 343, 428, 434,
447, 450–1
megaevolution 330–1
Mendel, G. 14, 32, 106, 280,
289, 296
Mendelian population genetics
see micromutation theory;
Neo-Mendelism
Mendelism 14, 109, 238, 276,
280–1, 289, 291–2, 295,
305, 312, 320, 323, 352, 355
mental faculties 165, 226–8,
232, 244, 261, 264–5, 347,
389, 391–2
metaphysics 6, 19, 34, 36, 40,
45, 51, 62–7, 88, 131, 151,
178, 187, 194, 225–6,
228–9, 234–5, 249, 261,

264, 273, 303, 318, 344,
351, 355, 362, 384–5, 392,
402, 407, 416, 422
microevolution 323, 325, 330–1
micromutation theory 12, 66, 88,
142, 145, 159, 178, 288–9,
348, 350, 379–80, 421–2
Darwin's 2, 76, 130–2,
139–40, 144, 160–1, 164,
166–7, 183, 185, 248,
279, 282, 291–2, 303,
306, 316, 402
Lamarck's 48, 52, 181
Neo-Mendelian 320–1,
323–5, 330, 332–5, 348,
350, 354, 356, 358–9,
364, 367, 376, 380, 416
Wallace's 208
see also corroboration;
falsification
Millhauser, M. 433
Milne Edwards, H. 131–2, 425
miracle 162, 184, 256–7, 317,
343, 388
misrepresentations 4, 66, 79, 88,
162, 195, 258–9, 406–11
mistakes 4–5, 19, 38, 42, 53,
88, 108, 113, 220, 268, 291,
293, 323, 345, 362, 402–6
Mivart, St G.J. 36, 91, 98, 135,
157, 198, 200–1, 236,
243–67, 272, 274, 276–7,
283, 385, 387, 413, 421, 441
molecular biology 8, 339–46,
365, 373, 376, 386, 419
molecular genetics 343, 365–6,
406
monster 70, 76, 81, 86, 105,
109–10, 158, 166, 197, 231,
249, 312, 363, 369
Morgan, T.H. 361, 449
morphogenesis 3, 67, 312, 345,
375–7
morphology 8, 38, 62–3, 66–7,
85, 88, 150, 152–3, 159,
161, 168, 234, 256, 279,
305, 312, 328, 340, 346–8,
368, 377, 404, 409, 419
Mudford, P.G. 428